Crisis Cities

Crisis Cities

Disaster and Redevelopment in New York and New Orleans

Kevin Fox Gotham

and

Miriam Greenberg

OXFORD
UNIVERSITY PRESS

Oxford University Press is a department of the University of
Oxford. It furthers the University's objective of excellence in research,
scholarship, and education by publishing worldwide.

Oxford   New York
Auckland   Cape Town   Dar es Salaam   Hong Kong   Karachi
Kuala Lumpur   Madrid   Melbourne   Mexico City   Nairobi
New Delhi   Shanghai   Taipei   Toronto

With offices in
Argentina   Austria   Brazil   Chile   Czech Republic   France   Greece
Guatemala   Hungary   Italy   Japan   Poland   Portugal   Singapore
South Korea   Switzerland   Thailand   Turkey   Ukraine   Vietnam

Oxford is a registered trademark of Oxford University Press
in the UK and certain other countries.

Published in the United States of America by
Oxford University Press
198 Madison Avenue, New York, NY 10016

Library of Congress Cataloging-in-Publication Data
Gotham, Kevin Fox.
Crisis cities : disaster and redevelopment in New York and New Orleans /
Kevin Fox Gotham, Miriam Greenberg.
  pages cm
Includes bibliographical references and index.
ISBN 978-0-19-975222-5 (hardcover : alk. paper)—ISBN 978-0-19-975221-8
(pbk. : alk. paper)   1. Urban renewal—New York (State)—New York.   2. Urban
renewal—Louisiana—New Orleans.   3. Disasters—Social aspects—New York
(State)—New York.   4. Disasters—Social aspects—Louisiana—New Orleans.
5. Urban policy—New York (State)—New York.   6.   Urban policy—Louisiana—
New Orleans.   7. Sociology, Urban—New York (State)—New York.   8. Sociology,
Urban—Louisiana—New Orleans.   I. Greenberg, Miriam.   II. Title.
HT177.N5G68 2014
307.3'416097471—dc23
2013035033

9 8 7 6 5 4 3 2 1
Printed in the United States of America
on acid-free paper

CONTENTS

PREFACE

The idea for *Crisis Cities* was sparked when we first met each other on a panel at the American Sociological Association Conference in 2006, a little under a year following Hurricane Katrina. We were presenting separate papers on the contradictions of post-disaster tourism strategies—Miriam in New York City after 9/11 and Kevin in New Orleans after Katrina. At the time, both of us had published articles and were finishing books (*Authentic New Orleans*, New York University Press, 2007 and *Branding New York*, Routledge, 2008) on the contentious history of tourism and marketing strategies in our respective cities, with a focus on the period of fiscal crisis and austerity that began in the 1970s and 1980s. And so we were particularly attuned to, and concerned about, the rapid embrace of "the tourism solution" once again following these two disasters. We bemoaned the instrumentalist logic of these globally oriented campaigns, whereby rebuilding the cities' commercial and tourist image appeared to take precedence over rebuilding the homes, businesses, and neighborhoods of dislocated populations. Yet speaking to each other after our presentations, we found striking similarities between our two cases that extended far beyond these particular contradictions.

First, we noted that both cities were using disaster aid to pursue a highly uneven approach to redevelopment writ large—one dependent upon, yet much broader than, tourism and marketing. From initial reports following 9/11, and again after Katrina, we saw public disaster funds in the form of Community Development Block Grants and lucrative tax abatements channeled to some of the most powerful private interests in our respective cities—including energy corporations, hotels, real estate developers, and financial firms. The physical manifestation of these funds—some still in the planning stage—were glistening office towers, luxury residential buildings, and high-end commercial districts, all of which were using taxpayer dollars in the name of broader "recovery." This investment, meanwhile, was occurring in neighborhoods that were already well-off, such as New York's Financial District and New Orleans's French Quarter. This, in turn, was driving rapid escalation of rents in targeted neighborhoods and adjoining areas, setting off or accelerating processes of gentrification. Yet little to no funds were going to affordable housing or small business loans for communities in neighborhoods like Chinatown and the Lower Ninth Ward, first devastated by the disaster and now threatened with displacement. These dynamics were more advanced in New York City five years after 9/11 than in New Orleans just one year following Katrina. But the similarity made us wonder: Was there a connection between these experiences? Was post-disaster redevelopment linked to broader processes of social and spatial restructuring? And was New York's path to be New Orleans's future?

In addition to similarity in the aftermath of the disasters, we observed similarities in the historical conditions that lead up to them. Namely, processes of uneven *redevelopment* seemed to be occurring on top of the uneven *development* that we had seen play such a large role in shaping both cities over the preceding decades, and that positioned certain communities to be far more vulnerable to disaster than others. As we knew from our own research and that of many others, contemporary inequalities can be traced in large part to urban transformations and policy shifts of the 1970s and 1980s. It is by now a well-known story: The federal government began dismantling Keynesian-era safety nets and urban programs and devolving risk to individuals and localities. Local governments, struggling to find alternative revenue sources, joined forces with growth coalitions to fortify downtown business districts and tourist destinations. Wealthy white residents concentrated in a handful of elite neighborhoods or fled for the suburbs. Low-income, disproportionately nonwhite, "inner-city" communities were left to fend for themselves, deprived of services and burdened with environmental hazards. And while economic growth returned in the 1980s and 1990s, it typically came without good middle class jobs and entailed the gentrification of low-income neighborhoods close to reinvested downtowns, all of which only intensified inequality. Now, it struck us that, in advance of 9/11 and Katrina, this inequality had created an uneven landscape of risk and resiliency—where the unequal fates of neighborhoods and communities following the disasters was, to a great extent, preconditioned by their unequal resources and power prior to them. This suspicion generated an additional question: should we analyze 9/11 and Katrina not as sudden disasters or exceptional events, but instead as moments of rupture shaped by and shaping the longer-term, polarizing dynamics of contemporary urban history?

Conducting preliminary research in the year following our first meeting, we were to answer the above questions in the affirmative. We came to see that we were indeed witnessing broader dynamics of crisis, urbanization, and inequality that only a comparative socio-historical and spatial analysis could make sense of. And so we decided to write this book—realizing that it would take us a number of years to see how historical dynamics ultimately played out for our different cities.

What we discovered, fundamentally, were widely divergent fates for different neighborhoods and communities that exacerbated preexisting inequalities. Prior advantages or disadvantages—in access to credit, insurance, and wealth; to stable and well-paid work; and to political influence— were compounded by inequitable access to post-disaster redevelopment aid. In terms of the latter, we discovered that policies pushed through in the crisis environment played a powerful role. Following 9/11, redevelopment agencies in New York City attained sweeping waivers of federal regulations governing the use of disaster and redevelopment funds—such that they no longer had to meet "public benefit" standards, be "means-tested," or be subject to "public oversight." City and state officials and partnerships lobbied for and won these waivers, inaccurately framing the primary economic victims of 9/11 as financial firms, which otherwise would not be considered "needy" or of a public benefit. Further they asserted that without these waivers the future of New York's, and the United States' financial center, was at risk—a threat that could never be disproven. After Katrina, these deregulations were extended to the entire Gulf Coast, on the basis of no argument beyond the New York precedent. This was a major victory, and source of legitimacy, for local growth coalitions who had long sought new flexible revenues to speed market-oriented redevelopment. Public redevelopment aid could now be used for projects not considered a public priority, and that, if not for the urgent, post-disaster context, would have been contested—from city marketing campaigns to corporate office towers. This, in turn, had the effect of driving wider market-oriented redevelopment citywide and, by leaving other needs unmet, dramatically augmented socio-spatial inequality.

Based on these discoveries and years of research in these two cities, we formulated our basic contention that New York and New Orleans have emerged as "crisis cities," representing a "neoliberal," or free-market-oriented approach to post-disaster redevelopment that is increasingly dominant for crisis-stricken urban regions around the country and the world. This approach emphasizes the privatization of disaster aid and resources, the placement of private sector elites at the helm of post-disaster planning, and the use of tax incentives and corporate stimulus instead of public outlay programs to bolster revitalization. Promoting a narrow policy repertoire of austerity, privatization, and devolution of disaster recovery responsibilities and funding to the local scale, the function of government in responding to disasters has become the restoration of investor confidence and profit making. Meanwhile, this approach forecloses or undermines public sector, "high-road" approaches oriented toward concern for equity, social justice and holistic community and environmental health and well-being. Thus, in our book, we problematize conceptions of "recovery" and "rebuilding," asking the questions: recovery and rebuilding for whom, and for what purpose?

Using a rigorous comparative historical methodology, our book contributes to scholarship on disaster, crisis, and redevelopment across the fields of sociology, geography, and urban studies. First, we demonstrate that despite vast differences in the type of disaster trigger (i.e., a terrorist strike and hurricane) and the intensity and scale of destruction, policymakers and government officials responded with strikingly similar, market-oriented strategies of recovery and redevelopment. This was reflected in the similar series of policies and regulations passed by policymakers at the local, state, and federal levels, facing intense lobbying from the private sector, such as: restriction in Federal Emergency Management Agency aid to needy communities; waivers of rules governing the Department of Housing and Urban Development's CDBG (Community Development Block Grant) program mandating that funds benefit low- and moderate-income people; expansion of "private activity bonds" and tax incentives to encourage the private sector to take the lead in the rebuilding efforts; and the establishment of new, public private redevelopment corporations, operated by unelected individuals drawn from the private sector, to oversee the distribution of disaster funds. Furthermore, both cities responded to the disasters with new citywide "rebranding" efforts designed to reimagine both cities as places of commercial rebirth and resilience.

Second, we show that the policy response to 9/11 and Katrina was not entirely new, but had precedent in New York and New Orleans's experience with fiscal crisis, government retrenchment, and social upheaval during the 1970s. It was then that political and economic elites in both cities first framed "crisis" as the legacy of "the old economy" based in blue-collar and unionized professions and a product of the "old political machine" that was corrupt and hostile to business. Elites in New York responded with a variety of entrepreneurial reforms to promote the growth of white-collar industries like tourism, finance, and real estate. Elites in New Orleans embraced similar reforms while also supporting new flood control structures to promote the urbanization of the wetlands. These reforms dovetailed with the implementation of new place marketing strategies designed to counter perceptions of urban decline and to enhance competitiveness with other cities and suburban areas. As we show, these reforms, along with service cutbacks, deregulation of industry, and anti-union assault did little to remedy growing social problems like concentrated poverty and environmental degradation. Rather, by shrinking the social safety net, reducing regulations, and contributing to the elimination of unionized jobs, these policies increased the vulnerability of the poor and low-income populations to future disasters and created the potential for more intense crises over time—laying the groundwork for the extreme dislocation that occurred following 9/11 and Hurricane Katrina.

Crisis Cities also develops a novel theoretical framework for analyzing post-disaster urban redevelopment processes as intensifiers of urban instability, vulnerability, and risk to hazards. In the chapters that follow, we employ the concept of *crisis driven urbanization* to understand how particular policy reforms, public-private actions, and socio-legal regulatory strategies have played a crucial role in creating and reproducing vulnerabilities as well as contributing to the uneven effects of the urban disasters. *Crisis driven urbanization* refers to the general approach employed by urban growth coalitions, aided by government and private interests at the local, state, and federal levels, to interpret and use "crisis" to advance and legitimize radical policy reforms and redevelopment projects that would be far more difficult to implement in normal times. Although financial strain and social problems may be common to many cities and societies, how organized interests define "crisis," attribute blame, and debate future policy alternatives depends on cultural, political, and social arrangements and framing strategies. Our concept draws attention to how an elite framing of crisis can affect policy and legitimize particular forms of urban redevelopment, and highlights the interaction between urban disasters, crisis, and state intervention and policymaking. That is, crises increasingly shape and constrain urbanization processes, while subsequent processes of urban redevelopment generate their own immanent contradictions and crisis tendencies on an even broader scale.

For case study examples, we sought out neighborhoods equally affected by the disasters but with widely divergent post-disaster outcomes. In New Orleans, the mostly white, upper-middle-class Lakeview and mostly black, working-class Lower Ninth Ward both suffered 12 feet of flooding when Katrina struck on August 25, 2005, yet the former recovered within three years, while the latter remains devastated. Similarly, the diverse communities in the Lower Manhattan neighborhoods surrounding the World Trade Center were all impacted economically, socially, and in terms of public health by the destruction, pollution, and street closures that lasted for months after 9/11. Yet ten years later, the "New Lower Manhattan," narrowly defined to include the wealthy and majority white neighborhoods adjoining the rebuilt Financial District, was at the apex of the city's growth in population and wealth, while in neighboring Chinatown, the collapse of its garment industry and related small businesses, combined with a spike in rents, led to an exodus of its majority working-class, Chinese-American residents. The divergent fates of these neighborhoods became extreme examples of broader, citywide trends. Socio-spatial inequalities that preceded the disasters were exacerbated in their wake. Moreover, "before" and "after" histories and geographies became inextricably linked, and together told a crucial story about the role of disaster and crisis in our time.

These powerful linkages were not, however, all-determining. To the contrary, we also witnessed how the post-disaster moment created an uncommonly potent space and time for collectively critiquing the cities' past, reimagining their futures and undertaking new and highly imaginative forms of activism and organizing. These were periods, after all, of profound rupture, and the suspension of "business as usual," and their openness and indeterminacy made our study of crisis particularly exciting. Here, too, history mattered, as grassroots groups and movements that had long organized in and for particular neighborhoods, communities, and causes came to see their common interest. Prevailing assumptions about the inevitable march of "neoliberalization" and fiscal conservatism were up in the air. Billions in discretionary funds being funneled to the two cities represented a last gasp, or new breath, of spatial Keynesianism and belief in an equitable urban future. At citywide visioning sessions, citizens were encouraged to "dream big." The possibility that these monies could be put to use to rebuild cities on a more socially just and environmentally sustainable foundation was envisioned, debated, and fought for.

Yet, these were also periods in both cities in which powerful growth coalitions, many of whose members were politicized during the 1970s fiscal crisis, became reinvigorated. Like grassroots movements, these elite groups also recognized the historical opportunity to dream big, but did so with privileged access to the redevelopment agencies through which public monies were channeled and policies written. And unlike in the past, they were now unburdened by public benefit, income, or oversight requirements. Thus, by necessity, a major target of grassroots organizing became the inequitable and often inscrutable process of redevelopment itself. There were some clear victories. Particularly egregious plans were uncovered and blocked—such as the Bring New Orleans Back Commission's "greening" proposal that would have replaced entire low-income neighborhoods with parks, or the plan in New York City for a high-speed train from Wall Street to Kennedy Airport costing untold billions. Many groups took matters into their own hands and created their own networks of mutual aid, social service provision, and even home building. Ultimately, however, these efforts were difficult to sustain and unable to shift what became, on the whole, a market-oriented and inequitable redevelopment agenda.

Nonetheless, the upsurge in what came to be called "disaster activism," as well as related research, reporting, and organizing—had long legs. These efforts helped expose the contested nature of redevelopment itself and underscored the fact that its rewards were the fruit of political struggle. Days after Katrina, NYC watchdog groups sent a letter of advice and solidarity to New Orleans, relaying lessons learned and offering support. Months later, the national Right to the City Alliance formed to address the injustice that New Orleans came to represent, and that was also felt by cities nationwide. Occupy Wall Street emerged a week after the tenth anniversary of 9/11, in the heart the "New Lower Manhattan," to protest the excesses of Wall Street. In the aftermath of Superstorm Sandy in October 2012, the broad-based Coalition for a Just Rebuilding was founded on the basis of hard-won knowledge from organizers involved post-9/11, post-Katrina, in Right to the City, and in Occupy. Clearly a new era of urban politics has emerged, one shaped by the trauma and solidarity felt in moments of crisis and by the dreams and disillusionment of redevelopment that came after. In this sense, the legacy of those struggles lives on—through the movements they formed, the futures they envisioned, and the consciousness they helped to raise. Our ability to research and write this book is also a fruit of this legacy.

ACKNOWLEDGMENTS

The comparative, socio-historical, and socio-spatial analysis we present in the pages of *Crisis Cities* required multiple methods and scales of analysis as well as the support and insights from a wide range of participants. We conducted participant and ethnographic field observations at community meetings and city visioning sessions and targeted interviews with key actors, including those at redevelopment agencies; public private partnerships; and civic, neighborhood, environmental, and activist organizations. We conducted primary analysis of government data from federal and state agencies; historical documents in our local municipal archives; redevelopment reports produced by watchdog organizations; and marketing reports produced by and for local economic development, tourism, and city marketing agencies. We consulted secondary sources, including journalistic accounts in books and periodicals, analyses produced by think tanks and consultancies, and scholarly books and articles. Finally, we analyzed the ever-evolving framing and representation of these two events and cities, as found in periodicals, media and popular culture, and city marketing campaigns.

In what follows, we lay out the multiple sources we consulted for this research and also use this as an opportunity to acknowledge some of the numerous individuals and groups who provided access to these data as well as advice and support along the way. Without the aid of these dedicated scholars, activists, city officials, analysts, archivists, librarians, agencies, and organizations, there is no way we could have conceived of, let alone completed, this book. We realize that the ultimate conclusions we draw from this analysis are ours alone and in some cases may deviate from the perspective of particular groups and individuals whom we consulted. And, needless to say, any errors we may make are ours alone.

We consulted an array of federal documents to understand everything from official estimates on the impacts of 9/11 and Katrina, to the content of federal disaster legislation, to the formulation and implementation of post-disaster redevelopment policy, waivers, and tax-increment financing. These included reports, analyses, and hearing transcripts from the Congressional Research Service, Office of the Federal Register, National Archives and Records Administration, Department of Homeland Security, Federal Emergency Management Agency, Army Corps of Engineers, Department of Housing and Urban Development, Government Accountability Office, and the Internal Revenue Service. At the state level, this included the New York and Louisiana Departments of Labor.

Much original data was gathered by consulting with the public and private city and state agencies that played a governing role in recovery and redevelopment.[1] These included the special authorities and coalitions created to lead redevelopment efforts for both cities, namely: the Lower Manhattan Development Corporation (LMDC), the Bring New Orleans Back Coalition (BNOB), and the Louisiana Recovery Authority (LRA). Central players also included local business-led partnerships, which lobbied for, helped populate, and/or worked closely with these authorities. In New York, these included the Association for a Better New York, the New York City Partnership, the Real Estate Board of New York, and the Downtown Alliance. In New Orleans, this included Greater New Orleans, Inc. (GNO, Inc.); the New Orleans Business Council; and the Downtown Development District (DDD). Also important were city and state agencies whose main job it is to liaison with the private sector, provide business incentives, and market the city and/or state. These included the New York City Economic Development Agency (NYCEDC), NYC & Co., Empire State Development Corporation, the Louisiana Bond Commission (LBC), the Louisiana Office of Community Development, the New Orleans Tourism and Marketing Corporation (NOTMC), and the New Orleans Metropolitan Convention and Visitors Bureau (NOMCVB). We greatly appreciate the many people within these organizations who helped us gain access to and make sense of this data. These included Randi Press and Peyton Sise of NYCEDC; George Fertitta, Jane Reiss, and Willy Wong of NYC & Co; Carl Weisbrod of the Downtown Alliance; Goldie Weixel of LMDC; Jennifer Day, Cathy Juarez, Kelly Schultz, and Stephen Perry of the NOMCVB; and Whit Kling of LBC. We also appreciate the speedy reply of LBC to our public records request in March 2011 for GO Zone data. Thanks also to Cornelia Schnall of Landov Media for permission to use images from *The Times-Picayune*.

A number of consultancies and think tanks provided reports that were used by the above organizations and so gave us insight into their process. These included the Urban Land Institute, the Brookings Institution, McKinsey & Company, and the Boston Consulting Group. Meanwhile, the data gathered by government watchdogs proved valuable for independent analysis of redevelopment governance, policymaking, and program implementation. In New York, this included the path-breaking work of

Reconstruction Watch (RW), the Fiscal Policy Institute (FPI), and Good Jobs New York (GJNY). For New Orleans, this included the Gulf Coast Reconstruction Watch (modeled on RW), the Bureau of Governmental Research (BGR), and the Citizens Road Home Action Team (CHAT). We also consulted useful reports, exhibits, and visioning sessions organized by nonprofit organizations, including some organizations created in response to the disasters. For New York City, these included 9/11 Environmental Action, the Labor Community Action Network (LCAN), the Beyond Ground Zero Network (BGZ), Committee Against Anti-Asian Violence (CAAAV), Chinese Staff and Workers, the Urban Justice Center (UJC), the Asian American Federation, the Civic Alliance to Rebuild Downtown New York, the Regional Plan Association, the Pratt Center for Community Development, the Municipal Art Society, the Community Service Society, the Center for an Urban Future, and the Architecture League of New York. For New Orleans, we consulted reports from the National Low Income Housing Coalition to examine the interaction of federal, state, and local governments in the implementation of policies to promote urban rebuilding.

We are extremely grateful to the many community and labor organizers, stakeholders, and advocates who provided assistance with data collection. In New Orleans, this included Melanie Ehrlich of CHAT, Michael Desjardins of the Mid-City Parkview Neighborhood Association, Seth Weingart of the Greater New Orleans Fair Housing Action Center, Arthur Johnson of the Lower Ninth Ward Center for Sustainable Engagement and Development, Darryl Malek-Wiley of the CSED and the Sierra Club, Davida Finger of the Loyola Law School, and Christy Kane of Louisiana Appleseed. In New York City, this included Wendy Cheung of CSWA and BGZ; Jennifer Vallone, Melissa Aase, and Katherine Chang of University Settlement; Helena Wong of CAAAV; Bettina Damiani of GJNY and RW; Sondra Youdelman of Community Voices Heard; Alexa Kasdan and Christopher Chaput of UJC; David Dysegaard Kallick of the FPI and LCAN; and Brad Lander and Ron Shiffman, then at PCCD. Rosten Woo and Valeria Mogilevich of the Center for Urban Pedagogy organized a helpful public conversation between Miriam and Willy Wong of NYC & Co.

Much research was conducted through library collections. For aid in the design of socio-spatial analysis for Chapter 5, we would like especially to thank librarian Frank Donnelly at Baruch College. Librarians at the Jack Brause Real Estate Library of NYU, government documents librarians at UCSC's McHenry Library and NYU's Bobst Library, and archivists at the New York City Municipal Archives, Xavier University Archives and Special Collections, and the 9/11 Archives at the Museum of the Chinese in the Americas provided great assistance.

Constant attention to media coverage of post-9/11 and post-Katrina events in the two cities for years after the two disasters enabled us to see continuities and turning points in the redevelopment process. We are very grateful to the dogged investigative and "city beat" reporters for local newspapers, public broadcasters, and online publications and blogs. Their accounts were enormously helpful in tracing the recovery policy debate (at local and national levels), identifying framing strategies and rhetoric employed by contending groups, and comparing events before and after the disasters. In addition to online sleuthing, we gained access to many of these accounts through Lexis-Nexis searches of the *New York Times*, the *Wall Street Journal*, the *Washington Post*, and the New Orleans *Times-Picayune*.

We also conducted in-depth interviews with more than one hundred respondents. Our interviewees included long-term residents, civil rights activists, neighborhood coalition leaders, city planners, and leaders of nonprofit organizations, city agencies, and development coalitions, as gathered through a snowball sample method. To protect the confidentiality of our interviewees we have either employed pseudonyms or avoided using names. To recruit informants for interviews, we attended dozens of community meetings and events in both cities. These meetings included neighborhood association meetings, coalition gatherings of civic leaders, community district meetings, and public meetings of social service organizations. We used an intensive, semistructured interview protocol that contained a set of general and specific questions. This gave participants room to articulate complex experiences and feelings, recall past events, and elaborate at length on different points.[2]

We used interviews to compare and contrast experiences, interpretations, and framing strategies that different community stakeholders, neighborhood coalition leaders, planners, and agency directors used to typify the immediate impacts and the long-term redevelopment in New York and New Orleans. We asked questions about the pace and trajectory of neighborhood recovery and the challenges and opportunities that different neighborhoods and organizations have faced in the years since the disasters. We sought to understand differing perceptions of the impact of 9/11 and Hurricane Katrina on each region, as well as on particular neighborhoods, public institutions, and market segments. We also asked about the impact of various government policies and programs on local neighborhoods, the bases of local community struggles and conflicts over the recovery process, and the role of federal and local governments in leading and/or impeding recovery and rebuilding efforts. Our interview format allowed us to probe for clarification when needed and helped create an opportunity to uncover rich data. Broadly, the interview data provided an added resource for triangulating data sources—that is, between archival data, government documents, and journalistic accounts—to enhance validity and reliability.

Special recognition goes to the many students who generously assisted in research. UC–Santa Cruz PhD and now assistant professor at Chico State Nik Janos was very helpful in thinking through theories of crisis, identifying secondary data, organizing newspaper articles on a variety of contentious issues, and compiling a list of relief organizations in the early years after Hurricane Katrina. We also thank Josh Lewis, longtime Lower Ninth Ward activist and now graduate student at the Stockholm Resilience Center, who helped us make connections with leaders of nonprofit organizations in the neighborhood and played a key role in organizing a series of focus groups with community stakeholders to understand peoples' conceptions and interpretations of "recovery" and "rebuilding." Tulane University undergraduate Ellyn Crane completed an excellent honors thesis on the Louisiana Road Home program and helped transcribe interviews and field notes. Special thanks are due to graduate students Alicia McCraw and Katherine Moon for editorial assistance and meticulous reading of the book at various stages, and to undergraduates Sara Denson, Elizabeth Ford, and Arielle Noffke for help with the tables in Chapter 5.

This book was enriched by innumerable conversations with dozens of colleagues. For taking time to talk with us, we give special thanks to Charles Allen, Tom Angotti, Andy Beveridge, Mike Blum, Julian Brash, Neil Brenner, Regina Bures, Jeff Busolini, Elsa Davidson, Bill Domhoff, Charles Figley, Farrah Gafford, Deborah Gould, Herman Gray, Lily Hoffman, Ann Holder, Dan Krier, Amy Lesen, Penny Lewis, John Liss, Richard Lloyd, Peter Marcuse, Steve McKay, John McLachlan, Douglas Meffert, Earthea Nance, Eric Porter, Jennifer Robinson, Gregory Smithsimon, Bill Swart, Andrew Szasz, Eric Tang, Lewis Watts, Mark Worrell, Wayne Zipperer, and Sharon Zukin. Thanks go to Richard Campanella for his superior map-making skills and stimulating conversation on the pace and trajectory of the recovery process in New Orleans. We are grateful to Shirley Laska for providing us with thoughtful commentary and suggestions for revision; our book has benefited enormously from her extraordinary guidance and detailed feedback.

Many colleagues hosted panels, symposia, and workshops that enabled us to present our initial findings and/or develop our theoretical framework. This included David Harvey and Neil Smith at the CUNY Center for Place Culture Politics, Eric Klinenberg and Metropolitan Studies at NYU, Jake Kosek at the Geography Colloquium at Berkeley, Andrew Harris at University College London, and Ayse Yonder at Pratt Institute. Kris Olds offered formative ideas on crisis theory on an AAG panel on "redevelopmentalities" conceived and organized by Ryan

Centner. During a sabbatical at the University of Buenos Aires, Miriam was assisted by Gabriela Merlinsky and the late Hilda Herzer, whose urban studies group pushed her to rethink the project within a Latin American context and provided valuable feedback on the material for Chapter 2, an earlier version of which was published in their journal *Quid 16*. The UC Santa Cruz Urban Studies Research Cluster created vital space to explore and hone the ideas in this book, thanks to support from the Institute for Humanities Research and a UCSC special research grant.

Ideas in two chapters originated in other publications. We developed our insights into the novel use of CDBGs and private activity bonds in chapter four in the writing of the article "From 9/11 to 8/29: Post-Disaster Response and Recovery in New York and New Orleans" for *Social Forces* (December, 2008, 1–24). Miriam developed the ideas for our discussion of Hurricane Sandy in the Conclusion in the writing of "The Disaster Inside the Disaster" for *New Labor Forum* (September 2013, 22, 3).

We are incredibly fortunate to have had the opportunity to work with James Cook as editor at Oxford University Press. We wish to thank him for his extraordinary enthusiasm and perseverance over the many years of bringing this book to publication. Editorial Assistant Peter Worger offered great advice on navigating the world of image acquisition. Copy-editor Cassie Tuttle read through the manuscript with great patience and precision. We are also indebted to OUP editor Dave McBride for long ago seeing links in our work and suggesting the possibility that we work together. Many thanks to the two sets of anonymous reviewers who read and responded to our initial proposal and final manuscript with remarkable expertise, care, and engagement.

Finally, Kevin thanks his family—Adele, Audrey, and Alexandra—for welcome disruption, refreshing disturbance, and appreciated interruption, all of which made this book possible. Miriam thanks parents Suzanne and Peter for endless encouragement and frequent childcare, Simona and Tamar for constant joy and inspiration, and Nathaniel for infinite wisdom, humor, and love, plus coparenting that quite a few times went over the half-way line.

LIST OF ACRONYMS

AAFNY	Asian American Federation of New York
ABNY	Association for a Better New York
ACORN	Association of Communities for Reform Now
ACS	American Community Survey
AEI	American Enterprise Institute
AFL-CIO	American Federation of Labor–Congress of Industrial Organization
AFSCME	American Federation of State, County, and Municipal Employees
BGR	Bureau of Government Research
BGZ	Beyond Ground Zero
BNOB	Bring New Orleans Back Commission
BPC/LM	Battery Park City/Lower Manhattan
BRG	Business Recovery Grants
CB1	Community Board 1
CDBG	Community Development Block Grant
CDC	Centers for Disease Control
CDL	Community Disaster Loan
CHAT	Citizens' Road Home Action Team
CPC	Chinese-American Planning Council
CSED	Center for Sustainable Engagement and Development
CSWA	Chinese Staff and Workers Association
CWE	Consortium for Worker Education
DA	Alliance for Downtown New York
DHS	Department of Homeland Security
EDC	Economic Development Corporation
EFCB	Emergency Financial Control Board
ESDC	Empire State Development Corporation
FEMA	Federal Emergency Management Agency
FIRE	Finance, Insurance, and Real Estate
GAO	Government Accountability Office
GIWW	Gulf Intracoastal Waterway

GNOCDC	Greater New Orleans Community Data Center
GNODRP	Greater New Orleans Disaster Recovery Partnership
GO Zone	Gulf Opportunity Zone
HHS	Department of Health and Human Services
HUD	Department of Housing and Urban Development
IA-TAC	Individual Assistance-Technical Assistance Contracts
IDB	Industrial Revenue Bonds
IHNC	Inner Harbor Navigation Canal
ILIT	Independent Levee Investigation Team (ILIT)
IPET	Interagency Performance Evaluation Taskforce
LB	Liberty Bonds
LCAN	Labor Community Advocacy Network
LDC	Local Development Corporation
LIHTC	Low-Income Housing Tax Credits
LMDC	Lower Manhattan Development Corporation
LP&VHPP	Lake Pontchartrain & Vicinity Hurricane Protection Project
LRA	Louisiana Recovery Authority
LTTC	Listening to the City
MAC	Municipal Assistance Corporation
MMRS	Metropolitan Medical Response System
MR-GO	Mississippi River-Gulf Outlet
MSA	Metropolitan Statistical Area
NAACP	National Association for the Advance of Colored People
NFIP	National Flood Insurance Program
NPN	Neighborhoods Partnership Network
NSF	National Science Foundation
NTA	Neighborhoods Tabulation Areas
NYCP	New York City Partnership
OUR	Organizing and Uniting Residents Waterfront Coalition
PAB	Public Activity Bonds
PPP	Public-Private Partnership
RAIN	Rehabilitation in Action for the Improvement of the Neighborhood
REBNY	Real Estate Board of New York
RPA	Regional Plan Association
RRG	Residential Recovery Grants
TARP	Troubled Asset Relief Program
ULI	Urban Land Institute
UNITE	Union of Needletrades, Industrial, and Textile Employees
UTNO	United Teachers of New Orleans
WTC	World Trade Center

Crisis Cities

CHAPTER 1

Comparing the Incomparable: Toward a Theory of Crisis Cities

In the first decade of the twenty-first century, the United States experienced two of the most devastating urban crises in its history—one set off by the terrorist attacks that destroyed the World Trade Center in New York City on September 11, 2001, and the other when Hurricane Katrina came close to destroying all of New Orleans in August 2005. In the months and years that followed, "9/11" and "Katrina" became shorthand for the two catastrophes. New York City and New Orleans, meanwhile, became paradigmatic cities of the new twenty-first century—urban microcosms of the spiraling mix of economic, political, environmental, and security crises occurring on a national and global scale. As we will argue in this book, they became *crisis cities*.

At first glance, the fact that New York and New Orleans share the status of crisis cities may appear no more than a coincidence of misfortune. Indeed, so many differences abound between these two cities and their unprecedented disasters that they may seem completely incomparable. To name a few of these oft-cited differences: the disaster in New York was "man-made," set off by a terrorist strike, while in New Orleans it was the "natural" result of a hurricane; the first event destroyed the World Trade Center and surrounding office buildings, while the second leveled New Orleans and extended throughout the Gulf Coast region; and finally, the immediate victims of 9/11 were the disproportionately white employees of the major corporations located in the Twin Towers, while those of Katrina were disproportionately poor, elderly, and African American.

These questions of differences in the trigger event, the scale of the two disasters, and the relative status of the victims are significant and require our critical attention. Yet we contend that these differences should be addressed alongside less visible but highly significant commonalities—commonalities that are all the more striking given the numerous points of divergence between the two events.

By commonalities, we do not mean simply the local contexts of history, geography, and demographics that many observers focus on to highlight the "exceptional" quality of the two cities and their respective disasters. It is indeed striking that both disasters occurred in port cities, each roughly three hundred years old. Moreover, each city is racially and ethnically diverse, multilingual, and with strong ties to diasporic communities around the globe. It is equally remarkable that both have rich and influential arts and cultural traditions that reflect this diversity, alongside progressive political traditions dating back to the nineteenth century and, in the modern period, a tradition of voting solidly Democratic in national elections. Because of all of these factors, New York and New Orleans are often viewed as "un-American cities" by those in more conservative, less diverse, non-coastal areas of the United States.

Yet, in what follows, we will analyze New York City and New Orleans in terms of commonalities that are at once less readily apparent and more widely shared by cities generally. These commonalities transcend distinctions typically ascribed to and used to categorize cities, for example, as "global cities" or "regional hubs," located on the coast or in the heartland, and industrial or post-industrial. The commonalities we examine also belie a conception of the city as a discretely bounded entity. Rather, we view our two cities as representative of a dynamic process currently unfolding—in diverse and context-specific ways—in many if not most cities and interurban areas all over the world. This dynamic, we argue, is rooted in a long-term mode of uneven, market-oriented urban development and redevelopment. This mode of urbanization has been catalyzed by, and itself helps create the conditions for, crises of various kinds across a multiplicity of urban spaces. We will refer to such spaces as *crisis cities*, and the process through which they are currently developing as *crisis-driven urbanization*.

Through this theoretical framework and the historical comparison of our two cases, we hope to advance the fundamental point raised by critical social theorists that "there is no such thing as a natural disaster."[1] Yet we will add that naming disasters "social" does not go far enough. We need tools to better understand the complex spatial and environmental histories behind disasters, as well as the reasons that certain disasters become full-fledged crises. In addition, we need to understand the ways in which crises present radical ruptures into which we can intervene to challenge the status quo in the way our cities are built, governed, inhabited, and imagined.

A major challenge facing those who wish to address these fundamental questions is the divided state of scholarship on disaster and risk on the one hand, and capitalist urbanization on the other. Thus, one of our first tasks in this opening chapter is to explore the insights from these scholarly literatures and what we might learn from a dialogue between them. In creating this dialogue, we will also lay out the theoretical frameworks that we will be deploying throughout the book.

CONCATENATED CRISES, DISASTER, AND RISK

The 9/11 and Katrina disasters, as well as the local, state, and national responses to them, exposed a new insecurity about the future of cities, demonstrating how catastrophic urban events can wreak havoc within the national and global economy and political system more broadly. Meanwhile, urban disasters of all kinds—whether triggered by ecological, biological, technological, industrial, infrastructural, market, or security failures or breakdowns—have increased markedly in the United States and globally in recent decades.[2] From these disasters, social, political, and economic "shocks" have spread and reverberated around the world, drawing attention to a wide range of hazardous, even deadly, conditions that now face urban citizens and ecosystems. Given the increasing interconnectedness of our globalized world, some have placed these local shocks in the context of "concatenated crises," noting the extent to which a multiplicity of crises can emerge simultaneously in different parts of the world, spread rapidly, and interact with each other in unpredictable ways.[3]

These concerns have sparked a large literature on urban disaster in general, and 9/11 and Katrina in particular. Researchers and scholars express concern that booming coastal population, changing climate, and sea level rise could dramatically intensify the destructiveness of urban disasters in the coming years.[4] In addition, weakening and aging public infrastructure projects such as dams, bridges, roads, water supply systems, and communication and transportation systems pose ominous threats to the safety and security of the United States and nations around the world.[5] Indeed, the exploding rate of planetary urbanization itself—and the "informal" manner in which the fastest growing cities currently develop in both the global north and south—is cited as a number one risk factor. As the United Nations has recently pointed out, more people than ever live at risk of earthquakes, droughts, floods, and other "natural" disasters mainly because of a surge in urban populations in both developing and developed nations, in combination with risks associated with global climate change.[6]

A crucial theoretical framework for many of these assessments is drawn from the wide-ranging literatures that comprise what might be called the social science of disaster—including the fields of sociology of disaster, environmental sociology, environmental anthropology, and environmental justice.[7] Through various methods and with varying forms of theorization, these literatures all seek to address the role of social and environmental policy, socio-cultural forces, and the politics of race, class, and difference in the production of risk and vulnerability. Typically drawing upon grounded case studies, critical scholars of disaster challenge common explanations circulated by pundits and the press—such as "act of God," "act of nature," and individual responsibility tropes. They also complicate the increasingly popular notion promulgated by academics and consultants that a "resilient city" can be achieved through technological fixes, upgraded emergency management, and/or visionary leadership.[8]

Rather, critical scholarship on disaster focuses on socio-economic, environmental, and cultural contradictions that generate and exacerbate disasters by making people, ecosystems, and cities vulnerable in the first place.[9] Socio-economic polarization and segregation, development in low-lying areas and flood zones, concentrated poverty and disadvantage, proximity to hazards, residential isolation, compromised immune systems, the belief in infallible technologies and "experts," and other factors are pointed to as the major agents of this vulnerability, producing in essence "disasters waiting to happen."[10] In addition, just as these contradictory conditions make some groups more vulnerable to disaster than others, vulnerabilities themselves reinforce these contradictions, exacerbating preexisting social, cultural, and environmental inequalities. By applying such analyses to targeted case studies, scholars have long demonstrated that low-income, poor, and marginalized people suffer more than the wealthy and well-connected when a major disaster hits and continue to be disadvantaged in the long wake of these events.[11]

In a related if more broadly historical fashion, "risk society" theorists—building on the path-breaking work of Ulrich Beck—stress the social construction and embeddedness of risk, risk assessment, and risk management.[12] Risk scholars show how modern societies' development of and reliance upon complex technologies and systems, dating back to the nineteenth century, has invariably created social and environmental conditions that subject people to hazards and pose unique risks to human health.[13] In the more recent work of Kathleen Tierney, Susan Cutter, Kenneth Hewitt, Mark Pelling, and Piers Blaikie, political and economic structures and power relations determine the ability to construct risk definitions, influence risk estimates, and shape and guide public discourse about risks.[14] Exemplary in this field is Charles Perrow's work on the "routinization of risks" in technological systems in late capitalism, which suggests that the complexity and tight coupling of systems inevitably results in "normal accidents" that may be catastrophic.[15] Seen from this critical perspective, growing risk and more frequent disasters over the last two hundred years are the consequence of the contradictions of capitalism and modernity: systemic inequalities, the fetishism of science and technology, the failure of democratic systems, and the ever-growing complexity of extra-local processes such as globalization and industrialization. Rather than disasters as discrete events with narrowly defined causes and effects, these scholars emphasize the role of larger political and economic structures as well as the compromised decision making of organized interests and government agencies that together produce conditions of risk and vulnerability.

Yet despite their critical orientation, and frequent mention of the urban concentration of risk clusters and of most contemporary disasters, the foregoing literatures on disaster and risk remain largely disconnected from critical urban and geographical theory. Missing, then, is a thorough socio-spatial analysis of the production of risk. This leaves a key question unexplored, namely, how are the social forces that produce systemic risk and vulnerability themselves embedded within longer histories of capitalist urbanization? Here, in our view, the broad and growing field of critical urban research—emerging in urban sociology, geography, urban political ecology, and "critical urban studies"—is of use.[16] Yet the reverse is also true: despite an emphasis on capitalist urbanization and its historic cycles of creative destruction, critical urban research has yet to focus on the dynamics of disaster, crisis, risk, and vulnerability, more generally, within these cycles.

This lack of theoretical linkage is also true of recent edited volumes on 9/11 and Katrina, despite their critical and timely analyses and findings. The short time horizon between the disasters and the analyses, and the individualizing, case study-based approach they mainly undertake militate against theoretical generalizability. The lack of historical and comparative focus makes it difficult to connect events to broader contexts of urbanization and social change.

In this book, we aim to build on these literatures and fill in these gaps by placing 9/11 and Katrina within a comparative history of urban transformation and the socio-spatial production of disaster. We seek to understand the broader social conditions that arise in the midst of periodic "states of emergency"—from the rapid formation of new political coalitions to the upsurge of cultural modes of legitimation and resistance. And we seek to test the role played by these conditions in catalyzing, curtailing, or more generally shaping patterns and processes of urban development and socio-spatial restructuring.

CRISIS AS RUPTURE AND FRAME

Key to what is to follow is what we mean by "crisis." Broadly speaking, we will be using the term in two distinct yet interrelated ways: as a historical period of rupture and as a framed event. First, we understand crises as historic periods involving large-scale and long-term breakdowns and ruptures in social, economic, and environmental systems. We emphasize that such breakdowns are suffered most intensely by those segments of societies, as well as those elements of ecosystems, that are historically most vulnerable. Here, we find it useful to distinguish conceptually between "disaster" and "crisis," with the former understood as a contingent event that under the proper conditions can trigger and be transformed into the latter. Thus, we distinguish between (a) particular disaster triggers such as terrorist strikes, earthquakes, hurricanes, and market downturns; (b) the immediate damage and destruction caused by this trigger; and (c) the crisis—that is, the large-scale and long-term breakdown—that such disasters frequently but not invariably become.

The ultimate development of a crisis is dependent upon the underlying *landscape of risk and resilience,* a landscape itself conditioned by the existing degree of inequality and risk and the strength or weakness of social and environmental protections.[17] In societies in which risk and inequality are minimal, disasters remain contained and do not result in full-blown social, economic, and environmental crises. Where risk and inequality are intense and widespread and protections are weak, crises will likely ensue. Thus traumatic events such as terrorist strikes and hurricanes can serve as triggers for disaster. But the subsequent damage and destruction as well as the potential for crisis originate in social conditions that may be far removed from the events themselves, such as environmental degradation; zoning that encourages settlement in hazardous areas prone to floods, fires, and earthquakes; lack of transportation to get out of harm's way; and other forms of social inequality. We argue that these conditions have historical and socio-spatial roots and are reproduced by political interventions at local, regional, national, and global scales.

Meanwhile, by creating a profound break in "business as usual," crises present what might be called a *radical rupture,* that is, historic opportunities for new forms of political intervention. Indeed, following political theorists like Colin Hay, we view crises as moments of simultaneous rupture and intervention, both of which interact in dynamic and unpredictable ways with political economic, spatial and cultural conditions, and create the possibility for innovation.[18] Suddenly, for instance, large public expenditures by regimes otherwise bent on austerity can appear to be common sense. That said, seemingly revolutionary breaks can also aid in the reinforcement of the status quo, perpetuating underlying contradictions. Here we follow William Sewell's notion of "eventful temporality," maintaining that crises display "both stubborn durabilities and sudden breaks, and even the most radical historical ruptures are laced with remarkable continuities."[19] As we know from Marx, capitalism itself is characterized by "the constant revolutionizing of production, uninterrupted disturbance of all social conditions, everlasting uncertainty and agitation."[20] Similarly, Joseph Schumpeter's term "creative-destruction" denotes a process of innovation, accumulation, and ultimately annihilation of capital, in the name of growth "that incessantly revolutionizes the economic structure from within, incessantly destroying the old one, incessantly creating a new one."[21] In this sense, as Sewell points out, capitalism may be thought of as both "hyper-eventful" and "still," prone to crisis and upheaval while maintaining certain constant, incessant conditions.[22]

We contend that a similar dynamic is at play in crises sparked by contingent events originating outside of the business-cycle, though within the broader, volatile, and uneven context of contemporary capitalism. In taking a broadly historical approach, we rely less on "economistic" Marxist analyses, which understand crisis as the inevitable result of inherent contradictions in the capitalist mode of production—for example, the falling rate of profit. Nor do we align with neoclassical economic analyses, which view crisis—if at all—as a temporary aberration in an otherwise rational market system. Rather, we adopt what we view as both a more nuanced and dialectical usage of the term "crisis," taking into consideration historically contingent events, forms of political intervention, and socio-spatial dynamics while contextualizing and analyzing these in relation to the creative-destructive tendencies of contemporary capitalism. This approach helps us frame key questions: What role do sudden disasters like hurricanes and terrorist strikes play against the larger and constant backdrop of capitalist urbanization? At the same time, what urban transformations do these radical ruptures potentially help to set in motion?

A second and necessarily related way in which we understand crisis is through processes of discursive narration and *framing*. Inseparable from crises as historical events are the crises we imagine, speak of, and represent through "frames." As coined by sociologist Erving Goffman, framing involves sorting and disseminating information and representations to draw attention to a major problem or grievance, convey a sense of urgency or severity of condition, and attribute blame and causality. Frames are those "schemata of interpretation" that enable individuals "to locate, perceive, identify, and label" events in the world at large.[23] Framing theory has also been advanced by media and cultural theorists, influenced by the Marxist cultural theory of Antonio Gramsci, who are interested in how practices of framing, narration, and articulation serve to reproduce ideology.[24] Studying the tactical use of mass media in Britain during the economic crises of the 1970s, Stuart Hall and colleagues argued that the framing of "crisis" situations, events, and populations is articulated with existing scripts of race and class and is used to reinforce power.[25] Thus, in framing a "state of emergency," certain "causes" and "culprits" must be identified, "disaster areas" designated, and "victims" worthy of aid named, all of which help generate moral categories of inclusion and exclusion and legitimate systems of power.

As Georgio Agamben has shown, crisis frames also underlay the modern "state of exception"—that is, the legal construct that invests individuals and governments with the authority to extend their power far beyond past limits and so to change or suspend existing law, diminish or supersede existing rights, and fundamentally alter established practice in a democracy, including through the imposition of martial law.[26] An overriding concern of all these theorists is that, despite their framing, "crises" and "states of emergency" are not in fact exceptional moments, aberrations of some soon-to-return normalcy. Rather, they are discursive devices to legitimate the imposition of a brutal political reality. As Benjamin famously stated in response to the use of the "state of emergency" to legitimate the rise of Fascism across Europe in the 1930s: "The tradition of the oppressed teaches us that the 'state of emergency' in which we live *is not the exception but the rule.*" Further, if we "attain to a conception of history that is in keeping with this insight... [w]e shall clearly realize that it is our task to bring about *a real state of emergency,* and this will improve our position in the struggle against Fascism."[27] A real state of emergency, in this sense, has the power to negate the appearance of emergency deployed by opportunistic regimes as well as to address and struggle against real conditions of oppression. Our interest in and use of the term "crisis" is in keeping with this insight. Of particular interest to us as urban scholars is how such states of exception or emergency are deployed in spatial terms and within the specific context of the city during periods of crisis—and how this deployment does or does not address the real state of emergency in which so many urban residents actually live.

Given the prevalent role of urban space in social struggles of the late capitalist era, the framing of crisis and emergency has frequently played out against an urban backdrop, creating an intertextual—if not a metonymic—relation between discourse of crisis and of the city. Robert Beauregard's interrogation of the American discourse of "urban decline" following

World War II, for instance, suggests that when we discuss "urban problems" in the United States, "we experience not an emotionally flat rendition of objectively specific conditions but highly charged stories built up of layers of personal and collective meanings."[28] Specifically, these stories are built upon two centuries of anti-urban discourse that frames cities and urban populations as inherently prone to and fundamentally to blame for crises of various kinds. Insofar as cities and urban populations increasingly bear the brunt of concatenated crises, this only increases the power and resonance of such discourse. And this, in turn, only increases the authority of those who seek to use crisis as an opportunity to impose a state of exception on cities and their populations. That is, it enhances their power to undo past social arrangements and supersede existing law, including those of public oversight, in order to transform neighborhoods, public space, and what Henri Lefebvre called the "right to the city." In the contemporary period, we have seen that crisis cities get "opened up" as preeminent spaces of capitalist experimentation, as David Harvey argues happened with New York City after the fiscal crisis of 1975.[29] Contemporary crisis cities become *sites of exception*, creating the possibility for the far-reaching extension of power, and of markets, into urban space.

In this sense, the two ways in which we understand crisis—as historic moment of rupture and intervention and as framed event—are always interrelated. The framing of crisis serves to make rupture intelligible, historically and spatially. Meanwhile, an array of social groups and movements do battle over different meanings and interpretations of crisis conditions and situations to legitimate or contest crisis-era political interventions and forms of urban redevelopment. In other words, the framing of crisis interacts dialectically with social conditions of rupture to create new opportunities for intervention and social transformation. Thus, we can view crisis cities as contested spaces in which opposing groups and interests battle to control the framing of crisis as a social reality, and so to prescribe and justify particular political interventions and visions of an ideal, post-crisis future.

The immediate consequence of post-disaster framing is in the setting of the priorities for disaster aid. For instance, research shows, and public debate underscores, the extent to which U.S. presidents designate areas as eligible for disaster relief and allocate much greater public assistance when political operatives define these areas as politically important. Thus, rates of disaster declaration and disaster expenditures are higher in swing states during election years and in states having congressional representation on Federal Emergency Management Agency (FEMA) oversight committees.[30] As sociologist Kathleen Tierney has observed, disaster declarations do not reflect the severity of disaster events but instead factors such as "election year politics, the 'CNN effect,' and states' ability to rapidly compile high-dollar preliminary damage estimates, which then become the basis of federal aid requests."[31] As a form of "disaster gerrymandering," the decision to declare a disaster and, consequently, distribute federal money may be motivated more by political strategy than public need.[32]

Over the longer term, the crisis frame can also be used to advance, legitimize, and "narrate" more radical policy reforms. In the aftermath of both 9/11 and Katrina, one of the most dramatic dynamics to be observed was the acceleration of a market-oriented mode of urban redevelopment that was actually catalyzed by the administration of federal disaster aid, a process that became popularly known as "disaster capitalism."[33] As demonstrated in Naomi Klein's *Shock Doctrine: The Rise of Disaster Capitalism*, these shifts were not limited to New York and New Orleans. Faced with a variety of calamities, powerful political and economic players in different parts of the world were all framing "disaster" to legitimize the rapid and far-reaching shift to free-market policies.[34] These remarkable similarities were no coincidence, but rather the result of an appreciation of the opportunity to exploit widespread shock, chaos, and trauma in order to impose new political and economic agendas. As Klein and others argue, powerful actors exploit the social uncertainty and instability caused by disasters to gain control over the policy-making arena and implement measures that support their interests. Crucial to this process is the framing of disasters to legitimize "market solutions," limit debate over "alternatives," and carry out controversial policies that would be resisted in normal times.

In this book, we embrace key aspects of the disaster capitalism thesis, including the focus on moments of crisis and the opportunistic frenzy that accompanies them. Yet, alongside the elite action emphasized by this thesis, we draw attention to the broad social and political conflicts and collective struggles that ensue over framing in the aftermath of disasters. Almost invariably, in the weeks, months, and even years following a disaster, there is heated contestation over the meaning and measure of both the crisis and the response, in what we will call *the spatial politics of redevelopment*. This includes engagement by an array of power brokers—often acting in concert through business-oriented public-private partnerships—as well as an array of citizens, from residents to professional groups to social movements. The "winner" of such contests is, of course, heavily conditioned by the political, economic, and media resources at their disposal. In a society of extreme inequality and in which most media is corporate and heavily concentrated, representational power tilts upward. Yet dominant scripts can also be "flipped"—and generally have been throughout the modern period. "Real states of emergency," as Benjamin might put it, may also be recognized, and in powerful ways. This historical dynamic has intensified in an age of social media and creative political tactics. We can think of the effort by Occupy Wall Street (OWS) in 2010 to reframe the economic crisis of 2008. However one measures the impact of this famously leaderless movement, OWS clearly succeeded in inserting a new, critical frame of elite governance and class divide—"the 1 percent" versus "the 99 percent"—into a mainstream debate long averse to the mention of capitalism and the language of class. And it did so in part by kicking off in a reclaimed public space at the heart of the "New Lower Manhattan," five days after the tenth anniversary of 9/11. The symbolic politics to emerge from crises can take surprising turns.

In addition to political contestation, we emphasize the historical cycles and spatial dynamics within which political interventions of all kinds play out. We view as highly significant the fact that previous rounds of crisis and restructuring create the regulatory environment, public-private mode of governance, and socio-spatial inequalities and vulnerabilities that lay the ground for the crises and spatial politics of subsequent generations.

CRISIS-DRIVEN URBANIZATION

In this book, we will refer to this contested, market-oriented, and cyclical mode of urban redevelopment as *crisis-driven urbanization*. With this focus, we wish to emphasize the socially, spatially, and historically rooted *process* of urbanization under conditions of crisis, rather than the finished form of the rebuilt city. In addition, we aim to reveal the vulnerability-producing dynamics of market-oriented state interventions and illustrate how, within certain socio-spatial and historic conditions, the actions of market and state agents have the potential to transform disasters into social and ecological crises.

Figure 1.1 presents five core dimensions of crisis-driven urbanization. The figure provides a starting point to analyze the socio-spatial conditions, policy repertoires, regulatory and discursive strategies, and land-use practices that generate risks and vulnerabilities to hazardous conditions and disasters as well as "systemic crises," including socio-economic downturns, ecological breakdown, and crises of overaccumulation, underconsumption, inflation, and so on. The figure also draws our attention to the importance of identifying different framings of crisis, short-term recovery and long-term redevelopment phases, and the progressive intensification of risk and vulnerability to crisis. The five phases identified in the figure are not mutually

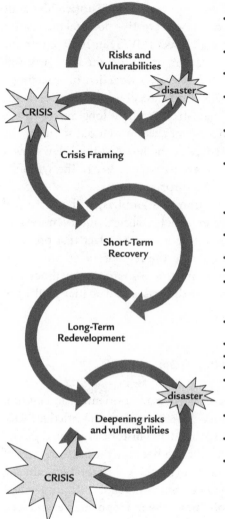

Risks and
Vulnerabilities

CRISIS

disaster

- Uneven landscape of risk and resilience, based in socio-spatial inequality and uneven development
- Public sector retrenchment, fiscal austerity, lack of resources to meet social needs
- Unsustainable land use, depleted ecosystems, increased vulnerability to hazards
- *Transformation of disaster into crisis*

Crisis Framing

- Individuals, groups, and political coalitions battle to frame "crisis" and "recovery" and to seize opportunity for political intervention
- *Victors of framing battle shape debate on appropriate mode of urban recovery and redevelopment*

Short-Term
Recovery

- Formation of public-private partnerships and multiscalar crisis regime
- Privatization, deregulation, devolution of disaster aid
- Contested recovery
- Post-disaster urban rebranding
- *Uneven recovery*

Long-Term
Redevelopment

- Entrenchment of market-oriented policies and modes of urban redevelopment
- Use of tax incentives as recovery strategy
- Contested redevelopment
- Utopian urban rebranding
- *Uneven (re)development*

disaster

Deepening risks
and vulnerabilities

CRISIS

- Intensification of risks inherited from previous rounds of uneven (re)development
- Increasing vulnerability of urban populations and ecosystems to future disasters
- *Escalation in number, intensity, and scale of future crises*

Figure 1.1
Crisis Driven Urbanization

exclusive and do not refer to clearly demarcated historical stages that follow a linear development. Rather, the phases are "ideal types," flexible concepts with no hard and fast temporal boundaries.

This framework has important implications in terms of building on and linking together literatures on risk and disaster with urban literatures—from sociology to geography to the emerging fields of "comparative" and "critical" urban studies—that seek to understand relations between urbanization and contemporary capitalism.

First, it inserts an analysis of crisis into studies of the contemporary capitalist or "neoliberal" city, showing how crises are both catalyzed by and catalysts of historical cycles of capitalism and urban restructuring. In addition, we argue that among the primary products of this mode of urbanization is an uneven and shifting landscape of risk and resiliency. Thus, a second set of implications has to do with literatures on the rescaling of risk and with this, the relation of crisis to social and ecological terrains of the contemporary city. We address each of these in turn.

Cycles of Crisis and Urban Neoliberalization

One of our core arguments is that the formulation and implementation of the political responses to the 9/11 and Hurricane Katrina disasters must be understood in the broader context of post-1970s neoliberal urban restructuring. While differences in conceptualization abound, most scholars agree that neoliberal restructuring involves a range of policies to engineer economic growth by privatizing public services and assets, deregulating major industries, reducing corporate taxes, and intensifying interurban competition for capital investment.[35] In the broader political culture, neoliberalism involves a conflation of democracy with free markets, skepticism of long-range and holistic government planning and policy making to ameliorate social inequalities; elimination of the concept of the "public good" in favor of "individual responsibility"; and the principled commitment by all levels of government to help the private sector grow and prosper.

As a theory of political-economic practices, neoliberalism holds that social betterment and progress will be maximized by promoting market transactions and bringing all human behavior and action into the orbit of market exchange.[36] In policy-making debates, valuable societal outcomes—such as equality, democracy, and social justice, as well as ecological concerns such as habitat depletion—that bring no capital return are marginalized as "nonmarket" issues and often dismissed entirely. We follow Neil Brenner, Jamie Peck, and Nik Theodore in conceptualizing neoliberalism as a contested and variegated pattern of urban and regional restructuring rather than an all-encompassing global structure.[37] We also concur with the emerging field of urban political ecology, advanced by Eric Swyngedouw, Maria Kaika, Mathew Gandy, and others, which understands neoliberalization as playing out within systems and spaces at once social and ecological, and involving metabolic dynamics and feedback loops at once impacting and impacted by human and nonhuman life.[38]

Of particular interest to us in these theories is their dynamic focus on historical processes of creative destruction. Neoliberal projects emphasizing the beneficence of the so-called "free market" and the corrosive effects of "big government" rose to prominence during the 1970s and 1980s as major policy and regulatory responses to economic crises that affected postwar U.S. and European societies. "Roll-back" strategies of welfare state retrenchment and federal defunding implemented in the early 1980s shifted to a new phase of "roll-out" neoliberalism of aggressive deregulation, reregulation, privatization, and financialization by the early 1990s.[39] Since the 1990s, governments have implemented a variety of "urban entrepreneurial" policies and regulatory strategies geared toward privatization as part of this rollout phase, including "enterprise" and "empowerment" zones, tax abatements and other incentives (tax increment financing districts, industrial revenue bonds, etc.), local development corporations, and public-private partnerships.[40] As these scholars assert, these processes have played out in path-dependent ways, with the local economic base, regulatory arrangements, political culture, and history of struggle having powerful effects on the scale, scope, and pace of reform. In this book, we add to this framework an increased focus on the impact of sudden disasters and contingent events, and also on longer-term crises. These crises are outgrowths of vulnerabilities rooted in neoliberalization as well as the concatenation of other crises and contingent events.

New York City and New Orleans are important examples of this decades-long crisis-driven process of neoliberalization, as well as uneven development. Uneven development refers to unequal patterns of metropolitan growth that reproduce racial and class-based inequalities and segregation, inner-city disinvestment, suburban sprawl, interurban competition for investment, and disparities both within and between cities. As reflected in the diverse scholarship of Mark Gottdiener, John Logan, Harvey Molotch, Gregory Squires, Neil Smith, Doreen Massey, Henri Lefebvre, David Harvey, and others, uneven development is a complex and contested process of socio-spatial transformation involving a relentless effort by private and public actors and growth coalitions to transform particular cities and regions into spaces of profit making and economic growth. The concept focuses on the harmful consequences of racial and class inequalities, discrimination, and social and environmental injustices that organize metropolitan areas in the United States. As the antithesis of sustainable development, uneven development is destructive because it threatens the basic social and environmental systems that are needed for human life and growth.[41] Based on our research, we will argue that uneven development in crisis cities is exacerbated by market-oriented post-disaster policies and politics and ultimately leads to what we will call *uneven redevelopment*—or the crisis-driven reproduction and intensification of patterns of uneven urban development.

Landscapes of Risk and Resiliency

Historical cycles of crisis-driven urbanization and uneven redevelopment also have profound implications in terms of shrinking protections against disasters of all kinds—market, natural, security—and hence the ballooning of risk. This involves a shift in the burden of risk away from the government and onto private citizens, or what some refer to as the "privatization of risk."[42] And it also involves socio-spatial shifts—that is, shifts from the federal to the local/urban scale, from the center of the city to the periphery, and so on—or what might be considered the *rescaling of risk*. These shifts emerge out of and help transform what we will term an *uneven landscape of risk and resiliency*. Following historic patterns of uneven development, the worst and most long-term effects of disasters are suffered by populations least equipped to protect themselves—poor and working class communities—while public-private partnerships ensure the resiliency and growth of wealthy, well-connected neighborhoods. Looked at cyclically, this also increases rent gaps between neighborhoods in the aftermath of crisis and so accelerates processes of displacement and gentrification, or what David Harvey terms "accumulation by dispossession" in urban form.[43] In the process of displacement and disinvestment, larger segments of vulnerable urban populations and ecosystems are also exposed to higher degrees of risk. These processes have profoundly transformed the face of New York and New Orleans. Indeed, with the bulk of redevelopment monies channeled into rebuilt luxury neighborhoods and tourism campaigns rather than areas most in need, these famously idiosyncratic cities have begun to resemble one another more and more.

This framework, we argue, has important implications for understanding the role of scale in critical urban studies. It is our contention that because neoliberalization processes play out unevenly across places and scales and in reaction to distinct events, what we need are context-sensitive inquiries into these dynamics in different cities and historical periods. Although there are cross-national similarities and generalized features of neoliberalization, we recognize that specific neoliberal policies and practices circulate unpredictability through multiple pathways to shape urban outcomes. Thus, there can be no "pure" form of neoliberalization that encompasses all urban contexts or constitutes a homogeneous and enduring pattern of urban and policy restructuring. Like other macrostructural trends, neoliberalization is a contested and contingent process of socio-spatial transformation that does not reach an end-state or final outcome.[44]

One of our basic arguments is that a new frontier of neoliberalization was opened up in conjunction with the 9/11 and Hurricane Katrina disasters and that a process of policy learning between the two events made this possible. Public-private partnerships and state officials developed a repertoire of entrepreneurial, market-oriented policies and regulatory strategies in New York. Similar ideas traveled to New Orleans to respond to the destruction and ultimate crisis there. Through a series of political maneuvers and policy struggles, neoliberalized strategies and regulatory experiments became exemplars, and ends in themselves, for evaluating the success of "recovery." We examine how policy relays were constructed and identify the place-specific constellations of social forces, historical precedents, and political struggles that shaped these efforts. In this sense, we do not view neoliberalization as a totality that encompasses all aspects of urban redevelopment or state activity, or as a deterministic, causal force. Rather, we use the term to contextualize local trends and to understand the political environment in which local struggles play out. Thus, we analytically probe and compare various institutions, regulations, and spatial practices that influence the reception of some neoliberal policies and the disavowal and contestation of others.[45]

It is with these broader linkages in mind that we refer to New York and New Orleans as *crisis cities*. The term refers not simply to cities in which crises have occurred, nor to the urban breakdown that occurs in the precise moment of disaster. Rather, it refers to cities that have been transformed over the long term, and on a broad scale, through the process of crisis-driven urbanization. The crises in question are both real and imagined, actually existing and framed, and may be sparked by any number of "triggering events"—from a natural disaster to a terrorist strike to a combination of these and more. Regardless, these cities are evidence of the fact that disastrous events are not the fundamental cause of crisis. Rather, they allow us to see more clearly perhaps than any other space in the contemporary period how crises are produced socially, environmentally, and in interaction with uneven processes of urbanization. As such, all cities are potential crisis cities. All cities are vital, local spaces to study how—in the global context of contemporary capitalism, uneven development, climate change, and planetary urbanization—crises create radical ruptures. In short, we study crisis cities as strategic sites in the creation of the political impetus for far-reaching, market-oriented forms of reimagining and redevelopment—as well as fertile ground for the contestation of these forms, and for the imagining and creation of alternative urban futures.

COMPARATIVE-HISTORICAL URBAN RESEARCH

In studying crisis cities, how does one attend to their historical and spatial interconnections as well as their particularities and local contexts? In our book, we use a comparative-historical approach to address this question. We compare post-9/11 and post-Katrina redevelopment efforts in New York City and New Orleans to identify and explain locally unique and peculiar aspects of post-crisis redevelopment outcomes in each city, as well as to reveal the general features of their pre-crisis history and post-crisis redevelopment process.

This approach contrasts with the numerous accounts that address these events individually and within a limited time frame and that, as a result, tend to produce motive-based and context-specific analyses. A conventional account focused on either 9/11 or Katrina would address the immediate cause and effect of the disaster in either locale and would cite local factors and individual actors as culprits or saviors. For example, one might argue that New York City's recovery in the immediate aftermath of 9/11 should be chalked up to a wartime allocation of scarce public resources, or the hubris of a neophyte CEO-Mayor, or the self-interested machinations of powerful elites or neighborhood groups. Such "what they were thinking" accounts are significant in interpreting agency, motivation, and class dynamics at the local scale. Yet they hold less water when multiple cases and longer historical periods are examined.

Our book aims to move beyond this limited focus on elites, political regimes, and neighborhood conflicts that isolated, historically de-limited case studies so often entail. We do this through the combined use of historical and comparative methods and by situating events within a broader process of urbanization. In terms of the latter, we do not approach cities as spatially fixed sites or view the territorial boundaries of the city as a relevant scale for analysis, comparative or otherwise. Such a framework enables us to do two things. One is to take crisis "pre-history" and "post-history" into serious account as constitutive *events*. The other is to foreground processes of socio-spatial restructuring and reimagining that exceed and explicitly challenge traditional city limits through the use of redevelopment policies and rebranding activities

This approach is inspired by the growing field of comparative research emerging within urban studies and the historical social sciences. In the urban field, we have learned from Janet Abu-Lughod's insightful and rigorous comparative analysis of Chicago, New York, and Los Angeles, which developed a historically rooted methodology to compare multiple cities along a range of issues. This work contributed to and helped provide grounding for existing urban theory through a comparative understanding of patterns of uneven development, federal-local connections, and the evolution of political institutions and governance structures.[46]

At the same time, our study positions comparison not just as a method per se, but also as a strategy of critique to challenge extant theories and thereby develop new theories of post-crisis urban redevelopment. Following the lead of geographers Jennifer Robinson and Colin McFarlane, we maintain that comparison offers investigators the opportunity to engage in analyses that can transform not just theory, claims, and knowledge but also the very objects of comparison, including cities and policies.[47] Whether studying New York, New Orleans, or any other city, we know that what happens on the ground is tied to connections and flows that stretch beyond the city limits, linked up with urban contexts in faraway places. These connections and flows themselves are crucial for comparing urban processes, not simply as influences on the outcomes in places but as important phenomena for understanding comparative knowledge transfer, policy making, and global restructuring.[48] To quote Robinson, "[t]he flows that connect cities are an important unit for comparing urban processes, not simply as influences on the outcomes in places, but as important phenomena in their own right."[49]

With this in mind, we proceed by drawing on comparative strategies proposed by historically oriented social theorists Charles Tilly and Philip McMichael, including "encompassing comparison," "variation-finding comparison," and "incorporating comparison." In the work of Charles Tilly, the goal of encompassing comparisons is to situate and explain local events within broader historical, socio-economic, and cultural contexts, structures, and processes, while the goal of variation-finding comparison is to "establish a principle of variation in the character or intensity of a phenomenon by examining systematic differences among instances." In the work of Philip McMichael, the goal of incorporating comparison is to explain how particular local events are "integral to, and define, the general historical process." Here, the aim is not to presume a " 'whole' that governs its 'parts,' " but rather to "give substance to a historical process (a whole) through the comparison of its parts. The whole, therefore, does not exist independent of its parts."[50]

While some scholarly applications of these comparative-historical strategies have viewed them as analytically distinct, we show how they can be fruitfully integrated and synthesized. We use the logic of "encompassing comparison" to explain how local developments in New York and New Orleans reflect, share characteristics with, and contribute to broader socio-economic and political trends happening on a supralocal or macrostructural level. Thus, we explain post-crisis outcomes with reference to local events and extralocal processes and developments including fiscal and economic crises and various policy orientations (for instance, fiscal austerity, devolution, deregulation, privatization). We use the logic of "variation-finding comparison" to examine the political-economic, cultural, environmental, and socio-historical differences between the two cities in an effort to explain variation in the pace and trajectory of the post-disaster redevelopment process. Finally, we use the logic of "incorporating comparison" to identify contingencies shaping redevelopment outcomes with an eye toward explaining these differences as products of and contributors to a continuously evolving process of neoliberalized, uneven development in and across time and space. We maintain that these three strategies of comparison are complementary and, in combination, can provide for breadth of generalization and depth of description to a degree that is not possible in large sample statistical analyses or individual case studies.

This approach does not just address the tensions between the general and the particular or between breadth and depth of analysis; it also aims to reposition comparison as a critical form of investigation. As McMichael puts it, we aim for a comparison that "becomes the substance of the inquiry rather than its framework."[51] For our purposes, such investigation will help situate and challenge existing theoretical approaches and empirical studies on the 9/11 and Hurricane Katrina disasters, as well as contest existing theorizations of the production of risk and vulnerability to disaster. Hence, we will use urban comparison both as explicit methodology and implicit theory to critically understand the long historical trajectories of crisis in New York City and New Orleans, how these trajectories differ, and how they have shaped broader historical dynamics. In so doing, we also eschew a historically limiting view of cities as discrete or self-enclosed and embrace one of urban space as open, relational, and embedded in cross-scale networks and flows of capital, commodities, people, politics, and ideas.

In short, our comparative-historical approach seeks to better understand the historical pre- and post-disaster trajectory of development in New York and New Orleans and, in so doing, reveal a larger story about contemporary dynamics of crisis cities. Such a comparative-historical approach has the potential, we think, to go beyond idiographic description while providing a check on universalism, and to highlight the crucial relationships that exist despite significant particularities between cases. Thus, across different cities and disaster contexts, we hope to trace the broader dynamics of crisis-driven urbanization that our two cases both reflect and have helped to create.

PLAN OF THE BOOK

The chapters of *Crisis Cities* will all be rooted in our historical-comparative methodology and will follow the arc of our theoretical framework of crisis-driven urbanization. We begin in Chapter 2 with a flashback to the period of crisis that lay the uneven ground for our two contemporary crises: the 1970s. It was then that both New York City and New Orleans, like cities nationally, experienced intense image and fiscal crises due to a spiral of problems. Global recession and oil crisis destabilized the U.S. economy and legitimated calls to implement austerity measures and cuts to cities. Local governments were faced with shrinking tax bases due to deindustrialization and suburban flight and with growing class and racial polarization and conflict. Public-private governing coalitions formed in both New York and New Orleans—as they did in other cities—and reacted to these crises in large part by adopting market-oriented urban development strategies. In New York, public-private coalitions pushed for "planned shrinkage" and slum clearance to spur the financialization of Manhattan, while in New Orleans, elites developed new land-use and water-control strategies to promote the urbanization of the wetlands. Both were crisis-driven political strategies to shift the socio-legal regulation of urban space to the supralocal—that is, federal government and transnational capital—in an effort to produce new spaces for investment and consumption. In addition to these spatial strategies, policy reforms were implemented to combat the power of organized labor and further the growth of white-collar industries like tourism, finance, and real estate. Rather than remedying crises, these spatial and policy interventions increased dependency on volatile industries, exacerbated inequality, and intensified the risks and vulnerability to trauma. By the 1980s and 1990s, in a national and global context of continued state retrenchment and privatization, a new geography of "risk versus resiliency" had emerged, creating the conditions for 9/11 and Katrina to produce such highly uneven impacts.

In Chapter 3, we move to the period immediately following 9/11 and Katrina: the phase of recovery led by the Federal Emergency Management Agency. We analyze the highly divergent framing of the disasters and their victims in New York and New Orleans—the former framed as "patriotic heroes" and the latter as "hopeless refugees." We then explore the policy implications of these frames. The militarized framing of 9/11 as an act of war facilitated the restructuring of FEMA under the newly created Department of Homeland Security. Major effects of this reorganization included the privatization and devolution of emergency management policy and the creation of new regulations (e.g., "direct result test limits") that sharply restricted aid itself. Despite the "positive" versus "negative" valence of the framing of New York and New Orleans following these two tragedies, both localities suffered comparable difficulties in accessing federal aid. Ultimately, the restructuring of emergency management in both cities followed and reinforced socio-spatial patterns of inequality and exacerbated uneven landscapes of risk produced in the 1970s.

In Chapter 4, our analysis moves from the phase of emergency management and immediate "recovery" to that of long-term "redevelopment," and the entrenched spatial politics that characterize this phase. We begin by exploring the complex forms of crisis framing and political intervention at work in this phase, including the historic upsurge of civic engagement, coalition building, and social movement formation, particularly at the grassroots level. These were accompanied, and ultimately out-maneuvered, by political mobilizations by newly created public-private partnerships— the Lower Manhattan Development Corporation and the Louisiana Recovery Authority. With the aid of federal-level waivers, these agencies were able to eliminate income targets "public benefit" requirements and public oversight from guiding recovery policies. This enabled two new forms of intervention: first, the channeling of Community Development Block Grant funds to private developers and second, the use of tax-exempt private activity bonds through the Liberty Zone and the Gulf Opportunity Zone to finance and promote private reinvestment, gentrification, and displacement. Using 9/11 as precedent, the policy response to the Hurricane Katrina disaster seized the opportunity to retrofit and extend identical market strategies on a regional scale. New York's post-crisis redevelopment may be seen as a prototype and New Orleans' as the first test case for the application of market-centered principles and spatial strategies to guide the institutional response to major urban disasters.

In Chapter 5, we examine the neighborhood-level impacts of uneven redevelopment in terms of the production of new, *uneven landscapes of risk and resiliency*. Drawing on 2010 census data, interviews, and other qualitative data, we compare neighborhoods in each city that experienced similar degrees of devastation as a result of the initial impact of the disasters, but that significantly differed in their contextual advantages prior to the events and in the recovery and redevelopment aid to which they had access subsequently. In New York, we compare the neighborhoods of Battery Park City/Lower Manhattan and Tribeca with Chinatown and the Lower East Side—neighborhoods whose economies were equally devastated by 9/11, yet with the former advantaged and aided as compared to the latter. In New Orleans, we compared the Lakeview neighborhood and the Lower Ninth Ward—both neighborhoods that experienced equal levels of flooding (up to 12 feet of water) as a result of the levee breaches, yet again, with the former advantaged and aided as compared to the latter. As our comparisons show, the feedback effects of past socio-spatial patterns of investment and disinvestment, combined with differentials in aid, explain variation in the speed and character of neighborhood redevelopment. While the intensity and scale of destruction caused by the disaster trigger is important to consider, we show that race, class, immigration status, and unequal access to recovery resources explain dissimilar redevelopment outcomes. Thus, just as relative risk versus resiliency is shaped by socio-spatial geographies of uneven development, current redevelopment projects in New York and New Orleans are reinforcing these geographies, creating new degrees of risk—and new potential for crisis.

In Chapter 6, we add an analysis of the media/cultural aspects of crisis-driven urbanization and uneven redevelopment, which, we argue, are inextricably intertwined with the socio-spatial, political, and discursive aspects discussed thus far. In short, we analyze the strategic and commercial representation of urban space following 9/11 and Katrina—a practice we refer to as *post-crisis rebranding*. We focus in particular on two stages of this process. First, we reveal the quiet and costly *retooling of branding infrastructure* that occurred in both cases, involving new public-private synergies, creative and corporate hires, local-global networking, and technological upgrades, as well as the expanded role of public funding and governance for city marketing. Second, we analyze the *redesign of the representational universe* of both cities that was made possible by this retooling. Post-crisis rebranding went beyond targeted campaigns to craft and disseminate a new, all-encompassing brand architecture that could operate at multiple scales—from the redeveloped neighborhood "subbrand" to the citywide "master brand." Initially, these efforts centered around "disaster tourism" and triumphalist marketing of redevelopment projects like the New Lower Manhattan and actor Brad Pitt's Make It Right Foundation homes in the Lower Ninth Ward. Over time, this shifted to a representational strategy that avoided reference to disaster and focused instead on explicitly post-crisis and utopian narratives of cultural diversity and urban sustainability. This rebranded landscape has served to frame, reify, and (to a degree) legitimize the controversial, contested, and uneven political and spatial interventions of crisis-driven urbanization.

In the concluding chapter of our book, we highlight our empirical findings, connect them with recent scholarly debates, and seek the broader lessons to be learned from this history. We show that socio-spatial patterns of damage, loss, displacement, and recovery from disasters are inextricably linked to political efforts to manage the contradictions and crisis tendencies of past investments in the production of urban space. Today such efforts embrace concepts of "urban sustainability" and "resilience" yet typically seek to marry these to the same market-oriented approaches of recent decades. Thus, growth coalitions and public-private partnerships mobilized in moments of disaster, while using enlightened rhetoric, play key roles in creating the conditions for crises—now and in the future—through modes of intervention, like privatization and deregulation, that at once privilege and limit scrutiny of market-oriented growth. In this way, New York and New Orleans have been affected by "wounds" inflicted not only through disasters but also through policies.[52] Without taking away from the destructiveness of 9/11 and Katrina, much collective trauma has resulted not from the actual terrorist strike and storm but from the savagely unequal approach to recovery, rebuilding, and redevelopment that followed. We point to the rise of novel forms and scales of "disaster activism"—as seen most recently in the aftermath of Superstorm Sandy with the rapid mobilization of Alliance for a Just Rebuilding, a coalition of groups that were radicalized by the contradictions of uneven redevelopment following 9/11 and Katrina. These groups seek not only to prevent a replay of the past but also to use the current crisis as an opportunity to envision a truly just and sustainable urban future.

Post-crisis political interventions are historically contingent and indeterminate, much like the moments of rupture in which they are hatched. While seeking to recognize patterns and context, we also recognize that we can never simply deduce the particular forms such intervention will take, nor the resistance and alternatives they might spark. Urban (re)development policies and their socio-spatial outcomes do not appear automatically or coherently in response to crisis conditions. Rather, they emerge within always-changing historical and environmental contexts and through the combined impacts of deliberate design, trial-and-error experimentation, the spread of ideas between cities and crises, and political coalition building, education, imagination, and struggle. This is why, we argue, it is so crucial to continue to study the ever-evolving dynamics of crisis cities, here and around the world.

In doing such a study, we take inspiration from the kind of multitasking disaster activism and scholarship that arises in these moments of radical rupture. By this we mean embracing a critical and creative sensibility focused on both short-term recovery and long-term redevelopment, on the present crisis and the histories that produced it, on neighborhood impacts and citywide revisioning, and on the local dynamics of crisis and those found in ordinary cities around the world that might otherwise, in "normal" times, appear entirely different.

"Tighten Your Belts and Bite the Bullet": The Legacy of Urban Crisis in New York City and New Orleans

On the afternoon of September 25, 1975, in a remarkable act of interurban solidarity, fourteen mayors from the U.S. Conference of Mayors met with President Gerald R. Ford in the Oval Office of the White House to plead with him to come to the aid of one of their members, New York City Mayor Abraham Beame. This meeting was actually a reenactment of an appeal made scarcely a year earlier, which then fell on deaf ears. See figure 2.1. Now buried by a $2.3 billion budget deficit, New York City was facing the possibility of the largest fiscal crisis of any sovereign government in history, and the mayors were urging President Ford to reverse his previously stated opposition to granting federal assistance.[1] His opposition was based largely on ideological grounds. That is, the solution to New York's problems, the Ford administration held, lay not in enhancing government expenditures but in what Ford's treasury secretary, William E. Simon, called "a radical new fiscal conservatism." This entailed two main reforms: deep cuts to public spending through austerity and layoffs combined with tax cuts and other pro-business measures to stimulate private investment. In the year since their previous meeting, New York City had gone down this road—cutting $1 billion in spending and laying off 30,000 workers in an effort to prove its credit-worthiness; but it was now in deeper fiscal trouble. The mayors present in 1975 were calling on Ford to now not only reconsider the fate of New York City but to also abandon this "draconian" approach to federal urban policy, which, they argued, was sure to affect them all.

Once again, the day's events, in which the mayors met with the president and testified before the Senate, was a grand act of political theater staged

Figure 2.1
President Gerald Ford Meeting in the Oval Office of the White House with the U.S. Conference of Mayors, August 14, 1974. New York City Municipal Archives.
In August 1974, New York City Mayor Abraham Beame and thirteen other mayors, including New Orleans Mayor Moon Landrieu, met with President Ford to press for a specific policy agenda—including transportation and housing aid and a federal anti-inflation program—and to discuss the economic plight of their cities with a particular focus on the example of New York City. Faced with rising unemployment, a shrinking tax base, and escalating expenses, the mayors called for federal leadership in addressing the "urban problem" exemplified by New York but affecting them all. At the meeting were, clockwise from the foreground: Mayors Richard Lugar, Indianapolis; John Oresis, Lewiston, ME; Richard Hatcher, Gary, IN; Abraham Beame, New York City; Ralph Perk, Cleveland; Eugene Peters, Scranton, PA; John Gunther, Executive Director, U.S Conference of Mayors; Mayors Peter Wilson, San Diego; Kenneth Gibson, Newark, NJ; Moon Landrieu, New Orleans; Joseph Alioto, San Francisco; President Ford; Mayor Tom Bradley, Los Angeles. Less than a year later, in July 1975, the mayors met again with Ford in an even more urgent appeal. Both efforts were to be unsuccessful.

to shift the anti-New York discourse then circulating in the media and on Capitol Hill, and the broader anti-urban discourse in which it was based. The moral of the mayors' story, intended both for the president and the nation, was that New York City—whatever anyone might think of it—was not alone in its plight. Rather, an unrelenting fiscal crisis was sweeping urban America and would continue without strong and proactive federal intervention. To make the case, Beame was again to be flanked by fellow members of the U.S. Conference of Mayors expressly chosen to represent a cross-section of American cities and regions—from Syracuse and Boston in the East; Chicago, Detroit, and Milwaukee in the Midwest; Anchorage, Denver, and San Leandro, California in the West; Houston and New Orleans in the South; and even San Juan, Puerto Rico. As they knew, the striking image of a diverse group of mayors meeting with President Ford and the Senate would garner headlines across the country. As newspaper articles from both 1974 and 1975 pointed out, the mayors were evidence of the fact that cities of all sizes, regions, economies, and demographics "felt they had a stake" in the survival of New York City.[2]

What was this stake? In the short term, the mayors feared a default on the scale of New York's would have a devastating effect on already-shaky municipal bond and credit markets. Citing the fact that New York City's crisis had already contributed to record high interest rates, the Conference of Mayors contended that an actual default would turn all U.S. cities into toxic assets. Mayor Moon Landrieu of New Orleans, as it happened, was then chairman of the Conference of Mayors and the organizer of this effort. Landrieu argued bluntly that New York's default would "make it difficult if not impossible for any city in the nation to borrow money" and so likely that they too would go bankrupt.[3] Mayor Coleman Young of Detroit observed that the mere possibility of default by New York had raised interest on his city's bonds from a previous high of 6 percent to a crippling 9.9 percent—and this despite a 20 percent reduction in municipal employees. Actual default by New York, Mayor Landrieu said, would be "catastrophic," causing "serious new economic burdens to local governments across the country."[4]

The mayors' immediate fear for their bond ratings was linked to a broader concern, one articulated succinctly by Mayor Young: "All the mayors here feel that New York's problems are symptomatic of a *national urban crisis* that has been overlooked in Washington." Detroit, he said, had already laid off 5,000 of 25,000 employees while still having to pay the aforementioned 9.9 percent interest on tax-exempt bonds, "which we consider extortion."[5] Other cities told of similarly major debt burdens and similarly drastic measures taken—mass layoffs, shuttered fire stations, deteriorating housing stock, and delayed bridge repairs. Denver Mayor William H. McNichols provided the conclusion to their testimony: "Every city in the nation is like a tenant in the same building.... If somebody says the third floor is going to collapse, you can't say that it is not going to bother me because I'm on the second floor."[6] From the mayors' perspective, if current conditions continued, the urban edifice built up over the preceding century—one that provided local residents with basic social services, sound infrastructure, a safe environment, affordable housing, and jobs—was at risk of collapse.

New York City was a particularly dramatic case of this national urban crisis. Yet notwithstanding President Ford's characterizations, New York was not exceptional. It was, more accurately, the tall tip of an enormous iceberg. U.S. cities saw their fates linked to New York months before the mayors' ceremonial visit to Washington, as the Conference made numerous efforts to publicize mounting urban problems and to push for more federal aid. Mayors warned that they would raise local taxes to offset proposed federal tax cuts."[7] The Conference presented a nine-point, $16 billion emergency economic recovery plan to much media fanfare.[8] Playing on the fears of urban uprisings in the 1960s, they warned of widespread rioting if federal officials did not act on the plan. As Mayor Henry Maier of Milwaukee put it dramatically: "there are some very conservative businessmen, not just mayors talking, who predict there is going to be blood in the streets of the cities. It would make the riots of the 1960s look like a Fourth of July Demonstration."[9]

INVOKING URBAN CRISIS

The national "urban crisis" invoked by Coleman Young and the nation's mayors in 1975 actually referred to a constellation of interwoven crises then transforming U.S. cities.

Beginning in the early 1960s, urban areas that had flourished in the post-World War II boom entered a phase of chronic industrial decline marked by increasing poverty and social antagonism.[10] Meanwhile, the fluctuating currents of metropolitan transformation and reform politics that marked the 1960s provoked increasing protest from social movements dedicated to challenging conditions of urban poverty, social exclusion, and residential segregation.[11] Indeed, the rise of the civil rights, fair housing, welfare rights, and other protest movements were largely a response to a decade of massive socio-spatial restructuring that included widespread displacement of people and destruction of urban neighborhoods as a result of highway building and urban renewal—a.k.a. "slum clearance" and suburban out-migration.[12] Intense and far-reaching demonstrations and campaigns to eliminate discrimination and inequality expressed people's hopes that urban social problems could be meliorated and democratic institutions could be reformed through the use of the federal government to address social justice and poverty.[13] Urban protest and mass agitation for government to remedy social inequalities translated into the passage of the Civil Rights Act of 1964, the Voting Rights Act of 1965, the creation of the Department of Housing and Urban Development in 1965, and passage of the Fair Housing Act of 1968 and other Great Society programs.

Yet, less than a week after President Lyndon Johnson signed into law the Voting Rights Act, rioting broke out in the Watts section of Los Angeles on August 5, 1965. For five days, the national media broadcast the violence and disorder as protesters looted stores and battled police shouting "burn, baby, burn." Over the next three years, rioting in America's cities brought to the surface intense grievances against marginalization, discrimination, and lack of opportunity. "The events of 1966 made it appear that domestic turmoil had become part of the American scene," wrote the authors of the Kerner Commission report. Forty-three violent disturbances, including three days of rioting in Chicago, left three people dead, and four nights of shooting and looting in Cleveland killed four people. By 1967, the number of events had climbed to 164, 8 of them ranked as "major" by the Kerner Commission on the basis that they involved "multiple fires, intensive looting, and reports of sniping; violence lasting more than two days; sizable crowds; and use of National Guard or federal forces as well as other control forces." Ninety percent of the more than eighty-three people killed were African American. Between 1964 and 1968, there were approximately 330 significant outbreaks of violence in 257 cities resulting in dozens of deaths and millions of dollars in damage and destruction.[14]

During these years, politicians, pundits, and the press constructed and deployed a discourse of "urban crisis" to stigmatize cities and their populations, and to blame "liberal" urban social policies and political leadership for the wave of unrest. Popular books such as James Q. Wilson's *Metropolitan Enigma* and Edward Bainfield's *Unheavenly City* proclaimed that cities were facing an escalating "crisis" of misery and social upheaval that demanded new public policy approaches and government action oriented toward discipline and restraint.[15] In 1969, President Richard M. Nixon declared that by supporting cities the federal government itself was the source of America's urban crisis and suggested that federal officials should return power to states and local governments, a philosophy he termed "New Federalism." Advocating for the devolution of policymaking and implementation, Nixon railed against the "bureaucratic monstrosity [and] cumbersome, unresponsive, ineffective" federal agencies that implemented urban policies. Condemning the spreading blight and escalating violence in cities, Nixon argued that the New Deal and Great Society programs implemented under Democratic regimes had "left us a legacy of entrenched programs that have outlived their time or outgrown their purposes."[16] Rejecting calls for renewed government intervention and comprehensive planning to remedy urban problems, Nixon claimed that federal policies themselves were the root cause of the poverty, unemployment, and related social ills that disproportionately affected cities.

By the early 1970s, however, it became increasingly clear that social issues were inexorably tied to economic ones and that local problems were compounded by those at the national and global scale. The place of the United States in the global economy was slipping, brought low by the flight of capital to newly industrialized nations, where wages were cheaper and unions scarce. In an effort to bolster the economic fortunes of the country, elected leaders eased administrative guidelines that prevented foreign access to U.S. financial markets and implemented statutes to deregulate various economic sectors. Exemplary of this deregulatory fervor was President Nixon's imposition of wage and price controls on August 15, 1971, to combat spiraling inflation. Nonetheless, a slowing economy, tipped by the oil crisis of 1973, led to a combination of stagnant wages and high inflation—also known as stagflation—which was to afflict the United States and much of the world for the rest of the decade. U.S. manufacturing, ailing since the 1960s, began its precipitous decline, illustrated by the jarring fact that 1975 was the final year in U.S. history of a trade surplus.[17]

Yet, despite evident structural roots to urban problems, divisive politics continued to surround the framing of the "urban crisis" itself—a volatile, contested label deployed constantly and heterogeneously across the political spectrum.[18] Fueling conservative anti-urban sentiment, the rapidly expanding mainstream media, from the old media of newspapers and film to the emerging "new media" of lifestyle magazines and documentary-style television news, actively exploited the negative image of cities through decontextualized invocations of impending chaos and "blood in the streets."[19]

Meanwhile, in the context of federal retrenchment and growing interurban competition for new resources, subjective factors like image and environment gained new importance as indicators of quality of life and business climate. As a consequence, urban "reputation"—for fiscal solvency, creditworthiness, and public safety—became a paramount concern for elected leaders and local elites. Thus, as media portrayals worsened, they contributed to "image crises," which expressed and reinforced the broader fiscal and financial crises that cities faced.[20]

Clearly, underlying this battle over the language of "urban crisis" was a broader ideological struggle to interpret the rapidly deteriorating economic and social conditions unfolding in most U.S. cities and to determine the appropriate political response. Urban leaders and social movements were coming to understand that the battle was not over the fate of a single city, but over the future path—political, economic, and cultural—that urban redevelopment would take. More broadly still, the debate over the nature of "urban crisis" was being used to frame the appropriate role of the state, if any, in future post-crisis solutions writ large.

In this context, urban fiscal crises became political opportunities to be exploited along partisan, regional, and ideological lines. It was easy to blame urban populations—disproportionately poor, working class, and nonwhite—for their own problems, to rally suburban residents against these populations, and to use fiscal crises as the rationale to reform urban policy and the welfare state more broadly. This opportunity was clearly on display during the mayors' trip to Washington in September 1975. Senator Hubert H. Humphrey of Wisconsin opened the Senate hearings with the pessimistic prediction: "the mayors should expect only indifference from Congress and hostility from the administration." Connecticut Senator Abraham Ribicoff put it more bluntly: "so far as they're concerned the cities can go to hell." Treasury Secretary Simon's "flinty" response to the mayors' pleas, calling simply for "further sacrifices," did not disappoint. Even if New York's sacrifices did not immediately prevent default, Simon added, they "could only be beneficial" for the larger example they would set for the rest of the nation's cities.[21]

And so, from the Rustbelt to the Sunbelt, U.S. cities heard the mantra from Washington, DC: "tighten your belts and bite the bullet."[22] "Belt tightening" referred to the demand that cities impose austerity budgets through which social services could be cut, municipal workers laid off, and public salaries and pensions reduced. "Biting the bullet" referred to the broader demand that cities accept the free-market doctrine over the longer term, making permanent the austerity regime. In effect, the national debate then heating up over the welfare state versus the free market was happening first in, and on the backs of, the nation's cities. And so emerged the bedrock terms later understood as the neoliberal credo: tax cuts, small government, and an end to "entitlement programs" for the poor and, by extension, for the cities in which the poor disproportionately lived. This era of disinvestment, as we will see, was to set the stage for uneven vulnerability to urban crises to come.

A TALE OF TWO CRISIS CITIES

Signs of economic decline began appearing for both New York and New Orleans in the 1960s, with a spike in the loss of manufacturing and commercial jobs in New York and a long-term erosion of tax revenue, manufacturing jobs, and population in New Orleans. For New York City, this was manifested in the loss of an interdependent web of industries, from textiles to longshoring, that had once made the city a national "goods-producing" hub. New York City lost 600,000 of such jobs between 1965 and 1973, with an average of 100,000 jobs lost every year from 1970 to 1975.[23]

During the main period of regional growth in the U.S. south, New Orleans experienced relative economic decline, particularly in manufacturing. The city had never been a major manufacturing center, except for shipbuilding, and even this limited industrial sector had been stagnant during the 1950s through the 1970s. Manufacturing declined every year but one in the decade between 1967 and 1977, and by 1978, only 11 percent of the labor force was employed in manufacturing, a figure that placed the city among the lowest in industrial employment among major U.S. cities.[24]

An often-cited economic analysis of the New Orleans economy by James Bobo of the University of New Orleans found that "the local economy has been in a period of relative stagnation from 1966 through mid-1975.... Unemployment has risen over the period [and] economic conditions have worsened." The report concluded:

> Extreme income inequality that exists in the metropolitan area is socially undesirable, because it tends to abet in economic stagnation and sub-employment, ensures the perpetuation of poverty and poorness, and exacerbates existing social problems.... More socially pernicious, however, it comprises the essential foundation of citizen alienation and vulnerability to rabble-rousers.[25]

Aside from the loss of "smokestack industries," however, other job losses were of greater concern to corporate and political elites in both cities, especially those in the corporate sector that leaders were actively trying to court. Such losses appeared especially dramatic in New York, which began experiencing a high-profile "exodus" of corporate headquarters in the late 1960s. Between 1966 and 1974, New York City lost more than seventy-five of the nation's most important business headquarters along with tens of smaller firms, and with them, tens of thousands of high-end service jobs.[26] In the current competitive environment, this loss translated as Connecticut's and New Jersey's gain and, even more frightening, signaled a broader and possibly permanent shift of economic advantage from the "Rustbelt" of the East and Midwest to the "Sunbelt" of the South and West. Between 1968 and 1974, New York's suburbs in Connecticut and New Jersey tripled their share of Fortune 500 companies while New York lost 30 percent of its share. Meanwhile, as New York State lost 20 percent—mostly from New York City—the Sunbelt gained 100 percent more headquarters over the same six-year period. In a comparison with ten other Eastern and Midwestern cities, New York City lost the most corporate headquarters overall. But as a percentage of the total, Detroit, Pittsburgh, Philadelphia, and St. Louis lost more, since they were more dependent on single industries. And New York was almost tied with Chicago and Boston, cities of comparable economic diversity, if not the same stature as capitals of corporate headquarters.[27]

In New Orleans, the shifting economic base alarmed local elites, who also perceived job losses as symptomatic of the city's declining ability to compete with other cities in the interurban struggle to attract jobs and investment. "The City of New Orleans faces a fiscal crisis," stated a 1966 report sponsored by the Bureau of Government Research (BGR), a local think tank. Rising deficits, increasing municipal wages and prices, and escalating public expectations for local government services threatened to wreak financial havoc to the extent that "the City will enter 1967 with an empty till." "Deficiencies in the City services are evident in almost every direction," and "the immediate prospects of larger State and Federal assistance to New Orleans are not good." In the absence of meaningful reform, the BGR feared that "the City must either raise more revenues or immediately face an increasingly serious deterioration of city services."[28] Already in 1966, the BGR was reporting that New Orleans was sure to face a major economic "disaster" by the mid-1970s if changes were not made in the structure of taxation.[29]

A declining white middle class and increasing city expenditures combined to aggravate the fiscal problems of the city and create a sense of political crisis. "If you follow economic trends and compare New Orleans with some other cities such as Atlanta, Dallas and Houston, you will see that New Orleans is competitively lagging behind," bemoaned Murray C. Fincher, President of the New Orleans Chamber of Commerce in 1968. "New Orleans is lagging in the race of major cities for economic development.... Studies bear this out.... The need to do something to promote commercial and industrial growth here [is] apparent." Echoing Chamber members' worries of declining profits, Fincher exclaimed: "[I]n the greater New Orleans area...we are experiencing major traffic problems, problems of air and stream pollution, problems dealing with housing, education, recreation, etc. for which solutions must be found." For Fincher and other Chamber officials, "[i]f the leadership of the metropolitan area does not now begin to take steps to establish priorities for curing these problems...by 1985 or sooner, this area is going to be in pretty bad shape."[30]

In both cities, deindustrialization, corporate flight, and job loss led to precipitous population declines. The city of New Orleans lost more than 34,000 residents during the 1960s, the first time the city had experienced a decade of population loss. While the suburban areas grew in population, the city lost more than 35,000 residents during the 1970s and more than 60,000 during the 1980s.[31] These population decreases were comparable proportional to New York's loss of 1 million residents between 1968 and 1982.[32] Already by the early 1970s, this intertwined drop in population, industry, and corporate headquarters had severely eroded the tax base of both cities, leading to a worsening quality of life, and earning both degrading monikers: "asphalt jungle" and "sunbelt in the swamp."[33]

The potential for fiscal crisis was exacerbated by new federal revenue-sharing formulas adopted in the 1970s that decreased the targeting of federal funds for disadvantaged inner cities as well as the failure of Presidents Nixon, Ford, and Carter to maintain support for low-income housing or to federalize healthcare. Cuts in healthcare caused particular pain for New York City, which was unique among cities for bearing 25 percent of public healthcare costs for its citizens.[34] With escalating healthcare costs and a growing poor population, the cost of covering the uninsured, on its own, constituted nearly half of the city's budget gap from 1975 to 1988, reaching 106 percent of the city's budget gap in 1978 and 109 percent during the Wall Street crash of 1987. As historian Jonathan Soffer put it bluntly: "If Washington D.C. had covered [healthcare], New York City would not have had a fiscal crisis, it would not have had to cut services, and the city government would have been in a far better position to deal with the public health-related problems of homelessness, AIDS, and drugs" that were to plague the city and the Koch administration in the 1980s.[35]

Escalating social problems fueled unrest and catalyzed an explosion of political activism, chiefly among the unemployed in the form of the welfare rights movement and among unionized workers in the form of strikes. Between 1960 and 1970, under mounting pressure from the welfare rights movement, New York City used Great Society and Model City programs to expand welfare rolls and extend services more widely to its poorest residents. This provoked what was arguably one of the highpoints in the "New York liberal tradition." Under the mayoralty of John V. Lindsay from 1966 to 1974, despite its falling fortunes, the city increased or maintained spending on welfare, housing, healthcare, education, and municipal payrolls.[36] During these years, the city also saw a dramatic increase in labor militancy, particularly among public sector unions. New York City workers participated in some thirty strikes and numerous other job actions between 1960 and 1975. Most of these occurred during Lindsay's two terms in office and were some of the most bitter strikes in the city's history, including transit (1966), teachers (1967 and 1968), sanitation (1968), drawbridge and sewage treatment plant operators (1971), police (1971), and firefighters (1973).[37]

In New Orleans, calls for "reforming" city government and solving the fiscal crisis also occurred in the context of a major escalation in labor activism. In the late 1960s, the state American Federation of Labor–Congress of Industrial Organization (AFL-CIO) formed the Louisiana Oil Field Workers and embarked on an aggressive campaign to unionize workers in the oil services industry. During these years, the Louisiana chapter of the American Federation of State, County, and Municipal Employees (AFSCME) lobbied the state legislature to increase taxes to support state workers' salaries. In addition, pro-union groups representing teachers, police officers, and firefighters pushed for collective bargaining rights and organized several strikes for union recognition, including a protracted teachers strike in New Orleans in 1969. A major upsurge of public sector organizing came in 1974 when three groups of school employees won the right to be represented by a collective bargaining agent. The first group, school teachers, selected the United Teachers of New Orleans, an affiliate of the National Education Association, the American Federation of Teachers, and the AFL-CIO, in a November election that followed a year-long fight to pressure the Orleans Parish School Board to allow such elections. The second group, maintenance employees, chose the Teamsters. And the third group, custodians, selected the AFSCME to represent them in contract negotiations with the school board.[38]

SPATIAL FIX AND SOCIO-SPATIAL RESTRUCTURING

Diminishing fortunes and escalating political tensions in New York and New Orleans motivated urban growth coalitions to launch several large-scale urban redevelopment projects aimed at reorganizing land uses and restoring profits and power. In New York, elites and planners adopted a proactive and entrepreneurial approach to expand rentable space on the tightly packed island of Manhattan. Using "slum clearance" grants and massive borrowing, newly created public-private partnerships defined working-class neighborhoods as "blighted" and used federal subsidies to clear residents and erect high-end office towers. In New Orleans, in a process akin to urban slum clearance, developers extended capital circulation into the swamps to clear wetland ecosystems for residential, commercial, and industrial uses.

We interpret these reform initiatives—for example, clearing slums and marshes in the name of "redevelopment"—as expressions of "creative destruction" and "spatial fix" in which political and economic leaders attempted to remedy the plethora of interconnected fiscal, socio-economic, and political crises by establishing new scales of urban and metropolitan regulation and accumulation.[39] Through levees and floodwalls, bulldozers and steel frames, and aided by powerful urban renewal policies and insurance subsidies, leaders in New York and New Orleans attempted to increase the liquidity of "disused" land and find outlets for surplus capital in a period of economic stagnation, while displacing risk for this new scale of speculative development onto taxpayers. These interventions were justified by stigmatizing wetlands and mixed-use neighborhoods as impediments to economic growth. Over time, however, these crisis-driven forms of geographical displacement and reconfiguration would produce heavy costs and new risks for local populations, eco-systems, and the public sector.

Local Development Corporations (LDCs) and the Financialization of Manhattan

The dream of transforming Lower Manhattan into a global financial center dates back to the 1920s, when prominent families in downtown banking and real estate, like the Rockefellers, Pratts and Dewinters, created the Regional Plan Association (RPA) and drafted plans to restructure the metropolitan region around a massive central business district stretching from the tip of Manhattan to Central Park.[40] The plan was scuttled by the stock market crash of 1929 and the subsequent depression and put on hold during the post-WWII boom. It was only in the mid-1960s, through the combined efforts of the administrations of Mayor John V. Lindsay and Governor Nelson Rockefeller—whose brother David was then at the helm of Chase Manhattan Bank—that the plan was taken up again. By now, the threat of corporate flight as well as desire for new investment opportunities motivated those in the finance, insurance, and real estate (FIRE) sector to pressure the city and state to provide incentives for big owners, renters, and financiers to stay in New York. This threat was felt acutely by the Rockefellers, both Nelson and David, given that their family was one of the largest landowners in Manhattan's downtown financial district. Under Governor Rockefeller's guidance, and with Mayor Lindsay's strong support, New York City and New York State undertook a novel form of "corporate welfare" designed to appease members of the city's FIRE sector and shore up Lower Manhattan's commercial real estate market. The project envisioned the greatest office and residential development in the city's history, concentrated on the southwestern tip of the Manhattan island and including Battery Park City and a new "World Trade Center." See figure 2.2.

Enlisted to support and push the plan through with a minimum of public scrutiny was the newly created New York and New Jersey Port Authority (PA), established and led by power broker Robert Moses. Federal funds—designated for mass transportation and "slum clearance"—were thereby appropriated for the project. In addition, the city and state adopted a highly unorthodox borrowing strategy: tax abatements for large real estate firms and outright subsidies of commercial property development through mortgage underwriting.[41] To this end, they formed "local development corporations" (LDCs), which enabled private companies to establish financial partnerships with government outside the normal channels of legislative oversight. The largest and most disastrous of these was the Urban Development Corporation, created by Governor Rockefeller in 1967, which went bankrupt in 1973, losing the state hundreds of millions of dollars and leading to a federal-level investigation of its practices. A number of

Figure 2.2
Financializing Lower Manhattan. New York Governor Nelson Rockefeller, foreground, and New York City Mayor John Lindsay, over his shoulder, with a model of the Lower Manhattan project, April 25, 1968. (*New York Daily News*)

other, smaller LDCs were created in the mid- to late 1960s and met similar fates during the real estate recession of the early 1970s.

In their short life, however, these LDCs were to play a powerful role. In order to finance the greatest office tower development in the city's history, private corporations borrowed billions of dollars in the short-term money market to enable these LDCs to get long-term mortgages. Between 1967 and 1973, over 66 million square feet were built in New York, an unprecedented rate of growth, and more than double any similar period between 1960 and 1992.[42] Most of this development occurred in Manhattan's downtown—in particular with the construction of the World Trade Center's (WTC) 10 million square feet of office space.

We can view this massive reorganization of urban space as a form of crisis-driven urbanization premised on refashioning land uses to remedy crisis conditions and create new socio-structural arrangements to encourage new forms of profitmaking and economic growth. It soon became clear that the construction of the massive high-rise WTC entailed not so much the clearing of "slums" as the deindustrialization of New York's still-thriving port district, the elimination of thousands of blue-collar jobs, and the destruction of a historically mixed-use and culturally rich district. The waterfront neighborhood had evolved over three centuries alongside what was, until this period, the most important commercial port on the Northeastern seaboard. It was a regional center for many of New York's longest-running industries, from tanning to beer brewing, coffee roasting to maritime, and, from 1921 through 1966, the electronics stores and warehouses of "Radio Row." One part of the area, known as "Little Syria," was also home to the nation's oldest Middle Eastern community. Oscar Nadel, a leader of the Downtown West Businessmen's Association, estimated in 1962 that 1,400 commercial enterprises doing an annual business volume of $300 million and employing 30,000 people were located in the 30-block site.[43]

Not surprisingly, the plans were to meet with opposition from many quarters. Local businesses, workers, and residents quickly organized, fighting displacement through highly publicized class action lawsuits and demonstrations. Urbanists and preservationists Jane Jacobs, Louise Huxtable, and Lewis Mumford deplored the loss of the "livable city" to the tyranny of modernism and published scathing articles in opposition.[44] City planners put out reports criticizing the design of "cities [with] extensive construction of tall buildings" for potentially worsening congestion, environmental conditions, and public safety.[45] State legislators held public hearings criticizing the Port Authority for the "impropriety" of investing public money into these "wasteful and lavish facilities." Officials called for legislation requiring the Port Authority to divest itself of the WTC and pay more attention to "its basic responsibility—mass transportation"[46] Hearings and a suit were brought by State Senator Franz S. Leichter, a Manhattan Democrat, and Assemblyman G. Oliver Koppell, a Bronx Democrat. Some of the plan's angriest opponents were private realtors in Midtown, which was then the regional and national office center. The main group representing Midtown realtors was the Committee for a Reasonable World Trade Center, led by Lawrence A. Wien, head of the syndicate that owned the Empire State Building. Realtors warned of the "glut" that would surely result from the additional 30 percent of Manhattan office space the towers would suddenly create. For the Committee, the special tax breaks and 5 percent financing advantage offered to buyers of space in the WTC was an "anti-competitive agenda" corrupting the real estate market.[47]

Yet in the end, aesthetic criticism, political resistance, and countervailing market tendencies were to no avail. Public and private leaders ignored the critics, deploying eminent domain to force out residents, workers, and

small property owners. When Robert Moses himself joined the opposition, criticizing the "appropriation" of his public agency for the sake of
high-end private office space, he was overridden by Governor Rockefeller
and removed from his post soon thereafter.[48] In 1968, following the RPA
plan, the PA began construction of four "superblocks" for the downtown
central business district.

With the zoning conversion from industrial to grade A commercial
real estate, the WTC served to raise real estate prices in the district up to
1,000-fold. Yet, with the building boom, mortgage money soon dried up,
as did the high-end rental market—just as Midtown realtors had warned.
Major financial and real estate families, such as the Rockefellers and the
Rudins, turned to lobbying the city to continue subsidizing mortgage
underwriting and actual rental of the new office space by government agencies.[49] To do so, the city began borrowing on the short term market. While
making up only 3 percent of the U.S. population, during the late 1960s and
early 1970s New York City held nearly half of all short-term debt borrowed
by U.S. cities.[50] Meanwhile using these short-term loans to cover operating expenses and make mortgage payments contravened generally accepted
accounting procedures—helping explain why New York was alone among
U.S. cities in borrowing for this purpose. Riskier still, the city did so in the
amount of $3 billion, equivalent to one-quarter of the city's entire budget,
half of the city's debt, and over three times the size of the city's total budget
deficit.

Making matters worse, despite the enormous upsurge in office and
luxury residential construction, the property tax levy was rapidly shrinking. By 1976, 40 percent of all real estate had become tax exempt, up from
28 percent in the 1950s, costing the city tens of millions of dollars annually. This was again due to lobbying efforts by real estate led public private
partnerships, which convinced the tax commission to lower assessments
on an annual basis. According to labor scholar Kim Moody, even a "modest
increase" in assessments "could have averted the Fiscal Crisis."[51]

Adding to this burden was the final price tag for the WTC, which,
when completed in 1977 for $900 million, was five years behind sched-
ule and $500 million over budget. This created a financing fiasco that
pushed New York even deeper into debt. Throughout the 1970s, the bulk
of the WTC's publicly financed units remained unsold, and if not for the
PA itself renting 56 floors—25 percent of the total space—the building would have remained almost entirely empty. In so doing, the Port
Authority forced the states of New York and New Jersey—renting space
above market rate and getting nothing back in taxes—to sink millions of
public dollars into this "white elephant."[52] Meanwhile, the huge buildings' maintenance costs far outpaced receipts to the extent that new lines

of credit had to be advanced by the city and state just to keep them open and running at a loss.[53]

These concatenated crises—real estate, financial, fiscal—were occurring at a time when the city was hemorrhaging manufacturing and commercial jobs, the foundation of its middle- and working-class communities. Multilevel forces, including interurban competition and local drivers of change, operated in a mutually constitutive fashion. Purposeful local policies of deindustrialization, such as those that had rezoned the port neighborhood, paved the way for tens of millions of additional square feet of private real estate throughout the city. This crisis-driven conversion of neighborhoods to commercial real estate exacerbated displacement and unemployment. The instability and loss of jobs, in turn, created additional demand for social welfare and public services, thereby increasing the strain on city finances. Thus, the multimillion dollar public debt incurred in building and maintaining this new symbol of downtown's financial might contributed heavily to the city's spiraling fiscal crisis of the mid-1970s.

Ecological Conquest and the Urbanization of the Wetlands

The federal government's response to the Hurricane Betsy disaster in 1965 reflected an emerging form of crisis-driven urbanization based on the idea that flood control structures and related socio-legal regulations—for example, levees, floodwalls, and insurance policies—could produce a new spatial fix to restore, extend, and intensify capital circulation.[54] The destruction caused by Betsy was unprecedented: the hurricane killed seventy-five people, flooded dozens of neighborhoods in New Orleans, and caused more than $1 billion in damage, the nation's first billion dollar hurricane.[55] Immediately, state and local officials lobbied Congress to pass the Flood Control Act of 1965, which authorized the Army Corps of Engineers (hereafter referred to as the Corps) to build the Lake Pontchartrain and Vicinity Hurricane Protection Project (LP&VHPP).[56] As originally planned, the LP&VHPP was to consist of massive physical barriers and flood control structures, including concrete floodwalls and levees around the metropolitan area to "protect" the region from hurricane storm surges. Levee enlargements and new floodwalls would span portions of Orleans Parish along St. Bernard Parish. Dozens of miles of levees would encompass the Chalmette and New Orleans East areas to encourage real estate development and stimulate the conversion of swampland into residential, commercial, and industrial land uses.

Although federally authorized, the LP&VHPP was a joint federal, state, and local effort, a public-private partnership in which governments sought to encourage private investment in building urban infrastructure in the swamps, wetlands, and marshes. Each parish (county) would contain a local levee district composed of state-appointed officials and operate as a state authority and local sponsor. The Corps was responsible for project design and construction of the approximately 125 miles of levees to protect communities in Orleans, Jefferson, St. Bernard, and St. Charles Parishes around Lake Pontchartrain. The local sponsors would be responsible for operation, maintenance, repair, replacement, and rehabilitation of the levees after the construction of the project, or a project unit, was complete.[57] Congress required the federal government to assume 70 percent of the construction cost and local sponsors to pay the remaining 30 percent. At the time of authorization in 1965, the Corps estimated that the hurricane protection project would be completed by the mid- to late 1970s and would cost approximately $80 million.[58]

Despite the rhetoric of hurricane and flood "protection," Corps officials and local sponsors planned and developed the LP&VHPP to mitigate the crisis tendencies affecting city and state governments. The LP&VHPP offered a new and extraordinary regulatory framework to enhance and accelerate the flow of capital into the wetlands using various water control and land-use devices. Congress required the Corps to perform "some form of benefit-cost evaluation...to justify the provision of the project purpose."[59] An "economic analysis" found in the Corps' 1962 "Interim Survey Report" stated that the "benefit-cost ratio is 18.9 to 1 for the entire project.... The majority of project benefits are derived from future land development and enhancement."[60] According to the Corps, a "high level of urban flood protection specified in Corps guidelines is not realistic unless net benefits would be maximized."[61] The Corps estimated that 21 percent of the property that the LP&VHPP aimed to protect was "existing developments," but 79 percent was for "future developments."[62]

The establishment of the National Flood Insurance Program (NFIP) (Pub. L. No. 90-448) in 1968 served as an additional socio-legal mechanism to transform swampland into a space of real estate investment. Passed as a result of the destructive flood surge in 1965 caused by Hurricane Betsy, the goal of the NFIP was to provide flood insurance protection for communities willing to adopt and enforce minimal floodplain management standards. The NFIP was also charged with identifying areas of high and low flood hazards and to set flood insurance rates for structures located in each flood hazard area. As a government insurance program "carried out by private insurance industry," Congress looked to the NFIP as a national policy to guide land development.[63] Prior to 1968, few insurance companies would insure property in flood- and hurricane-prone areas, a situation that impeded residential and commercial development in many coastal regions and flood zones in the United States. By providing subsidized private flood insurance, the federal government made it possible for private insurers to write policies in areas at risk for flooding and hurricane damage.[64]

Political and economic elites framed the urbanization of the wetlands using the vocabulary of ecological conquest, infusing the rhetoric of economic growth and progress with the stigmatization and destruction of the surrounding marshes and swamps. In previous decades, urban growth and sprawl had been hemmed in by bayous, wetlands, and lakes. By the 1970s, however, federal and state investments and lucrative subsidies were overcoming geographical constraints to real estate development and opening up the region to far-flung urbanization. In a 1974 report to Congress, the Corps proudly proclaimed that the LP&VHPP "will hasten urbanization and industrialization of valuable marshes and swamps by providing for further flood protection and land reclamation."[65] As a result, areas such as New Orleans East, St. Bernard Parish, and other outlying areas "would be rendered more suitable for urban use as a result of the project works. This effect will be reflected in increases in value of these lands, which increases are called 'enhancement benefits,' since they do represent additions to the Gross National Product." At the same time, the Corps warned "urbanization of the project area would proceed at a much reduced rate if the hurricane protection plan was not implemented."

The promise of extending capital circulation into the swamps was akin to the urban slum clearance that was taking place in Lower Manhattan and many other cities around the United States during the 1950s and 1960s. Instead of clearing blighted housing and mixed-use commercial districts for more profitable purposes, city leaders and the Corps degraded and disparaged the wetlands, thus providing justification for clearing the swamps for residential, commercial, and industrial development, a process of "creative-destruction" in Joseph Schumpeter's famous formulation.[66] This justification drew strength from the dual authorities of law and engineering science, especially the so-called "benefit-cost analysis," to legitimatize the inherently ambiguous concepts of flood "risk" and hurricane "protection" and create the appearance of certainty and security out of the cacophony of claims about economic "growth" and "value."

Ultimately, slum and wetlands clearance activities were designed and implemented by policymakers to both mitigate crises and create new bases of profit making. Like targeted policies of deindustrialization and rezoning and investments in office infrastructure that served to increase the liquidity of urban real estate in Lower Manhattan, local growth coalitions in New Orleans looked to invest in flood-control structures, including levees and floodwalls, and flood insurance as a socio-legal means to increase the liquidity of swampland real estate. Clearing physical structures and clearing wetlands operated as analogous political mechanisms to overcome the spatial and temporal barriers to capital circulation. Like urban renewal policies in cities, the policies governing the draining of the wetlands aimed to absorb the risks and costs of land development so that capitalists would not have to do so. In addition, the building of floodwalls and levees to control water flow and facilitate new property development enabled state actors to match distant real estate investors with new profit-making opportunities. In short, there was an elective affinity between slum clearance and wetlands clearance activities. Both operated to open up new markets, speed production cycles, and reduce the turnover time for buying and selling parcels of urban and wetland property.

The construction of the Mississippi River-Gulf Outlet (MR-GO) in the 1960s operated as another weapon in the arsenal of planning tools to pulverize and transform the wetlands into abstract, homogeneous, and quantifiable spaces to enhance tax revenues and profit making. Planned in the 1950s and constructed in the 1960s, the Corps designed and built the seventy-five-mile MR-GO as a navigation canal to connect the port of New Orleans with the Gulf of Mexico. See figure 2.3. The project dredged 290 million cubic yards of earth, 60 million more cubic yards than was dredged to create the Panama Canal. A 1957 newspaper article in the *New Orleans States News* proclaimed, "the [MR-GO] is a chance for the industrial development of St. Bernard parish as a supplement to the great industrial growth of neighboring Orleans."[67] The Corps considered the MR-GO as a fundamental and strategic component of the LP&VHPP that "was predicted to encourage the development of port facilities and related economic activity." By building a hurricane levee along the banks of the MR-GO, the Corps believed their flood protection efforts would produce "the new tax base that would generate the funds to make the local cost share payments" to fund the LP&VHPP.[68] Yet, over time, MR-GO dramatically increased salinity in the marshes and gradually devastated the wetlands, producing a harbinger of future social-ecological disaster.[69]

The LP&VHPP project, MR-GO, and the NFIP introduced a new conjuncture of regional development that profoundly transformed the surrounding ecosystem and generated new risks and environment consequences. Whereas in 1950 New Orleans's population comprised 660,000 persons on 90 square miles of urbanized land, by 1990 this had grown to 1.04 million people on 270 square miles. Prior to the 1960s, Lake Pontchartrain to the north and vast wetlands to the west, south, and east had inhibited New Orleans's growth and development.[70] After the 1960s, the Greater New Orleans metropolitan area would sprawl across former

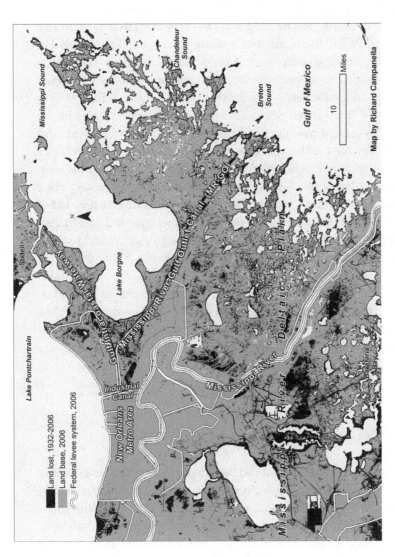

Figure 2.3

Map of Mississippi River Gulf Outlet (MR-GO) showing erosion of the wetlands and land loss since 1932. (Richard Campanella)

Since Hurricane Betsy in 1965, critics have attacked the MR-GO as a "superhighway for hurricane storm surges" because of the channel's susceptibility to deluge by storms. In 1998, forty years after construction of the MR-GO, the St. Bernard Parish Council unanimously adopted a resolution to close the canal. In 2007, the U.S. Congress singled out MR-GO's complicity in Katrina's devastation and ordered the Corps to close the canal and to develop a plan for ecosystem restoration. Before closure in 2008, MR-GO had contributed to the erosion of 20,000–65,000 acres of wetlands, as much as 100 of the 500 square miles of wetlands that had previously stood to the southeast of New Orleans, an area that was in the bullseye of Hurricane Katrina's storm surge that engulfed the city and region. All told, the construction and operation of the channel negatively affected more than 618,000 acres (965.6 square miles) of habitat—an area almost three times the size of New York City's five boroughs.

wetlands and marshes, consuming swampland at more than three times the rate of population growth. The transformation of bayous, marshes, and swamps into large-scale residential communities accelerated during the 1960s and 1970s as Jefferson Parish added 47,000 housing units and Orleans Parish added 29,000 units.[71] In New Orleans East, commercial and residential development skyrocketed as the previous wetlands were cleared to make way for 22,000 new housing units and tens of thousands of people. In St. Bernard Parish, the number of housing units more than doubled in the forty years after the completion of the MR-GO. Throughout the metropolitan area, populous new suburbs sprang up across former wetlands along the lake and to the east—all areas that would flood in 2005.

Overall, the crisis-driven restructuring of socio-physical space in the 1960s and 70s created new risks and vulnerabilities for governments and residents in the New Orleans region. The urbanization of the wetlands resulted in a "great risk shift" in which more and more households were dependent on floodwalls, levees, and flood insurance to protect their major financial investment, their home.[72] The region-wide management of land-use and water control through such structures operated as a "spatial fix" to remedy the fiscal crisis of the state and overcome the socio-spatial barriers to capital accumulation. Yet, federal investments in the LP&VHPP and the NFIP drained not only the wetlands but also the tax revenue from Orleans Parish as floodplain development encouraged people and industries in the city to relocate into the new federally subsidized suburbs. The eroding tax base, in turn, created new financial risks and vulnerabilities for the city as diminishing revenue constrained policymaking and, even more problematic, provided fodder for some to argue for lucrative tax incentives and other market-centered policies to spur urban revitalization.

FISCAL CRISIS AND NEOLIBERAL REFORM

The financialization of Manhattan and the urbanization of the New Orleans wetlands reflected an emerging socio-spatial strategy—and ostensible spatial fix—to solve the fiscal crisis of the local state and re-create the social conditions for profit making and economic development. In addition to these two strategies, elected officials and economic elites in both cities attempted to catalyze new growth through a series of tax incentives, cuts to public services, and curtailments in labor organizing. This last strategy was particularly significant given that the power and militancy of unions, both public and private sector, had been expanding in the postwar period. As noted above, New York and New Orleans were centers of such growth in union strength through the 1960s. There as elsewhere, labor organizing had the effect of driving up the size, earnings, and political power of the working and middle classes but, from the perspective of economic elites, had driven down the competitiveness of the local "business environment." Thus, disrupting labor power was essential to the advancement of a broader pro-growth agenda. Together with entrepreneurial officials at the levels of city and state, mayors and elected leaders in New York and New Orleans framed the fiscal crisis as an opportunity to promulgate their preferred approach to market-centered urban revitalization. On one hand, they argued that fiscal crisis necessitated new austerity measures to reduce wages, institute layoffs, and curtail public spending. On the other hand, they used fiscal crisis discourse to legitimize expanding the role of public-private partnerships in urban governance, as well as to redevelop the space of the city for new economic purposes and affluent demographic groups. In so doing, they intensified a market-centered approach to urbanization that, arguably, had helped to produce the crisis in the first place.

The New York Crisis Regime

Once the fiscal crisis hit in the summer of 1975, New York governor Hugh Carey together with a team of advisers from New York City's tourism and FIRE sectors, took over the city's affairs and created two powerful, supra-governmental state agencies to oversee the city's budget, contracts, and policy.[73] First was the Municipal Assistance Corporation, also known as "Big MAC," a temporary financial institution headed by nine board members from the private sector that was authorized to sell up to $3 billion in bonds. To defray risk, the board gained control over city sales and stock transfer taxes and could withhold these vital monies if the city was not demonstrating sufficient "restraint"—that is, imposing large enough cuts to public spending.[74] To further ensure cutbacks were made, a second institution, the Emergency Financial Control Board (EFCB), was created. Here, elected officials were in the majority but were subject to veto power by three bank and corporate representatives.[75] The EFCB had a mandate to develop a financial plan for the city, to reject city spending and labor contracts considered excessive, and even to remove the mayor and other officials if they defied EFCB directives. Together, the MAC and EFCB advanced an agenda that was doggedly pro-business, antiwelfare state, and anti-union, while shifting attention away from the role of "corporate welfare" in the city's default, and the notion that corporate sacrifices should play any role in the city's recovery.[76]

Following MAC and EFCB directives, Mayor Beame imposed scores of austerity measures in 1975, including, among others: a transit fare hike,

limits on rent control, cuts to welfare benefits, the closing of public facilities, wage freezes, and the elimination of thousands of city jobs. Specifically,
the city called on workers to forgo a 6 percent pay increase scheduled for
July 7 or accept, with proportional pay reductions, a four-day workweek.
After the unions rejected the proposal, Beame called for a huge reduction
in City University of New York admissions, the closing of library branches
and health facilities, and the immediate elimination of 38,000 city jobs.[77]
Staunch opposition by community-union alliances was overcome, largely
by including labor leaders, who voted against their own membership,
within the MAC.[78]

While serving as powerful "political symbolism," the cuts saved relatively little money, especially in the midst of tax cuts.[79] Thus, while seen as a
"very positive step" by Treasury Secretary Simon, New York's austerity did
not accomplish their purported goal: convincing the White House that the
city could balance its books. President Ford and the Treasury Department
developed a plan that enabled the federal government to compensate major
banks while voiding union contracts. Then, On October 29, 1975, Ford
announced he was "prepared to veto any bill that has as its purpose a Federal
bailout of New York City to prevent default."[80] The next morning, the *Daily
News* ran its infamous headline: "FORD TO CITY: DROP DEAD."

The legacies of the fiscal crisis were severe and sweeping. Among the most
striking was the disempowerment of New York City's public sector unions.
This was made clear when the unions' carefully tended pension funds were
used to "save the city" by buying $2.5 billion in unsellable municipal bonds.
Union leadership, working with the corporate boards of the crisis regime,
forced their members to accept this deal, thus placing them at great financial risk, and putting them in the compromised position of being creditors
to their own employers in city management. A second, related legacy was
the empowerment of an unelected, business-dominated "crisis regime." The
latter included MAC and EFCB, as well as activist public-private partnerships like the Association for a Better New York (ABNY) and the New York
City Partnership (NYCP), and entrepreneurial government agencies like
the Office of Economic Development (OED) and an expanded Convention
and Visitors Bureau (CVB). These entities were to constitute what critics
and supporters alike came to call a "permanent" or "shadow government"
of the city's elites.[81] The OED, soon to change its name to the Economic
Development Corporation (EDC), and CVB, soon to change its name to
NYC & Co., became an expanding beachhead for the interests of FIRE and
tourism within City Hall. Perhaps most significantly, this new model of
public-private governance—unelected, far-reaching, and with little public
oversight—served as a precedent for the creation of similar, ad hoc groups
to arise in future crisis periods.

Planned Shrinkage

With the decline in investment opportunities, and expanded powers, the crisis regime turned to a new form of spatial fix through a host
of blight-clearance policies broadly referred to as "planned shrinkage."
Compared to the period of office tower construction in the 1960s, this
phase of creative destruction was to be less architecturally grandiose but
even more socially and spatially disruptive. "Planned shrinkage," originally
developed by Roger Starr, Director of the Department of Housing and
Urban Development, was a controversial tactic that applied, as Starr put it,
a "triage" approach to urban development. Through discriminatory budget
policies, city services were curtailed in the poorest districts, thus "shrinking" the populations demanding the most services while freeing resources
to be concentrated in more affluent areas where the tax base was stronger
and ostensibly more resilient.

This harsh budgetary calculus was joined by new land-use policies. The
New York Housing and Development Administration ceased building new
public housing, reduced support of existing housing, and sold off large
stretches of publicly held land. In so doing, New York City was participating
in what was a nationwide phenomenon in the 1970s, after federal funding
for construction of public housing was ended by the Nixon administration
in 1972. At the same time, New York's housing cuts were intensified by
MAC and the RPA's "Blighted Areas Plan" in 1976.[82] This created a zoning
category of "blight" whereby "visual signs of decay" could be used to make
large areas—usually poor and with a mixed-use economic base—eligible to
be "blacktopped," their populations "removed," and their land rezoned for
industrial or commercial use—essentially warehousing the properties for
future reinvestment.[83] Meanwhile, banks "redlined" entire neighborhoods
surrounding the supposedly blighted area—that is, lowered credit ratings
and stopped loans, thus making it nearly impossible for existing residents
and businesses to invest or maintain properties in these communities.[84]

Also in 1976, the Beame administration created the Office of Economic
Development (OED) as a means of "spurring new investment and cutting
red-tape" for businesses dealing with the city. OED was empowered to,
among other things, issue subsidies and tax breaks to spur new investment
in particular areas and as a means of boosting credit ratings and enticing
further loans for businesses in these areas. As part of the planned shrinkage agenda, OED strategically centralized such incentives in Manhattan's
downtown and Midtown business districts.

Thus, in practice, planned shrinkage, in conjunction with austerity measures, meant that the impact of fiscal crisis would be socially and spatially
managed through the unequal distribution of public resources and private

investments. The heaviest burden would be borne by communities in the Bronx, Brooklyn, and the Manhattan neighborhoods of the Lower East Side, Chinatown, and Harlem—communities that were primarily poor, working class, and nonwhite. Elected leaders and policymakers would instead target resources toward the upkeep and security of the central business districts, tourist destinations, and more affluent, white enclaves.

The implementation of planned shrinkage and austerity was criticized as racist, classist, and anti-union, and strenuously contested by many groups—from politicized teenage graffiti writers to the rank and file of police and fire unions and from city planners and architects to the black and Latino caucus in City Council.[85] Yet, ultimately, the policies were pushed through, leading to many of the nightmare scenarios opponents warned of. The combination of service cuts, financial disinvestment, ongoing job loss, and inflation led to a vicious cycle: landlords could not afford to maintain their buildings, renters could not afford to pay rent, and thousands of properties were simply abandoned. According to one study, of 200,000 housing units abandoned between 1967 and 1977, 130,000 were abandoned between 1975 and 1977.[86] Realizing that they could make more money by burning down their buildings and collecting insurance than by maintaining them, desperate landlords.sparked an "epidemic" of arson throughout the city's poorest districts, one exacerbated by the closing of firehouses in targeted neighborhoods.[87] The fires were met with a citywide crime wave, one left largely unchecked outside the wealthier areas of Manhattan.

Ultimately, while planned shrinkage did help accelerate a demographic shift in New York City, it was one that (at least in the short term) was the opposite of what its engineers had envisioned. Most of the approximately 1 million New Yorkers who vacated the city between 1970 and 1980 were working-class and middle-class whites who relocated to the expanding suburbs of Westchester County, Connecticut, and New Jersey—not the mostly poor and working-class communities, disproportionately non-white, who were targeted by these policies.[88] Instead, the latter had few mobility choices and were most likely to stay behind in deteriorating neighborhoods, which would be disadvantaged for generations to come.

The Politics of Fiscal Crisis in New Orleans

By the 1970s and 1980s, New Orleans's fiscal crisis had become a major battleground in which various contending groups and socio-political alliances struggled to influence the form and trajectory of socio-spatial restructuring in a context of chronic deindustrialization, population decline, and eroding revenues. Exacerbating the city's financial problems were the implementation of Reagan era cutbacks and the passage of several Louisiana statutes that imposed powerful new fiscal austerity measures upon Louisiana cities during the 1970s.[89] These fiscal constraints included a reduction in local governments' ability to collect income from property taxes; a statute that two-thirds of both houses of the state legislature had to approve any increase in an existing local tax; and an expanded exemption on homeowners' property taxes. The state legislature increased this homestead exemption from $50,000 of assessed valuation in 1974 to $75,000 in 1982.[90]

Rather than helping to remedy social problems, state government statutes and socio-legal regulations aggravated the fiscal crisis of local governments in Louisiana, further undermining their redistributive capacities and entrenching a regressive tax situation. State-imposed constraints on the expansion of the local property tax put pressure on city leaders to rely on sales taxes as the main source of tax revenue, a major structural constraint pushing the formation of tourism-oriented policy experiments.[91] In the two decades after 1964, the percent distribution of property taxes for New Orleans dropped from 33.3 percent of total revenue to 9.8 percent, while the percent distribution of city sales tax increased from 33.5 percent of total revenue in 1964 to 57.3 percent in 1984.[92] The increasing reliance on sales taxes for revenue provided little opportunity for public sector–led growth and, more important, imposed a greater burden on the poor than on the rich.

Confronted with legal and political constraints on revenue raising and spiraling inflation during the late 1970s and early 1980s, political and economic elites called for across-the-board layoffs, reductions in wages, and curtailments on public spending. A 1975 memorandum from New Orleans's Chief Administrative Officer Richard Kernion explained to city council members that pay for city employees would not increase for at least five years due to stagnant revenue flows. According to Kernion, "the Administration is reminding the Council that the level of services must be reduced in 1976 through 1980 to offset the anticipated deficit since the Charter requires that the budget for each year be balanced and no deficit exist at the time that the budget is prepared for that calendar year."[93]

In response to sharp reductions in federal aid in 1980, Mayor Dutch Morial laid off seven hundred city workers, closed three fire stations, cut food stamps, and introduced an array of new programs championing reliance on voluntarism. Among these programs were a reserve police officers voluntary patrol program, neighborhood watches, taxis on patrol, neighborhood anticrime councils, and "adopt-a-playground" projects. What distinguished these otherwise diverse programs stressing extensive voluntarism was the substitution of paid city employees with unpaid citizen volunteers, thus disguising cuts in various city services. A year later, in June 1981, the Morial administration reduced the staff of the Comprehensive

Employment and Training Act (CETA) program by 57 percent and halted CETA training services to 1,000 unemployed residents.[94]

It seemed that Mayor Morial was following the lead of Mayor Abe Beame who had imposed austerity measures in New York City during the summer and fall of 1975. Just as Beame forced deep cuts in services and wages for municipal workers, Morial exacted major concessions, declaring that "what we're trying to do is retain the functional capacity of the city to provide services by dealing with the reductions in a selective fashion." Yet critics assailed the uneven and selective nature of the budget cutbacks, arguing that Morial's rhetoric of "prudent and sound fiscal management" was a smokescreen to deflect attention away from the use of increased user charges, new accounting techniques, replacement of paid labor with voluntary labor, and personnel reductions and attrition.[95]

By this time, New Orleans was caught in a protracted and unrelenting fiscal crisis, forced to slash funding for public services while financially pressured to develop new strategies for engineering urban redevelopment. Federal cutbacks acted in tandem with the dramatic loss in urban population and restrictive statutory and constitutional limitations on the city's taxing authority to further exacerbate the fiscal problems of the local government. A staggering $30 million deficit greeted Mayor Sidney Barthelemy when he took office in 1986. Shortly thereafter, the new mayor laid off 1,200 city employees, a measure that reduced the deficit to $10 million. In October, City Council implemented a four-day workweek for 5,800 employees, an austerity measure that reduced their wages by 20 percent for the rest of the year.[96]

Reductions in federal and state aid were especially severe and created a new historical context where the city was forced to rely on a series of "stopgap" revenue measures to balance the budget. These short-term fixes included refinancing the city's long-term debt, adopting partial-year budgets, failing to fund state-mandated court and correction agencies, and not paying court-awarded judgments. The city's attempt to solve its fiscal problems also included periodic service reductions, layoffs, cost-control measures, and deferred employee pay raises and building maintenance. Like other cities experiencing fiscal stress, New Orleans also privatized various functions of government, contracted out services to nonprofit organizations and the private sector, and implemented various "reinvention" techniques to increase the efficiency of government. None of these fixes redressed the city's recurring annual deficit of $30 million to $40 million.[97]

The Business Assault against Organized Labor

In the eyes of New Orleans's vulnerable upper classes, urban population loss and spiraling fiscal crisis were omens of looming urban obsolescence that necessitated bold planning and action. While there were many policy options for addressing the city's fiscal woes and other social problems, public and private sector alliances chose to zero in on combating the power of organized labor. Brown and Root, a nonunion international construction company, worked with oil firms to form the Louisiana Oilfield Contractors Association (LOCA) and set up the Louisiana chapter of the Associated Builders and Contractors (ABC), a national employers' association dedicated to combating unions in the construction industry. These new organizations were joined by the Public Affairs Research Council (PAR), a "business-oriented voice of enlightened self interest," to target specific pro-labor legislators for electoral defeat.[98] During the 1969 legislative session, members of the LOCA and ABC formed the Louisiana Political Education Council (LAPEC) to "break labor's grip on the capitol."[99] In 1975, the LOCA, ABC, LAPEC, and the Louisiana Chamber of Commerce formed the Louisiana Association of Business and Industry (LABI), a powerful business alliance dedicated to reforming state labor laws and promoting right-to-work legislation.[100]

During the 1970s, the LABI and other business organizations and their political allies launched a barrage of highly coordinated attacks against organized labor, arguing that unions were antidemocratic organizations that were responsible for the state's loss of jobs and revenue. The publisher of the New Orleans *Times-Picayune* newspaper, Ashton Phelps, railed against "compulsory unionism" as "fascistic" and called for the LABI to "focus the opposition" and curtail the "huge power unions already have to disrupt commerce and tie up industry and production." Demonizing labor operated as a framing strategy used by business organizations to turn public opinion against unions and build public support for business solutions to social problems. As Phelps argued:

> [I]n these days where the public is faced with serious threats of strikes on many fronts including such tender areas as teachers, firemen, policemen, bus drivers, and sanitation workers, there is less and less sympathy for and more and more aggravation at the results of union power.[101]

Assertions that unions were authoritarian threats to freedom and liberty bent on destroying Louisiana and the American way of life formed the crux of the business assault against organized labor. As Louisiana Governor Edwin Edwards told Ed Steimel, leader of the LABI:

> People are tired of pressure from labor unions; they are tired of hearing public employees unionize and threaten to strike. Unemployment is high, and you can be sure that labor will get the blame; they are simply not accepted.[102]

The passage of statewide right-to-work legislation in 1976 was instrumental in establishing a new socio-regulatory context for the development of a low-wage, anti-union tourism economy. Combating the growth of unionization constituted the structural linchpin of government and private sector efforts to build New Orleans's tourism sector and attract corporate investment. By the 1970s, transnational hotel firms such as Hilton, Sheraton, Marriott, and Hyatt had emerged as major corporate actors in the crusade to weaken organized labor. In 1981, Hyatt workers became the first hotel workers in the city to vote for a union in more than twenty-five years. Five years later, however, Hyatt still had refused to sign a contract with the mostly black and Hispanic workers represented by the Service Employees International Union (SEIU). By this time, the AFL-CIO had entered the skirmish and launched a nationwide boycott of nonunion Hyatts because of the company's refusal to sign a contract at the New Orleans Hyatt Regency. "If you have a conscience, you'll definitely sleep better someplace else" than Hyatt, read a SEIU leaflet publicized to draw attention to the plight of local hospitality workers receiving poverty-level wages and paltry benefits in the nonunion hotel sector.[103]

URBAN BRANDING AND THE TURN TO TOURISM

Through the 1980s, the retrenchment of the welfare state combined with deep cuts in federal resources for cities imposed powerful new fiscal constraints upon cities. These constraints were compounded by policies and projects at the local-scale, as we have seen. This lead to major budget cuts during a period in which social inequalities and urban conflicts intensified in conjunction with rapid urban and regional restructuring. Business leaders and government officials in New York City and New Orleans now sought to employ a variety of market-centered policy experiments, to revive their moribund economies. Business-led groups in both cities—including existing Convention and Visitors Bureaus (CVBs) and Chambers of Commerce as well as newly created public-private partnerships like ABNY—mobilized politically around a two-pronged strategy of redevelopment. First, they sought to neutralize negative imagery through advertising and marketing. Second, they promoted and lobbied for pro-business political and economic restructuring and neoliberal reforms. We refer to this dual visual and material strategy as urban branding.

In terms of representation, urban branding involved the cultivation of new synergistic campaigns coordinated by public and private sector organizations to reshape the identity of both cities. In New Orleans, the Chamber of Commerce formed an "Image Improvement Committee" in

1974 to launch an internally focused public relations campaign that, they hoped, would have wider effects. They explicitly targeted "metropolitan Orleanians," most of whom, they believed, had "either an erroneous or poor image of their area." This, they feared, was affecting attitudes of those beyond the city's borders regarding the city's climate for business. What was urgently needed, according to the Chamber, was an "attitude adjustment program...a P.R. program to create a progressive attitude [among] the citizens of this four-parish area," which would help to "create a positive business image among key business decision-makers in this country and abroad."[104] Ultimately, these promotional efforts would dovetail with the formation of the New Orleans Image Development, Inc., a public-private partnership established in 1982 by Mayor Ernest (Dutch) N. Morial to improve the city's image not only in the eyes of residents but also internationally. As Morial noted, "many agencies have their image campaigns, but none have fully succeeded in overcoming some negative perceptions of the city. Negative perceptions of the city begin with its citizens and persist outside of New Orleans."[105]

For New York's city marketers, the initial effort was launched by ABNY in 1971 with the "Big Apple" campaign. This was a traditional "booster" campaign based in PR stunts—like handing out golden apple lapel pins at train stations and having corporate executives clean the streets in front of their buildings—as well as big events like the Democratic National Convention (DNC) and the Bicentennial celebration. Yet, given the scale of the city's competition, as well as its epic image crisis, such local events were insufficient. Instead, city marketing "jumped scale" and was taken over by the New York State Department of Commerce, which in 1977 helped finance "I♥NY," the city's first international, year-round marketing campaign.[106] The new effort was based on professional market research that urged the city to use cultural attractions to eclipse crime reports and images of a resurgent Wall Street to send business the message that "New York had purged itself and changed its ways." Thus, cutting-edge television and print campaigns featured Broadway shows. New York magazine's artistic director, Milton Glaser, designed a logo. And in a masterful sleight of hand, the newly built World Trade Center—still mostly empty and costing the city millions—was featured in the campaign as a symbol of the city's resurgence. In this way, marketers presented New York City as a hip cultural capital and a thriving financial center—rather than a crisis-ridden, strike-infested, industrial-age city.

In the context of deepening socio-spatial polarization, New York and New Orleans, as well as other U.S. cities, adopted a variety of tourism-oriented strategies to promote themselves as places of entertainment, leisure, and consumption. In New Orleans, the 1984 Louisiana World Exposition stimulated construction of lavish new consumer spaces including the Riverfront Mall (designed by James Rouse).[107] The number of hotel rooms climbed to 20,000 in 1985 and 25,000 in 1990, five times the 4,750 rooms that existed in 1960. The number of convention delegates increased ten times in the two decades after 1960, from 58,000 in 1960 to 580,000 in 1980. The opening of a new convention center in 1985 provided a new facility to accommodate large conventions and spurred major growth in the number of conventions, trade shows, and visitors.[108] In 1970, New Orleans attracted 200 conventions and trade shows; by 1980, that number was up to 800 and in 1985 the city attracted more than 1,000 meetings and about 650,000 conventioneers.[109]

Much like New Orleans, by the late 1970s, New York City was "quietly becoming [a] world tourist haven," as a local newspaper put it in 1978.[110] Total numbers of travelers increased from 16.5 million to 19.8 between 1976 and 1988, buoyed by the building of the long-awaited Javitz Convention Center in 1984, alongside a glittering complex of luxury hotels and tourism facilities. Meanwhile, business travelers, convention goers, and international tourists—the segments of the tourism industry that spent the most and stayed the longest—arrived in increasing numbers. While the glut of new rooms meant hotel occupancy rates grew only slightly, visitor spending rose appreciably, from $.5 to $2.65 billion between 1976 and 1988. By the late 1980s, tourism and tourism marketing had become the "second pillar" of New York City's economic base, next to FIRE and business services.

Nonetheless, this growth of the "new economy" had highly contradictory effects. In what became known as the "jobless recovery," the service jobs being created were far fewer than the manufacturing-based jobs being replaced. In addition, new jobs tended to be "bifurcated" at the high and low end of the skill and income ladder, exacerbating socio-economic inequality. New Orleans was a classic case. The city lost far more jobs than it gained— a decline of 44,000, or 12 percent, of all jobs between 1979 and 1998—as losses in construction, manufacturing, transportation and public utilities, wholesale and retail trade, and FIRE were not offset by vaunted "growth" in tourism and related services. Indeed, the New Orleans service sector grew by 76 percent, and the FIRE sector grew by 69 percent between 1970 and 2000, a shift that revealed a major change in the structure of the metropolitan economy. In 1970, manufacturing and transportation accounted for 12 and 10 percent, respectively, of the metropolitan area's employment. Over the next thirty years, both industries' shares dropped precipitously to only 6 percent. In contrast, the service and retail sectors together expanded from 38 percent of employment in 1970 to 52 percent of employment in 2000.[111]

In the immediate aftermath of its crisis, New York City saw rapid job growth, with 141,000 new jobs created between 1982 and 1984. But, as

Emanuel Tobier pointed out at the time, new jobs were concentrated in FIRE and business services, that is, in "businesses that require white collar skills that many poor do not have."[112] Indeed, between 1967 and 1982, New York City's tourism sector, in which healthy job growth might have been expected given growing revenues, *lost* 45 percent of its workforce due to industry consolidation, a higher percentage than in any other sector. Meanwhile the new tourism and service jobs paid far less than the blue-collar jobs lost. In short, new tourism and service-oriented jobs did not adequately replace the loss of well-paying, entry-level jobs in manufacturing, commercial, and port industries.

The combination of pro-business policies, an antiredistributive agenda premised on battling unions, and a polarized "new economy" helped produce marked socio-economic inequality, characterized by scholars at the time as the "dual city" phenomenon.[113] Much like the extremes of wealth and poverty that occurred at the height of the "Gilded Age" of the late nineteenth century, sharp differentials in earnings coincided precisely with the "boom years" of 1977–1987. New York's wealthiest 10 percent saw their incomes grow over 20 percent in the 1980s and another 15 percent in the 1990s. This top tier accounted for a third of all income gains over the time period, while the top 20 percent accounted for half of such gains. Meanwhile, the poorest 20 percent saw their incomes decline by 17.5 percent over the same period and found themselves worse off not only relative to wealthier people but also as compared to their earnings in the 1970s.[114] While most famously described in New York, the same phenomenon occurred in New Orleans, and U.S. cities generally, in this period.[115]

THE URBANIZATION OF RISK

Despite their otherwise significant differences, both New York and New Orleans witnessed similar forms of crisis driven urbanization in the 1970s, as factions of finance and real estate capital and government leaders attempted to revalorize space and remedy fiscal crisis through a combination of slum and wetlands clearance, attacks on organized labor, the imposition of austerity measures, and urban rebranding campaigns. We can view these reforms as crisis mitigation strategies designed to establish new forms of corporate profit making and investment and to neutralize organized efforts by workers to improve their economic status and working conditions. Rather than resolving crises, however, these reform initiatives generated a host of new governance problems including, among others, environmental destruction, misallocation of public funds, and the growth and spatial concentration of low-income groups.

Table 2.1 POVERTY RATE FOR ALL PERSONS BY NEW ORLEANS AND NEW YORK
CENTRAL CITIES AND METROPOLITAN STATISTICAL AREAS (MSAS), 1969–1999

	1969	1979	1989	1999
New Orleans MSA	20.2	17.6	21.2	18.3
City	26.8	25.6	30.6	27.9
New York MSA	11.9	16.8	17.5	13.6
City	14.9	20.0	19.2	22.6
United States	13.7	21.2	13.1	12.4

Sources: Madden, Janice Fanning. "Changes in the Distribution of Poverty across and within the U.S. Metropolitan Areas, 1979–89." *Urban Studies* 33, no. 9, 1996: 1581–1600; Ortiz, Elaine. "Who Lives in New Orleans and the Metro Area Now?" Greater New Orleans Community Data Center, September 26, 2011, accessed March 11, 2012, http://www.gnocdc.org/Demographics/index.html; Levitan, Mark, and Susan S. Wieler. "Poverty in New York City, 1969–99: The Influence of Demographic Change, Income Growth, and Income Inequality." *Federal Reserve Bank of New York Economic Policy Review.* July 2008, accessed March 2, 2011, http://www.ny.frb.org/research/epr/08v14n1/0807levi.pdf.

Indeed, the most striking demographic shift for New York and New Orleans in the decades after 1970 was the growth of extreme wealth alongside extreme poverty. New York City's poverty rate rose dramatically during the 1970s (table 2.1). In 1969, 14.9 percent of New York City residents lived below the poverty line, a rate comparable to the nation's 13.7 percent. By 1979, one in five city New York City residents, or 20.0 percent, lived in poverty. In 1999, the poverty rate stood at 22.6 percent, more than 7 percentage points above the 1969 level and nearly ten points above the U.S. rate of 12.4 percent. In New Orleans, the city poverty rate was already high in 1970, at 26.8 percent, but rose even higher to 30.6 percent in 1989 before declining slightly to 27.9 in 1999. As table 2.1 shows, the poverty rates in the central cities were much higher than for their entire Metropolitan Statistical Areas (MSAs) for each time period. The table also shows widening gaps between rates of inner-city poverty and rates of metropolitan poverty for New York and New Orleans. The poverty rates of both cities were greater than the national average from 1969 through 1999.

These rates also had unequal effects across racial and age categories, with African Americans and children being hit the hardest. In New York, poverty rates tripled for both of these groups between 1969 and 1984, reaching 40 percent and 50 percent respectively.[116] In New Orleans, African American poverty rates rose to almost four times that of the white population. Indeed, rising poverty rates for New Orleans overall may be attributed to the rise in black poverty, which remained at 38 percent between 1979 and 1999 even while white poverty decreased from 9.5 percent to 6.1 percent over the same time period. Meanwhile, by the mid-1990s, just as in New York City, more than half the children living in New Orleans, 51.6 percent, were living below the federal poverty level. By 2000, metropolitan New Orleans was the sixth poorest out of the one hundred largest metropolitan areas.[117]

Ultimately, for post-1970s New York and New Orleans, the growing concentration of poverty reflected dramatic and troubling socio-spatial disparities that interlocked with growing risks and vulnerabilities to disaster. For New York, budget cuts, austerity, and the implementation of neoliberal reforms were signifiers of the inequalities that underpinned the progress of crisis-driven urbanization and the financialization of Manhattan. In New Orleans, federal flood insurance subsidies and investments in the LP&VHPP to encourage the urbanization of the wetlands enabled more people and jobs to locate outside the city, further isolating poor African Americans in the urban core and contributing to growing racial and class polarization on a regional scale. By the 1980s, a new geography of risk was emerging both within and across the two cities as service cuts, deindustrialization, and government retrenchment worsened the quality of life for those not benefiting from the gains of the "new economy." The increasing concentration of poverty meant that marginalized communities would face the greatest risks to health and livelihood from disasters, no matter if the trigger was a hurricane or a terrorist strike.

CHAPTER 3

Constructing the Tabula Rasa: Framing and the Political Construction of Crisis

The September 11, 2001, World Trade Center attacks and Hurricane Katrina in New Orleans on August 25 and 26, 2005, are now considered among the most catastrophic urban disasters in American history. With the first designated the nation's worst act of domestic terrorism and the second the nation's worst natural disaster, their rapid succession brought to the forefront the concatenated crises and escalating risks that characterize our contemporary urban age. In the process, New York and New Orleans became emblems of this age. At first glance, this shared status may appear no more than a coincidence of misfortune. And indeed, as "9/11" and "Katrina" have become a part of our shared cultural lexicon, the particularities of these two catastrophes are by now common knowledge. Yet upon closer examination, we find that it is necessary to understand both the differences and similarities between the two events to fully appreciate their devastating and transformative impact. In what follows, we briefly outline some of the singular aspects of each event—from the disaster trigger to the scale of devastation to the political framing of the disasters and their primary victims. Also explored here is how emphasis on these manifold differences has obscured and distracted critical attention from important similarities between the two disasters, namely, their economic impact on low-income communities and marginalized neighborhoods, placed at risk by previous rounds of restructuring. We then turn to an examination of another important similarity and one that compounded these unequal impacts: the privatization and devolution of emergency management and disaster response. Remarkably, political justification for this common approach was aided in different ways by the distinctive initial framing of the two events.

9/11

The "September 11 attacks" (9/11) were the result of coordinated suicide missions carried out by al-Qaeda terrorists on the United States. Nineteen al-Qaeda operatives hijacked four commercial passenger airplanes and intentionally crashed two of them into the Twin Towers of New York City's World Trade Center (WTC), immediately killing everyone on board and many others working in the buildings. Within two hours, both 100-story towers collapsed, destroying nearby buildings, damaging others, and killing many more people. The hijackers crashed a third airplane into the U.S. Pentagon in Arlington, Virginia, and a fourth, redirected to Washington DC, crashed into a field in rural Pennsylvania after passengers and flight crew attempted to retake control of the plane. All told, nearly 3,000 victims and the nineteen hijackers died as a result of the attacks. These victims included all airline passengers and crew,184 people at the Pentagon and 2,752 people at the WTC. At the WTC, 2,349 were civilian casualties, including nationals of over 70 countries and 403 "first responders," including 343 firefighters and 60 police officers from New York City and the New York-New Jersey Port Authority.[1]

Given these figures, it is understandable that official reports and news coverage of the attacks on the World Trade Center focused mainly on first responders and high-end service and financial workers. Indeed, approximately 40,000 jobs and 10 million square feet of high-end office space were immediately lost with the destruction of the Twin Towers. Thus, not surprisingly, popular understandings of the events were shaped by the notion that the primary impact of 9/11 was felt by the mostly upper-middle-class New Yorkers working in the towers and the police and firefighters who rushed in to save them. Within this frame, the response to 9/11, in which civil servants acted with incredible valor in the face of terror, and after which financial firms based at the WTC made a remarkable recovery, was dubbed "heroic" and a "success." The city of New York, uniformed public-sector workers, as well as the financial firms of Lower Manhattan all became a source of national pride.

Yet while not inaccurate, this understanding of the impact of 9/11 on New York City obscures a more complicated picture. When measured in total jobs and percent of revenue lost, the major blow of 9/11 was felt not by the disproportionately white and well-off finance workers, but by disproportionately nonwhite, low-wage workers and the businesses that employed them, whether in the Towers, in the blocked-off streets of Lower Manhattan, or in related trades throughout the city. In the months following the 9/11 attack, 300,000 New Yorkers lost their jobs throughout the city.[2] This included service workers in the Twin Towers whose jobs were immediately destroyed; workers in airlines, hotels, and security whose jobs were dependent upon tourism and finance; and the owners of, or workers in, small businesses that were shuttered due to their proximity to Ground Zero. The latter were dominated by the retail, wholesale, and light manufacturing industries of Chinatown and the Lower East Side.

Overall, of the 100,000 jobs lost one month following the attacks, 60 percent paid less than $11 per hour, a rate that remained about the same as, if not greater as total job losses rose.[3] Significantly, these job losses were concentrated in manufacturing and retail or in the low-wage service sector, which was supposed to replace New York's once thriving, unionized, blue collar economy. In addition, workers in these sectors tended to live as renters in the neighborhoods that had been hardest hit by the spatial fix and planned shrinkage of that earlier period: from Chinatown and the Lower East in Lower Manhattan to the outer-borough neighborhoods of Upper Manhattan, the Bronx, and Queens. For low-income workers in these precarious sectors and neighborhoods, with their lack of insurance and health benefits and the already insecure nature of their employment and housing, and for small businesses with their low profit margin, the disruption of 9/11 was particularly devastating.[4]

KATRINA

Less than four years after the events of 9/11, on August 29, 2005, Hurricane Katrina struck the Gulf Coast causing catastrophic destruction over 90,000 square miles and flooding over 80 percent of the city of New Orleans, with some parts of the city under 12 feet of water during September 2005. The Katrina's storm surge punctured the Mississippi River Gulf Outlet (MR-GO) in approximately twenty places, flooding much of east New Orleans and almost all of St. Bernard Parish and the East Bank of Plaquemines Parish. The major levee breaches in the city included breaches at the 17th Street Canal levee, the London Avenue Canal, and the Industrial Canal. As a result, nearly 228,000 occupied housing units, reflecting almost 50 percent of the metropolitan area's total, were flooded. These included 120,000 owner-occupied units (39 percent of the metro total) and 108,000 units occupied by renters (56 percent of the metro total).[5]

Long-term processes of crisis-driven urbanization reflected and reinforced an institutionalized system of class and racial segregation that ensured minority residents and the poor would suffer the most from the collapse of the federal government's levee system. Though they made up 45 percent of the metropolitan population, African American and other minority residents accounted for 58 percent of the residents who lived in flooded neighborhoods. By contrast, whites, who made up 54.8 percent of the metropolitan population, comprised 42 percent of those who lived in flooded neighborhoods.[6]

In the years since Hurricane Katrina roared ashore, governments have spent billions of dollars to repair a fractured levee system that was supposed to protect people and property from the risks of hurricanes and floods. For decades, the federal and local governments fronted huge sums to drain the swamps and subsidize private-led land development based on tenuous promises of future value generation and enhanced tax revenue. Rather than resolving fiscal crises and mitigating economic stagnation, however, state interventions to mobilize the swamps and marshes as arenas of real estate investment generated new crisis tendencies and imperiled future profit making. The Lake Pontchartrain & Vicinity Hurricane Protection Project (LP&VHPP) cost more than $700 million federal dollars and nearly $200 million in locally generated funds over a forty-year period. In the first year after Katrina, the federal government paid out $800 million to repair the LP&VHPP, more federal money than had been spent in the previous forty years to build the system. As of 2011, the Corps had spent more than $8 billion on levee design and reconstruction, including building the world's largest drainage pumping station on the West Bank of the Mississippi River.[7] Elected officials and Corps leaders boasted that post-Katrina federal investments gave New Orleans "unprecedented protection."[8] Overall, to date, Congress has authorized approximately $14.6 billion worth of repairs and upgrades to the shattered flood protection system, a huge amount compared to prior expenditures in the decades before Hurricane Katrina.

As a vehicle of uneven development, the LP&VHPP normalized and disguised risk in the built environment, increased vulnerability to hurricane damage, and concealed hazardous flood conditions. The Corps' official report on the Katrina disaster, conducted in its 2006 Interagency Performance Evaluation Taskforce (IPET), concluded that the "hurricane protection system in New Orleans and southeast Louisiana was a system in name only."[9] The levees, floodwalls, and other physical structures were an incomplete and inconsistent patchwork of protection, flawed in design and construction and not built to handle a hurricane anywhere near the size of Katrina. Notwithstanding the failure of the levees, the system unfortunately performed quite well in devastating the wetland ecosystem and spreading catastrophic flood risk over a vast metropolitan region, making

(a)

Figure 3.1a
Flooding of New Orleans at the 17th Street Canal
Source: *The Times-Picayune*, Landov Media.

communities and populations more vulnerable to seasonal rains, hurricanes, and tropical storms. Today, government funds to rebuild the levee system are part of larger effort to promote urban renewal, community rebuilding, and reinvigorate devalued flooded property. As a major crisis management strategy, the Corps' levee rebuilding efforts are a direct response to previous state-led interventions to urbanize the wetlands under the guise of remedying fiscal crisis and engineering new growth and development.

Thus, the devastation caused by these two epochal catastrophes, distinctive though they were, can both be found to have roots in the similarly uneven landscapes of risk versus resilience that were produced in preceding decades in both cities. Of interest to us here is how these inequalities were then exacerbated through the highly politicized and market-oriented approach to "recovery" pursued in both cities. Over the years, as both New York and New Orleans have experienced a series of interconnected crises related to 9/11 and Hurricane Katrina, planners and elites have attempted to construct the two cities as tabula rasa, or "blank slates" for social and spatial redevelopment. In doing so, they have exploited both disasters as opportunities to advance a neoliberal model of urban recovery premised on the application of the policies of devolution and privatization to the process of emergency management and disaster response. Devolution refers to the decentralization and transfer of authority, responsibility, and funds from the federal government to states and lower levels of government. Privatization can take the form of outsourcing public services

(b)

Figure 3.1b
Plaque Demarcating Levee Breach Caused by the Army Corps of Engineers (Levees.org)
Since 2010, a grassroots group, Levees.org. has campaigned to install Louisiana State Historic Plaques on city property at
each of the levee breaches in New Orleans. This plaque at the 17th Street Canal explains why the flood protection system
failed and what happened as a result. Several lawsuits against the Corps for failing to properly construct and maintain
the levee system were dismissed. In the case involving the breach at the 17 Street Canal, U.S District Court Judge
Stanwood Duval, Jr., concluded: "While the United States government is immune for legal liability for the defalcations
alleged herein, it is not free, nor should it be, from posterity's judgment concerning its failure to accomplish what was its
task.... This story—50 years in the making—is heart-wrenching. Millions of dollars were squandered in building a levee
system with respect to these outfall canals which was known to be inadequate by the Corps' own calculations." Today,
organizations like Levees.org are part of an emerging global network of activist groups dedicated to drawing public attention to the omnipresent flood risks that communities face. Since 2006, Levees.org has established satellite locations in
California, Oregon, Illinois, Florida, and New York. (*Source*: photograph by Kevin Gotham)

to private third parties, contracting out goods, providing direct grants to
third parties, and depending upon nonprofit organizations, corporations,
and/or quasi-governmental entities for service delivery. While devolution
and privatization have a long history—and indeed were seen in embryo in
the "tighten your belt and bite the bullet" policies of the 1970s—what is
new here is the attempt by governments to use them for emergency management and recovery and ultimately as vehicles of long-term post-crisis
redevelopment.

In the immediate emergency management period under FEMA,
which is the focus of this chapter, these two strategies impeded the
restoration of housing stock and public infrastructure, as well as compensation for small businesses and low-income residents. In so doing,
devolution and privatization revealed the role of disaster frames in
what David Harvey has called "accumulation by dispossession," that
is, the use of state actions and policy to distribute income and wealth
upward through the direct transfer of productive public assets to private

companies, and by depriving vulnerable residents of their assets, income, or rights.[10] Ultimately, these dynamics were to intensify through processes of post-crisis redevelopment, which will be explored in the following chapters. The process was set in motion, however, during this initial post-disaster recovery phase and so deserves special attention. The first significant step taken in this phase was the framing of the disasters themselves, which was to play an important role in legitimizing the targeting of recovery aid.

POLITICAL FRAMING AND THE FEDERAL RESPONSE TO 9/11 AND HURRICANE KATRINA

In the early years after the 9/11 and Hurricane Katrina disasters, a variety of political actors and media outlets constructed and deployed several framing strategies to typify the two disasters, define the victims, assign responsibility for the traumatic conditions, and identify remedies and solutions. Table 3.1 shows how these various framing strategies applied to New York City and New Orleans after the disasters. Diagnostic framing involves sorting, organizing, and disseminating information to draw attention to a major problem or grievance, convey a sense of urgency or severity of condition, and attribute blame and responsibility. Prognostic framing suggests a series of solutions, strategies, and tactics to remedy the problem(s).

Power relations, institutional interests, and politics shape the social construction and framing of disasters and crisis conditions. In the pioneering work of cultural theorist Stuart Hall, frames are cultural representations that reflect institutional structures of information production and dissemination.[11] As such, framing strategies express relations of power linked to conflicts over material and cultural resources. What is important is not simply that frames help shape how people interpret political issues, but that some groups and interests have the resources and capacity to frame these issues differently and make particular interpretations more prominent and significant than others in media and political discourse. How different groups and actors define and frame disasters has important consequences for how people view disaster victims and disaster-impacted communities. Just as politics and institutional practices influence the construction of "crises," framing strategies can constrain political debate and influence the selection of some kinds of policies rather than others to respond to and remedy crisis conditions.

Table 3.1 DOMINANT FRAMING STRATEGIES FOR POST-9/11 NEW YORK AND POST-KATRINA NEW ORLEANS

	Type of Tragedy	Status of the Victims	Diagnostic Frames	Prognostic Frames
New York City	Global and national tragedy	Heroes of a global tragedy	Terrorist strike as act of war	Privatize domestic security functions; establish Department of Homeland Security (DHS)
New Orleans	Local and regional tragedy	Refugees who are responsible for their plight	"Natural" disaster; and an act of God; policy and government failure	Devolve and privatize emergency management policies and functions; Pressure cities to assume responsibility for rebuilding themselves

Framing 9/11: Heroes and an Act of War

Two of the most significant framing strategies used to interpret the 9/11 disaster were the construction of the terrorist strike as an act of war and the celebration of victims and first responders as heroes of a national tragedy. Early on, elected officials, pundits, and government agencies played critical roles in diagnostically framing the 9/11 terrorist strike as an attack on the homeland by an enemy force. On the morning after the terrorist assaults of September 11, 2001, President George W. Bush declared: "The deliberate and deadly attacks which were carried out yesterday against our country were more than acts of terror. They were acts of war. This will require our country to unite in steadfast determination and resolve.... This will be a monumental struggle of good versus evil, but good will prevail."[12] In these remarks and many others, Bush defined the problem of the September 11 disaster in terms of "us" versus "them," using militaristic language to mobilize the country for a "war against terrorism." President Bush, Vice President Richard Cheney, Secretary of State Colin Powell, and other officials used these same words many times in the days and months following September 11; George W. Bush invoked "war" twelve times in his State of the Union speech on January 29, 2002.[13]

The act-of-war frame was particularly potent in helping to define the victims as national heroes,[14] As Ground Zero still smoldered just days after the 9/11 attacks, President Bush stood with a bullhorn in one hand and his arm around retired New York City Fire Department firefighter Bob Beckwith cheering "USA! USA! USA!" with patriotic onlookers celebrating the nation's strength and resilience in the wake of the attacks. With moments of silence punctuated by somber music, readings of names, and tears, Americans held solemn memorial services in the following months to honor the victims of the terrorist attacks. "Time is passing. Yet, for the United States of America, there will be no forgetting September the 11th," as President Bush expressed in November 2001. "We will remember every rescuer who died in honor. We will remember every family that lives in grief." As President Bush remarked in September 2005, in presenting families of the victims with the 9/11 Heroes Medal of Valor:

> We witnessed the courage of some of the finest people our country has ever produced. And their sacrifice will always be remembered.... Four years ago, America saw the unparalleled heroism of our nation's public safety officers. We lost brave rescue workers who gave their lives so that others could live. We lost many other citizens who assisted in the rescue efforts, and whose courage and sacrifice that day made them extraordinary.[15]

Seven years after the attacks, Bush was still invoking the hero narrative remarking on the commemorative anniversary in 2008, "On a day when buildings fell, heroes rose," according to the president. "One of the worst days in America's history saw some of the bravest acts in America's history."[16]

Significantly, the heroes framed in these accounts were primarily of three types: uniformed public safety officers, workers in the World Trade Center, and the immediate families of these two groups. In terms of the workers, as many noted, "large corporate tenants of the Twin Towers—Cantor Fitzgerald, Marsh & McLennan—have naturally loomed large in reports of the tragedy."[17] This had the significant effect of transcending class distinction, since both working-class and non-working-class "heroes" were celebrated in dominant accounts. Yet excluded from this frame were the two-thirds of tenants in the towers working in small firms, the fleet of low-level service and commercial workers upon whom all the towers' firms depended, and, as we shall soon see, the thousands of small businesses and low-income tenants "beyond ground zero" who were also profoundly affected by the attack.

Diagnosing the 9/11 terrorist attack as an "act of war" with heroes straddling the class divide helped build public support for and unite the country behind several prognostic solutions. Despite local protests mobilized behind the slogan "Our grief is not a cry for war," 9/11 became a rationale for the "global war against terrorism," the 2003 U.S. invasion of Iraq, and the establishment of a new Department of Homeland Security (DHS). The administration might have identified other policy remedies and chosen other ways of interpreting and responding to the attacks. But the mobilization of war rhetoric was carefully scripted to obtain virtually unanimous assent from Congress and the media. In addition, by implying the necessity of a strong federal and military response, this strategic framing helped legitimize the expansion of presidential and executive branch authority on a number of political fronts.

One front for which this diagnosis provided new political opportunity was in the area of privatization of disaster response, an agenda that had long been championed by conservative policymakers. In the wake of the 9/11 tragedy, according to Peter Dreier, Bush used concerns over national security to create a quota mandating that government agencies outsource at least 425,000 (later upped to 850,000) federal jobs to private contractors. In December 2001, Bush rescinded rules forbidding businesses guilty of breaking federal laws, including labor, environmental, consumer protection, civil rights and tax laws, from signing outsource employment contracts with federal agencies.[18] Several months later, the Homeland Security Act of 2002 moved twenty-two federal agencies and 170,000 federal employees under the control of the new DHS. Shortly after the establishment of the DHS, several senior deputies took lucrative jobs for the private sector as homeland security lobbyists. As documented by Charles Perrow, "the number of lobbyists who registered and listed 'homeland,' 'security,' or 'terror' on their forms was already sizeable at the beginning of 2002, numbering 157, but jumped to 569 as of April 2003."[19] Over the next several years, outsourcing to the private sector by DHS increased at a faster pace than annual budget increases, rising from $4.2 billion in 2003 to $13.7 billion in 2009.[20]

Policymakers and officials in the Bush administration also seized upon the chaos of the 9/11 disaster to push for the development of new public-private partnerships linking the federal government with a web of private contractors and subcontractors. The Homeland Security Act of 2002 eliminated the cabinet-level status of FEMA and separated national security from the administration of emergency management functions (e.g., disaster mitigation and response capacities).[21] From the beginning of fiscal year 2003 through fiscal year 2005, over $1.3 billion in new or expanded programs entered into FEMA, while the DHS and the White House transferred programs with funding of nearly $1.5 billion out of FEMA. After DHS absorbed FEMA, three-fourths of every grant dollar provided by FEMA for local preparedness and first responders went to terrorism-related measures—in other words, $2 billion in grants to prevent terrorist attacks but only $180 million for natural disasters.[22] In addition, FEMA's incorporation into the DHS resulted in a reallocation of more than $800 million in federal grant money for state emergency management offices to state homeland security offices for use in counterterrorism from 2001 to 2005.[23]

Overall, the establishment of the DHS and reorganization of FEMA represented a major shift in domestic security and emergency management functions. Programmatic changes combined with reallocation of funds were components of a larger transformation of FEMA from service origi-nator to service purchaser (through contracts with private companies) and service arranger (through partnerships with lower levels of government, private sector, and nonprofit sector). To be sure, these changes were begin-ning before the September 11 disaster under the precepts of the "reinvent-ing government" movement of the 1990s. What was different after 9/11 was the acceleration and expansion of these programs through an elaborate web of public-private networks empowered to manage and deliver domes-tic security and emergency management services. Thus, the DHS and a transformed FEMA offered new opportunities to further political agendas unrelated to disasters and terrorist threats. The "war on terror" and fram-ing of the 9/11 victims as "heroes" of a global tragedy were important ele-ments in building political support for war and militarization, as well as for new disaster-related outsourcing and privatization mechanisms. As we shall see, these mechanisms would have profound effects on how emergency response was to be carried out on the ground in both New York City and New Orleans, despite differences in the framing of the two events.

Framing Hurricane Katrina: Refugees and Civil Unrest

In contrast to the framing of 9/11 attacks as an act of war and of 9/11 victims as heroes, media reports and political narratives surrounding Hurricane Katrina deployed a civil unrest frame that focused on images of social breakdown and was infused with an anti-urban discourse that emphasized the responsibility of the storm's disproportionately poor African American victims for their own plight. Shortly after the levee breaks, media outlets around the world described the descent of New Orleans into anarchy and lawlessness, with "hundreds of armed gang members killing and raping peo-ple" and storm victims shooting at rescue crews.[24] Various news reporters described the New Orleans Convention Center—which became an unof-ficial refuge for storm victims due to lack of any other suitable emergency space—as "a nightly scene of murders, rapes and regular stampedes."[25] Such reports constructed some of the disaster victims as "lawless, violent, exploitative, and almost less than human."[26] Statements made by city offi-cials—including the mayor and police chief—helped to fuel some of the more extreme myths of mayhem during the New Orleans disaster, includ-ing reports of rampant murder, "babies being raped," and armed thugs tak-ing control.[27]

Closely related to the civil unrest frame was the stigmatization of residents as "refugees," a term usually reserved for non-citizens of a particular country forced to leave their foreign country of origin. An Associated Press (AP) story that ran the day Katrina roared ashore applied the "refugee" label to the more than 9,000 people seeking shelter in the New Orleans Superdome, and a later AP story referred to an "unprecedented refugee crisis" unfolding in the storm's wake as thousands of people were forced to flee their homes. Not surprisingly, civil rights activists such as Reverend Al Sharpton, Reverend Jesse Jackson, NAACP President Bruce Gordon, and others objected to the use of "refugee" for disproportionately African-American victims of the storm, on grounds that the label carried with it a racial stigma, and put displaced people at risk of being deprived of their rights as U.S. citizens.[28]

Conservative pundits and elected leaders deployed diagnostic and proscriptive framing strategies that were based in this initial characterization of Katrina's victims. In stark contrast with post-9/11 New York City, the primary objective in New Orleans was to discourage the federal government from taking a strong leadership role in responding to the disaster. A key diagnostic strategy framed the alleged chaos in New Orleans as evidence of the disastrous effects of liberal social policy in fomenting pathologies of dependency and crime. Although lacking supporting evidence, this argument was appropriated by popular media outlets, including talk radio programs and the Internet to further stigmatize Katrina evacuees and New Orleans broadly.[29] Conservative commentator Bill O'Reilly stated: "Many, many, many of the [homeless] poor in New Orleans . . . weren't going to leave no matter what you did. They were drug addicted. They weren't going to get turned off from their source. They were thugs, whatever."[30]

Conservative think tanks such as the Heritage Foundation, the Manhattan Institute, the Cato Institute, and the American Enterprise Institute (AEI) obsessed on dramatic reports of criminal activity and looting as symptomatic of a pathological culture of government corruption and welfare dependency that defined New Orleans.[31] According to Manhattan Institute analyst, contributor to the New Orleans City Journal, and onetime New Orleans resident Nicole Gelinas:

> New Orleans can't take care of itself even when it is not 80 percent underwater; what is it going to do now, as waters continue to cripple it, and thousands of looters systematically destroy what Katrina left unscathed? . . . The city's government has long suffered from incompetence and corruption. . . . New Orleans teems with crime, and the NOPD can't keep order on a good day.[32]

Joel Kotkin, writing in AEI's monthly magazine, *The American Enterprise*, declared that New Orleans had become "useless to the middle class, and toxic for the disorganized poor." Kotkin went on use the city as representative of urban America more broadly:

> Today's liberal urban leadership across America needs to see the New Orleans storm not as just a tragedy, but also as a dispeller of illusions, a revealer of awful truths, and a potential harbinger of things to come in their own backyards. Look beyond the tourist districts. Few contemporary cities are actually healthy in terms of job growth or middle-class amenities. Most are in the grips of moral and economic crisis. If we are lucky, the flood waters of Katrina will wash away some of the '60s-era illusions that fed today's dysfunction. Honest observers will recognize that this natural disaster, which hit the nation so hard, was set up by the man-made disaster of a counterproductive welfare state.[33]

A related, prognostic framing strategy used victim-blaming rhetoric to argue that residents needed to take care of themselves and that those who did not evacuate should face the consequences of displacement and be punished. As then Senator Rick Santorum expressed on September 6, 2005,

> I mean, you have people who don't heed those warnings and then put people at risk as a result of not heeding those warnings. There may be a need to look at tougher penalties on those who decide to ride it out and understand that there are consequences to not leaving.[34]

The conservative, anti-urban, and punitive ideologies expressed by O'Reilly, Gelinas, Kotkin, Santorum, and other pundits were neither isolated nor confined to the media. They were institutionalized within the disaster relief operations of the federal government. Within several months of the disaster, federal officials working at FEMA attempted to limit housing assistance by defining displaced residents as transient homeless populations rather than hurricane victims with real housing needs. According to an February 3, 2006, e-mail from one official, FEMA was "[n]ot a bit interested in providing new funding to the State for shelter purposes— convinced we are dealing with a pre-disaster homeless population that HUD and [Louisiana State government] must come to grips with. Further extension will only delay resolution of the issue." AIn another e-mail dated February 13, 2006, stated:, "[M]any folks will go ahead and find an alternative housing plan when they are told the [rental assistance] program is ending.... even if to stay with family and friends while their final plans are coming together."[35] Underlying FEMA's position was the implication that needy New Orleans residents were lacking in personal responsibility.

According to one FEMA press release from August 8, 2006, less than one year after the disaster,

> FEMA has done everything it can to help the survivors of the Katrina [disaster]....
> Ultimately, it is the responsibility of each individual to take charge of their own recovery
> from a disaster, and move on.[36]

A final and related prognostic framing strategy raised the question of whether the federal government should spend *any* money to help aid the city. While government officials want to "do whatever is necessary to address this national disaster," proclaimed Senator John McCain, "we also have to be concerned about future generations of Americans. We're going to end up with the highest deficit, probably, in the history of this country."[37] Some officials seized on the city's location near the Gulf Coast as a reason not to invest in recovery efforts. As former House Speaker Dennis Hastert remarked, "[i]t makes no sense to spend billions of dollars to rebuild a city that's seven feet under sea level...., It looks like a lot of that place could be bulldozed." When asked about rebuilding the city, Hastert said, "I don't know. That doesn't make sense to me."[38] In campaigning for president in 2008, Senator John McCain told CBS News' Dante Higgins that he was not sure he would rebuild the Lower Ninth Ward neighborhood if he were elected president: "That is why we need to go back and have a conversation about what to do—rebuild it, tear it down, you know, whatever it is."[39]

Ultimately, the dominant framing strategies applied to Hurricane Katrina, and with this the government response to the disaster, reflected the prerogatives and intentions of powerful political interests who opposed a proactive and interventionist state. The framing of Katrina victims as refugees helped construct a view of the victims as undeserving of government aid and resources. In addition, the unsubstantiated and later discredited atrocity tales coming out of New Orleans provided political ammunition to conservative politicians to kill legislation calling for generous public resources and a strong federal role in leading a large-scale and comprehensive rebuilding effort.[40] Finally, the framing of the disaster in terms of policy and government failure was used to denigrate the public sector and support initiatives giving the private sector greater authority to implement emergency management policies.

This framing stood in stark contrast with that of 9/11, helping to explain why the latter received proportionally more aid and, as we will see, greater flexibility in terms of cost-sharing and loan forgiveness. Nonetheless, these very different frames also lead, in their particular ways, to a similar result: separating deserving from undeserving recipients of aid, and legitimizing the overall devolution and privatizing of federal emergency management.

RESTRUCTURING EMERGENCY MANAGEMENT POLICIES AND FUNCTIONS

Explaining similarities and variations in the federal response to the two disasters means adopting a holistic and context-embracing approach aimed at explaining how specific crisis management strategies and processes recur or diverge in the different cities. Table 3.2 presents an overview of FEMA's response to the disasters in New York and New Orleans. As the nodal point of the federal emergency response and management system, FEMA directs federal agencies to support state and local assistance efforts; provides technical assistance, advice, and damage and needs assessments with local and state governments; and manages the planning and distribution of federal resources through federal and state government programs and charities and philanthropic organizations. The table compares modifications in eligibility rules for disaster assistance, problems and limitations with post-disaster federal response, and post-disaster rebuilding strategies. It reflects process-oriented comparative research in which we analytically juxtapose differences in federal and local policy, response, and the post-disaster redevelopment trajectories, so as to trace emerging patterns of crisis driven urbanization in both cities.

New York: FEMA Responds to 9/11

In the years following the September 11 disaster, government reports praised FEMA's "positive" and "effective" response to the terrorist strike and commended the agency for its "successful" efforts to assist city leaders to rebuild Lower Manhattan. Several general assessments of FEMA's long-term response to September 11 suggest that there were few, if any, sustained complaints that federal aid was not forthcoming in the years after 9/11. Histories of the 9/11 period describe FEMA as having "stepped up and responded well" and FEMA's response as being "relatively well-regarded."[41] Former FEMA Director James Witt proudly stated that "FEMA responded extremely well in 9/11 in New York, as well as the Pentagon." "I was at FEMA in 2001 when we responded to 9/11," remembered former director Michael Brown, and "we did an excellent job in that disaster."[42] In commenting on a draft of a 2003 Government Accountability Office (GAO) report on FEMA public assistance to New York City, the acting director of FEMA's Recovery Division noted that "FEMA officials are proud of the agency's response in delivering public assistance programs to NYC and state, and that they are satisfied that FEMA's authority was adequate and flexible enough in most circumstances to meet the response

Table 3.2 RESTRUCTURING FEDERAL EMERGENCY MANAGEMENT FUNCTIONS

	New York	New Orleans
Modifications in eligibility rules for disaster assistance	Full federal funding of disaster response and recovery costs (local and state cost-shares waived by federal government); Bush Administration forgives disaster loans to New York City	100 percent of cost shares not waived until 21 months after Hurricane Katrina disaster. Bush Administration and Congress prohibit loan forgiveness to communities. Prohibition not lifted for New Orleans until November 2010. Prohibition still in place for suburban parishes as of January 2012
Restructuring Strategies	Institutional separation and splintering of emergency management and domestic security policies and functions; devolve emergency management functions via the establishment of the Department of Homeland Security (2002)	Acceleration of government efforts to devolve and outsource the implementation of emergency management functions; devolution of federal emergency management functions closely intertwined with the application of privatization strategies in which responsibility for disaster "recovery" is coordinated with, or accomplished directly through, non-government organizations, quasi-government organizations, and private firms
Limitations of and problems with post-disaster federal response	Imposition of "direct result" test limits benefits; mistakes in eligibility determinations; errors in allocation of recovery funds; shortchanging aid requests; predisposition to deny government reimbursement requests; federal government denies responsibility for addressing long-term environmental liabilities	Public assistance programs defined by continually changing requirements, procedures, deadlines, and litigation that resulted in court ordered reinstatements of previously denied benefits; predisposition to deny government reimbursement requests; inconsistent guidelines, arbitrary rule changes, and explicit rule violations; protracted financing disputes with state and local governments, institutions, and businesses

and recovery needs of New York."[43] Overall, the GAO and Congress held that FEMA's post-disaster response was effective and successful.[44] These reports and analyses praise the very positive lessons of the recovery effort, including the extraordinary rescue, recovery, and cleanup effort after the collapse of the WTC.

Yet the congratulatory tone of various reports and official statements belied the considerable suffering endured by the thousands who fell outside the frame of heroic 9/11 victims—low-wage workers, displaced residents, and small businesses. As these groups attempted to navigate the federal bureaucracy and access disaster assistance in the weeks and months after the 9/11 tragedy, they faced repeated extensions, changes to procedures, and errors. This threw these already vulnerable groups into a cycle of despair and anxiety as they struggled to rebuild their lives and communities.

This lack of access can be tied in part to a single major policy change that FEMA implemented after 9/11: the new requirement that people prove that their hardship was a "direct result" of the September 11 attacks. In previous disasters, including hurricanes and wildfires, FEMA merely asked applicants to show that their losses were "a result" of the catastrophe. FEMA officials defended the new "direct result" requirement as fiscally responsible: "You have to draw the line somewhere or all 289 million Americans would be eligible" for federal disaster assistance, according to FEMA director Joseph Allbaugh.[45] On the one hand, this policy change reflected the novelty of this type of urban disaster for FEMA—that is, one with diverse and large-scale economic impacts versus one with geographically contained property damage. On the other hand, it reflected the restrictive framing of the disaster's deserving "victims" as corporate office workers in the towers and uniformed civil servants.

In addition, this narrow frame was reinforced by the designation of the FEMA "disaster area" as the blocks immediately surrounding the site of the fallen towers, dubbed "ground zero." This area was first represented through the creation of a map for buildings needing cleaning after September 11, on which the northernmost cut-off was Chambers Street.[46] Ultimately, areas "south of Canal Street"—some 10 blocks to the north—became the official limits for aid. This disaster designation reflected what many argued was a lack of geographic and cultural sensitivity, and led to the exclusion of low-income residents, workers, and small business-people who were mostly located in surrounding neighborhoods outside these limits. In particular, it excluded most of Chinatown and the Lower East Side, two neighborhoods heavily affected by dust and debris of the falling towers, and caught in the "frozen zone" south of 14th Street where streets were closed by the National Guard for months following 9/11. See figure 3.2.

As will be discussed in greater detail in Chapter 5, these restrictions of geography and "direct impact" were to set a problematic precedent for future rounds of aid, charitable giving, and redevelopment funding. In the short-term, they were reflected in FEMA's inability to provide adequate emergency aid. This was epitomized by its cornerstone program, Mortgage and Rental Assistance (M.R.A.). In the crucial first eight months following

(a)

(b)

Figures 3.2a and b
Chinatown business slows due to street closures
These images, from the exhibit "Chinatown POV: Reflections on September 11th" at the Museum of the Chinese in the Americas (MOCA), show how areas extending far beyond Ground Zero, such as Chinatown, were immediately affected by the fall of the Twin Towers. Local photographers documented Chinatown's proximity to the attack and to the cloud of dust and debris that soon blanketed the neighborhood, as well as a) the hundreds of workers waiting outside establishments lacking business, and b) the role of police barricades in blocking main access points, in this case Chatham Square. (*Source*: Corky Lee. Images courtesy of MOCA)

9/11, FEMA records indicated that the agency turned down seven of every ten people who applied for M.R.A.s, a far higher number than in other major relief efforts.[47] Analyzing the reasons behind the denials, one sees that the agency had little appreciation for the economic impacts of the disaster

Table 3.3 WINNOWING DOWN REQUESTS FOR EMERGENCY FEDERAL AID POST-9/11

Applicants sent M.R.A. packets	**31,578**
M.R.A packets not returned	**20,610**
M.R.A packets returned	**10,968**
Initial applications approved	2,854
Cases pending initial review	284
Request to applicant for additional information	521
Initial applications denied	7,309
Reasons for denials:	**7,309**
Various reasons	2,011
Loss of income not directly linked to disaster	3,299
Delinquent mortgage/rent paid by other agencies	91
Delinquency predated disaster	521
Not yet facing eviction or foreclosure	1,387
Appeals processed	**1,416**
Appeals approved	324
Appeals denied	1063
Pending review	29
Applications for continued assistance	**819**
Applications approved	381
Applications denied	422
Pending review	16

Eight months after 9/11, the Federal Emergency Management Agency had only approved 29 percent of the New York area applications to its Mortgage and Rental Assistance (M.R.A.) program, a crucial safety net for those who lost their jobs after the World Trade Center attack and a main source of disaster aid for low-income residents. Here is how applications had been processed as of April 8, 2002.
Source: Federal Emergency Management Agency; Diana Henriques and David Barstow, "Change in Rules Barred Many from Sept. 11 Disaster Relief," *New York Times*, April 26, 2002, A1.

for small-business owners and low-income residents or for the precarious financial situation of applicants—as many were penalized for having a prior "delinquency" on their rent or because were "not yet facing" eviction or foreclosure. See table 3.3.

By 2003, FEMA had doled out less than $65 million to help struggling families in the disaster area pay their bills, buy food, and avoid eviction, a miniscule amount of what the agency distributed in months after other major disasters. FEMA spent more than $1.4 billion on public assistance to help families affected by the California Northridge Earthquake in 1994; $1 billion for those affected by Hurricane Georges that struck Puerto Rico and a dozen other islands in the eastern Caribbean and Florida, Louisiana, Mississippi, Alabama, and Georgia in 1998; and $220 million for those affected by floods in Michigan in 1999. While the federal government paid the amounts over years, most of the payments occurred in the first months after the disasters. For FEMA Director Allbaugh, the low numbers of victims seeking aid were not due to the new stringent requirements but to "proud New Yorkers" who had been reluctant to seek help.[48]

While FEMA television advertisements promised aid to "all those who need it," the agency's rules governing eligibility were confusing to many residents. "There's really no guidance anywhere that the public has seen," according to Jackson Chin, associate counsel at the Puerto Rican Legal Defense and Education Fund. "There is nothing out there that helps the applicant make the case that their job loss was directly linked Sept. 11."[49] "It's as if they assume them criminals first," commented Wing Lam, Director of the Chinese Staff and Worker's Association in Chinatown, on FEMA's penchant for denying claims. Facing foreclosures and potential homelessness, some victims stopped seeking aid rather than submit to humiliating FEMA interviews that required victims to provide verification from the bank that they were being evicted. "When you're emotionally battered," according to one person, "and you go to the people who are supposed to help you, and you get more emotionally battered by them, you have to say to yourself, 'Is this worth my sanity?' "[50]

The "direct result" requirement represented a major break from long-standing policy and created excessive burdens for victims to prove that the catastrophe was responsible for their job losses, destroyed homes, or other hardships. Some argued that the new "direct result" policy was not peculiar to FEMA but was becoming a pervasive policy orientation shared by other branches of federal government. As the chairwoman of the New York City Arts Coalition and the information officer of the New York City Arts Recovery Fund wrote:

> The Federal Emergency Management Agency was not alone in imposing the "direct result" test, which limited benefits to those who could prove that their lost income was a "direct result" of the attacks. The Labor Department established the same criteria for eligibility for disaster unemployment insurance for the self-employed. Most artists, and we suspect most other self-employed people, were rejected when they filed for this insurance. Our experience shows that nonprofits (with the possible exception of the large academic institutions and large health care facilities), small businesses and the self-employed have not been served well by the government relief efforts.[51]

New York lawmakers assailed the federal response to the September 11 disaster, questioning whether FEMA was genuinely trying to get people the assistance they needed. According to Congresswoman Carolyn B. Maloney, FEMA's mismanagement of individual aid programs for New Yorkers who were affected by the disaster "left thousands without needed housing aid and with limited assistance for lost and damaged property from the disaster."[52] As a result, "[t]housands of people have lost trust in [FEMA] because of prior rejections and false promises."[53] Other New York lawmakers accused the federal government of not doing enough to alleviate the loss of tax revenue and municipal job losses caused by the disaster. Pointing out the multibillion dollar gap that remained between what New York lost as a result of the economic impacts of 9/11 and what the federal government provided in aid, twelve New York members of Congress called for congressional hearings to determine the adequacy of the federal response and the additional aid necessary. According to a May 21, 2003, letter to Speaker Hastert from Majority Leader Bill Frist and Minority Leaders Nancy Pelosi and Tom Daschle:

> Significant deficiencies in the federal response to New York after 9/11 have left New Yorkers, as well as their city and state, suffering severe financial hardship directly as a result of the attacks.... In addition, federal disaster response guidelines need reform immediately, so that the uneven response that occurred in New York does not happen again. Right now, New York City and State face drastic choices including job cuts and raising taxes to close budget gaps that were caused in a large part because 9/11 happened in lower-Manhattan. Terrorist attacks are national issues that deserve a full federal response, not a partial and uncoordinated response that leaves the locality most hurt, grappling with billions of dollars in losses.[54]

We can view the intense conflicts and struggles between FEMA and New York City residents in the context of the dramatic restructuring of emergency management functions that occurred in the years before and after the September 11 attacks. Ironically, the patriotic framing of 9/11 and its primary victims may have only contributed to this restructuring. Unlike previous rounds of devolution that marked other presidential administrations, a hallmark of the Bush administration was the combination of intense federal investment to create a resource-rich Department of Homeland Security, with the vertical decentralization of and cut-backs to emergency management operations. This legitimized new, more stringent guidelines for emergency aid. In addition to the imposition of the novel "direct result" test, FEMA determined that a distinction would be made between preexisting problems and pre-disaster conditions versus problems caused by the disaster, a distinction that executive branch officials would continue to use during and after Hurricane Katrina. Thus, the eligibility criteria for disaster aid required "a clear link between physical damage to the business or industry caused by the disaster and an applicant's loss of household income, work, or employment regardless of geographic location."[55]

The devolution of emergency management functions closely intertwined with the outsourcing of disaster aid to private charities. In the months and years after 9/11, FEMA officials explained that the agency spent comparatively little on financial aid to victims of the terrorist attacks because private charities and insurance filled the void and spent so much. As reported by the *New York Times*, FEMA officials accused charities of bowing to intense public pressure and hastily distributing money to the same victims FEMA was ready to assist. The unfortunate result, according to FEMA, was that private charities distributed tens of millions of dollars in private donations to people eligible for FEMA assistance. Charity officials dismissed FEMA's criticism as a veiled attempt to deny aid and restrict assistance. "FEMA is saying, in effect, that the victims of September 11 should be penalized and not get benefits that other disaster victims have gotten because the charities were quick to supply aid?" asked Joshua Gotbaum, chief executive of the September 11 Fund, the second largest charity responding to the attacks.[56] Yet whether the confusion was due to the charities' failure to coordinate with FEMA or FEMA's failure to communicate with the charities is irrelevant. The devolution and outsourcing of disaster management functions exacerbated the problem of displacement by splintering the delivery of services among disconnected government, private, and quasi-private agencies, a process that would continue, on a much larger scale, with Hurricane Katrina.

New Orleans: FEMA Responds to Hurricane Katrina

In the days after the collapse of the Army Corps of Engineers levee system in New Orleans, the Bush administration was faced with a spiraling crisis of legitimacy as it became clear that the federal government was ill-prepared and incapable of launching a major relief effort, despite spending billions of dollars on "homeland security" in the years after the 9/11 disaster. As New Orleans began to flood, tens of thousands of poor residents asked their leaders for food, water, and shelter. In turn, executive branch officials castigated and insulted residents for not leaving the city when they were told. Despite the fact that most poor, sick, and elderly residents had stayed because they had no means to escape, on September 1, Michael Chertoff, Secretary of Homeland Security, asserted that "the critical thing was to get people out of [New Orleans] before the disaster.... Some people chose to not obey that order. That was a mistake on their part."[57]

The inability of the federal government to respond to the disaster in an expeditious fashion revealed the failures of a devolved and privatized system of emergency management that had been built after the 9/11 disaster. "Two days after Katrina hit, Marty Bahamonde, one of the only FEMA employees in New Orleans, wrote to [FEMA Director Michael] Brown that 'the situation is past critical' and listed problems including many people near

death and food and water running out at the Superdome," the main shelter of last resort in the city. "Brown's entire response was: 'Thanks for the
update. Anything specific I need to do or tweak?'"[58] President Bush, who
had appointed Brown in 2003, praised the FEMA director after the storm
with the infamous line, "Brownie, you're doing a heck of a job."[59] Shortly
afterward, Brown was forced to resign when political leaders accused him
of being aloof and unresponsive to the disaster.

Whereas conservative media outlets blamed state and local governments
and tried to emphasize positive features of the federal relief effort, images
of widespread devastation and slow initial response undercut efforts to
convey an image that the executive branch was in charge and dealing effectively with the disaster. Thus, the problems of Katrina became personified
in Michael Brown as the FEMA director was demonized by media outlets
and became the scapegoat for the feeble government response to the crisis.
Scapegoating Brown was useful in zeroing public attention in on the actions
of a lone individual as the source of the problem rather than the privatized
and devolved system of emergency management that proved to be incapable of protecting and caring for flood victims.

Meanwhile, behind the scenes, FEMA officials were engaged in highly
organized damage control effort to manage media information about the
crisis in New Orleans and deflect responsibility for their poor response to
Hurricane Katrina. Essentially, the agency embraced a blame-the-victim
ideology that castigated the sufferers as undeserving of aid, a position that
was identical to the agency's response to the 9/11 disaster. Central to this
stigmatization and condemnatory approach was the decision not to extend
housing aid to displaced residents for more than six months. In December
2005, FEMA announced that it would terminate housing assistance for displaced persons and end its motel/hotel shelter program by January 7, 2006.
Over the next several months, the agency was the target of numerous legal
actions involving claims of improper or inadequate housing and claims of
discriminatory treatment of displaced residents on the basis of race and
ethnicity. Several of these cases were class action lawsuits brought on behalf
of tens of thousands of people denied aid, and seeking to compel FEMA
to provide assistance or stop the agency from taking assistance away.[60] As
a result of this litigation, at least 1,063 evacuee households obtained housing benefits, and all evacuees who could reasonably be located received a
detailed notice and an opportunity to appeal. For instance, in *McWaters
v. FEMA*, filed in November 2005 on behalf of a class of all Alabama,
Louisiana, and Mississippi applicants for public assistance, the court found
that FEMA had not adequately informed the applicants of the scope and
conditions for housing assistance. As a result, the court blocked FEMA
from ending its hotel/motel lodging shelter program.

The court condemned FEMA's arbitrary and capricious efforts to end the hotel/motel shelter program and recognized the intense hardship these decisions caused to evacuees. According to the court,

> FEMA has changed the relevant dates for the Short-Term Lodging Program at least three times (from November 30, 2005 to December 15, 2005 to January 7, 2006) since taking over the program for the Red Cross in late October. These actions have resulted in some evacuees getting Notices to leave their hotels and motels in a haphazard fashion, creating considerable anxiety for those persons most directly affected by FEMA's inconsistencies.[61]

The court highlighted the harsh effects of FEMA's decisions on those most in need of government aid and came to the conclusion that "the arbitrary January 7, 2006 termination of benefits is directly aimed at those who have virtually no resources, economic or otherwise."[62] In short, the decision by FEMA to arbitrarily terminate rental payment benefits—in this case and in many others—expressed victim-blaming assumptions that displaced residents were responsible for their own post-disaster housing problems, and the federal government was decidedly not.

Multinational Corporations Respond to Hurricane Katrina

Hurricane Katrina provided the first major test of the newly established Department of Homeland Security (DHS) that executive branch officials and managers designed after 9/11 to make the nation safer and more secure from terrorist strikes and other disasters. Following the formation of the DHS and the absorption of FEMA into that much larger bureaucracy, emergency management functions and responsibilities came to be viewed as assets that could be contracted out and privatized, a policy shift that created new opportunities for corporations and private contractors to maximize profits. Notably, a distinctive feature of the federal government's response to the devastation caused by the levee breaches was its heavy reliance on large private corporations to implement the federal, state, and local recovery strategy and policy.[63]

Immediately after Katrina, FEMA formalized relationships with private sector contractors by entering into no-bid contracts for $100 million each with four transnational corporations: Fluor Enterprises, Inc. (Fluor), Shaw Group (Shaw), CH2M Hill Constructors, Inc. (Hill), and Bechtel National, Inc. (Bechtel). FEMA contracted with these and other corporations to use hotels and cruise ships to house displaced residents during the immediate

Table 3.4 FEMA CONTRACT OBLIGATIONS FOR HURRICANE KATRINA, 2005–2006

Contract Obligations	Total	Percentage of Total	Percentage of IA-TAC Contract
Total FEMA Contract Obligations	$10.8 billion		
Other Obligations	$7.5 billion	70%	
IA-TAC Contract Obligations	$3.2 billion	30%	
Fluor	$1.3 billion	12%	43%
Shaw	$830 million	7.7%	26%
Bechtel	$517 million	4.8%	16%
Hill	$63 million	0.6%	15%

IA-TAC stands for "Individual Assistance-Technical Assistance Contract"
Source: U.S. Department of Homeland Security, Office of Inspector General, *Hurricane Katrina Temporary Housing Technical Assistance Contracts*, 2-3.

months after the disaster and then relied on contractor-installed trailers and mobile homes and a contractor-administered rental program after 2006. From September 2005 through 2006, FEMA ordered over 150,000 trailers to house residents displaced by Hurricane Katrina.[64]

By early December 2006, FEMA had obligated approximately $3.2 billion to Individual Assistance-Technical Assistance Contracts (IA-TAC) organized by multinational corporations for hurricane relief. These contracts included $1.3 billion for Fluor, $830 million for Shaw, $63 million for Hill, and $517 million for Bechtel (see Table 3.4). The government entered into contractual arrangements to reimburse the firms for funds they spent without defining the terms and conditions associated with a contract or task order. In January 2006, FEMA conducted an assessment and identified several problems with the use of private contractors including "contractors have invoiced the government for the cost of services in excess of the allowable level of reimbursement permitted."[65]

During this time, FEMA officials lamented the escalating dollar amounts for the contracts, noting that that all of the contracts were nearing their ceilings. At the time of the January 2006 assessment, the ceiling for each of the four contracts had been raised to $500 million. FEMA estimated that the ceilings on three of the four contracts would need to be raised even higher to complete the work assigned. FEMA officials complained that the agency had too few contract management personnel to sustain the workload; staffing levels were "fluctuating greatly"; and the agency had "little ability to plan and project accurate staffing levels." FEMA officials also expressed concern that "high turnover is hurting effectiveness, frustrating staff, housing managers and contractors"[66]

FEMA correspondence suggests that the contract ceiling issue posed a serious threat to the New Orleans recovery operation. In January

Table 3.5 FUNDING INCREASE FOR FEMA IA-TAC CONTRACTS FOR HURRICANE
KATRINA, SEPTEMBER 2005–SEPTEMBER 2006

IA-TAC stands for "Individual Assistance-Technical Assistance Contract"
Source: U.S. Department of Homeland Security, Office of Inspector General, *Hurricane Katrina Temporary Housing Technical Assistance Contracts*, 2-3.

2006, two of the four contractors, Shaw and Fluor, threatened to cease disaster-related recovery operations if FEMA did not raise the $500 million ceilings. In a February 2006 e-mail, officials with the Shaw Corporation noted that the firm "will have to shut down in 4–5 weeks without a ceiling increase." Fluor complained of "potential demobilization due to contract ceiling amount" and opined that "the citizens of Louisiana will have to suffer even more if we are forced to demobilize." A month later, in March 2006, FEMA raised the Fluor ceiling to over $1 billion and the Shaw ceiling to $950 million. Work continued to be tasked to these contractors without FEMA performing cost estimates and negotiating prices. As table 3.5 shows, funding increased dramatically from September 2005 to August 2006.[67]

The heavy reliance upon manufactured housing, or what came to be known as "FEMA trailers," was a conscious policy choice that had far-reaching and long-lasting negative consequences. The federal government spent more than $5.5 billion on trailers, including fees paid to contractors who installed and maintained such housing.[68] By 2008, a FEMA investigation concluded that manufactured housing, when compared to repair of rental units, was "less cost-effective" and "does not ensure permanent housing."[69] Notwithstanding the high costs, trailers contained high levels of formaldehyde that exposed residents to considerable health risks, provoking Amnesty International and the Sierra Club to condemn FEMA and motivating Congress to launch hearings and investigations into the health hazards of the toxic trailers.[70] Yet as early as October 2005, the Occupational Safety and Health Administration (OSHA) tested for and found formaldehyde in FEMA temporary housing staging areas. In late 2007, FEMA and the Centers for Disease Control (CDC) again conducted air quality tests of 519 trailers and confirmed that the trailers posed a serious danger to residents still living in them. Thus, the negative health effects of the trailers were neither unforeseen nor surprising. Rather, FEMA officials ignored and downplayed the toxicity and health risks of the trailers, decisions that generated extensive social costs and harmful health consequences for displaced disaster victims.

Exploitative Cost Shares and No-Forgiveness Loans

The federal response in the New York City area after the terrorist attacks differed significantly from the traditional approach FEMA had used in providing assistance after other major disasters. The three significant differences were the elimination of local sharing of disaster response and recovery costs; the size and type of projects funded; and capped amounts of federal funding that released unspent funds to state and local governments to cover recovery costs. In past disasters, FEMA paid 75 percent of the costs—the minimum provided for under the Stafford Act[71]—and affected state and local governments were required to pay the remaining share. FEMA provided for 90 percent of all public assistance costs for the Northridge, California, earthquake in 1994 and for assistance after Hurricane Andrew 1992. At the discretion and direction of President Bush, however, FEMA provided 100 percent of all public assistance costs in the New York City area, the first time an entire FEMA public assistance operation was 100 percent federally funded.[72]

Yet after Hurricane Katrina, the federal government was to return to past practice. Affected states and localities were required to pay 10 percent of rebuilding and individual assistance costs. This was to constitute one of the most serious financial burdens for New Orleans and other Gulf Coast cities. Given the massive scale of the disaster, even the relatively low cost share of 10 percent created insurmountable difficulties for cash strapped governments. Moreover, FEMA's public assistance program required governments to pay up front and then submit receipts for reimbursement, an arrangement that made it difficult for localities to plan and rebuild due to disaster-devastated finances, evacuated workers, and eviscerated tax bases. Interesting, the Disaster Mitigation Act of 2000[73] allowed FEMA to pay for large public assistance projects on the basis of estimates rather than waiting for reimbursement of actual costs. Yet FEMA never promulgated the rule necessary to implement the reform.[74]

As a result of FEMA's burdensome and exploitative cost-share and reimbursement practices, debris removal, restoration of public services, repair of police and firefighting facilities, reopening of schools, and other services needed for residents to move back into their homes and communities were delayed in many Gulf Coast cities. For example, the FEMA cost share alone for the state of Louisiana in 2006 was $1 billion, of which the state had paid some $400 million (out of the state's $7 billion in tax revenues). This FEMA share did *not* include costs for increased demands for social services, additional support for economic development and recovery, costs for bringing buildings up to safety code, and payment for facility repair. Louisiana communities also faced the loss of revenues needed to finance normal operating expenses, a point that was brought home when New Orleans Mayor C. Ray Nagin announced on October 4, 2005, that he would have to lay off 3,000 municipal employees—50 percent of the city's work force—due to lack of revenue.[75]

State and local officials lobbied aggressively, pleading with the White House to adjust the federal cost share to 100 percent. Officials wondered why Congress provided New York with 100 percent federal cost share to recover from 9/11 but required the state of Louisiana and city governments to pay 10 percent of their costs even though the damage and destruction far exceeded the cost of other disasters, and were the fault of the failure of federally funded levees in the first place. "It is all about the severity of the impact and the need to treat Louisiana fairly," as one Louisiana official noted before Congress in January 2007. According to this official:

> At the local level, some of our parishes have had their economic heart torn out through the loss of tax base, residents, and economic vitality. Some of our communities are struggling to survive. Based on this severe impact, *and the fact that much of the damages we experienced were the result of the failure of Federal levees which should have held in the face of a Category 3 event like that which we experienced*, we need the Administration's and Congress' support to adjust the Federal cost-share to 100%.... After the tragedy of 9/11, Congress provided New York with 100% federal cost share to recover from the disaster. They looked at magnitude of what the city was facing and leaned forward to cover much of the expense.... We are doing what we can, but there are limits to what a state the size of Louisiana can do for itself. We are stretched and are nearing the breaking point. The federal government should waive this state cost-share responsibility, as they did for New York following 9/11, and increase the federal cost share to 100% for all disaster relief programs (emphasis in original).[76]

On May 22, 2007, the Bush administration granted 100 percent of cost shares. By this time, already strapped state and local governments had absorbed cost-sharing burdens for twenty months following the 2005 storm. Yet the White House limited the cost-share waiver to projects for which a request for assistance form had been submitted as of the date of enactment. Thus, unless local governments had submitted a request for assistance form, the cost share was not retroactive, a policy decision that left them unable to access needed federal recovery dollars for projects they had already started.

The burdensome effects of federal policies and socio-legal regulations continued through the Community Disaster Loan (CDL) program that provided interest-bearing loans to Gulf Coast city governments to revive their communities.[77] From the start of the CDL program in August 1976 through September 30, 2005, the federal government canceled repayment of 97 percent of the $233.5 million in principal advanced through the CDL program. But at the direction of the Bush administration, Congress altered the CDL program to bar forgiveness of loans and thereby compel Gulf Coast cities to pay back the federal loans with interest. In 2005, FEMA approved 136 special CDLs totaling $739 million for Louisiana communities, including $120 million for New Orleans. The Emergency Supplemental Appropriations Act of 2006 (Pub. L. No. 109-234), enacted on June 15, 2006, included an appropriation to support an additional $372 million in CDLs.[78]

The unprecedented legislation requiring repayment of the CDLs incensed elected officials who derided the no-forgiveness loans as cruel and insulting. The federal government was treating New Orleans "in some second-class fashion," complained Louisiana Senator Mary Landrieu. "The Gulf Coast states have been basically forced by the Republican leadership in the House to accept help under conditions that have never been imposed on any state, city, region, county, sheriff, mayor ever before in the history of the country," Landrieu protested. On the Senate floor, Senator Hillary Rodham Clinton, D-NY, recalled how Congress provided New York City with $20 billion after the 2001 terrorist attacks "without telling New Yorkers that, 'Well, you're just going to have to figure out how you're going to repay when you're not even sure there's another attack coming.' The same good will should be given residents of the Gulf Coast." Rep. Bobby Jindal, R-Kenner, LA was "greatly disappointed by the change in precedent" for loan forgiveness. "The federal government has forgiven over $227 billion in loans for other communities. What makes my city or the Gulf Region any different?" wondered Rep. William Jefferson, D-New Orleans.[79] In February 2007, a year and a half into the recovery process, Governor Kathleen Blanco derided the debt as an "injustice," noting that state and local governments

Table 3.6 FEMA COMMUNITY DISASTER LOANS (CDL) FOR
THE NEW ORLEANS REGION, JANUARY 2010

Governments	Loan Amount
Jefferson Parish	
Hospital districts	$102 million
Public school system	$77 million
Parish government	$66 million
Law enforcement	$22 million
Orleans Parish	
City of New Orleans	$240 million
Sewerage and Water Board	$63 million
Schools	$59 million
Regional Transit Authority	$55 million
Criminal Sheriff	$18 million
Levee District	$10 million
New Orleans Aviation Board	$9 million
Port of New Orleans	$7 million
Plaquemines Parish	
Sheriff	$13 million
Schools	$11 million
Parish Government	$8.9 million
St. Bernard Parish	
Schools	$36 million
Parish Government	$18 million
Sheriff	$9 million
St. Tammany Parish	
Schools	$69 million
Sheriff	$13 million
Parish Government	$12 million
Fire Districts	$7 million

Source: Department of Homeland Security. Table adapted from Tilove, Jonathan, "FEMA Loan Forgiveness Is in the Works for Louisiana and Mississippi." *The Times-Picayune*, March 30, 2009 (updated January 15, 2010).

elsewhere never had to repay such federal disbursements after other disastrous events, including Hurricane Andrew (1992) and the September 11, 2001, terrorist attacks. "This is an issue of fairness," she remarked.[80]

The federal government's regulation prohibiting loan forgiveness pushed the burden of rebuilding onto local governments, many of whom faced destroyed assets and scattered work forces, the outcome of the flooding when the federally built floodwalls collapsed. By the end of 2008, Louisiana had accumulated almost $1 billion in CDL debt, while New Orleans owed $240 million to the federal government. Other parish governments and public entities, including school districts, law enforcement, and fire districts, had also amassed tens of millions of dollars in federal debt to finance their operations and rebuild their communities (see table 3.6).

On January 15, 2010, more than four years after the destruction caused by the Corps' levee system, Vice President Joe Biden announced that the federal government would forgive hundreds of millions of dollars in community disaster loans. "You're going to get your money," he told an audience of state and local officials who applauded his statements.[81] Shortly after the vice president's visit, however, FEMA published rules stating that the agency would not forgive loans unless local governments could prove that they were unable to meet their operating costs for the three years following the storm.[82] After more than five years of political wrangling, in November 2010, the federal government agreed to cancel the $240 million CDL owed by New Orleans.

In the years since the vice president declared that the federal government would forgive disaster loans, local communities have struggled to overcome fiscal crisis and rebuild their communities that had sustained heavy damage from the storm. As of May 2011, about fifty-two parishes, school systems, hospital districts, and other government entities had applied for the relief pledged by the vice president. Thirteen had their loans canceled and ten had them partially canceled. Twenty-nine of these government entities, more than 50 percent, were told by FEMA that their loans would not be canceled.[83] FEMA forgave $602 million in Katrina-related loans, but as of March 2012, the agency contended that it could not grant loan forgiveness to Jefferson Parish and other suburban parishes because they had budget surpluses after the deluge. Congress allows FEMA to grant loan forgiveness only for city governments with three full fiscal years of deficits.[84] In late 2012, the House of Representatives stripped from a Hurricane Sandy aid package a provision added by Senator Mary Landrieu that would have authorized FEMA to forgive the Katrina disaster loans. Finally, in March 2013, Landrieu added the provision to a Senate spending bill for the remainder of the 2013 fiscal year. This time, the House passed the bill to restore the possibility of loan forgiveness and nullify legislation in 2005 that made it impossible to forgive disaster loans under any circumstances.[85]

Scholars have long known that the framing of "crises" is neither neutral nor benign but reflects the political interests and prerogatives of claims makers and institutional actors. How extreme events are constructed has important consequences for victims and communities since disaster definitions can determine the allocation of resources, influence the policy response, and thereby transform cities. Thus, on the one hand, in the context of Katrina and 9/11, we can understand and explain variation in cost-share waivers and disaster loan forgiveness through reference to the different crisis-framing strategies applied to the two cities. On the other hand, we can see how similar results in terms of the market orientation of recovery policy over the longer term can be arrived at via very different framings and local contexts of disasters in the short term.

For New York City, the decision by Congress to waive cost shares and forgive payment for loans dovetailed with constructions of 9/11 victims as national heroes of a global tragedy. This framing strategy reflected the White House's interests in gaining public support for the establishment of the DHS, and the reorganization of emergency management functions to further privatization agendas. Although the private sector has long been involved in assisting governments in responding to disasters and crisis situations, the DHS represented a new and powerful vehicle for entrenching market-centered prerogatives into emergency management policy.

For New Orleans, government antipathy toward granting waivers of cost shares and forgiving payment of disaster loans expressed views that New Orleans communities were responsible for their own recovery even though Katrina's destruction was caused by the collapse of the federal government's levee system. Insofar as possible, government officials sought to frame the damage and destruction as a problem of individuals and local municipalities rather than as a societal problem created by economic and political arrangements and policy orientations. Moreover, a strong and proactive federal response to Hurricane Katrina would have been antithetical to political ideology stressing corporate leadership, private sector implementation of emergency management policy, and the sacrosanct status of market-centered programs and regulatory strategies as solutions to post-disaster rebuilding. Thus, diagnostic framing that stigmatized New Orleans as exemplifying welfare state failure and flood victims as undeserving of aid disadvantaged New Orleans relative to New York in accessing federal funds. Yet the cities' distinct crisis frames contributed in their own ways to a similar prognosis: that the private sector is most capable of responding to disaster and managing crisis situations.

REGULATORY DEFICITS AND THE CONTRADICTIONS OF POST-9/11 AND POST-KATRINA POLICY REFORMS

In the years since the 9/11 and Hurricane Katrina disasters, many scholars and government investigations have identified the limitations of federal programs for post-disaster individual and housing assistance.[86] One popular explanation for the inadequacies of the federal response to Hurricane Katrina, and one that echoes assertions made following 9/11, was the overall lack of coordination among various agencies and organizations that slowed the delivery of aid and impeded long-term rebuilding.[87] A second explanation contends that FEMA assistance programs and procedures are designed for small-scale disasters and cannot be easily adapted or scaled to large disasters in highly urbanized areas with concentrated populations.[88] There are three major limitations associated with these explanations, which we think apply equally to our analysis of 9/11 and Katrina and have implications for urban disaster response more generally.

First, these explanations impute a monolithic status to program design and do not answer why policymakers and government officials decided not to alter programs and policies in the face of pervasive governance failures and policy limitations. Five years after Hurricane Katrina, government hearings and reports were still asking questions about why the government response was weak and sluggish. As John Conyers, Jr., the U.S. Representative for Michigan's 13th congressional district, put it in July 2010,

> Katrina is still very visible.... We all knew that when the President told Federal Emergency Management Chief Michael Brown the classic phrase, "Brownie, you're doing a heck of a job," it was the biggest incorrect assessment of one of his people in the Administration of maybe all time. The compliment would still be premature because 5 years later, we can't point to what's going right with the government's response to Katrina.[89]

Ultimately, the problems of post-disaster recovery and rebuilding include FEMA but also other executive branch agencies. This is particularly the case in terms of FEMA's response to Katrina, as the agency was by this point reporting to the DHS, and subcabinet and cabinet officials were involved in formulating and implementing post-Katrina policy decisions. The president, vice president, and other executive branch officials were aware of FEMA's emergency management policy, understood that the agency failed to meet basic community recovery needs, and recognized in the years after Katrina that FEMA's policies and actions had dysfunctional effects. The White House, DHS, or Congress could have redirected priorities and changed policies to remedy the limitations of emergency management programs, expedite the delivery of resources, and speed recovery. Thus, the lack of coordination and nonscalability explanations do not explain why the federal government chose to follow some legal and policy directives such as refusing to waive cost shares or forgive payment of disaster loans. Moreover, these explanation ignore examples of highly coordinated activities—for example, between the federal government and private contractors—that actually slowed the delivery of aid and exacerbated the pains of displacement.

Second, the two standard explanations for FEMA's failures ignore the dominant force of market-centered ideology, especially devolution and privatization strategies, in guiding the formulation and implementation of emergency management policy. The limitations and hurdles built in to the federal response—for instance, changing eligibility requirements, procedures, and deadlines; predisposition to deny government reimbursement requests; explicit rule violations; and protracted financing disputes with state and local governments and institutions—are hardly evidence of the lack of coordination among agencies or irregularities in standard policy procedures. Nor was the combination of these problems with long processing time, low amounts of aid, and the punitive and discriminatory treatment of victims in New York and New Orleans due to a lack of coordination or difficulty in scaling recovery activities. Rather, these outcomes were entirely consistent with federal efforts to privatize and devolve emergency management functions and responsibilities and belied rhetoric of greater "efficiency" of the private sector used to justify these efforts.

Third, the two popular explanations miss the central importance of history and past decision-making in shaping FEMA's operational plans and policy strategies. As we have pointed out, the historical backdrop of 9/11 and the subsequent creation of the DHS decisively shaped the development of policies to respond to Hurricane Katrina. That is, the emphasis on outsourcing government aid and resources and devolved program implementation emerged not because of the peculiarity of the disaster trigger (e.g., a hurricane) or the scale of destruction. Rather, these policy strategies emerged on the basis of previous policies and regulatory approaches developed after the September 11 disaster. The incorporation of privatization and devolution priorities and logics into the DHS formed the basis for making future decisions about what should be the appropriate federal response to a major disaster.

Overall, post-9/11 decisions to shift emergency management responsibilities from government to the private sector not only had major negative consequences for New Orleans but also have resulted in a major transformation in the way the federal government views disasters and disaster victims. In particular, outsourcing addresses disaster victims as isolated customers, clients, and consumers. In doing so, such privatization obscures liability and accountability for problematic post-disaster outcomes and renders null and void claims from disaster victims and communities that they have a democratic right to aid and recovery resources as members and citizens of a sovereign nation-state. By prioritizing the goals and interests of subcontracted corporations, privatization allows such groups to use public resources to achieve what are essentially private aims. As a result, business approaches stressing restoration of private profits take precedence over public-sector regulation, democratic oversight, and broader community recovery needs. Moreover, privatization creates new institutional relays through which business interests can commandeer public resources and directly shape the content and implementation of policy. Ultimately, the market-centered ideology that endorses the use of devolution and privatization strategies serves to stymie public debate on alternative courses of urban rebuilding based on, for example, public investment, redistribution, and social justice.

Since 9/11 and Hurricane Katrina, privatization and devolution have proceeded in tandem to skew spending priorities and fracture the delivery of disaster assistance among levels of government and nongovernmental entities, including private companies. FEMA's establishment of a Private Sector Division in 2007 reflects federal efforts to cultivate public-private networks to support greater private-sector influence over and input into the process of disaster policy formulation and implementation.[90] In 2008, FEMA began outsourcing much of the agency's logistics to private contractors who are now in charge of acquiring, storing, and moving emergency supplies. This arrangement, known as third-party logistics, reflects the agency's interest in creating and strengthening networks with the private sector to deliver resources and plan for disasters. The federal-level privatization of disaster provisions dovetails with state-level attempts to contract out emergency management operations to large retailers such as Walmart and Home Depot to provide water, ice, medical aid, and other critical supplies during disasters. After seeing the sluggish response to Hurricane Katrina, the state of Texas established its own emergency management division to plan for catastrophes and provide disaster aid when needed, the assumption being that FEMA will provide nothing. "If they can get supplies that way," a FEMA spokesperson told the *Houston Chronicle*, "that's just one last thing we don't have to coordinate for."[91]

In recent years, pundits and elected officials have praised FEMA reforms, including greater integration of disaster preparedness and response functions, restrictions on possible FEMA reorganizations by the DHS, and the establishment of a "national preparedness goal" and national preparedness system. Other reforms have included strengthening regional offices; improving logistics to ensure timely delivery of goods and services; improving contracting and information technology systems; providing assistance to disaster-affected areas and populations; improving preparedness; and preventing waste, fraud, and abuse.[92] In May 2009, President Obama appointed W. Craig Fugate, a former emergency manager in Florida, to lead FEMA, hoping a new director with experience in disasters could help restore credibility to an embattled agency. For proponents, these reforms have created a more efficient and rationalized agency that is better able to respond to disasters and deliver aid to victims.

Yet it is important to recognize that these reforms in no way challenge the longstanding emphasis on privatization and devolution in emergency management policy, and indeed intensify FEMA's reliance on private-sector implementation of disaster aid. Thus current reforms do not address nor aim to fix the underlying contradictions that bedeviled post-9/11 and Katrina recovery efforts.

Identifying similarities and differences in post-disaster redevelopment policy efforts and outcomes in New York and New Orleans implicates comparison as both a research method and a critical strategy for revealing the assumptions and limitations of particular empirical claims about the 9/11 and Hurricane Katrina disasters. Typical case study accounts of the two disasters tend to embrace an event-centered conception in which each disaster's immediate and disruptive impacts and subsequent response and recovery efforts become the main objects of analysis. While useful and important, this conception concentrates analysis in time and space and obscures the deep historical roots of both 9/11 and Hurricane Katrina. Moreover, case study approaches miss the multiple and multi-scalar processes and contradictions that connect the two disasters and that lead to longer-term crisis and successive rounds of redevelopment.

What is distinctive about our comparative historical approach is that we problematize conventional notions of "disasters" as discrete events or static occurrences. In place of these models, we reveal that disasters are processes that unfold over time, are contested politically, and interact with local socio-spatial conditions. Indeed, precisely because disasters are temporal processes, they may interact with one another—generating concatenated crises—such that the relative timing of that intersection can play a decisive, if not all-determining, role in shaping trajectories and outcomes. As we point out, entrenched policy orientations, framing strategies, and the feedback effects of past decisions can affect the subsequent trajectories and outcomes of urban rebuilding. As such, comparison reveals that post-crisis recovery periods are not just about physical or infrastructural rebuilding but also about reinforcing and perpetuating power relations and social inequalities, all of which can create new patterns of risk and vulnerability to future disaster.

Crisis as Opportunity: Tracing the Contentious Spatial Politics of Redevelopment

"That's alright. You guys in New York can't get a hole in the ground fixed and its five years later. So let's be fair." So remarked New Orleans Mayor C. Ray Nagin in response to CBS correspondent Byron Pitts when questioned about the slow pace of the rebuilding process in New Orleans in August 2006.[1] Confronted by Pitts' accusations that his administration was taking too long to clean up New Orleans, Nagin defended the city's post-Katrina response by remarking on New York City's failure to rebuild Ground Zero. While pundits blasted Nagin's statement as callous and some New Yorkers reacted angrily, few disputed the accuracy of his assertion. The exasperation was captured on the front page of the satirical newspaper *The Onion*, which showed a photo of Ground Zero under the headline, "NYC Unveils 9/11 Memorial Hole."[2]

Five years after the terrorist attacks on the World Trade Center towers, many New York City residents wondered when, or if, they would see progress on the long-planned "Freedom Tower" and September 11 memorial. Asked by CBS anchor Bob Schieffer why the rebuilding was taking so long, New York Governor George Pataki replied, "this is hallowed ground. And we have to act very respectfully and prudently." Others noted, however, that a glut of office space was slowing the New York City rebuilding effort, a result of the demand made by World Trade Center's primary lease-holder, Larry Silverstein, and endorsed by Governor Pataki that the 10 million square feet of commercial real estate be replaced on the site. As David Dyssegaard Kallick, a fellow at the Fiscal Policy Institute, commented: "It's a kind of a vanity project for the governor because there's not a market demand."[3] Local and state inertia was compounded at the federal level. *The Onion* article concluded with the faux voice of Governor Pataki articulating a pattern many were starting to see in Washington DC: "And of course, I commend President George W. Bush, whose administration provided the kind of ample, unquestioning financial support to the rebuilding project for which they are famous, from New York to New Orleans.... Mr. President, you as much as anyone have made the dream of this hole a reality."

Post-crisis periods are frequently characterized as unparalleled moments of political opportunity, and rightly so. In the aftermath of collective trauma, such moments present the sudden, urgent possibility for civic engagement to repair, reimagine, and transform the urban landscape. New visions of a future city can be considered; large-scale urban development, previously off the table due to bureaucratic inertia, lack of funding, and entrenched interests, can suddenly be discussed; new solidarities and broad-based coalitions can be formed; and longstanding social injustices can be addressed and potentially remedied. Yet just as suddenly and urgently, contentious political realities impose themselves. Who will govern redevelopment projects and programs? Who will their primary beneficiaries be? And will these projects and programs—massive in physical and financial scale— challenge or reinforce the reigning political, economic, and cultural status quo? Such questions suggest that political conflicts over redevelopment are deeply spatialized as people negotiate and renegotiate meanings of and control over urban space at the same time that they attempt to rebuild their communities.

We use the phrase "spatial politics of redevelopment" to illuminate the various socio-spatial conflicts and political struggles tied to collective assertions of what Henri Lefebvre called "the right to the city."[4] In the case of New York City and New Orleans, struggles to control post-crisis redevelopment decisions are intimately linked to territorialized forms of inclusion and exclusion that empower some actors, alliances, and organizations at the expense of others. Tracing the contentious spatial politics of redevelopment implicates urban space not merely as an arena of collective action but as an object of struggle, as people battle over the meanings of "community," "recovery," and "rebuilding." In many ways, these contests are just part of the broader spatial context of urban politics. As Erik Swyngedouw has suggested, "the continuous reshuffling and reorganization of [urban space] is an integral part of social strategies and struggles for control and empowerment,"[5] a point underscored in Marxian terms by Mark Gottdiener when he notes that "social relations also are spatial relations; we cannot talk about one without the other."[6] Yet, as we see in our cases, the unique historical context of post-disaster civic engagement intensifies and complicates these ongoing spatial struggles. In the disaster's immediate aftermath, as citizens come together to mourn, pick up the pieces, and affirm the survival of their cities, there is often a desire for consensus and healing. With this frequently comes the idea that taking a critical, political stance on redevelopment would be unnecessary, if not divisive and disrespectful. Meanwhile, the political stakes could not be higher. The prospect of large-scale, subsidized redevelopment mobilizes a range of groups—in particular, growth coalitions with an inside track on the formation of redevelopment agencies, policies, and decision-making processes. Grassroots, labor, and neighborhood-based groups quickly realize that they cede this ground, and these spatial politics, at their peril. Thus, in both New York City and New Orleans, we found that the always contentious relations of socio-spatial development became even more so. They produced what Henri Lefebvre referred to as an "explosion of spaces," in which a multiplicity of meanings of and visions for the city erupt and enter into conflict as different constituencies fight to set the path of post-crisis redevelopment.[7]

CIVIC ENGAGEMENT AND CRISIS ORGANIZING

One of the most striking dynamics in the aftermath of 9/11 and Katrina was the sudden burst of civic engagement—at the grassroots, among the elite, and at all levels in between. This engagement was rooted in the circumstances and structures of feeling that are particular to post-crisis moments—a collective sense of trauma, desire for solidarity, love for neighborhood and city, as well a sense that the moment constituted a once-in-a-lifetime opportunity to have a voice in the future shape of the city. As Tom Angotti described in a reference to post-9/11 New York, there was, in the early months, a "flowering of participation in the public discussion about how to rebuild."[8] As Wynton Marsalis put it in reference to post-Katrina New Orleans: "When we saw our city go under water, it's like seeing something happen to your mama. You wish you had something more to give than time."[9]

In the early recovery stage, this "something to give" took the form, primarily, of mutual aid. People from around the city, the nation, and the world stepped up to offer moral support and to donate goods and services, expertise, and labor—from carpentry, to pizza making, to childcare, to emergency medical treatment—to help with local recovery efforts. There were spontaneous gatherings, organizing meetings, and jam sessions in public spaces of all kinds.[10] Famous examples included packed crowds of New Yorkers who filled Union Square in New York and Jackson Square in New Orleans twenty-four-hours a day, for weeks, to collectively grieve, find strength, and pay tribute to the hundreds of fellow citizens whose faces and stories, emblazoned on fliers and in newspapers, lined makeshift memorial walls. In New Orleans, too, an array of citizens, organizations, and visitors came together to support one another, share knowledge, and pick up the pieces of their city and communities.

In subsequent months, with mechanisms for disbursing disaster aid tested and formal redevelopment efforts underway, this flowering grew into a cross-pollinating political landscape, with diverse groups united in their desire to see their interests and needs represented in these efforts. Alongside mutual aid, there was now an upsurge in social movement organizing oriented toward longer-term, community-based efforts and focused on broader, structural change. Gatherings now took the form of urban visioning sessions and "crash courses" in what was required to actually rebuild the infrastructure of the city. Rachel Luft has termed such mobilizations "crisis organizing." Though the term was coined in reference to the political landscape of post-Katrina New Orleans, it applies equally well to New York City. In both cases, "new grassroots relief and reconstruction groups... sprang up rapidly out of preexisting movement networks" as community-based organizations, settlement houses, labor unions, and other activist, social service, and professional groups sought to connect urgent post-disaster needs to their ongoing mission as well as to join forces in order to contend with the enormous scale of this need.[11] This initial mobilization seeking a voice in recovery priorities soon shifted to proactive politics as newly formed coalitions sought a place at the table in redevelopment decision-making. While many in the two cities stressed the need for conciliation in the immediate months after the disasters, these coalitions, frequently drawing on members' long histories of organizing, saw the need for politics.

In New Orleans, it was in this early period that groups like the Common Ground Collective, one component of The People's Hurricane Relief Fund, mobilized an estimated thirteen thousand volunteers—mostly young activists and college students—to "provide services, distribute supplies, gut flood-devastated houses, and conduct bioremediation" in New Orleans.[12] Under the slogan "solidarity not charity," the organization explicitly sought to distinguish itself from the bands of volunteers and "voluntourists" who were largely disconnected from local community-based groups and their ongoing struggles. Another important example was the rapid organization of displaced residents protesting the shuttering of public schools and the razing of public housing developments.[13]

Following 9/11, similarly innovative grassroots coalitions formed in New York City among preexisting but heretofore unconnected organizations and groups.[14] Here, the focus was not on mobilizing thousands of volunteers for rebuilding since the recovery effort was more geographically concentrated and the physical destruction less extensive than in New Orleans and along the Gulf Coast. Rather, the focus was on having a voice in the priorities of rebuilding more broadly. Four coalitions led by middle-class professionals—including architects, designers, and academics—became influential, particularly on questions of the redesign of Ground Zero: Civic Alliance to Rebuild Downtown (Civic Alliance); Imagine New York; New York/New Visions; and Rebuild Downtown Our Town.[15] Meanwhile, groups like Labor Community Advocacy Network (LCAN), Rebuild with a Spotlight on the Poor (Spotlight), and Beyond Ground Zero (BGZ) focused on including the needs of the poor and people of color—communities disproportionately impacted by the 9/11 disaster but largely unacknowledged as victims—at the center of their recovery efforts. Further, these latter three groups argued for a "high-road" approach that included affordable housing, living-wage jobs, and improved public health and environmental conditions within the definition of recovery and redevelopment.

Spatial politics were central to the surge in collective action in both cities. In New York, this was particularly true of coalitions like LCAN, BGA, and Spotlight, whose organizing was largely focused on expanding the narrow definition of disaster-impacted areas and populations. As we saw in the last chapter, this definition was established with FEMA's initial disaster designation. It was to continue with the creation of the Lower Manhattan Development Corporation (LMDC), the chief public-private organization in charge of distributing federal funds. Once again, LMDC's definition of "Lower Manhattan" was focused on Ground Zero and neighborhoods immediately adjacent—that is, the sixteen square blocks of the World Trade Center site and the affluent and mostly white neighborhoods of the Financial District, Battery Park, and Tribeca south of Canal and west of Broadway. Groups representing heavily impacted populations outside this zone came to see the necessity of conceiving of their "community" on a larger scale, both culturally and geographically. See figure 4.1.

In New Orleans, in an unprecedented show of civic engagement and unity, residents formed the Neighborhoods Partnership Network (NPN), a citywide network of neighborhood coalitions, nonprofit organizations, and other activist groups to assist communities in accessing limited resources and information and to work toward shared goals. Meanwhile, Catholic, Mennonite, Salvation Army, and other faith-based relief groups linked up with large secular nonprofit organizations such as the Red Cross to form the Greater New Orleans Disaster Recovery Partnership (GNODRP), the first time in U.S. history in which major religious and secular nonprofit groups established a region-wide network to coordinate work and share

Figure 4.1
Organizers for the coalition Beyond Ground Zero posted notices for a rally and march through Lower Manhattan seeking more disaster aid for Chinatown and the Lower East Side. June 5, 2002. Above their poster is a drawing honoring the victims of 9/11. This was an early moment in which community response moved beyond mourning to include crisis organizing and coalition building. (*New York Times*)

resources.[16] In addition, resident groups, together with the NAACP and Louisiana Association of Communities for Reform Now (ACORN), organized broad-based opposition to the call by the Mayor Nagin's administration and the Bring New Orleans Back (BNOB) Commission for a smaller city footprint and a moratorium on rebuilding in flooded areas. Later, the Citizens' Road Home Action Team (CHAT) and Levees.org organized to draw attention to the problems of federal and state housing recovery programs and the decision-making that contributed to the levee failures. In addition, local activists formed the Lower Ninth Ward Center for Sustainable Engagement and Development (CSED), a community-based center housed in the neighborhood, to plan recovery efforts focused on community sustainability. Through their national and global networks, leaders and activists with CHAT, Levees.org, and CSED fought vigorously for a more democratic and inclusive post-Katrina planning process.

ELITE MOBILIZATION AND THE PERFORMANCE OF PARTICIPATION

A major challenge facing grassroots groups in both cities was contending with the equally dramatic political mobilization going on among business-led groups and related growth coalitions.[17] This mobilization process following 9/11 and Katrina was remarkably similar to that of the fiscal crisis period of the 1970s. Then, as we saw in Chapter 2, powerful players in the place-based industries of real estate, finance, tourism, and marketing, together with entrepreneurially minded city and state officials, created civically engaged public-private partnerships (PPPs) that both advised the city and advocated for longstanding economic development interests. Although 9/11 and Katrina were not primarily fiscal crises, the disruption they created caused a similar opportunity for elite intervention and the realization of long-held dreams. As one *New York* magazine architecture critic put it shortly after 9/11: "No one asked for the opportunity," but many soon realized that "deploying the equivalent of fifteen Empire State Buildings in New York represents a powerful tool for reshaping the city."[18] New Orleans developer Joseph Canizaro tied the language of real estate opportunity to that of social cleansing: "I think we have a clean sheet to start again. And with that clean sheet we have some very big opportunities." Louisiana Congressman Richard Baker (R-LA) made the business agenda more explicit: "We finally cleaned up public housing in New Orleans. We couldn't do it, but God did."[19] New Urbanist architect Andres Duany of the Duany Plater-Zyberk company, a major consulting firm leading planning groups in the city, took a more liberal stance in his celebration of the opportunity to intervene, remarking in April 2006 that "New Orleans is the planning Super Bowl."[20]

As in the 1970s, industry-led groups were also leading lobbyists for their cities at state and federal levels of government and so had a major advantage over grassroots groups in shaping the policy responses and structures of governance that would prevail during the crisis and beyond. Indeed, many of the very same PPP's and agencies most active during the 1970s, and which since had become enmeshed in the urban business establishment, again assumed a central role. In New York, these included the Association for a Better New York (ABNY), the New York City Partnerships (NYCP), the Economic Development Corporation, NYC & Co., and the Empire State Development Corporation (ESDC). They were joined by groups that had formed at later stages, like the Association for Downtown New York, a business improvement group created in 1995, motivated by the recession of the early 1990s to represent the interests of Wall Street and Tribeca. Members of these groups quickly engaged in their own process of "crisis organizing," though largely on behalf of the powerful interests of the business community. The numerous coalitions they formed in the immediate days and weeks following 9/11 included the Crisis Communications Committee, Wall Street Rising, and the NYC Rebuild Taskforce. Arguing that business interests represented the interests of all local citizens—or as NYCP director Kathryn S. Wilde would later put it: "Wall Street is our Main Street"[21]—these groups both advocated for greater aid for New York and lobbied for their own members to be at the helm of new governing bodies that oversaw this aid and subsequent redevelopment. As we shall see, they were to be remarkably successful, helping to both create and then dominate the board of the powerful Lower Manhattan Development Corporation (LMDC).

Unlike the early post-9/11 planning process in New York City, which was dominated by a well-organized cadre of PPPs with relatively clear business-centric redevelopment goals, the post-Katrina planning and redevelopment process was marked by widespread political conflict and social antagonism. From the beginning, a mixture of ad hoc commissions, planning organizations, and community groups battled to frame the city's "recovery" and control the allocation of federal resources. Both Louisiana Governor Kathleen Blanco and New Orleans Mayor C. Ray Nagin created separate recovery commissions to develop plans to guide long-term rebuilding. Governor Blanco spearheaded the creation of the Louisiana Recovery Authority (LRA) by executive order on October 17, 2005, initially with a twenty-six-member board, which was later expanded to thirty-three members. Mayor Ray Nagin created the seventeen-member Bring New Orleans Back (BNOB) Commission on September 30, 2005, just one month following Katrina, with the goal of preparing a rebuilding plan by the end of 2005. The New Orleans City Council created its own commission and voted to extend an existing housing-related contract with Miami-based Lambert Advisory LLC and the local firm, Shedo LLC, to develop plans for the city's flooded neighborhoods. Not to be outdone, Lt. Governor Mitch Landrieu (the eventual mayor of New Orleans) instituted a fourth planning commission. Of the four commissions, Nagin's BNOB Commission and Blanco's LRA proved most consequential, and both adopted ambitious and far-reaching proposals to transform the socio-spatial character of the city.[22]

From the start, New Orleans and Louisiana governments and their commissions disagreed on many aspects of the recovery, including how to plan, what should be the funding priorities, and who should control the allocation of funds.[23] Governor Blanco and the LRA advocated splitting up billions of dollars in federal aid and distributing it around the state to fund rebuilding efforts in rural areas damaged by Hurricane Rita and in other areas damaged by Hurricane Katrina. Nagin and the BNOB Commission disagreed, arguing that New Orleans should receive the bulk of federal money since Hurricane Katrina was much more severe than Hurricane Rita, which hit the western region of the state a month later, in September 2005. Against the wishes of Nagin, who advocated a city-run agency to control recovery efforts, the Louisiana state legislature approved the creation of the LRA in 2006, and the agency became the chief distributor of money from the Department of Housing and Urban Development (HUD) to tackle the state's housing crisis.

The creation of the LMDC in New York and the LRA in Louisiana alongside a broader upsurge in civic engagement illustrates the contentious spatial politics of redevelopment and the "explosion of spaces" associated with struggles over rebuilding in both New York City and New Orleans. State governments in New York and Louisiana created "independent," quasi-public authorities to guide the redevelopment process, while at the same time privileging entrenched and, they would argue, strategic, private sector interests. Tracing the implementation of redevelopment policies and distribution of aid reveals the contradictory and deeply contested nature of this arrangement in each city—as the establishment struggled to assert its position and vision over and against challenges by emerging grassroots groups and broad-based coalitions. In this sense, redevelopment politics remind us of what Edward Soja refers to as a "competitive conflict between the old and the new, between an 'inherited' and 'projected' order" that so often typifies urban redevelopment generally. This conflict "implies flux and transition, offensive and defensive positions, a mix of continuity and change"—in the redevelopment of Los Angeles for Soja, and also in New York and New Orleans following these disasters.[24]

Civic Engagement and the Lower Manhattan Development Corporation (LMDC)

In the weeks after September 11, elite coalitions mentioned above, representing the interests of New York City business, particularly those of Lower Manhattan, came together to coordinate a common response. One of the first results was the following statement, issued by the Association for Downtown New York (DA), ABNY, NYCP, and REBNY:

> We know it is important that downtown remain and grow as a powerful engine of the city's, region's, and nation's economies. The best living memorial to those who perished in the World Trade Center attack is to make sure that lower Manhattan emerges from this tragedy as a spectacular center of the global economy. The rebuilding effort must assure that this function is secured and enhanced.[25]

These groups went on to form a joint venture, the NYC Rebuild Taskforce, advocating the full restoration of the 11 million square feet of office space lost. This should take the form, they argued, of a new "commercial icon" that would serve as a "flagpole" for the financial industry and in patriotic defiance of terrorism. As with the original building of the WTC in 1973, debates became heated over the quantity of office space being proposed—whether the city needed it and whether the market could support it. Should New York "rush to rebuild" on the site or take its time and use the redevelopment process as an opportunity for better planning? Should the new building seek to replace the office space that had been destroyed or seek a "smaller footprint"—especially given market tendencies disfavoring Lower Manhattan over the previous decade. Was commercial office space the best way to honor the lives of those lost, or, as many victims' families and average New Yorkers argued, should the site be dominated by a memorial? And most crucially from the perspective of grassroots groups, should the emphasis of redevelopment be on the sixteen square blocks of the former WTC site at all, or should it look farther afield, "beyond Ground Zero," to include the needs of the many diverse communities impacted by the event?

These were thorny questions to be sure. Yet overhanging all of them was the thorniest of all: who should decide? This list was long: the mayor? the governor? victims' families? Larry Silverstein, who was the leaseholder of the site? the Port Authority, which was the owner of the site? Lower Manhattan business interests? rival Midtown business interests? Lower Manhattan residents of the wealthy Community Board 1, including Tribeca and Wall Street? Lower Manhattan residents of the working-class Community Board 3, representing the Lower East Side and Chinatown? And what of the desires of the range of New Yorkers—whether those in labor unions, community-based groups, professional associations, or average citizens—who were represented by the range of grassroots coalitions described above?

Faced with this situation, Governor Pataki and Mayor Bloomberg, designated by the federal government to oversee the disbursement of $21 billion of federal rebuilding funds, quickly created the Lower Manhattan Development Corporation (LMDC) on November 30, 2001, as the lead planning agency and mediator. A subsidiary of the Empire State Development Corporation (ESDC), the famously opaque economic development arm for New York state, the LMDC acted as a cross between a secretive independent authority and a public-facing neighborhood planning board. As detailed in a watchdog report entitled "Who Are These People and Where Did They Come From?," Pataki and Bloomberg appointed LMDC board members who were almost entirely white males of the business world.[26] Yet as a recipient of public monies, LMDC was also responsible to seek "public feedback and participation" in its decision-making process—something with which its board members were not overly familiar.

The challenges of this split personality were apparent from the start when the LMDC was tasked with launching the redesign of the World Trade Center site. In April 2002, the LMDC ceremoniously sent out requests for proposals to twenty-four major Manhattan architecture firms in what was extolled as an "open, public" process. Yet when the resultant entries proposed a range of positions on how to include office space at the site—some fully restoring the space, some banishing offices in favor of a memorial, most falling somewhere in between—the LMDC quickly withdrew the request.[27] On July 16, 2002, the LMDC then revealed that, without any public involvement, it had commissioned plans for fully restoring the 11 million square feet of office space, unveiling six models drafted by Beyer Blinder Belle, a hand-picked commercial architecture firm.[28]

These plans were met with instant and near universal disapproval by architectural critics, with many reminded of the business-led approach to urban renewal through which the original WTC was designed in the 1960s. Ada Louise Huxtable, a vocal critic of the original World Trade Center, called these plans "*deja vue* all over for those of us who remember the urban renewal destruction of Lower Manhattan in the 1960s."[29] In her view, "[t]he only concept apparent in the six concept plans released by the PA and LMDC is the restoration of all the commercial real estate by dumping it back in the same place in a slightly different form." Even some among the elite, such as Mayor Bloomberg, were taken off guard, given the disregard for the wealthy residential communities of Lower Manhattan that had been growing since the 1980s as well as the competition this would pose to Midtown, where Bloomberg's own corporate headquarters and development ambitions were focused.[30]

Then, on July 20 and 22, 2002, the Civic Alliance, a group organized by the Regional Plan Association along with more than eighty-five other civic groups, sponsored a massive event entitled "Listening to the City" (LTTC) to add the voice of the public into this debate.[31] It appeared to be similar to other public forums occurring around the five boroughs, including "Imagine New York" and "New York, New Visions," which sought to catalog diverse visions for rebuilding and contribute to a thoughtful, democratic, comprehensive planning process. Like the other fora, the Civic Alliance event included venerable planners like the Pratt Institute Center for Community and Environmental Development, established community-based organizations, newly created coalitions like LCAN and BGZ, and throngs of interested citizens. See figure 4.2.

LTTC sought to balance the complex mix of feelings that motivated so many to attend, such as "pain, sadness, and disruption" with a sense of

Figure 4.2
The front page of the report from the "Listening to the City" event of July 20 and 22, 2002, attended by some five thousand New Yorkers wishing to weigh in on the question of post-9/11 redevelopment for the World Trade Center site and beyond.

"opportunity born out of tragedy" to participate in shaping the future of the city. The report that came out of the event described the nature of this opportunity in moving terms:

> Last month, more than 5,000 people came together to make a difference in the city that they love. Total strangers sat with each other at diversely assembled tables and over the course of a day shared their stories and emotions, puzzled over plans and the challenges facing this city and our region.... [Our goal was to achieve] a rebuilt city that is more accessible, more equitable, and more successful than it was before. The tragedy of September 11 demands that the rebuilding process leave "business as usual" behind and be conducted in an open manner, drawing upon broad and diverse input from across the region.[32]

Yet part of what set this forum apart from others was the fact that it received institutional support from the LMDC, HUD, the Port Authority, and Deputy Mayor Dan Doctoroff, as well as powerful business interests. Additional sponsors included foundations like the Rockefeller Brothers Fund as well as major New York City-based corporations and banks like AOL Time Warner and JP Morgan Chase. Generous financial support enabled the Civic Alliance to rent out the Javitz Convention Center for the two-day event and conduct additional online forums and professional media outreach. This support helped in hiring consultant America Speaks, a national organization founded in 1995 to conduct "21st Century Town Halls" that used trained facilitators and state-of-the-art interactive technology to "give citizens an opportunity to have a strong voice in public decision-making" via tightly choreographed forms of participation.[33]

The results were, by all accounts, spectacular. The huge convention hall was filled with hundreds of tables around which groups of ten deliberated over questions of the design, governance, and economic priorities of the planning process. Their responses were then fed into computers, tallied, and projected on giant screens. All major media outlets in New York City, as well as many from around the world, covered the event. Organizers and participants alike spoke of this as being their first experience of "direct democracy" in action. Participant Erin Doyle, who spent three years working for organizations that promote democracy in the former Soviet Union, spoke for many when she said: "Most of all I was proud of making my voice heard and honored to have the opportunity to participate in an historic process, the result of which will stand as a great symbol of the freedoms we Americans hold so dearly and take, all too often, for granted."[34]

Interestingly, however, a majority of the participants polled at the meeting lacked confidence "that those in power would hear their voices"—a significant issue, given the powerful financial and real estate interests that also had a stake in Lower Manhattan.[35] In response to this concern, Roland Betts, a member of the LMDC board, real estate developer, CEO of the waterfront recreation center Chelsea Piers, and former fraternity brother and business partner of George W. Bush, told the July 20 gathering: "Everyone seems to fear that the real meeting is going on in some other room . . . . Let me tell you something—this *is* the real meeting."[36]

In part, this was true. The first half of the event was devoted to analyzing the newly released Beyer Blinder Belle plan—and to roundly denouncing it as an uninspired, overly commercial design that killed the life of the street, had too little space for a memorial, and most damning, "looked like Albany." As the *New York Times* reported, powerful officials, from the LMDC to Governor Pataki, who "were surprised by the fervor of the [negative] reactions" to their original plan, were "likely to be listening closely."[37] And indeed, the public's design concerns did bear some fruit—at least initially. In September 2002, the LMDC cited opinions gathered at LTTC in launching a new international competition with more flexible guidelines that allowed for reduced space for offices and placement of up to 40 percent of office space within the thirty-block area around the World Trade Center site. Eventually, the LMDC selected Daniel Libeskind's heavily symbolic 1,776-foot "Freedom Tower" in 2003 and Michael Arad's memorial "Reflecting Absence" in 2004. Ultimately, however, even the selection of these new designs was to be a pyrrhic victory. WTC owner Larry Silverstein, referring to Liebeskind's design as always no more than a "master plan," brought in his own architecture firm to reconceptualize the Freedom Tower and alter the memorial to allow more space for offices.

Yet all of this missed a crucial point. For the majority of participants in these public debates over the future of Lower Manhattan, design of the WTC site was never their primary concern. Networks like LCAN and BGZ had been growing in influence, their message widely embraced; and a vocal majority of those present at LTTC urged the LMDC to think beyond Ground Zero and use the funds to create affordable housing and living wage "liberty jobs" throughout Lower Manhattan, including Chinatown and the Lower East Side.

The official LTTC report by the Civic Alliance did reflect some of these concerns—including a pie chart showing majority support for housing and transportation[38] and, while avoiding the term "equity," acknowledging that rebuilding should "enable everyone to benefit from the large public expenditures that will be made in Lower Manhattan; and...ensure that the end result is a community that reflects values such as diversity and opportunity that help define New York."[39] Yet, in statements by LMDC officials and reporting of the event by major media present, the public's desire for "spectacular design" became the focus, with no mention whatsoever of their desire for affordable housing and jobs. In terms of what was reported by the media, an LCAN member, present at the event, noted that "we didn't expect [housing and jobs] to be the major story, but we were stunned by their total omission."[40] He surmised that part of the explanation lay in the perhaps not accidental scheduling of the day. The morning was focused on "rebuilding the site" while the discussion of housing and jobs, called "rebuilding lives," was left until the final, late afternoon time block. By that time, reporters had already rushed back to the office to write the articles that would come out the next morning.[41] This poor planning may also be seen as a reflection of LMDC's interest in using the event to legitimate their development agenda. Deputy Mayor for Economic Development and Rebuilding Daniel Doctoroff, liaison to the LMDC, was present throughout the entire event and is cited prominently in reports. As the former head of New York City's 2008 and 2012 bids for the Summer Olympics and a major force behind efforts to develop a stadium on Manhattan's West Side, Doctoroff was famously associated with grand development plans. He may well have known better when he said: "If I had to sum up what I heard today in one phrase, it would clearly be: Don't settle. Do something great."[42]

In subsequent months, the predilection by officials to focus on "great design" for the World Trade Center site and its immediate neighbors in the Financial District and Tribeca was to become official policy. The LMDC was obliged by its federal contract to hold a certain number of public meetings in different neighborhoods, or what they would call— building on the Civic Alliance event—"listening tours." Yet these were to be invitation only events that excluded many of the representatives of low-income communities and mixed, if not outnumbered, those who did get a seat with staunch advocates for business development. As we shall see, this was aided by federal-level deregulation that made independent authorities like the LMDC—and LRA—unaccountable to public scrutiny.

Thus, the upsurge in post-crisis civic engagement was to reap contradictory rewards. Grassroots efforts at events like LTTC helped to change the terms of the debate but did so only insofar as these terms helped legitimate the redevelopment priorities of powerful real estate interests and coalitions. Public concerns about uninspired design were heard loud and clear, though this was ultimately used to push an agenda—packing 10 million square feet of office space into 16 square blocks—that the public opposed. Meanwhile, broader and more urgent demands for equitable development were ignored. In essence, democratic participation was performed rather than practiced, with the result of reinforcing public doubts about the very possibility of "democracy" itself. The LTTC was emblematic of a seemingly "public" redevelopment process that, in effect, served to legitimize a real estate war for Lower Manhattan. As one leader of Good Jobs New York recalled:

> Five thousand people showed up. What do you envision lower Manhattan to be? It was housing, it was jobs, it was recreational space. And what are they squeezing in there? Office space. I'm not saying office space shouldn't be part of that. We need a place for commerce to happen. But it was like the square peg into the round hole.... After all our talking, all their "listening"...it seemed like a handful of people went into a room by themselves and came up with a plan without talking to anybody.[43]

Civic Discontent and the Louisiana Recovery
Authority (LRA)

Post-Katrina framings, planning debates, and civic discussions over recovery and rebuilding in Louisiana and New Orleans followed a similar trajectory as in New York after 9/11, if one that was even more contentious. Packed public hearings, antagonistic city council meetings, and rancorous state legislature debates dealt with controversial issues surrounding the future of the city: What does planning for recovery mean? Who will control the formulation and implementation of policies to guide rebuilding? How will local, state, and federal governments work together to allocate funds? Will some neighborhoods benefit and others suffer from the distribution of government largesse? Should leaders adopt a triage approach and begin rebuilding on higher ground? How should governments guard against haphazard development? What about the voices and interests of displaced residents who now live in other parts of the United States: who will advocate for them and their neighborhoods?

Aggravating the pains of displacement were calls from the nationally based Urban Land Institute (ULI) and Mayor Nagin's BNOB Commission for a smaller city footprint and moratorium on rebuilding in flooded areas, a proposal that civil rights activists condemned as an elite strategy to prevent poor, African American residents from returning to the city.[44] One major point of contention was the New Orleans *Times-Picayune's* publication of a "green-dot" map (see figure 4.3) that suggested vulnerable areas where parks and green spaces might be created. Planners envisioned the green-dot map not as a final outcome but as a nascent land-use tool that would evolve after the approval of a government buyout program and the conclusion of a citizen-driven planning process. Yet neighborhood coalitions reacted negatively to the release of the BNOB proposal in December 2005 and the publication of the green-dot map in early 2006, arguing that "greening" was the death knell of New Orleans's historic and culturally unique urban neighborhoods since the map seemed to infer that tens of thousands of homes would have to be demolished, rather than rebuilt, to make way for new parks and green space.[45] Activists contended that the greening of flooded neighborhoods was a vehicle for citywide gentrification and a planning device to exclude rather than include diverse groups in the rebuilding of the city.

Soon after the formation of BNOB, residents began packing into meetings of their neighborhood associations and demanding a more inclusive and democratic planning process. During an October 2005 public meeting to discuss which neighborhoods should be redeveloped first, protestors shouted down Mayor Nagin and BNOB Commission members with chants

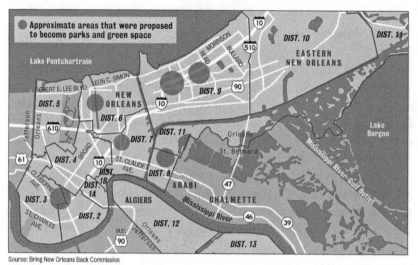

Source: Bring New Orleans Back Commission

THE TIMES-PICAYUNE

Figure 4.3
Green-Dot Map in New Orleans
The infamous "Green-Dot" map appeared in the New Orleans *Times Picayune*, January 11, 2006, showing neighborhoods that BNOB and the ULI designated as green space. Neighborhoods surrounding the green dots would have to "prove viability" in order to receive public services and reinvestment resources. The map sparked widespread protest by civic groups fearing that the city would clear homes and convert their beloved neighborhoods to green space. (*Source: The Times-Picayune*, Landov Media)

of "Cooperation, not corporations! We demand representation."[46] The specter of greening shaped an emerging confrontational strategy adopted by neighborhood coalitions to challenge exclusion and marginalization. "I saw that my neighborhood was to be cleared as green space, and I said, 'Oh, hell, no,'" recalled Reggie Lawson, a coordinator with the Faubourg St. Roch Improvement Association. "This was my home, and I had no intention of moving, nor could I fathom a reason why I should move."[47] Vera Triplett, who, along with several others, founded the Gentilly Civic Improvement Association in November 2005, said she initially believed city officials and planners' claims as she considered the costs of whether to rebuild in her home in Gentilly, a green-dotted neighborhood swamped by water pouring through breaches in the London Avenue Canal. "But my husband and I felt very strongly that unless they could prove to us unequivocally that we were placing ourselves and our children in danger—and they couldn't—then we were not going to allow anyone to unilaterally dictate where we couldn't live," she said.[48]

For displaced residents of the Lower Ninth Ward, plans calling for a building moratorium sent an unsettling message that they might face increased risks to safety and security if they moved back. Indeed, as late as August 2006, Mayor Nagin continued to warn against rebuilding in the Lower Ninth Ward and two sections of eastern New Orleans, though he refused repeatedly to define the sections. As Nagin told New Orleanians:

> I've been saying this publicly, and people are starting to hear it: low-lying areas of New Orleans East, stay away from. Lower 9th Ward…. People are starting to hear it. That's what I'm telling people (in the Lower 9). Move closer to the river.[49]

On the other hand, however, the mayor argued that property rights were sacrosanct and that the city would issue construction permits to allow rebuilding in all parts of the city. Residents assailed the city's contradictory messages. "I encourage the mayor to stand up and say something other than, 'Let the market decide,'" complained Nagin critic Reed Kroloff, Dean of the Tulane University School of Architecture. "That's planning not to plan. Let the mayor say, 'Here's some guidance.' Why let this happen randomly? Why not encourage it to happen intelligently?"[50] For Nagin, the laissez-faire approach was working exactly as intended. "The market is reacting properly," he stated in 2006. "If you get the information out there, the marketplace is going to make a good decision."[51]

For many residents, the city's decision to permit reconstruction in all sections of New Orleans seemed to offer tacit assurance that city officials would neither deny public services nor convert neighborhoods to green space. Frustrated by the befuddling messages from elected leaders, many residents took the initiative and moved ahead with rebuilding their homes. "I felt strongly that I was not going to let the city government tell me where I could live," recalled one Ninth Ward resident. "Hell, I had a mortgage to pay and a job here. I wanted to rebuild and get going with my life. I was not going let a corrupt city government deny my right to return."[52] According to another neighborhood leader:

> The green-dot plan was a form of class and racial redlining that was meant to tell residents to stay away. The city did this so they could rebuild whatever they wanted with black people and poor people out of the way.[53]

At the same time, another resident recalled:

> I remember when I went to see if I could get a permit to rebuild my mother's house. I asked one person working at the permit office, "if you are going to tear it down and build a park, why should I get a permit to rebuild?" The person told me that he could issue a permit for the address, which did not make much sense to me. But I took it and I rebuilt the home. I love New Orleans. I was born here. This is my home.[54]

Amid the panic and fury of residents whose neighborhoods had been overlaid with green dots, the map quickly met its demise. Along with it went a suggestion that City Hall temporarily quit issuing building permits across a broader swath of the city while residents cemented their rebuilding plans. Notably, the green-dot controversy spurred an unprecedented outpouring of civic activism in the name of protecting property rights and beloved neighborhoods. The controversy also changed the nature of the planning debate by forcing city government to jettison the idea of neighborhood clearance in the name of greening. Yet, as in New York, the post-disaster planning process fueled skepticism and contributed to public mistrust. City Councilwoman Cynthia Willard-Lewis, who represented the hard-hit Lower Ninth Ward and Eastern New Orleans, recalled that the green dots made many of her African American constituents remember the civil rights era, thinking they would need to fight for equal access all over again. The maps, she said soon after they were unveiled, "are causing people to lose hope."[55]

Meanwhile, the contentiousness of political debates occurring at the state and local levels was largely a sideshow to congressional and executive branch efforts to force Louisiana and New Orleans officials to adopt a New York-style rebuilding program to distribute federal resources for urban redevelopment. Within a month after Hurricane Katrina roared ashore, the federal Department of Housing and Urban Development, in "[e]xpanding distribution and direct action," recommended "the Lower Manhattan Development Corporation as a model" for the state of Louisiana and stated:

> [I]n increasing the administrative cap, Congress is signaling its intent that the States under this appropriation also be able to carry out activities directly. Therefore, HUD is waiving program requirements to support this. HUD is also including in this Notice the necessary complementary waivers and alternative requirements related to subrecipients to ensure proper management and disposition of funds.[56]

Following this recommendation, in October 2005, the Louisiana state legislature created the Louisiana Recovery Administration (LRA), a new public authority to access and distribute Community Development Block Grant (CDBG) funding to assist in planning and revitalization efforts. Like the LMDC, the LRA was set up to operate outside the normal system of checks and balances with a board composed of business owners and executives, some of whom lived outside of Louisiana and the Gulf Coast states.[57] The state of Louisiana via the Office of Community Development (OCD) granted the LRA wide authority to plan and implement the state's post-Katrina redevelopment goals. This authority included the right to "receive, prioritize, create guidelines for and disburse to other agencies and organi-zations" all disaster recovery-related CDBG funding.[58] The Public Affairs Research Council of Louisiana celebrated the LRA as the panacea for New Orleans's recovery:

> The LRA is modeled after the Lower Manhattan Development Corporation, which was created as a state government unit responsible for post-9/11 development. The intent of the federal legislation that makes the block grants available to Louisiana is clearly that the funds should flow through an entity like the LMDC, which in Louisiana's case is the LRA. The New York experience shows that this model for post-disaster research and planning can work.[59]

REDEVELOPMENT THROUGH THE COMMUNITY DEVELOPMENT BLOCK GRANT PROGRAM: THE CASE OF POST-9/11 NEW YORK

Both the LMDC and the LRA represented novel, public-private corpo-rations whose initial mandate was to funnel federal aid to New York and New Orleans through the Community Development Block Grant (CDBG) program. Established by Congress in 1974 through the Department of Housing and Urban Development (HUD), the CDBG program awards funds to the affected state or local government to administer themselves, thereby affording states and localities broad discretion and flexibility in deciding how to allocate the funds and for what purposes. Policymakers designed the program to help states meet "urgent community development needs," such as by aiding them in the "prevention or elimination of slums or blight" through the creation of affordable housing and in remediating "conditions [that] pose a serious and immediate threat to the health and welfare of the community." As such, HUD originally intended grantees to use at least 70 percent of the CDBG funding for "activities that principally benefit of low- and moderate-income persons."[60]

Over the last two decades, the flexibility of the CDBG program, com-bined with increasing cuts to most other sources of federal funding for localities, has made it a highly desirable funding source for cash-strapped cities and states, particularly in times of disaster. Starting with Hurricane Andrew in 1992 and the Midwest floods in 1993, Congress allowed HUD to use the program to support post-disaster redevelopment. Nonetheless, the amounts of CDBG assistance for this purpose were relatively small— never exceeding $50 million—and the core HUD regulations surrounding the use of the grants remained intact.

The 9/11 attacks, and intense lobbying by powerful local growth coalitions, motivated Congress to alter the structure and operation of the CDBGs in three major ways. One programmatic change was to dramatically increase the amount of disaster aid channeled through HUD. In November of 2001, HUD allocated $3.483 billion in CDBG funds to New York City and New York State, representing more than ten times what Congress had allocated for any other individual disaster since the federal government began keeping records in 1992. After Hurricane Katrina, Congress appropriated $19.7 billion for Gulf Coast rebuilding assistance, the largest amount in the history of the program.

Second, beginning with 9/11 and replicated with Hurricane Katrina, Congress allowed states to establish new entities to coordinate and oversee rebuilding efforts and to serve as policymaking bodies responsible for distributing CDBG funds. Under the leadership of Governor George Pataki, New York State complied with this regulation by creating the LMDC to oversee all rebuilding efforts. The LMDC structure was that of an independent authority that was both extremely powerful and largely immune from public oversight. Beyond simple program implementation and documentation—the extent of local agencies' responsibility in the past—the LMDC was empowered to serve as the lead policymaking body responsible for planning and implementing redevelopment within the state through the administration of both grants and bonds.

The final, most far-reaching shift in the post-9/11 use of CBDGs was in terms of regulation. The devolution of responsibility to the state and local level gave powerful political actors in New York a legal mechanism to control the delivery of aid and, most important, lobby for waivers of HUD regulations pertaining to the program. In early 2002, in response to lobbying efforts by the New York City delegation, HUD waived the requirement that 70 percent of the CDBG funds be for activities that benefit low- and moderate-income people. Indeed, under this waiver, the LMDC was not obligated to appropriate *any* CDBG funds for low- and moderate-income people affected by the events of 9/11. HUD's explicit expectation for New York City was only that the LMDC "make a good faith effort to maximize benefit to low- and moderate-income persons." Yet, in addition, and undermining another basic goal of the CDBG program, HUD waived "public benefit standards," which made future funding contingent upon predetermined benefits of economic development activities to a broad "public"—such as, for instance, the creation of a given number of new, full-time, low- and moderate-income jobs.[61]

In a final move, HUD waived "citizen participation requirements" that mandated public hearings for citizens to comment on CBDG plans; lifted major restrictions on how the ESDC and LMDC should monitor and evaluate the distribution of HUD grants; and "removed requirements for consistency" with a "consolidated plan." HUD also eliminated the provision that the LMDC prepare and submit normal performance reports on a regular basis.[62] In short, the LMDC's implementation of the CBDG program did not contain requirements for notifying the public about how the funds were to be spent nor any mechanism to hold the state of New York accountable for the use, or misuse, of funds. As a result, the LMDC positioned itself as a quasi-public agency with the authority to operate outside the normal system of legislative checks and balances, and with no obligation to provide public benefit or help low-income people. This authority was especially significant given the unprecedented sum of $21 billion at its disposal.

This radical restructuring of CDBGs occurred over two phases: the initial *recovery phase*, when large grants were made for short-term business and residential recovery programs, and the subsequent *rebuilding phase*, when grants were made for longer-term and more varied economic development projects. The restructuring was to have different but equally consequential impacts in each phase.

In the recovery phase, $2.4 billion was allocated, mainly in the form of Business Recovery Grants (BRGs) and Residential Recovery Grants (RRGs). Empowered by deregulation, the LMDC was to structure both grants in ways that were primarily beneficial to corporate and developer interests. With BRGs, the LMDC redefined "small business" as any company with *fewer than 500 employees* rather than the typical 25, and with no restrictions on annual revenues. An investigation by the *New York Times* and our own evaluation of the LMDC reports revealed the disturbing results of this new formulation. Close to 40 percent of the BRGs went to major corporations with hundreds of employees, which together represented only 15 percent of those affected. These firms received on average two times what small businesses received. And this is despite the fact that none of the former suffered great losses in the long run, while hundreds of the latter were put out of business entirely.[63] As noted in one *New York Times* article: "The inconsistencies in the [Business Recovery Grant] grant program... did not result from fraud. Rather, they were the outcome of regulations drafted quickly by New York State officials, based on laws that were hastily written in Washington—all in an effort to quickly distribute badly needed money to suffering businesses."[64]

Compounding such "inconsistencies," the largest employers also received multimillion dollar cash incentives in the form of RRGs to commit to Lower Manhattan for at least seven years, regardless of whether they intended to leave in the first place. Incentives included $40 million for the Bank of New York, $25 million for American Express, and $23 million for the New York Board of Trade.[65] These RRGs, unbound by income targets, had perverse effects: landlords took advantage of tax breaks granted to large corporate tenants by raising rents, as well as by evicting lower-income tenants and small businesses to make room for those who could afford the new higher rents.

Activists from grassroots coalitions condemned the inequities and lack of transparency surrounding these grants. LCAN's newly created watchdog organization, Reconstruction Watch, detailed the many ways landlords were gaming the system. For instance, to incorporate the incentives for renters provided by RRGs, landlords simply raised rents and then refused to renew two-year leases to low-income tenants so as to free the space for higher-income tenants with larger subsidies.[66] Thus, CBDG grants for "small business" actually provided a new, legal means to evict low-income tenants in Lower Manhattan. More than four years after the disaster, Daniel H. Bush, director of 9/11 Recovery and Victim Advocacy for New York Disaster Interfaith Services, a federation of faith-based disaster relief agencies, noted that "while the LMDC acted quickly allocating funds to corporate business retention and aiding the real estate market, immigrants and low-income individuals were forced to seek other means of sustenance and support for their families." According to Bush, the LMDC's redevelopment initiatives "did nothing to alleviate the struggle of low-income families for housing. Many have faced eviction proceedings since 9/11."[67]

This inequity was only exacerbated in the subsequent *rebuilding phase* beginning in 2004. Here, $1.3 billion of more discretionary funding was at stake, yet the opportunity for public input was delayed for two years by the lobbying efforts of Governor Pataki, the Downtown Alliance, and the NYCP. They sought to direct the entirety of the CDBG funding toward a $6 billion dollar rail link between Lower Manhattan, the suburbs, and John F. Kennedy airport, which critics argued would have mainly benefited commuters, tourists, and business travelers—not the local communities most impacted by the disaster.[68] The proposal was finally jettisoned, yet the lobbying behind it created a formidable barrier for civic groups, small businesses, and others trying to push their own priorities.

This was not, however, the only challenge facing groups without ties to the LMDC board. Small-business groups reported tremendous difficulty in accessing information about the status of their funding proposals and numerous bureaucratic obstacles to receiving grants.[69] From the Ground Up, a grassroots support group representing six hundred Lower Manhattan small businesses, railed against inadequate funding for struggling businesses and called for an end to federal rules requiring that grants be taxable. Along with other small business advocates, they argued that businesses allied with the LMDC were adopting a top-down, "growth-first" approach to redeveloping Lower Manhattan that sought the return of major corporations and large firms—or attraction of new ones—to the exclusion of small business.

More Kafkaesque hurdles awaited those who tried to protest LMDC events. As mentioned above, a limited number of LMDC public hearings were held in 2003 as part of the agency's reporting requirement, though these were invitation only. Even if those able to gain invitations advocated for housing and jobs, the hearings resulted in nothing more than written reports, with no follow-up required.[70] LMDC board meetings were still, by law, open to the public, yet the public had no right to speak unless they could get on the agenda, which was prepared in advance and extremely long. Members of grassroots coalitions who regularly attended the meetings recalled that board members with interests in particular projects would recuse themselves, often multiple times in a single meeting, and invariably have their projects approved in their absence. Meanwhile, local groups' demands for housing and jobs were ignored. This forced the use of creative, if ultimately ineffectual and undocumented, tactics. As one coalition leader recalled:

> We would sneak in sheets in our handbags that we would hold up throughout the meeting saying, "Build Our Community!" But if you look at the minutes it was like we were not even there. So, making them even *feel* accountable was like a herculean task. Now it is almost 10 years later and we're all still like "so where is that money?"[71]

Finally, in 2006, $50 million of the original $1.3 billion in long-term rebuilding funds was approved for affordable housing, though critics argued that the definition of "affordable" was still too expensive for low-income people, and measures of "success" were vague.[72] From (fiscal) 2009 to 2011, only about 8 percent of the units developed by the city were meant for households that earned 40 percent of the area median income, even though that income group represented more than a third of all New York households. Meanwhile, 56 percent of the city's affordable units were built for households making 51 to 80 percent of the area median, although that group represented only 17 percent of all households.[73] In the end, the "affordable housing plan" used such a narrow and restrictive definition of "affordable" that the neediest local residents—once the target of CDBGs— were excluded from the program altogether.

Thus in 2007, when LMDC provided an additional $37 million for "community enhancements" like "healthcare, education, community services, recreation and cultural projects"—it was a bittersweet victory for grassroots coalitions.[74] Some important local institutions serving low-income residents of public and subsidized housing did finally receive aid.[75] Yet Mayor

Bloomberg's comments on the enhancements indicated a broader purpose: "Lower Manhattan is one of the fastest-growing central business districts in the country and is one of our City's hottest residential markets. As we watch the transformation of this community into a twenty-four hours a day, seven days a week place to be, it's important that we continue to offer support to organizations that improve the quality of life here, and enrich our entire city."[76] Given the LMDC's lack of support for affordable housing, "quality of life" improvements were to increasingly benefit the new, more affluent residents moving in to these "hot" real estate markets rather than the low-income communities that had fought for them in the first place.

LIBERTY BONDS

In addition to direct grants, President Bush's post-9/11 Job Creation and Worker Assistance Act of 2002 created the Liberty Bond program, making available up to $8 billion worth of tax-exempt bonds as an additional mechanism to aid New York City's reconstruction after the terrorist attacks. The mayor and governor could each decide to allocate up to $4 billion over the next three and a half years, or until 2004, with no stipulation that they must spend all money. Ultimately, $6 billion was spent.[77]

Liberty Bonds (LBs) are a form of tax-exempt qualified private activity bonds (PABs), previously known as Industrial Development Bonds (IDBs), and a popular form of private-sector subsidy dating back to the 1970s.[78] The use of such bonds is justified by the argument that the government's provision of cheap capital for development will encourage new investment and, in so doing, will provide a net public benefit.[79] This goal, however, has long been in tension with the highly profitable nature of the bonds, which, compared to taxable corporate bonds, provide large investors with major savings. Indeed, as a result of widespread abuses of IDBs in the 1970s and early 1980s, Congress created more restricted parameters, including caps on the amount of bonds available to each state annually, known as "annual state ceilings," and public use restrictions on "qualified" tax-exempt facilities. Congress codified these reforms in the Tax Reform Act of 1986.[80] Such facilities are listed in the U.S. Tax Code and include privately owned and operated properties upon which the public depends, such as transportation facilities, public works facilities, affordable rental housing, and electric and gas utilities.[81]

Through the LB program, and again spurred by the lobbying of the LMDC, the federal government was able to essentially rewrite this law, doing away with all state ceilings and "public interest" requirements governing PABs. This "re-regulation" thus facilitated uses of tax-exempt bonds

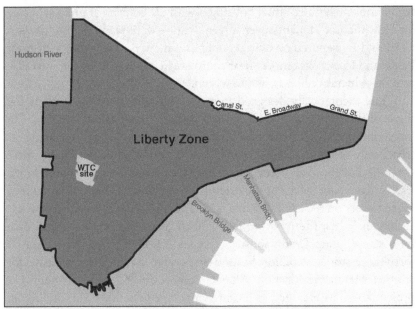

Source: GAO.

Figure 4.4
The New York Liberty Zone
The New York Liberty Zone, enacted by the Job Creation and Worker Assistance Act of March 9, 2002, provided for the issuance of $8 billion in tax-exempt "Liberty Bonds" within this zone south of Canal Street, in Lower Manhattan. In a change to IRS regulations governing such "qualified private activity bonds," the size of Liberty Bonds could exceed previously established state ceilings, and their use no longer had to meet "public interest" requirements. This created a major incentive to develop market-rate, or "luxury," commercial and residential real estate within the zone. (*Source*: Government Accountability Office)

that had not been possible since the pretax reform era of the 1970s— namely, underwriting highly profitable, market-rate development. The lifting of caps occurred mainly within the HUD-designated "Liberty Zone," bounded on the north by Canal Street, East Broadway, and Grand Streets. See figure 4.4. Another innovation was the federal decision that, unlike traditional "enterprise bonds," 25 percent of the funds, or in this case, $2 billion, could also be spent *outside* the Liberty Zone and within New York City. Also new was the sheer scale of the program. In granting $8 billion over three and a half years, New York City received almost four times the total amount of all PABs disbursed *nationwide* over a similar period. PABs were given to the city at approximately seven times the rate that would have been available to the entire state (i.e., $8 billion versus $1.2 billion).

Thus, for the first time, the PAB tax exemption could be used for *commercial development*, something that had not previously met "qualified" PAB restrictions as it did not serve the "public interest," and could do so on a broad scale.[82] This was to have far-reaching effects. Traditional "80/20" regulations governing rental housing—with 20 percent of units set aside for "low-income" tenants over fifteen years—were waived. And, as with CDBGs, LBs required no official public comment period, giving Governor Pataki and Mayor Bloomberg near complete freedom to decide how to allocate these lucrative bonds, and to whom.[83]

While theoretically designed to create jobs and assist workers, as the name of the statute implies, LBs were assailed by a range of critics as "an indiscriminate handout to businesses" and "a pass-through to landlords [that] only resulted in higher rents."[84] Who were the major beneficiaries? Over 40 percent of all bonds, or $2.59 billion, went to a single developer, Larry Silverstein, owner of the original World Trade Center, to build new office towers on the site (see table 4.1). The second largest beneficiary was Goldman Sachs, the most profitable Wall Street firm, based downtown for over 130 years. Goldman Sachs received $1.65 billion to finance a new forty-three-story, $2 billion headquarters after it threatened to leave for another Manhattan location. After Goldman threatened to abandon the project, the state enlarged its incentive package to include $115 million in tax breaks and cash grants in what critics described as "the most egregious example of corporate welfare in city history."[85] As Bettina Damiani, director of Good Jobs New York, commented at the time: "Well, we certainly reinforced the status quo, which is that if [Wall Street and the real estate industry] are doing well, by golly, we all are.... Here's my motto for downtown: Bring free-market capitalism back to Lower Manhattan."[86]

Table 4.1 shows the issuance amount and various projects approved for Liberty Bonds. Almost 60 percent of the bonds, or $3.8 billion, were for three projects relating to the World Trade Center site. Meanwhile, $650 million of tax-exempt financing went to Bank of America for building a new tower on West 42nd Street—outside the zone—and this despite the fact that the company admitted publicly that it never intended to leave New York.[87]

Meanwhile, the Liberty Zone reproduced the uneven geographic benefits achieved by earlier forms of post-9/11 aid. The Canal Street boundary, first established by FEMA and used by the LMDC in distributing CDBGs, was used again for Liberty Bonds. This again cut off the bulk of affected low-income residents and small businesses north of Canal Street, while creating yet greater advantage for the relatively well-resourced businesses and real estate developers to the south.

The impacts of uneven redevelopment on Lower Manhattan will be explored in the following chapter. But for now, we wish to highlight how this cumulative neoliberalization—through FEMA, CDBGs, and the PABs—along with the geographic exclusions it reproduced, incensed and galvanized grassroots coalitions and crisis organizers. They mobilized to challenge what they saw as the use of public policy to force taxpayers to

Table 4.1 LIBERTY BONDS (DOLLARS IN MILLIONS)

Project (commercial only)	Developer	Issuance Amount	Date of Issuance
Atlantic Terminal-Bank of New York York Tower	FC Hanson Office Associates	$90.8	February 2003
1 Bryant Park-Bank of America	One Bryant Park/Durst	650.0	November 2004
InterActive Corp	HTRF Ventures	80.0	August 2005
7 World Trade Center	7 World Trade Company	475.0	March 2005
Downtown Hotel Site 26	377 Greenwich	38.9	December 2004
Battery Park City National Sports	The Goldman Sachs Group	1,650.0	October 2005
Museum	TNSM	52.0	August 2006
Moinian Hotel	123 Washington	50.0	October 2007
Silverstein Properties	World Trade Center Properties	2,593.5	December 2009
PA-1 World Trade and Retail Space	1 World Trade Center WTC Retail	701.6	N/A
Front Street*	Yarrow (NYS HFA)	8.0	June 2003
2 Gold Street*	Rockrose (NYC HDC)	7.2	September 2003
90 West Street*	B.C.R.E. 90 West Street (NYC HDC)	3.0	March 2004
TOTAL		$6,400.0	

Note: * commercial portion of residential project
Source: Figures compiled by the New York City Independent Budget Office, *The Aftermath: Federal Aid 10 Years After the World Trade Center Attack*, http://www.ibo.nyc.ny.us/iboreports/World Trade Center2011.pdf, accessed January 23, 2012.

subsidize tax-exempt private real estate investment for the wealthy and to further disadvantage their communities. Adopting the slogans "Rebuild NYC = Rebuild our Lives" and holding aloft symbols of the impacts of redevelopment in the form of shelter pillows and eviction notices, organizers sought to remind the LMDC, Congress, and the broader public of the ongoing suffering in Lower Manhattan that wasn't being addressed by the prevailing real estate-focused approach—and that was, indeed, being exacerbated by it. See figure 4.5.

In a 2006 congressional hearing, Bettina Damiani, the aforementioned director of Good Jobs New York and a member of BGZ, noted that by then, "the vast majority of Liberty Bonds [have been used] to finance high-end office space and luxury housing projects." She also

(a)

(b)   (c)

Figures 4.5
Post-9/11 Redevelopment Protests
(a.) Chinese Staff and Workers Association and Beyond Ground Zero march through Lower Manhattan, June 2002, to demand equitable aid and health care for low-income communities beyond the narrowly defined disaster area.
(b.) Rebuilding with a Spotlight on the Poor leads protest on Wall Street in front of a joint session of Congress held on first anniversary of 9/11, September 2002, to demand use of Liberty Bonds to build affordable rather than "market rate" housing.
(c.) Labor Community Advocacy Network holds a Town Hall near City Hall, July 28, 2003, to call for creation of new "liberty jobs" to help low-wage workers who lost jobs and income due to the post-9/11 economic crisis.
Courtesy: CSWA, Community Voices Heard, and University Settlement.

provided an analysis of how deregulations and restrictive zoning might have predicted this outcome:

> Tax-exempt bonds are often an invaluable resource for a wide range of businesses that require government assistance to finance capital projects. However, it would not be an understatement to say that the allocation of $8 billion in Private Activity Bonds— aka Liberty Bonds—has primarily benefited the real estate industry. Split between

residential and commercial, the Congressional design of the Liberty Bond program all but ensured that the bonds would exclusively subsidize large real estate projects while neglecting the affordable housing crisis in New York City and the capital needs of industrial businesses and small commercial developments outside Lower Manhattan.[88]

One might well question the use of billions of dollars of state-subsidized investment in New York City's high-end real estate market as a solution to the post-9/11 economic crisis. We are reminded that those who suffered most during this time were wage laborers, small businesses, and low-income tenants, all of whom ended up either ineligible for bonds and grants or unable to attain them in any significant amount. If nothing else, post-9/11 redevelopment programs appear to have created a unique opportunity to use public resources to prop up the Lower Manhattan real estate market, and to do so without public oversight. This was to set a powerful precedent, as policies and practices developed to rebuild New York post-9/11 would soon be applied to New Orleans in response to the destruction caused by the levee breaches. Given the scale of devastation there, the scope of these policies would be extended in the process.

THE LOUISIANA ROAD HOME PROGRAM

Following the model established in New York, HUD and Louisiana officials strategically framed the problem of "recovery" and "rebuilding" as dependent on the deregulation and liberalization of rules on program implementation and funding. Shortly after the disaster, and as in New York, elected leaders lobbied for and received HUD permission to lower the requirement that 70 percent of CDBG money benefit low- and moderate-income people in this case to 50 percent. Additionally, HUD waived requirements for citizen participation, rules for submitting annual performance reports, rules against use of subrecipients to carry out recovery activities, and requirements that state and local economic development activities follow a strategic or consolidated master plan. Waivers freed HUD from the legal obligation to monitor whether Louisiana or other Gulf Coast states were providing broad "public benefit" or "housing development" for low-income people displaced by Hurricane Katrina. HUD also neutralized federal oversight responsibilities by granting waivers to laws governing the program's checks and balances system, that is, mechanisms for "grantee accountability" (e.g., performance reports) and "citizen participation" (e.g., public hearings).[89]

Administrative waivers had the most far-reaching consequences when, in June 2006, the LRA signed a three-year $750 million contract with Virginia-based ICF International to manage the "Road Home" program,

Table 4.2 LOUISIANA ROAD HOME HOMEOWNER PROGRAM STATISTICS, AUGUST 2012

Total Applications Received	229,432
Total Eligible Applications	148,455
Total Applications Eligible for Benefits Calculation	130,111
Total Applications with Funding Disbursed	129,901
Total Funding Disbursed	$8.96 Billion

Source: Louisiana Road Home Program, https://www.road2la.org/, accessed August 3, 2012.

thereby privatizing the largest housing recovery program in U.S. history. Under the Road Home program, Louisiana would use $4.2 billion in block grants with other federal money to pay eligible homeowners for their uninsured, uncompensated damages—up to $150,000—to repair or rebuild their homes.[90] Homeowners could also opt to sell their properties and relocate within or outside the state. In an August 23, 2006, press conference to launch New Orleans's first Road Home housing assistance center, Louisiana Governor Kathleen Blanco proudly claimed credit for the program, announcing that "the governor's Road Home program is up and running, full speed ahead," before a room crowded with dozens of local and out-of-town reporters. "This is a most joyful day."[91] From 2006 through 2012, the Road Home Program received over 229,000 applications and distributed $8.96 billion in funds to eligible homeowners (see table 4.2).

Yet ICF International's implementation of the Road Home program aggravated the wounds of forced displacement and intensified conflicts among elected leaders, residents, and government agencies. Early on, critics pointed to the long turnaround time from initial application to actual ICF contact with residents, incorrectly calculated grant awards, bogus calculations to appraise prestorm home values, slow progress in awarding grants to needy homeowners, mismanagement of a program to help mom-and-pop landlords repair damaged rentals, and demeaning antifraud rules that required applicants to be fingerprinted before they received funds. Interesting, during the first years of program implementation, the LRA did not require ICF to evaluate the quality of the organization's policies, programs, and strategies. In addition, the Road Home contract did not contain requirements for ICF to deliver certain services to applicants by a specific time. The LRA left it up to ICF to develop its own measurements of success and then refused to oversee and monitor the contractor.[92]

Community discontent with the Road Home program reached a crescendo in December 2006 when the Louisiana House of Representatives voted 97–1 to approve a resolution demanding that Governor Blanco cancel ICF's three-year, $756 million contract. Lawmakers repeatedly questioned the company's competence while the bill's sponsor, Rep. J.P. Morrell, D-New Orleans, called ICF's performance "morally reprehensible." "In Lakeview, in Gentilly, in the 9th Ward, this is a road to nowhere," said Rep. Peppi Bruneau, R-New Orleans, who spoke in favor of the measure.[93] Governor Blanco balked at firing ICF and, in December 2007, increased the size of ICF's contract from $756 million to $912 million despite unrelenting negative publicity about the program and continuing problems with ICF's performance. News outlets complained that the Blanco administration made the increase without disclosure to the legislature or the public. Thus, the governor rewarded ICF with a multimillion dollar raise when only one year prior, the legislature had passed a resolution assailing the Road Home program and calling for the firing of ICF for widespread program failures.[94] Significantly, just days before giving ICF the huge raise, the Blanco administration moved to discontinue funding legal services to help low-income people work through Road Home application obstacles in order to receive their grants.[95]

Overall, CDBG program waivers, combined with the privatization of program implementation, had two major effects on the post-Katrina redevelopment process in New Orleans. First, waivers created lucrative opportunities for ICF and its subcontractors to advance their profiteering interests and accumulation agendas with little public oversight and democratic accountability. Three months after winning the Road Home contract, ICF announced that it would sell its stock publicly for the first time in its thirty-seven years of existence. ICF's annual revenue increased fourfold between 2005 and 2007, and gross profit nearly tripled. In 2007, ICF's chief executive was awarded a $1.5 million performance bonus. Later that year, in August 2007, the corporation reported that its second-quarter revenue had quadrupled to $190 million, and the company's stock had shot up 70 percent since September 2006. Large corporate subcontractors received the lion's share of CDBG resources, with three dozen subcontractors collecting 62 percent of the $592.7 million the state paid ICF by March 10, 2008. Interesting, the recipient of the most money ($84.9 million) was the Shaw Corporation whose founder and chairman, Jim Bernhard, once led the Louisiana Democratic Party and was a leading campaign contributor to Governor Kathleen Blanco.[96]

Second, program waivers helped establish and legitimate a novel federal-state relationship whereby HUD and state agencies like the LRA could insulate themselves from legal obligation to ensure compliance with fair housing antidiscrimination statutes. The formula for computing the grants for homeowners, which was adopted by the LRA and approved by HUD, provided that the grant amount be the lower of two values: (1) the home's prestorm value (minus any other compensation the applicant received for loss to the structure, such as insurance proceeds), or (2) the cost of repairing damage to the home (minus any other compensation the applicant received for loss to the structure). Consistent with the statutory and regulatory framework of the CDBG-DR (Disaster Recovery) program, the LRA proposed and developed this Road Home grant formula and the details of the Road Home program in consultation with HUD and subject to HUD's ongoing approval and oversight.

The HUD-approved Road Home formula that the LRA used to allocate grants to homeowners had a discriminatory impact on thousands of African American homeowners by tying recovery dollars to the values of their prestorm housing instead of the actual cost to repair damage. In November 2008, civil rights groups and a class of plaintiffs filed a federal class action lawsuit charging the LRA, HUD, and the executive director of LRA with unlawful racial bias and discrimination in the design and implementation of the Road Home program.[97] The crux of the complaint was that the Road Home program discriminated against African Americans since homes in predominantly African American neighborhoods had lower values than those in white communities, even when comparing and controlling for condition, style, and quality of homes.

In essence, the design and implementation of the HUD-funded Road Home program reinforced racially segregated housing patterns, as grants for African Americans were more likely to be determined on the prestorm value of their homes rather than on the cost of damage from the storm.[98] To buttress their claims, civil rights activists drew on 2008 data showing that homeowners in the Lower Ninth Ward, a predominantly black neighborhood, faced shortfalls on average of over $75,000 between the available rebuilding resources and the cost of rebuilding each home. At the same time, homeowners in Lakeview, a predominantly white neighborhood, faced shortfalls on average of $44,000 per home.[99]

In response to the filing of the lawsuit, HUD argued that it lacked political authority to require CDBG recipients like the LRA to enforce federal fair housing laws once the federal government dispersed funds—a position that was contrary to the legal duty that Congress imposed on HUD to affirmatively promote fair housing in federal housing programs. During the years when LRA contracted out the Road Home program to ICF, LRA officials claimed that HUD and the Louisiana state legislature were responsible for overseeing program implementation. According to LRA Executive Director Andrew D. Kopplin:

> We do not run the Road Home or any programs at the LRA. Our job is to recommend
> expenditure recommendations of Federal grant funds to the governor and the Louisiana
> Legislature and to set broad policy guidelines for the programs they approve.

In turn, ICF claimed that they were not responsible for the problematic outcomes and unequal effects of the program because, as one high-ranking ICF official put it: "The Road Home Program is a recovery challenge unprecedented in its scope and complexity. It was designed and approved by the State of Louisiana, and ICF has been implementing this program at an accelerated pace for the past 7 months, but only for 7 months."[100]

In addition, the LRA argued that it was not subject to the antidiscrimination requirements of the Fair Housing Act, even though Congress refused to allow the waiver of fair housing and nondiscrimination requirements when it funded the CDBG program. By accepting CDBG funds, the state of Louisiana was required to enforce fair housing statutes in the implementation of the federal program. Yet the privatization of the CDBG program allowed state managers to evade responsibility and accountability for distributing federal funds fairly and in compliance with civil rights mandates. A major effect was to subvert the original intent and goals of the CDBG program to use federal resources to benefit low- and moderate-income people. A related outcome was to open up new prospects for private contractors to siphon public resources to promote their profiteering agendas without regard to larger public and community needs. Through the years, the allegations of the exploitative and discriminatory nature of the program have been a source of intense neighborhood opposition and collective resistance, with nonprofit organizations joining with neighborhood coalitions and national civil rights organizations to launch dozens of coordinated protests throughout the city. See figure 4.6a and b.

RETROFITTING THE LIBERTY ZONE TO THE GULF COAST: THE CASE OF THE GULF OPPORTUNITY ZONE

To supplement CDBGs, the federal response to Katrina, modeled on the post-9/11 redevelopment package, included the use of tax incentives, deductions, and exemptions to spur recovery in the Gulf Coast region. In December 2005, the U.S. Congress passed H.R. 4440, Pub. L. No. 109-135, the Gulf Opportunity Zone Act of 2005 (GO Zone Act), to provide tax incentives and other financial incentives for businesses in Louisiana and other states affected by Hurricanes Katrina and Rita. Under the GO Zone Act, the state of Louisiana was responsible for allocating $14.9 billion in

Figure 4.6
Road Home Protests
(a.) Within a year of the debut of the Road Home program in 2006, activists were launching major protests throughout the New Orleans region charging that the program ignored the majority of New Orleans residents who were renters and exacerbated the affordable housing crisis. (b.) On May 30, 2010, two activist groups, Survivors Village and May Day NOLA, staged a protest to call attention to the failure of local and national officials to address the massive displacement and dispossession of New Orleans residents. Source: Communities Rising, Archive for May, 2010. "Survivors Village Claims Road Home Property," blog of Survivors Village New Orleans. Accessed November 11, 2013. http://communitiesrising.wordpress.com/2010/05/

tax-exempt private activity bonds between 2006 and 2011. While the state also implemented other tax relief measures, including low-income housing tax credits (LIHTC), the amount of these provisions paled in comparison to the huge amount of tax-exempt bonds to finance recovery efforts. The GO Zone Act authorized $323 million in LIHTC tax credits; $350 million in GO Zone tax credit bonds, a newly created category of tax credit bonds; and $7.88 billion in additional advance refunding bonds.[101]

Following precedent set by federal tax relief acts passed after 9/11, elected leaders and state managers waived existing rules and restrictions and made generous tax exemptions available to all developers, regardless of the "public benefit" of their projects. The GO Zone represented a further loosening of restrictions around the use of PABs. As the Government Accountability Office (GAO) reported:

> The liberalized use for GO Zone tax-exempt private activity bonds in comparison to qualified private activity bonds subject to annual state volume caps is broadly similar to private activity bond authority awarded in the New York Liberty Zone. Whereas the Liberty Zone provision divided the authority between the state and local levels and set specific limits on retail and residential rental property, the GO Zone provision did not set aside any portion to be allocated for specific localities or set dollar caps on certain categories of use. The GO Zone Act of 2005 provided states with broad discretion in allocating GO Zone tax-exempt private activity bonds.[102]

Congress has long provided tax relief to individuals and businesses affected by major disasters. What was new after the 9/11 terrorist strike and the Hurricane Katrina levee failures, however, was the effort by Congress to spatially target disaster-related tax provisions. The Liberty Zone tax benefits package was the first ever targeted to a specific disaster-impacted geographic area. The GO Zone represented a regional extension of the urban Liberty Zone program and used market-centered strategies and tax incentives to prime the private sector to rebuild New Orleans and the Gulf Coast. Unlike the Liberty Zone, the Katrina GO Zone contained a heterogeneous mix of urban and rural communities spread across more than 60,000 square miles of territory in eighty-nine counties and three states (Alabama, Louisiana, and Mississippi), with an estimated population (in 2003) of

---

(b.) On June 27, 2013, fifteen members of the Road Home Action Network Team (RHANT) organized a protest to draw attention to the exploitative nature of the Road Home program and advocate for a federal investigation of what they described as systematic mismanagement of the $13.4 billion program.

Source: Times-Picayune, Landov Media.

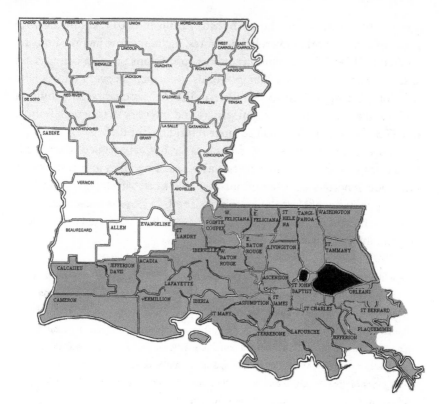

Figure 4.7
Louisiana GO Zone
The Louisiana Gulf Opportunity (GO) Zone represented the application of the logic, goals, and principles of the Liberty Zone on a wider scale, encompassing thirty-one parishes in southern Louisiana. Like the Liberty Zone, the GO Zone program used market-centered strategies and tax incentives to stimulate community recovery, a policy orientation that reflected the longstanding belief that alterations to the tax code can be effective strategies for generating targeted economic development and reinvestment. In designing the GO Zone, poli\cymakers imposed a package of tax relief onto a vast region with widespread differences in the population concentration, poverty status, income levels of residents, and disaster damage and impacts. *Source*: Kevin Fox Gotham.

more than 5.7 million people. Figure 4.7 shows the parishes (counties) eligible for GO Zone bonds under the GO Zone Act.

In the weeks after Hurricane Katrina roared ashore, President Bush proclaimed that the new GO Zone he proposed would "provide immediate incentives for job-creating investment, tax relief for *small* businesses, incentives to companies that create jobs, and loans and loan guarantees for *small* businesses, including minority-owned enterprises, to get them up and running again."[103] Despite the intent to help small businesses, the evidence suggests that not all firms benefited from GO Zone tax benefits. Some smaller businesses and disaster-impacted firms were excluded from using GO Zone bonds because of their small-scale operations and lack of capital. "If you

Table 4.3 LOUISIANA GO ZONE TAX-EXEMPT PRIVATE ACTIVITY BONDS (PABS)
RANKED BY ISSUANCE AMOUNT, 2005–2011

Project Type	Developer/Company	Issuance Amount (in millions of dollars)	Location (Parish)
Petrochemicals & Environmental Technologies	Marathon Oil Corp.	$1,000	St. John the Baptist
Petroleum Coke Gasification Project	Lake Charles Cogeneration Project	$1,000	Calcasieu
Manufacturing	NuCor Steel Louisiana	$600	St. James
Petrochemicals & Environmental Technologies	Exxon Capital Ventures, Inc.	$300	East Baton Rouge
Petrochemicals & Environmental Technologies	Valero Energy Corporation Project	$300	St. Charles
Petrochemicals & Environmental Technologies	Exxon Capital Ventures, Inc. Project	$200	East Baton Rouge
Petrochemicals & Environmental Technologies	Westlake Chemical Corporation Projects	$198	Calcasieu

Source: Prepared by the authors using data from the Louisiana Department of Treasury, Louisiana Bond Commission. Data was released through public records request initiated by the authors.

didn't have the money you couldn't qualify to get money," according to the State Bond Commission director.[104]

Large petrochemical companies in the western part of the state received a disproportionate share of GO Zone bonds. As table 4.3 shows, Marathon Oil Corporation, NuCor Steel, Exxon, and Valero Energy Corporation received approximately $2.4 billion in bonds, more than a quarter of all bonds allocated. If we also include the Lake Charles Cogeneration facility, a petroleum coke gasification project located in Calcasieu Parish, the amount of GO Zone bonds going to promote growth in manufacturing and oil increases to $3.4 billion, almost half of all GO Zone bonds.[105] None of these projects were located in the New Orleans metropolitan area. See table 4.3.

Through their diverse resources, economies of scale, and specialized legal staff, large businesses could interpret and navigate the labyrinth of regulations to access bonds and pursue new investment opportunities within the GO Zone. Small businesses, on the other hand, had limited access to GO Zone bonds because they had far fewer resources and, in many cases, could not meet the credit standards for tax exemptions. Moreover, small businesses were not well capitalized and had low levels of reserves and discretionary income. These points corroborate Graham's findings on the lackluster recovery of small business in Lower Manhattan after the 9/11 disaster.[106] Small businesses were often uninsured or underinsured, subject to rent increases, and faced varying degrees of physical damage and social loss. In the heavily damaged areas of Louisiana, small businesses endured the emotional toll of multiple interconnected crises—for example, a devastating hurricane, a subsequent economic recession, an eviscerated customer base, construction obstacles, and the sheer uncertainty of how to navigate a massive government bureaucracy to mitigate these crises.

Overall, the GO Zone made it possible for large businesses to take advantage of benefits offered under the GO Zone Act, even though Congress and policymakers designed the legislation to promote recovery and rebuilding for all businesses in the most disaster-devastated areas. The huge size of the GO Zone effectively neutralized the intended effects of the GO Zone Act since geographic targeting proved both overinclusive and underinclusive. Even within the GO Zone, some areas experienced little disaster damage, while other areas like New Orleans were forced to suffer with devastated infrastructure and destroyed communities for years after the disaster.

LEGACIES OF THE POST-9/11 AND POST-KATRINA REDEVELOPMENT PROCESS

Less than one month after Hurricane Katrina, and close to the four-year anniversary of 9/11, a number of the grassroots coalitions that had formed in New York City to address issues of redevelopment sent out an open letter to "members of Congress and concerned individuals and groups on the Gulf Coast." With an urgent tone, they wished to impart the "lessons learned" from their own experiences as quickly as possible, in the hopes that with post-Katrina redevelopment, unlike that following 9/11, "the poor and disenfranchised people of the region are not left out of the process." To this end, they began with Lesson #1: "Decisions made now could restrict options later." The letter explained:

> In New York many of us hesitated to criticize program design because we didn't want to seem ungrateful or (in the post-9/11 world) divisive. As it turned out, however, when we got into debates later on, the early design of the programs severely limited our ability to influence the decision-making process.[107]

With historical perspective on post-Katrina redevelopment, it is clear that elected leaders and officials did not heed these warnings—or at least not in the way New York's grassroots coalitions had hoped. Deploying a narrow market-centered framework for "recovery," growth coalitions in New Orleans, as in New York, were quickly able to shape the terms of the debate. They effectively argued that redevelopment should be defined as top-down economic development, that prime real estate and office space should be replaced, that the zone of the disaster should be constrained to those areas that were most affluent prior to the event, and that public discussion should be limited to questions of physical design rather than inclusive, equitable development. Policymakers jettisoned long-held "needs-based" CDBG tenets and outsourced the program implementation to public-private corporations and private contractors to spur more flexible private-sector investments, with the result being a highly uneven process of recovery and redevelopment—after 9/11 and again after Katrina. Ultimately, programmatic changes in the CDBG program enabled powerful political actors in New York City to control the disbursement of federal redevelopment monies and incentives while marginalizing redistributive concerns and prerogatives, a process replicated in New Orleans. Thus, both in New York and New Orleans, civic engagement morphed into pitched battles over redevelopment priorities as it became clear that the "flowering" of public participation in town halls and hearings was being "weeded" by elites rather than seeded at the grassroots.

The experience of post-crisis organizing was transformative in geographic, cultural, political, and historical terms. New forms of coalition building recharged and redirected progressive urban movements. Slogans such as "We are all New Yorkers" and "Solidarity Not Charity" expressed a new common sense: that community-based groups could join with diverse local and national organizations and across traditional neighborhood boundaries to take on issues of citywide planning. This shift in consciousness was to have long-lasting impacts—not least in sparking the national Right to the City Coalition in 2006 and in preparing the ground for a new scale of organizing following subsequent disasters.

Yet in the short-term, politically powerful coalitions—such as the Downtown Alliance in New York City and the BNOB in New Orleans—were able to blunt this discourse of equity, inclusion, and solidarity by framing themselves as "civic groups" and "partnerships" between the private and public sector, and as simply another "community of interest" within the larger, diverse mosaic. Meanwhile, by positioning themselves at the helm of redevelopment authorities such as the LMDC and the LRA, these groups could also transform the urban fabric of both cities in radical and fundamentally unaccountable ways. As a result, the post-crisis redevelopment process could be insulated from democracy itself, while the privatization and devolution of disaster aid could be championed as "best practice" for promoting recovery and rebuilding.

CHAPTER 5

Landscapes of Risk and Resilience: From Lower Manhattan to the Lower Ninth Ward

A s geographers and urban scholars have long understood, the production of urban space is associated with the generation of a historically specific landscape in which particular places, territories, and scales are mobilized as forces of production and consumption. The resultant patterns of investment and disinvestment, devalorization and revalorization, and ensuing socio-spatial inequality are never stable and enduring but constantly shift through the dynamics of uneven development.[1] Of interest to us in this chapter is how uneven development relates to the process of *redevelopment*—that is, those historically contingent acts of state intervention into degraded and/or disaster-stricken urban spaces in the name of rebuilding and "better use." Here, spaces labeled as "blighted," "damaged," or otherwise "obsolete" are targeted for repair, redesign, and repurposing using the rhetoric of "renewal," "revitalization," and "progress."[2] These urban redevelopment initiatives, we argue, are major sites for orchestrating the production of space, including geographical distribution of wealth, population, and socio-economic activities, and so act as both an expression and catalyst of uneven development.

Over the decades, notions of crisis have played a key role in marshaling funds and building consensus for new urban redevelopment projects to promote growth and revalorize deteriorated spaces. Whether the nationwide "urban crisis" of the 1960s, "fiscal crisis" of the 1970s, "financial crises" of the late 1980s and 2000s, or the periods of crisis following sudden disasters, crisis frames help initiate a phase of intense debate and policy experimentation in which powerful actors, organized interests, and political alliances promote competing urban visions and redevelopment strategies. As we saw in the last chapter, once implemented, urban redevelopment projects can radically alter land uses, unify some growth coalitions and fragment others, and transform the socio-spatial organization of cities. As such, urban redevelopment is associated with a series of regulatory dilemmas: on one hand, redevelopment initiatives can promote new forms of economic growth to alleviate crises and promote widely shared benefits; on the other, they can intensify socio-spatial inequalities, thereby threatening the social conditions for sustainable urban and community development.

In her often-cited book, *The Shock Doctrine: The Rise of Disaster Capitalism,* Naomi Klein singles out a progenitor of neoliberalism, Milton Friedman, as popularizing the idea that crises are drivers of social transformation. According to Friedman, "[o]nly a crisis—actual or perceived—produces real change. When that crisis occurs, the actions that are taken depend on the ideas that are lying around." The "basic function" of political leaders, then, is to "develop alternatives to existing policies, to keep them alive and available until the politically impossible becomes the politically inevitable."[3] For Friedman, writing in the 1970s, these alternatives should move policy in a free-market direction and away from the regulated, welfare-state capitalism of the mid-century. While we have placed greater emphasis on the politically contested nature of crisis moments, rather than their inevitability, we nonetheless concur that they have provided unique opportunities for neoliberalization, with far-reaching effects. In our case, we address the impact on cities when urban policymakers, inclined in a neoliberal direction, seize the opportunity to guide the rebuilding of disaster-impacted cities. A key question for us is: what happens when preexisting, market-oriented urban development plans, as well as policy solutions, are the ideas "lying around" for resurgent growth coalitions to apply to post-disaster redevelopment?

In this chapter, we explore these conflictual dynamics in terms of their socio-spatial impact on uneven redevelopment at the neighborhood scale. To do so, we identify neighborhoods that reflect differences both in terms of their preexisting socio-spatial conditions and in the pace and trajectory of their recovery. Clearly, nearness to the disaster triggers—for instance, the terrorist strike and hurricane levee breaches—are important in understanding the intensity of the destruction. Yet we hypothesize that contextual factors—historic, social, spatial, and political—also influence variation in redevelopment patterns. Thus, we examine neighborhoods that are similar in terms of the immediate impact of the disaster but differ in their contextual situation prior to and following these events. *Pre-disaster*, we are interested in the existing landscape of risk and resilience that produce differing degrees of vulnerabilities, understood in terms of socio-economic and race-based inequalities as well as tendencies toward gentrification and displacement of poor and working class populations. *Post-disaster*, we are interested in the degree to which neighborhood populations had access to aid and other long-term redevelopment resources or were marginalized or otherwise excluded from aid. We then use the interaction of these pre- and post-disaster conditions to explain the long-term, unequal impacts of redevelopment on the demographic, economic, and housing characteristics of the neighborhoods.

We use the phrase "landscapes of risk and resilience" to refer to pre-existing socio-spatial, environmental, cultural, and political economic conditions that weaken or strengthen the ability of particular places to cope with and adapt to crises. The notion of resiliency refers to the adaptive capacity of a social system or unit to withstand shocks and protect against other hazards by reorganizing and innovating. Risk implies threat of harm caused by socio-economic or environmental crises or other trauma. Racial disparities and class inequality, as well as the degradation of urban ecosystems, track closely with the uneven geography of environmental and socio-economic risk versus resilience. These landscapes are further shaped by development projects, as fought for by a range of local and supra-local actors, which invest resources in some places, spaces, and scales over others. The resultant patterns of socio-spatial and environmental inequality express the basic processes of uneven redevelopment.

We address the following questions: What contextually specific and historically produced factors explain variation in neighborhood redevelopment outcomes? Specifically, how have preexisting socio-spatial, political, and demographic landscapes, in combination with uneven recovery aid and redevelopment policy, shaped trajectories and patterns of post-disaster neighborhood development? In New York City, we compare four neighborhoods whose economies were similarly devastated by 9/11: Battery Park City/Lower Manhattan and Tribeca on the one hand, and Chinatown and the Lower East Side on the other. In New Orleans, we compare two neighborhoods that experienced similarly devastating levels of flooding (up to 12 feet of water) as a result of levee breaches: the Lakeview neighborhood and the Lower Ninth Ward. In contrast to their similarities immediately following the terrorist strike and levee breaches, the comparison neighborhoods were highly distinct in their preexisting socio-spatial conditions and class and racial characteristics and in the resources to which they had access for the purpose of "recovery."

NEW YORK AND THE "NEW LOWER MANHATTAN"

There is no better example of what Henri Lefebvre has termed the "production of space" than the shifting boundaries of what is considered "Lower" or "Downtown" Manhattan. The term "Lower Manhattan" was originally used to designate the altitude and latitude of the low-lying southern tip of the island of *Manahatta* where the native Lenape tribes found the most plentiful grounds for fishing and hunting and where the Dutch and British based their colonial settlements in the late seventeenth and early eighteenth centuries. It was also a northern U.S. center for the African slave trade—the site of defensive walls and buildings built by slaves under the Dutch, of a slave market and slave revolt under the British, and of some of the first plots of land in the United States owned by freedmen.[4] Over the course of the eighteenth, nineteenth, and early twentieth centuries, the port neighborhood expanded and became both home and commercial hub for successive waves of immigrants from the Middle East, Europe, and China. Little Syria, Chinatown, Little Italy, and the mostly Jewish Lower East Side emerged as New York City's most densely populated neighborhoods and as important economic and cultural centers for the larger region.[5]

Beginning in the mid-twentieth century, as the New York City population and economy continued to expand northward, the definition of Lower Manhattan shifted further. "Downtown" was distinguished from "uptown," "lower" from "mid" and "upper" Manhattan, as neighborhoods rapidly developed to the north. Meanwhile, the scale of "downtown" grew with the scale of the city. It wasn't until the entire island of Manhattan was settled up to 207th Street, with the completion of the north/south subway line in 1932, that the popularly conceived limit of "downtown"—now included in novels, songs, and tourism guides—finally rested at around 14th Street.

These broad conceptions of Lower Manhattan and downtown, however, were historically at odds with narrower, business-oriented definitions of the area. Much like the "City of London" created in the 1500s, the New York financial industry had remained based in the well-defended "city" of its inception: the colonial and postcolonial district that grew up around the Stock Exchange on Wall Street between the early eighteenth and early twentieth centuries. As explored in Chapter 2, Wall Street area landowners and their corporate clientele had sought over the course of the twentieth century to reinforce these boundaries, banding together in an effort to eliminate nonfinancial uses in the district as well as to distinguish the downtown financial district from the newer business district that arose in Midtown in the 1930s—an effort that reached its zenith with the construction of the World Trade Center in 1973. This agenda, however, did nothing to alter the fact that multiple definitions of "Lower Manhattan"—popular and business-related—coexisted over time.

The 9/11 terrorist strike and subsequent response dramatically altered and transformed meanings and definitions of Lower Manhattan. One major driver of this transformation was the drawing of the "Liberty Zone" boundaries for recovery aid irrespective of economic need in relation to the wider impact of the disaster. Thus, a restricted definition of "Lower Manhattan" as south of Canal and/or Chambers Streets, and more or less coterminous with "Ground Zero," emerged as dominant. This new exercise in border construction extended beyond the limits of the old financial core, yet only slightly. Well-off residential areas to the west and northwest—namely Battery Park City, Tribeca, and a small portion of Chinatown—were included. The mainly working-class residential and commercial districts of Chinatown and the Lower East Side to the north and northeast, up to Houston or 14th Street, were excluded, despite the severe impacts suffered by these communities.

For the purpose of our study of neighborhood-level impacts of redevelopment post-9/11, we determined the following criteria for selection had to be met: (a) location in what is commonly understood as "Lower Manhattan," south of 14th Street; and (b) significantly negative economic impact as a result of 9/11 and subsequent security measures. These criteria enabled us to compare Lower Manhattan neighborhoods impacted by 9/11 that were both included and excluded from the Liberty Zone. Using 2010 census figures, we were then able to narrow the study down to four Neighborhood Tabulation Areas (NTAs) south of 14th Street: (1) Battery Park City/Lower Manhattan (BPC/LM); (2) Soho/Tribeca/Civic Center (Tribeca); (3) Chinatown; and (4) the Lower East Side.[6]

LOWER MANHATTAN SINCE THE 1970S

"Over the past decade, New York City has come roaring back, faster and stronger than anyone thought possible." So remarked Mayor Mike Bloomberg in a September 6, 2011, speech in Lower Manhattan sponsored by the Association for a Better New York (ABNY).[7] Calling the rebuilding of Lower Manhattan "one of the greatest comeback stories in American history," Mayor Bloomberg was actually referring to a particular part of Lower Manhattan: Battery Park City and the Financial District. Introducing a slide show of spectacular new development projects in these two neighborhoods, he said, "Our goal was to turn a financial district that became a ghost town after 6 PM into a vibrant and dynamic 24/7 community. We believed that if we could create new housing, new schools, new parks, and new infrastructure, we could attract new residents, new visitors, and new businesses. And as we'll see...they've come in droves."[8] Unmentioned in this celebration were other parts of Lower Manhattan that already had "vibrant and dynamic 24/7 communities" prior to 9/11, albeit ones that were struggling and low income: Chinatown and the Lower East Side. Also unmentioned was the fact that these neighborhoods were far worse off on this tenth anniversary of 9/11 than before the disaster, and were increasingly falling behind their neighbors in the ascendant BPC/LM and Tribeca. A major factor driving this process of uneven redevelopment was the extent to which inequity in post-disaster aid reproduced and exacerbated a prehistory of uneven development between the two areas.

The Financial District and Battery Park City

The idea to transform LM/BPC into a tourist destination and a diverse, live/work district was hardly new. To paraphrase Milton Friedman, the idea had been "lying around" for decades, but it would take a series of crises— first the recession of 1989–1992, and then 9/11—to make the idea a reality. As we noted in Chapter 2, earlier efforts to redevelop the financial district focused not on diversification but on the goal of the Rockefellers and other local finance, insurance, and real estate (FIRE) elites for the complete "financialization of Lower Manhattan." This plan took a major hit with the crisis in the 1970s, itself aggravated by the city's overdependence on and generosity toward the financial sector, as epitomized by the debt-financed, state-subsidized construction of the World Trade Center itself. Amid their massive, half-empty office towers, developers sought a dual approach that combined FIRE with tourism, devising city marketing campaigns that reimagined Lower Manhattan as a hip, twenty-four-hour entertainment, business, and tourist destination.[9] With the deregulatory boom of the 1980s, however, the financial district returned to business as usual, and concerns about image and tourism receded.

The stock market crash of October 1987 and subsequent economic recession of the early 1990s devastated Lower Manhattan, creating a sense of crisis and thereby motivating some to create new networks and organizations to promote urban revitalization. One former president of the Alliance for Downtown New York (a.k.a. Downtown Alliance or DA) whom we interviewed recalled that the so-called "recession of 1989–92" was, for Lower Manhattan, "a true depression." FIRE declined more than it had since the 1930s, and firms began fleeing Lower Manhattan for Midtown and the suburbs in numbers not seen since the 1970s. According to this person, the prevailing psychology of the time was "which corporation's going to be the last one to turn out the lights?"[10] Soon thereafter, in 1995, the Downtown Lower Manhattan Association created a Business Improvement District (BID), the Alliance for Downtown New York (DA), with the goal of revitalizing the economy of the neighborhood. To this end, the DA hired Carl Weisbrod, a highly esteemed urban planner involved in the Times Square redevelopment project, as its first president, a post he held until 2005. Weisbrod was also named a board member on the LMDC in 2002 by Mayor Bloomberg.

Whereas during the 1970s crisis, local boosters sought a solution split between financialization and tourism marketing, in the early 1990s "depression era," the DA realized the area needed to broaden its economic base far more. This realization reflected a new appreciation of the cyclical, risky nature of high finance, growing competition from other regional financial centers, and opportunities presented by emerging sectors. As the former president of the DA put it, the DA realized the need "to do what any good financial advisor would tell you: diversify your portfolio."[11] The need to diversify was particularly urgent for the DA's founding members, all large enterprises with major sunk investments in the neighborhood, including Chase Manhattan Bank, Goldman Sachs, the Port Authority, and the New York Stock Exchange. Revitalizing and expanding the local economy was also a major concern of local realtors and homeowners in newly developed Battery Park City and Tribeca and their representatives on Community Board 1 (CB1), all of whom were worried about rents and property values.[12]

Thus the DA, together with CB1, worked assiduously to catalyze a shift in the neighborhood that would both support traditional FIRE firms and attract new uses, industries, and consumers.[13] The six goals of the DA included: first, "maintain and enhance Lower Manhattan's role as a first class business district, both for smaller companies and headquarters"; second, "diversify" the economic base of the neighborhood beyond FIRE; and third, bring residential development into the neighborhood, turning a "9 to 5" area into a "lively mixed-use district operating 7 days a week." Corollary goals were to bring better and more lively retail and cultural uses into the area and to enhance the waterfront, "one of the great waterfronts of the world which was not achieving its full potential." The final goal was to attract commuter rail to Lower Manhattan that would connect it to the northern suburbs of Westchester and Connecticut, thus placing it in proximity to the homes of senior Wall Street executives.[14]

The conversion of commercial land to residential use was the leading edge of this dramatic socio-spatial project to alleviate crisis and promote the gentrification of the area. Initial growth was sparked by the city's 1995

Lower Manhattan Revitalization Plan and lobbied for by the DA and CB1, which gave tax breaks for property conversions from commercial to residential use for both neighborhoods. A *New York Times* profile of the Financial District, "If You're Thinking of Living In..." appeared on September 9, 2001, and detailed the impact of the plan over the preceding six years. "Most of the area's apartments can be found in recently converted skyscrapers, some of which once housed the headquarters of leading American companies," with more than 5,000 apartments in fifty-one formerly commercial buildings so converted.[15] To attract young, single stockbrokers and new families, real estate agents marketed the neighborhood for its ample transportation and sleekly designed, Internet-wired housing.

Nonetheless, the district's reputation as stodgy and service deprived was hard to overcome. This was foreshadowed by Jane Jacobs' 1961 critique of the area as exemplary of American urban planning that "killed the street." Jacobs famously wrote: "To see what is wrong [with American urban planning], it's only necessary to observe the deathlike stillness that settles on the [Financial] District after 5:30 and all day Saturday and Sunday."[16] While seen as a "very speculative area" by the late 1990s, new apartments were marketed as rentals rather than sales since "real estate people" still considered the neighborhood "secondary," "transitional," and "alternative"—all terms they "don't like to hear."[17] After the stock market crash and recession of 2000–2001, the still struggling district "felt the brunt of the downturn more quickly than the neighborhoods uptown," and rental prices fell 15 percent in one year.[18]

Yet, the subsequent decade of post-9/11 redevelopment was to bring with it the long-sought conversion of the southern tip of Lower Manhattan and do so far more quickly than local residents, boosters, and FIRE elites ever imagined. The preexisting goals of the DA and CB1—both for the neighborhood and the World Trade Center site itself—were to precisely match the new goals of the LMDC. This synergy was aided by the fact that many DA members and the head of CB1 sat on the LMDC board and that tens of billions of redevelopment aid dollars were made available to them. As the former DA president and LMDC board member told us in September 2011, "progress [toward goals set in the 1990s] was greatly accelerated" by the rebuilding effort, "and frankly, if we haven't already, we're well on our way to securing achievement of all of our original goals."[19]

Chinatown and Lower East Side

The three decades before 9/11 also had profound impacts on the neighborhoods of Chinatown and the Lower East Side, though placed them in a strikingly different position on the eve of 9/11 than that of the Financial District and Tribeca. To some extent, the history of these two neighborhoods should be understood separately. In Chinatown, a process of population and economic expansion had been underway since the 1970s—a process that was different both from the Lower East Side to the north and the finance-dependent neighborhood to the south. Indeed, as urban sociologist Peter Kwong characterized it, the 1970s and 1980s was a period of "boom" for New York's Chinatown that was distinct from the rest of New York City and, further, other "Chinatowns" around the United States.[20] This boom was driven by a number of local and global factors, including the rapid growth of New York's fashion and garment industry; the influx of new immigrants from mainland China, Southeast Asia, and Hong Kong to work in this industry; and the multiplier effects of this growth and immigration on local retail and restaurant industries.

A "large pool of manual labor and service jobs" put New York's Chinatown in a position to "pre-select immigrants of working class origin." Unlike other Chinatowns, New York's Chinatown attracted "poorer, less skilled, and less educated immigrants" while also providing an environment in which these immigrants could create a relatively autonomous ethnic enclave.[21] Meanwhile, the decline in agglomeration and real estate prices throughout Lower Manhattan, which spelled recession for the Financial District, fueled Chinatown's rise, providing inexpensive space for factories, showrooms, small businesses, and housing. What had been for a century a small, "precapitalist," service-oriented neighborhood occupying never more than six blocks had, between the mid-1960s and mid-1980s, ballooned more than sevenfold, attracting a quarter of all Chinese immigrants entering the United States.

The growth of Chinatown to some extent displaced the Lower East Side, which had been the historic heart of the city's garment industry since the late nineteenth century as well as the city's oldest and largest immigrant neighborhood. In the post-1965 period, the area also experienced massive in-migration, in this case by poor and working-class Puerto Ricans and African Americans. The availability of affordable housing, both in tenements and newly built public housing, as well as jobs attracted these immigrants. Yet unlike in Chinatown, the Lower East Side's manufacturing-based economy was in decline, having been outcompeted by Chinatown, and was negatively affected by the broader deindustrialization of the city's economy. Residents faced the additional pressure of displacement when the newly hip East Village became the center of rapid, "post-recession gentrification," driving up rents and leading to widespread evictions.[22]

Pro-landlord development policies and zoning regulations, such as those that provided tax abatements for conversions and renovations and others that auctioned city-owned buildings to private developers, aided the gentrification process.[23] By the late 1980s, the Lower East Side had been segmented into the upscale, mostly white East Village, the increasingly poor black and Latino neighborhoods of Alphabet City, and the mostly Jewish and Chinese co-ops south of Delancey. Then, in the mid-1990s, as upscale SoHo pushed back efforts of working-class Chinese encroachment and young professionals and businesses started moving south in search of cheaper space, the same forces that gentrified the East Village moved southward into the Lower East Side and Chinatown, bringing to an end the latter neighborhood's thirty-year expansion.[24] Internal divisions grew as landlords and larger businesses created Local Development Corporations in an effort to accelerate gentrification. Rising rents drove up the cost of factory space for the garment industry and led many lower-income residents to relocate out of Manhattan—in the case of Chinatown to new enclaves in Sunset Park, Brooklyn, and Flushing, Queens.

Yet even after three decades of gentrification and deindustrialization in the Lower East Side and the beginning of such processes in Chinatown, both neighborhoods were still known for their large, low-income populations, working-class jobs, and the dense concentration of subsidized and relatively affordable housing. Indeed, by simply holding on, they had emerged as the last working-class outpost in Manhattan south of 96th Street. Beginning in the mid-1990s, many started to push for these two neighborhoods to join forces. "Antidisplacement" and proaffordable housing coalitions began forming, framing their struggle in broad spatial and class terms. Similar to the Downtown Alliance (DA), which formed in the same period, coalitions like Rehabilitation in Action for the Improvement of the Neighborhood and the Lower East Side Joint Planning Council sought to represent neighborhood residents, workers, and businesses in the face of an existential threat.[25] Yet distinct from DA, an alliance of businesses and financial bodies with considerable social capital, these coalitions were explicitly grassroots. Their focus was to bring together tenants' rights groups, homesteaders, community development agencies, religious organizations, and unions in what would be called a "right to the city" framework.

Thus, on the eve of 9/11, something that all the neighborhoods of Lower Manhattan had in common was a history of political organizing among local groups that transcended traditional geographic boundaries—linking Tribeca to the financial district and Chinatown to the Lower East Side. Yet economically and demographically, the neighborhoods were moving in opposite directions. BPC/LM and Tribeca were in a process of slow, albeit sluggish, expansion and growth. Their middle- and upper-middle-class residential populations were increasing incrementally with the aid of city-sponsored residential revitalization programs. Chinatown and the Lower East Side, on the other hand, were pushing back against gentrification-induced displacement. Their populations were fighting to stay in their homes and at their jobs, contending with city policies that favored market-oriented redevelopment, and doing so with far fewer resources. In the face of the coming crisis, these contrasting demographic, political, and economic conditions represented an uneven landscape of risk and resiliency.

POST-9/11 INTERVENTION: DEFINING THE DISASTER ZONE AND CIRCUMSCRIBING AID

A maelstrom of destruction greeted the approximately 300,000 residents and workers of Lower Manhattan south of 14th Street on September 11, 2001. In the loft district in Tribeca and the towers of Battery Park City, locals witnessed the two hijacked airplanes crash into the World Trade Center towers from their own windows. In adjacent Chinatown and the Lower East Side, neighbors watched from the balconies of tenement apartments and the roofs of public housing. As the massive buildings collapsed to the ground, clouds of dust and ash littered the streets, covering storefronts, automobiles, and playgrounds throughout the entire area. Traumatized residents gave similar accounts. In Tribeca, Barrie Mandel, a senior vice president of the Corcoran Group who had lived and sold real estate in Tribeca since the 1980s, recalled: "After 9/11 there was a sense of paralysis in the neighborhood—of 'Oh, my God, what has happened, and will it happen again, and is it safe to live here?' "[26] Likewise, in Chinatown and the Lower East Side, where many residents had direct experience of war in their home countries of Cambodia, Vietnam, China, El Salvador, or Poland, people recounted fearing that this was the beginning of protracted and potentially bloody conflict.[27] Yet despite widespread fears and doubts, very few Lower Manhattan residents chose to leave as a result of 9/11. Rather, as Ms. Mandel put it: "most people decided, one person at a time, 'Yes, it could happen again,' but they decided to stay and help merchants reopen their businesses, and help the neighborhood come back and revive."[28]

The economic challenges facing these neighborhoods were daunting. This was so in the 16-block zone of the WTC itself, soon to be referred to as Ground Zero, where thousands of jobs, millions of square feet of office space, and massive amounts of infrastructure were immediately lost. But, contrary to common notions and media depictions, the disaster was felt, both environmentally and economically, far beyond the site of initial impact. The toxic cloud of ash and dust created by the disaster and spread by the wind contaminated job sites, schools, parks, and residences throughout Lower Manhattan south of 14th Street, as well as parts of northern Brooklyn.[29] Meanwhile, neighborhoods throughout the area were equally afflicted by service cuts and infrastructural breakdowns—including telephone and Internet service disruptions, electricity outages, and bridge, tunnel, and subway station closures. This isolation was reinforced by the designation of 14th Street as the northernmost border of the "frozen zone," or security cordon, where police and military checkpoints restricted access, disrupted commuter van service, and limited parking spaces for weeks— and, in the case of Chinatown, where the police headquarters was based, for years.[30] Thus, this group of neighborhoods was avoided by visitors, shoppers, clients, and workers, while most small business that depended on foot traffic and deliveries—from taxi service to green grocers to garment factories—ground to a halt for weeks.[31]

These socioeconomic impacts were felt most deeply in Chinatown, a neighborhood with high concentrations of small businesses and "distinctive characteristics" that increased vulnerability to sudden disruptions.[32] Most businesses were cash based, operated on thin profit margins, relied on large quantities of orders, and did not have insurance. Most workers were "low skilled" and faced language barriers, limiting their employability and wage potential "even in good times." Most supported large extended families "amplifying the effects of individual job and wage losses." And most tended to pay a higher than average percentage of their income on housing, further "increasing dependence on employment."[33] Businesses and workers lacked credit history, and in some cases documentation, blocking their access to private loans or grants. Not surprisingly, the impact figures in Chinatown are particularly striking. In the first two weeks after 9/11, there was a 60 to 100 percent drop in business across the major industries of garment manufacturing, restaurants, and retail. Three months post-9/11, a third of all workers were still unemployed, and an additional 40 percent were underemployed. Restaurants reported declines of up to 70 percent and retail of 55 percent; forty garment factories had closed.[34]

Thus, the workers, residents, and businesses of Chinatown and the neighboring Lower East Side would seem like natural targets for federal aid, alongside their neighbors in Tribeca, Battery Park City, and the Financial District.[35] Yet it soon became apparent that this was not the goal of federal or local aid agencies. As the New York Times reported of the first public hearing held by the LMDC at Pace University on May 23, 2002, "what quickly emerged was a growing schism between two groups that live and work within a mile of each other."[36] Most of the people that spoke at this meeting "expressed anger that hundreds of millions of dollars had been set aside for large corporations and the well-off residents of Battery Park City and Tribeca, at the expense...of small businesses and the more needy residents of Chinatown and the Lower East Side."[37]

Significant here was the timing. Feelings of frustration and anger were "infrequently discussed during the cleanup and recovery at the World Trade Center site" due to a broadly felt desire for solidarity at that time as well as a political climate that silenced dissent. But once "the focus turned to rebuilding, the protests...gained in volume" as FEMA and the LMDC implemented new eligibility restrictions reportedly meant to exclude victims from aid and channel tax breaks and other resources to wealthy businesses.[38] Some of these restrictions, designed by FEMA, were enacted in the early recovery period; others, designed by the LMDC, were enacted in the rebuilding process. Taken together, these restrictions were to become, in the language of the Asian American Federation of New York (AAFNY), "barriers to recovery" that were nearly insurmountable for many low-income immigrant communities of Lower Manhattan.

The first mechanism of exclusion was a cultural and racialized one, that is, exclusion on the basis of the "distinctive characteristics" of immigrant communities mentioned above. These distinctive characteristics included language barriers, particularly among first generation Chinese and Latino residents, as well as the nonstandard bookkeeping and lack of credit history typical of immigrant small businesses.[39] Surveys conducted by Asian Americans for Equality, for instance, showed that FEMA rejected approximately 70 percent of Chinatown's loss claims, with rejections attributed to a combination of language problems and lack of proper documentation.[40] Little in the way of culturally sensitive, multilingual outreach was done to target Chinese- or Spanish-speaking communities or small businesses. In addition, scholars found that economic hardships were exacerbated by a "post-9/11 anti-immigrant climate," which was reinforced by the policies stemming from the USA Patriot Act signed into law on October 26, 2001.[41] These two factors contributed to an increase in racial profiling by police in immigrant communities in New York City, a statistically disproportionate upsurge of layoffs among undocumented (and documented) immigrants, an increase in deportations, and increased scrutiny of and requirements for documentation from the immigrant workers, residents, and disaster-aid seekers of the Lower East Side and Chinatown. Meanwhile, fear of undue scrutiny became an obstacle for many seeking aid, a fear that went unaddressed by FEMA and the LMDC.

In addition to cultural and racialized barriers to aid eligibility, residents of the Lower East Side and Chinatown faced geographic ones as well. As discussed in previous chapters, geographical exclusion began with FEMA's decision, just two weeks after 9/11, to limit the "disaster area" from all of New York City to "Lower Manhattan south of Canal"—thereby excluding 80 percent of Chinatown, 100 percent of the Lower East Side, as well as the

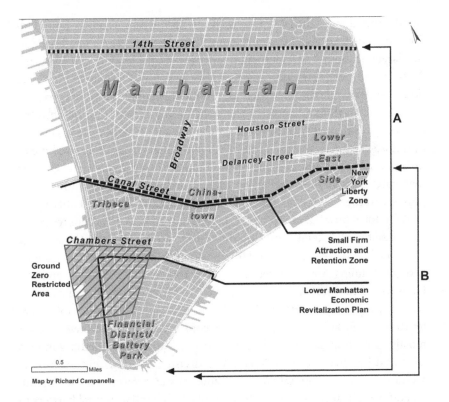

Figure 5.1

Map of 9/11 Impact versus Disaster and Redevelopment Assistance

The "A" bracket, the area south of 14th Street, encompasses all areas most severely impacted by 9/11. 14th Street was the boundary for the "frozen zone," which cut off roads and services for weeks following 9/11, thus devastating small businesses within the zone. This is also the area in which public health was most heavily affected by toxic dust and debris spread by the fall of the Twin Towers. The area in the "B" bracket, south of Canal Street and closer to Ground Zero, encompasses the area that received the bulk of disaster aid and redevelopment assistance. This restricted boundary was first set by FEMA as the northernmost limit of its disaster designation (originally set at Chambers Street and pushed up to Canal). FEMA's Canal Street boundary set a precedent. It was used by major aid organizations like the Red Cross. And it was adopted by the LMDC as the limit for $21 billion in Community Development Block Grants and Liberty Zone tax credits. This excluded the majority of Lower Manhattan's low-income residents, small businesses, and factories—located south of 14th Street and north of Canal—from aid. (*Source*: Lower Manhattan Development Corporation. Map courtesy of Richard Campanella)

rest of the city from most forms of assistance.[42] This arbitrary border was then adopted by the Red Cross in channeling charitable donations, by the New York City Department of Health in creating its WTC Health Registry, and by the lead agencies disbursing $20 billion in federal funds, including the LMDC, which designated Canal as the northernmost border of its Liberty Zone.[43] See figure 5.1.

As noted in Chapter 4, the explicit use of public resources for high-end real estate development became enshrined in public policy when policymakers and elected officials eliminated public benefit and needs-based requirements that historically applied to disaster aid, block grants, and Private Activity

Bonds. This allowed the LMDC to use Canal as the northernmost boundary for disbursing CDBGs and Liberty Zone tax breaks as well as to tier this aid so that larger economic development grants were available south of Chambers. Thus, "Small Firm Attraction and Retention" were available up to the Canal Street border, while the far heftier "Economic Revitalization" grants program was cut off north of Chambers. The same tiering of aid occurred with the LMDC's Residential Grant Program.[44] As a result, for tens of thousands of businesses, workers, and residents affected north of Canal, there was little to no aid. Implicit in this mapping was the notion that the economic impacts that mattered were those facing the financial industry, large downtown businesses, and the well-to-do residential communities of BPC and Tribeca.

A few local social service providers and union-sponsored groups receiving special state and federal grants provided aid to areas outside of these zones. These included New York Safe Horizons, which provided aid, counseling, and job training for displaced workers throughout Chinatown, and the Consortium for Worker Education (CWE), which ran a disaster relief/wage subsidy program for workers throughout New York City whose jobs were impacted by 9/11.[45] These groups were considered highly effective by their mostly low- to middle-income beneficiaries. Both exemplified arguments advanced by advocates that "relation to disaster," "needs," and "economic sector" should be more salient than geography in determining aid eligibility and that aid agencies should be attentive to potential cultural barriers to seeking or receiving aid.[46] These two groups also represented a strategy of leveraging disaster aid to build a "high road" economy of living wage jobs for working- and middle-class people.[47] As Bruce Herman, director and architect of the CWE program put it, aid programs should be "structured to privilege the best jobs in the community" rather than those at the very high and very low end of the wage spectrum.[48] Yet funding for this approach, which ran counter to the market-centered strategy pushed at the federal, state, and local scales, did not survive past 2003. In post-9/11 New York City, as we have seen, the preferred approach entailed leveraging public disaster aid to attract and retain high-end businesses and luxury residences in a narrow swath of already affluent Lower Manhattan. This exclusionary aid, combined with the preexisting landscape of risk and resilience, was to play a dramatic role in exacerbating uneven development and displacement.

THE UNEVEN REDEVELOPMENT OF
LOWER MANHATTAN

By the tenth anniversary of 9/11, census data revealed what people on the ground had long known: the post-9/11 rebuilding process had driven

LM/BPC and Tribeca in a starkly different direction from Chinatown and the Lower East Side. Between 2000 and 2010, while New York City as a whole showed modest population growth of 2.1 percent—considerably less than had been predicted by city officials[49]—the population of Tribeca's 75 block neighborhood swelled by more than a third, to 14,190, according to census data. Meanwhile the population of BPC /LM doubled, growing by more than 97 percent, making it the fastest growing neighborhood in the city (see table 5.1). Indeed four of the ten fastest growing census tracts in the city were found to be south of Chambers Street. The new residents of the area were far wealthier, too, with a median household income of $136,000, nearly one-fifth higher in inflation-adjusted dollars than a decade ago.[50] The opposite population and income trends had occurred in Chinatown and the Lower East Side. The population of Chinatown dropped by 4,531 residents, a decline of 8.7 percent and the first significant population decline in the neighborhood's history. The Lower East Side's population plateaued, showing no significant growth (see table 5.1).

Meanwhile, in both of the latter neighborhoods, socio-economic indicators showed a disturbing portrait of persistent poverty, stagnant incomes, and displacement—a pattern that stood in stark contrast to high levels of affluence and inmigration in the Soho/Tribeca/Civic Center and Battery Park/Lower Manhattan areas. By 2010, more than a quarter of the families in the Lower East Side and Chinatown lived below the poverty line, whereas only 3.7 percent of the families in the Battery Park/Lower Manhattan area lived in poverty, according to five-year poverty rate estimates from the American Community Survey (ACS) (see table 5.2). With the exception of slight increase in in Battery Park/Lower Manhattan, 2010

Table 5.1 TOTAL POPULATION, NEW YORK CITY NEIGHBORHOOD TABULATION AREA, 2000–2010

Geographic Area	2000 Number	2010 Number	Change, 2000–2010
New York City	8,008,278	8,175,133	166,855 (2.1%)
Manhattan	1,537,195	1,585,873	48,678 (3.2%)
Battery Park City,	20,088	39,699	19,611 (97.6%)
Lower Manhattan			
Soho, Tribeca,	36,757	42,742	5,985 (16.3%)
Civic Center,			
Chinatown	52,375	47,844	–4,531 (–8.7%)
Lower East Side	72,258	72,957	699 (1.0%)

Note: Neighborhood Tabulation Area (NTA) is a composite of census tracts according to commonly designated neighborhoods, designed by the New York City Department of City Planning. NTAs used here are: MN24, MN25, MN27, & MN28.
Source: U.S. Census Bureau, 2010 and 2000 Census Public Law 94-171 Redistricting Files Population Division—New York City Department of City Planning (Feb. 2012)

Table 5.2 POVERTY STATUS OF FAMILIES FOR NEW YORK NEIGHBORHOODS, 1999 AND 2010

Neighborhoods	Poverty Status in 1999 of Families (income of families below poverty level)	Poverty Status in 2010 of Families (income of families below poverty level)	Change in poverty status from 2000–2010
Battery Park City, Lower Manhattan	109 (2.9%)	232 (3.7%)	123 (56%)
SOHO, Tribeca, Civic Center, Little Italy	833 (11.8%)	692 (9.7%)	–141 (-17%)
Lower East Side	4848 (29.4%)	3353 (25%)	–1495 (-30%)
Chinatown	3002 (27.1%)	2954 (29%)	–48 (-1.6%)
New York County (Manhattan)	53,792 (17.6%)	43,397 (14.5%)	–10,395 (-19%)
New York City	535,935 (11.5%)	501,076 (10.8%)	–34,859 (-6.5%)

Source: U.S. Census Bureau. Poverty Status in 1999 and 2010 of Families (income of families below poverty level). Prepared by Social Explorer. March 24, 2012

census data show declining numbers living in poverty across the neighborhoods, indicating the outmigration of the poor from these communities due to the combined impact of post-9/11 economic decline, lack of access to aid, and gentrification. Meanwhile, poverty rates at the tract level remained as starkly uneven as they had been a decade earlier. Seven out of fourteen census tracts in the Lower East Side registered rates of poverty in excess of 20 percent. Six out of eight census tracts in Chinatown had poverty rates of 20 percent or higher. All eight census tracts in Chinatown, and thirteen out of fourteen on the Lower East Side, had median household incomes below the median family income for New York County (Manhattan) as a whole in 2010 ($64,971), in contrast with Soho/Tribeca or Battery Park/Lower Manhattan where they were well above. The numbers show how histories of inequality between the neighborhoods were reproduced rather than alleviated by post-9/11 demographic and socio-economic transformations.

Population and socioeconomic trends in both areas were accompanied by equally dramatic shifts in the racial composition of the neighborhoods, particularly with the in-migration of whites. Tribeca and BPC/LM saw their white populations increase by 41.4 percent and 90 percent, respectively. Chinatown remained mostly Asian (63 percent), compared to 16.3 percent white, but it became less Asian and more white, with a 15 percent drop in the Asian population, and a 42 percent increase in the white population. It also lost 15 percent of its Hispanic population. Similarly, the Lower East

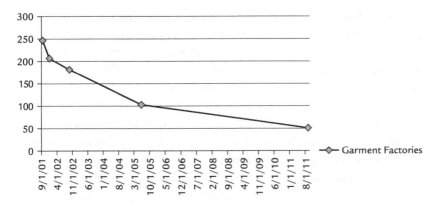

Figure 5.2
Decline in Chinatown Garment Factories Post-9/11
Sources: Asian American Federation of New York, "Chinatown After September 11th: An Economic Impact Study"
(An interim report, in collaboration with the Fiscal Policy Institute) April 4, 2002; Asian American Federation
of New York, "Chinatown One Year After September 11: An Economic Impact Study" (in collaboration with the
Fiscal Policy Institute) November, 2002; Barbara Ross, "Chinatown's garment biz shrivels, tourist traffic dwindles
in lasting blow of 9/11." *New York Daily News.* September 5, 2011 http://articles.nydailynews.com/2011-09-05/
local/30136943_1_chinatown-partnership-mott-st-asian-american-federation/2

Side remained majority Hispanic, yet lost 10 percent of its Hispanic population while gaining 18 percent more whites.[51]

These demographic shifts were emblematic of the gentrification-induced
displacement of the poor and non-white, driven by post-9/11
market-oriented policies emphasizing tax incentives, Liberty Bonds, and
upper-income housing investment. As we have seen, the Chinatown economy was flagging in the 1990s and devastated in the aftermath of 9/11.
This decline was then exacerbated over the decade to come as neighborhood businesses were largely blocked from disaster aid. The most dramatic
impact was on the area's largest, oldest, and most symbolically central
employer: the garment industry. Garment shops were vulnerable in the
1990s, and, beginning just a month after 9/11, their numbers began to
plummet (see figure 5.2). In large part this was due to the fact that 80 percent of the shops were located north of Canal Street and thus were ineligible
for loans and tax credits. Of 246 Chinatown garment shops in 2001, fewer
than 50 garment shops remained in 2011, a loss of more than 80 percent of
the industry. The number of garment workers, the great majority of whom
were unionized, dropped by a similar proportion over the same period,
from 14,000 to 2,000. This decline was felt throughout the entire area. As
May Chen, former leader for the textile union, Union of Needletrades,
Industrial, and Textile Employees (UNITE), put it: "9/11 permanently
changed Chinatown by essentially damaging the garment industry and the
community.... And there was a ripple effect."[52]

This ripple was powerful. Through the scale and relative strength of salaries in the garment industry, garment shops had been an economic multiplier for the area, driving business in local restaurants and retail stores as well as in the local service sector. But now these establishments, already weakened by the loss of visitor and tourist foot traffic after 9/11, lost the business of their most loyal customers in the factories once these former employees moved away.[53] Thus, rapid post-9/11 deindustrialization brought with it the decline in related services and small business, both in Chinatown and throughout the Lower East Side.

The decline in small business and retail was a common feature not only in Chinatown, but also the Financial District. Despite popular representations of economic impacts in the Financial District primarily falling on financial firms, the area's many small businesses—from diners to shoe repair shops to family-owned hardware stores—were also heavily impacted. Indeed these impacts were used to bring more federal aid to the Financial District. According to a 2002 survey by the Alliance for Downtown New York (DA), a sample of 20 percent of the DA's retail population within the area from City Hall to the Battery, from the East River to West Street, showed that average revenues were down 42 percent, mainly because of the decrease in the commercial workforce. By 2003, 55 percent of survey respondents had lower revenues than one year prior, and the percentage of those "very likely" to renew their leases in Lower Manhattan had dipped from 51 percent to 39 percent. These businesses had greater access to post-disaster aid than similar businesses in Chinatown. Almost all recipients depended on disaster aid funds to cover ongoing costs such as rent, salaries, and utilities.[54]

Yet, beginning in 2004, retail rents began to climb in the Financial District and throughout Lower Manhattan because of the uneven distribution of redevelopment aid and related economic development incentives. Of $539 million in business-recovery grants (BRGs) distributed through 2006, only $62 million, or 11 percent, went to owners of small businesses, with the remainder going to large brokerage firms and corporations.[55] Meanwhile, through changes made to the definition of "small business," corporations with as many as five hundred employees—as opposed to the previous limit of twenty—were able to receive grants from the Small Business Administration and further expand their operations.[56]

The heady mix of incentives, tax breaks, and sky-high profits was rapidly transforming all of Lower Manhattan, and the Financial District especially, into the symbolic heart of the post-crisis terrain the Bloomberg administration called "New York as luxury product."[57] The combination of Liberty Bonds with unfettered federal grants helped finance the "largest luxury-housing boom in recent New York City history."[58] From 2001 to 2006, the residential population of the Financial District increased

60 percent, while the median income for neighborhood residents shot up to the highest in New York City. With the assistance of Liberty Bond subsidies, co-op prices in the Financial District climbed 50 percent after 2001, faster than any other part of the city over this period.[59] Between 2004 and 2007, a "Lower Broadway luxury retail corridor" emerged, concentrated along Wall and Broad Streets. Hundreds of new businesses moved in, existing ones with the requisite capital expanded, and retail rents rose by an astounding 171 percent. Despite receiving relatively more aid than similar establishments in Chinatown and the Lower East Side, the majority of small businesses in the district—many decades old—could no longer hold out. New tenants occupying their vacated spaces, and featured in the DA's annual "State of Lower Manhattan" report, included BMW in 2005, Sephora in 2006, and Hermes and Tiffany's in 2007. By 2011, this Manhattan neighborhood, famously lacking in nightlife, counted "38 Zagat-rated restaurants and a bastion of high-end steakhouses and chef-driven eateries," including Delmonico's and Cipriani Wall Street.[60] See figure 5.3.

NEW MONEY IN THE LUXURY CITY

Related to this bounty of public subsidies, rapidly growing profits on Wall Street were a significant factor driving up Lower Manhattan rents. Enabled by a remarkable combination of federal and local aid, as well as far-reaching federal deregulation of financial transactions, Wall Street firms were in a position to create a booming global market in "the next big thing": mortgage-backed securities. Between 2003 and 2006, fees for the bundling, rating, and selling of these exotic securities doubled annually. By 2006, Wall Street bonuses *alone* totaled nearly $24 billion—equal to the entire post-9/11 federal aid package. The same year, and while other sectors in the city were still flagging, the finance industry reached a historic peak of 200,000 people employed. Meanwhile, corporations that were major players in the housing market and major beneficiaries of post-9/11 aid—including the Bank of New York, Goldman Sachs, and Moody's Investors Service—were building millions of square feet of new office space downtown as well as expanding into Midtown, where, through their lobbying, Liberty Bonds were also accepted.[61]

By 2008, bundled mortgage products were revealed as toxic assets, and the recent practices of Wall Street firms—from investment to sales to insurance to credit rating—were revealed as overly risky and in many cases illegal. The national housing bubble burst, bringing the stock market down with it. The economic crisis had an enormous effect in the downtown area,

Figure 5.3
The "New Lower Manhattan" Had Arrived

This is the cover of the Downtown Alliance's "State of Lower Manhattan" 2008 annual report seven years after 9/11. The cover was typically devoted to a single glossy image of the Financial District or Lower Manhattan skyline. This year, it was devoted to statistics describing seven years of meteoric and multifaceted growth in the New Lower Manhattan. The interior of the report includes images, stories, and more statistics illustrating all the elements on the cover—including historic spikes in tourism, grade A office space, and residential population, as well as the creation of a new "downtown luxury retail corridor." (Courtesy of Downtown Alliance)

bringing commercial rents down 17 percent the final quarter of 2008. But over the longer term, the crash did little to dampen speculation or cause a market correction. Post-9/11 rent subsidies and tax breaks for premier tenants were still high and were now met with federal Troubled Asset Relief Program (TARP) financing, along with a new round of incentives from Mayor Bloomberg's entrepreneurial economic development agency intent on blunting the financial toll of the crisis. Indeed, this latest crisis was to push the city to finance and manage some of the largest real estate deals yet for Lower Manhattan and to finally realize the longstanding dream of the Downtown Alliance for economic diversification. Unprecedented incentives were used to lure new industries like media and biotechnology—most famously Conde Nast, which was inspired to move from Midtown to the new, uncompleted WTC on the basis of $42 million in cash grants, thirteen floors of grade A office space, plus promises to reroute streets to allow their employees to travel easily by car to the building.[62]

By the end of 2010, rents were climbing again, pushing out the small businesses—even smaller luxury boutiques—that remained in Lower Manhattan. National chains like Bed Bath and Beyond, Whole Foods, and Barnes & Noble opened glamorous, capacious stores in former banks and office buildings. Duane Reade, with its new move toward custom-branded drugstores, built its largest and most opulent pharmacy ever, replete with hair salon, sushi bar, and an on-staff doctor to fit the new vibe of the area.[63] By 2011, the Downtown Alliance, which had used the plight of small businesses to lobby for post-9/11 aid, was celebrating the arrival of "a new class of retailers."[64]

The flood of new money on Wall Street had strong ripple effects in Lower Manhattan and beyond, bringing formerly fringe working-class neighborhoods—Bushwick, Crown Heights, East Harlem, and, more immediately, Chinatown—into the limelight as desirable "new frontiers" and creating a new scale of risk. As Alyssa Katz, an investigative journalist and housing expert who closely followed this process described: "Developers raced to catch the wave, armed with funds not just from the local banks that usually back speculative construction but from some of the biggest names on Wall Street. New York City made the *Scarface* mistake: It got high on its own supply."[65]

With the crash of 2007–2008, it became clear that this speculative fever far outstripped real demand. The Right to the City Coalition surveyed downtown Brooklyn, Bushwick, Harlem, the Lower East Side, the West Village/Chelsea, and the South Bronx and counted more than six hundred incomplete or largely empty luxury condominium buildings, with two bedrooms priced typically in the six figures.[66] This was more than most residents of these communities could hope to earn in a lifetime, leaving many doubled up in substandard housing or homeless. This prompted a new organizing drive: "People Without Homes for Homes Without People," demanding the city make condo buildings available for affordable prices to those in need of them—a policy that never took off.[67]

The greatest percentage increase of luxury housing in the city was to be found in the new, 24/7 post-9/11 financial district. As we have seen, the seeds of Lower Manhattan's gentrification were planted in the 1990s. Nonetheless, the speed and scale of growth in the subsequent decade, as well as the transformation of what was primarily a financial district into a mixed-use residential one, was extraordinary. By 2004, just two years after breaking ground, developers had constructed more than 5,800 apartments, doubling the units built in the preceding decade. By 2010, according to the census, BPC/LM more than doubled its total housing stock—including conversions and new construction—adding 12,477 units, or 105 percent more than existed in 2000.[68] As table 5.3 shows, the huge increase

Table 5.3 TOTAL HOUSING UNITS AND VACANCY STATUS, NEW YORK CITY NEIGHBORHOOD TABULATION AREAS (NTA), 2000–2010

	2000			2010			Change 2000–2010		
	Total Housing Units	Occupied Housing Units	Vacant Housing Units	Total Housing Units	Occupied Housing Units	Vacant Housing Units	Total Housing Units (% change)	Occupied Housing Units (% change)	Vacant Housing Units (% change)
Soho, Tribeca, Civic Center, Little Italy	18,738	17,346	1,392	23,081	20,923	2,158	4,343 (23.2%)	3,577 (20.6%)	766 (55.0%)
Battery Park City, Lower Manhattan	11,779	10,208	1,571	24,256	20,717	3,539	12,477 (105.9%)	10,509 (102.9%)	1968 (125.3%)
Chinatown	18,642	17,949	693	19,565	18,494	1,071	923 (5.0%)	545 (3.0%)	378 (54.5%)
Lower East Side	30,068	28,660	1,408	31,846	30,578	1,268	1,778 (5.9%)	1,918 (6.7%)	−140 (−9.9%)

Source: Table PL-H2 NTA, Total Housing Units and Vacancy Status, New York City Neighborhood Tabulation Areas, 2010, http://www.nyc.gov/html/dcp/pdf/census/census2010/t_pl_h2_nta.pdf.

in housing units in BPC/LM was matched with a 125 percent increase in vacant housing units, an indicator of the increasing inability of people with modest incomes to afford housing in the rapidly gentrifying area.

In the nine years following 9/11, Tribeca's housing stock grew by a substantial 4,343 new units, or 23 percent. For both neighborhoods, this represented an increase in both owner-occupied and vacant units. With the latter at 125 percent for BPC/LM and 55 percent for Tribeca, it was clear that rates of new construction outpaced even highly accelerated rates of population growth in the area. As in other parts of the city surveyed by the Right to the City movement, this fact was evidenced by newly built, state-of-the-art condominium towers standing largely empty during the market downturn of 2008–2009. Residential property values, like the commercial market, took a dip during this period but, aided by city subsidies, stayed strong. In 2006, median residential sales prices had jumped 75 percent.[69] By 2010, it was up by 120 percent.[70]

Thus, it was noted early on that Liberty Bonds, which "were meant to revitalize Lower Manhattan," were "transforming it, too"—into a luxury enclave.[71] Of the more than 12,000 units of new, subsidized apartments, the total number of "affordable" units was just 77—and even of these, 33 were targeted at "low income," and 44 were "middle income," with the latter capped at 150 percent of median family income. This was despite early modest promises from the LMDC that $50 million dollars would be allocated to build more than 200 units of affordable housing and to rehabilitate 2,854 more.[72] "Post-2001 New York has not been terribly kind to the $51,000-median-family-income New Yorker," according to a *Washington Post* article written at the time. "It would take a microscope to find affordable housing in downtown Manhattan."[73]

THE NEXT GENERATION: RESILIENCE OR DISPLACEMENT?

The rapid transformation of Tribeca and BPC/LM into emblems of the luxury city between 2000 and 2010 explains the new groups moving in: educated, upper middle class, mostly white, between 18 and 50 years of age. As in the 1990s, many of these were singles seeking proximity to jobs on Wall Street and new local jobs in multimedia. Yet now, the number of young families was also growing, by an average of one hundred per year since 2000. Ten years after 9/11, downtown had been transformed from the Financial District to the "diaper district" and Tribeca from an elite artists' enclave to the "Land of the $800 Stroller."[74] The 2010 census bore out these claims, with increases in children under age 18 by almost 21 percent in Tribeca (from 4,151 children in 2000 to 5,016 in 2010), and 123 percent in BPC/ LM (from 1,966 children in 2000 to 4,390 children in 2010).[75]

In addition to incentives and jobs, this influx was largely driven by investments by the LMDC and Economic Development Corporation (EDC) in family-oriented services that were historically lacking in Lower Manhattan, namely, schools, parks, childcare, and community centers. Julie Menin, the chairwoman of CB1 and sole member of the LMDC representing "community needs," worked assiduously with her constituents to ensure children and families were a priority and had a voice in the rebuilding.[76] Ten years hence, she saw something in these new amenities, and the local baby boom they helped cause, that was akin to what Mayor Bloomberg saw in rebuilt commercial towers of Lower Manhattan: a living monument to resilience. "When we look back at the rebuilding efforts," Menin argued, "the many new schools, parks, playgrounds, ball fields and community centers are the real testimony to our community's ability to persevere."[77]

Extending Menin's argument: to what does the lack of new community-oriented services and amenities in Chinatown and the Lower East Side testify? For, with the exception of a refurbished playground in Chinatown's Columbus Park, no new parks, schools, or community centers were built in these neighborhoods post-9/11, despite a longstanding need. Indeed, this lack of public investment exacerbated already dire conditions on the ground. As documented in a 2008 report by the Committee Against Anti-Asian Violence (CAAAV) and the Urban Justice Center, these conditions included joblessness catalyzed by post-9/11 deindustrialization; real estate speculation and gentrification driven by growing rent gaps and residential rezoning; and increased evictions and tenant harassment by landlords eager to eliminate rent-controlled units.[78] See figure 5.4. As a result, the exact opposite demographic shift occurred in Chinatown and the Lower East Side between 2000 and 2010—a marked *decline* in the populations of young people, as low-income families could no longer afford to stay. The percentage of people younger than 18 years of age declined 28 percent in Chinatown and 18 percent in the Lower East Side, in stark contrast to their neighbors to the west.[79]

The main hope for a substantial community-oriented investment in the Lower East Side and Chinatown came in 2005 in the form of $150 million worth of LMDC funding for the redevelopment of two miles of East River waterfront—the second largest community-oriented grant offered by the LMDC after the $800 million grant for the 9/11 Memorial.[80] This funding stretched from Battery Park in the Financial District, through the disused piers of South Street Seaport, to the dilapidated East River Park, which provided coastal access to the co-ops and housing projects of Chinatown and the Lower East Side. The funds came from the $2 billion in federal

Figure 5.4
Converting Chinatown
CAAAV and the Urban Justice Center wrote a report in 2008 based on six years of research documenting the multiple impacts of the lack of disaster and redevelopment aid, disinvestment, and gentrification following 9/11. These impacts, intensified by market pressure from redevelopment aid downtown and by commercial and residential rezoning in the East Village, brought about the conversion of Chinatown from a semi-industrial, working-class, Asian American neighborhood into one oriented increasingly toward tourism and high-end real estate. Manifestations of this conversion include, from upper left, counterclockwise: tenants organizing against mounting landlord abuses and evictions; shuttered storefronts of small businesses forced to close; protests against lack of translation for disaster aid documents; new luxury development in a former factory building on Canal Street; organizing by tenants rights advocates; new luxury development alongside tenements on Hester Street; and, center, new tourist kiosks on Canal Street.
(Courtesy CAAAV and the Urban Justice Center)

CDBGs administered by the LMDC. The proposal for the massive project came from the EDC, which saw this stretch of coastline as key to Mayor Bloomberg's larger effort, outlined in the blueprint "PlaNYC 2030," to rezone and redevelop valuable waterfront land across New York City for economic and "greenway" development linked to tourism, recreation, and real estate.[81] Given its link to these larger processes of rezoning and redevelopment, the plan is an important example of the long legs of crisis-driven urbanization at the local scale.

Park neighbors in the Lower East Side and Chinatown were not consulted in the planning phase. Upon learning of the plan, concerned local groups, who had long depended upon and sought to rehabilitate their waterfront, quickly formed Organizing and Uniting Residents (O.U.R.) Waterfront Coalition, conducted their own visioning sessions, and drafted their own alternative "People's Plan for the East River Waterfront."[82] Based on O.U.R. Waterfront Coalition analyses, the "People's Plan" was oriented toward spaces, amenities, and services that were deemed more "affordable," "accessible," and attuned to community concerns than those in the EDC plan.[83] The former included public basketball courts, barbecue pits, and playgrounds; low-cost or free classes and trainings; and pavilions dedicated to cultural centers, educational annexes, small businesses, and an "anti-eviction center."[84] To maintain the public orientation of the waterfront space, O.U.R. proposed that the space be governed by a nonprofit or the Parks Department rather than the EDC. These alterations responded not only to concerns over the affordability and accessibility of the park itself. The "People's Plan" spoke also to broader concerns that the new park might feed the "increased gentrification" and "forced displacement" of low-income people in surrounding neighborhoods—a process accelerated by the "flood of new development and construction...in the wake of 9/11 and...facilitated by pro-real estate City policies under Mayor Bloomberg."[85] Vision sessions echoed these concerns:

"One of my main concerns is whatever gets built in the space will determine who comes there and who gets to benefit from the space...."

"Most of the housing along the river is low-income housing; I am concerned that the development will impact this housing...."

"We want the waterfront to be for everyone. Like for me, I'm poor but I still want to be able to use the waterfront."[86]

As of 2011, the first phase of the project, including a spectacular esplanade with award-winning innovations in lighting, landscaping, and seating, was constructed according to the EDC plan.[87] Meanwhile, in the face of O.U.R. resistance, the plan's other "community-oriented" features were put on hold—stalling almost 50 percent of the budget and leaving many dangerously "blank spaces" along this coveted and contested stretch of waterfront. Thus, much like interior streets, businesses, and demographics, the East River waterfront came to represent the uneven and top-down redevelopment of Lower Manhattan after 9/11. Despite state-of-the-art design, this development came to be viewed by local residents not hopefully as a sign of resilience and sustainability, but anxiously as a potential harbinger of the final stage of gentrification and displacement for a low-income community clinging to its toehold in Lower Manhattan.

NEW ORLEANS: TRIUMPH AND ANGUISH IN DISASTER-DEVASTATED NEIGHBORHOODS

Similar to what was soon to occur in New York City on the tenth anniversary of 9/11, celebrations of "Katrina V" and the "New Orleans Miracle" in August 2010 extolled the vigorous recovery and resilience of the city and region. Numerous news stories and reports buoyed these assessments. Typical among these was the often-cited Brookings Institution report, "An Overview of Greater New Orleans: From Recovery to Transformation."[88] Based on a comprehensive examination of the region using twenty key indicators, researchers observed that the New Orleans area "has become more 'resilient,' with increased civic capacity and new systemic reforms, better positioning the metro area to adapt and transform its future."[89] According to the Greater New Orleans Community Data Center (GNOCDC), New Orleans weathered the Great Recession better than most places. The metropolitan area experienced a 0.1 percent decrease in jobs from June 2008 to June 2012 at the same time the nation lost 3.0 percent of all jobs. In addition, "[e]ntrepreneurship has spiked" with 427 of every 100,000 adults starting a business during 2008–2010, compared to 333 of every 100,000 adults nationally. As reported by the GNOCDC, "blight is rapidly declining in New Orleans," down from 65,428 blighted residential addresses in March 2008 to roughly 35,700 in March 2012.[90]

According to the U.S. Census Bureau, New Orleans was the fastest growing large city in the country between 2010 and 2011. In each of the seven parishes that make up the New Orleans metropolitan area, "a greater share of public school students post-Katrina are attending schools that meet state standards of quality. This is most notable in the city, where that share grew from 28 percent in 2003 to 59 percent in 2009."[91] By July 2011, the Census Bureau estimated New Orleans' population at 360,740, or 74 percent of its 2000 population of 484,674. The metropolitan area, with 1,191,089 residents, had 90 percent of its 2000 population of 1,316,510. Overall, according to the Brookings Institution, "New Orleans is rebounding and, in some ways, doing better than before" the Hurricane Katrina disaster.[92]

Yet, as others noted with some concern, what did these pronouncements of "rebound" mean in the context of significant, ongoing problems—such as population displacement, persistent socio-economic disparities, and omnipresent flood and storm risks? Despite billions of dollars spent rebuilding and upgrading levees and floodwalls, for instance, researchers contended that the hurricane and flood protection system was still inadequate to protect the city from catastrophic flooding and hurricane damage.[93] A report commissioned by the state of Louisiana on the collapse of the LP&VHPP found that post-Katrina repairs on the failed levee system "still provide a substantially lower level of protection than was originally authorized in 1965."[94] Dr. Bob Bea, co-director of the University of California, Berkeley, Center for Catastrophic Risk Management, and member of the National Science Foundation-funded Independent Levee Investigation Team (ILIT), "pointed out that 'the repaired sections of the hurricane protection system are the strongest parts,' but that 'strong pieces embedded within weak pieces do not translate to a reliable system.' "[95] The hurricane flood defense system "was and continues to be an assembly of disjointed and defective components."[96]

Since the repairs to the levees, reports of weak spots and incomplete protection continued to alarm residents and leaders. Such concerns, along with fears of increased vulnerability due to climate-change-driven sea level rise, implicated the LP&VHPP as a harbinger of future catastrophe. It was noted that, because contemporary risks can have a long latency period, the adverse effects of design defects in the levee system may lie dormant, ready to unleash a torrent of destruction when the next hurricane roars ashore. Meanwhile, hidden environmental risks embedded within regional patterns of uneven development coincided with serious financial risks for renters and homeowners as housing costs spiked dramatically following the levee breaches. Based on American Community Survey (ACS) data from the U.S. Census Bureau, the GNOCDC found that for renters, post-Katrina housing is largely unaffordable. According to the GNOCDC, 60 percent of renters in the city paid more than 30 percent of their pretax income on rent and utilities in 2010, compared with only 50 percent of renters nationwide. Moreover, 31 percent were severely cost burdened, paying half or more of their incomes on housing, compared with 25 percent nationwide. Overall, renters across the entire New Orleans metropolitan area faced a housing affordability crisis more severe than in other metropolitan areas.[97]

The release of the 2010 Census revealed a vast and continuing human trauma marked by regional depopulation and prolonged displacement. A month before Katrina, about 484,674 people called Orleans Parish home, according to census estimates. That figure had declined to about 210,000 in 2006 and rebounded to 343,000 in 2010, a decline of 29 percent from 2000 to 2010 (see table 5.4). Jefferson Parish ranked as Louisiana's second most populous parish in 2010, though it lost ground over the decade as the percentage of residents declined by five percent. Other metropolitan parishes saw sizable declines: heavily flooded St. Bernard Parish lost

Table 5.4 POPULATION BY PARISH IN NEW ORLEANS METROPOLITAN AREA,
2000 AND 2010

Parish	Population, 2000	Population, 2010	Change, 2000–2010	Percent Change, 2000–2010
Orleans Parish	484,674	343,829	–140,845	–29%
Jefferson Parish	455,466	432,522	–22,914	–5.0%
Plaquemines Parish	26,757	23,042	–3714	–14%
St. Bernard Parish	67,229	35,897	–31,322	–47%
St. John the Baptist Parish	43,044	45,924	2880	7.0%
St. Charles Parish	48,072	52,780	4708	10%
St. Tammany Parish	191,268	233,740	42,472	22%
Metropolitan Statistical Area (MSA)	1,316,510	1,167,764	–148,746	11%

Source: Greater New Orleans Community Data Center analysis of data from Decennial Census 2000 and 2010, "What Census 2010 Reveals about Population and Housing in New Orleans and the Metro Area," updated April 15, 2011, http://www.gnocdc.org/Census2010/index.html, accessed July 14, 2011.
Notes: Data for the New Orleans Metropolitan area is based on the sum of data for the seven parishes that make up the New Orleans-Metairie-Kenner Metropolitan Statistical Area (MSA) (Jefferson, Orleans, Plaquemines, St. Bernard, St. Charles, St. John the Baptist, and St. Tammany).

47 percent of its population while Plaquemines lost 14 percent. In contrast, St. Tammany Parish, the destination for many St. Bernard displaces, witnessed a 22 percent increase in population. Regional census data indicate that more than 146,000 residents had still not returned, having scattered to Atlanta, Houston, and points beyond.[98] Even amongst those who returned, uncounted thousands relocated within the region in unfamiliar communities because old ones were flooded and never rebuilt.

Critical analyses and pronouncements of continuing risk and vulnerability alongside celebrations of resilience and recovery are interconnected with questions of indicators and scale. When looking at entrepreneurialism, housing costs, and average incomes, for instance, one can find improvement. When looking at population, storm protection, housing affordability, and income inequality, however, one finds worsening conditions. In addition, the question of scale complicates generalizations of resilience and recovery en masse. When looking at the greater metropolitan region as a whole and using averages, resilience appears to be a major trend. When closing in on the neighborhood scale, however, and looking at neighborhoods comparatively, the impact of the starkly unequal nature of levee protection, socio-economic growth, and population trends becomes apparent.[99] Thus, in the crisis of post-Katrina redevelopment, one sees the production and reproduction of burdens on some neighborhoods alongside benefits

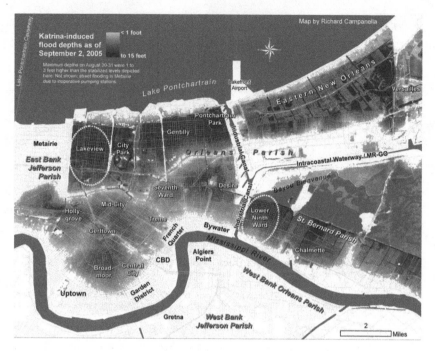

Figure 5.5
Map of New Orleans: Post Katrina Flood Depth

for others, a disparity that belies claims of resurgence for the metropolitan region as a whole.

THE CHANGING FACE OF TWO NEIGHBORHOODS

When Hurricane Katrina struck the New Orleans region, the Lower Ninth Ward and the Lakeview neighborhood both became symbols of the mass destruction caused by the levee breaches. As in other areas in the city, up to twelve feet of floodwater engulfed the two neighborhoods and repopulation and physical rebuilding were slow (see figure 5.5). Yet despite similarities in levels of flooding, census figures and our research show vast differences in pace and trajectory of the post-Katrina recovery and rebuilding process in each neighborhood. Both neighborhoods experienced dramatic population declines but at very different rates.[100] In Lakeview, the population fell almost 35 percent between 2000 and 2010, dropping from 9,781 residents to 6,394 residents. During the same time, the Lower Ninth Ward registered a population decline of almost 80 percent. According to

Table 5.5 POVERTY STATUS OF FAMILIES IN 2000 AND 2010 FOR NEW ORLEANS, LAKEVIEW, AND THE LOWER NINTH WARD

	2000	2010	Change
New Orleans	26,988 (23.7%)	12,170 (19%)	-14,818 (54%)
Lakeview	72 (1.4%)	15 (1.4%)	-57 (-79.2%)
Lower Ninth Ward	1,112 (32%)	99 (23.5%)	-1,013 (91.1%)

Source: U.S. Census Bureau. Poverty Status in 1999 and 2010 of Families (income of families below poverty level). Prepared by Social Explorer, March 24, 2012.

the 2010 census, only 2,842 Lower Ninth Ward residents lived in the neighborhood out of a pre-Katrina population of 14,008.[101]

Following the levee breaches that caused the flooding in the city and region in 2005, both neighborhoods saw a similar dynamic as in Lower Manhattan after 9/11: a modest decline in poverty rates combined with an entrenchment of longstanding patterns of socio-spatial inequality. Table 5.5 shows the poverty status of families living in New Orleans, Lakeview, and the Lower Ninth Ward in 2000 and 2010. While the table shows declines in rates of poverty for families in New Orleans and the Lower Ninth Ward, the latter shows stubbornly high rates (32 percent in 2000 and 23.5 percent in 2010) compared to the much lower figure for Lakeview (from 2.7 percent in 2000 to 1.4 percent in 2010). The decline in the rate of family poverty for New Orleans, the Ninth Ward, and Lakeview also reflects the fact that the poor were the most vulnerable to flood damage and least likely to have the resources to return to the city after the deluge. Meanwhile, despite these declines, census tract data show sharp differences between the two neighborhoods in terms of their post-Katrina poverty status. In 2010, median household income for Lakeview was $69,294, well above citywide figure of $37,468 and the metropolitan area figure of $44,014. In contrast, the Lower Ninth Ward registered a median family income of $21,206, well below the city and metropolitan area level, thus designating the area as a neighborhood of extreme poverty. Overall, for Lakeview and the Lower Ninth Ward, the decline in poverty rates was due to the flood-induced displacement of poor residents and the in-migration of more affluent residents in the years after deluge.

The above population and demographic figures are not simply expressions of the damage caused by Hurricane Katrina. The post-Katrina spatial structure of the metropolitan area is the result of decisions made by key institutional actors about where various kinds of housing would be rehabilitated and reconstructed. Moreover, municipal land-use regulations and the actions of city leaders have determined the kinds of housing that should be removed (e.g., public housing) and which neighborhoods should be redeveloped and repopulated. There were also, of course, individual decision-makers in the housing market, and people determined for themselves where they would relocate to in the city and metropolitan area. The cumulative result of these individual decisions influenced the ways in which populations distributed themselves in the post-Katrina landscape. But the impact of these individual decisions pales in comparison to the impact of powerful institutions and land-use actors whose actions and decisions about construction, investment, and disinvestment had sweeping and far-reaching consequences for tens of thousands of people. And as in New York City, variations in neighborhood recovery outcomes point to the different race, class, and socio-spatial histories of the two communities and the importance of understanding repopulation and redevelopment trends in the larger socio-historical context of uneven development.

Divergent Paths of Neighborhood Redevelopment: Lakeview and the Lower Ninth Ward

Throughout most of New Orleans' French and Spanish colonial history, the Lakeview area was one of undeveloped swampland. Early commercial development began in the 1830s when Irish indentured servants cut the New Basin Canal through the swamps, thus enabling commercial shipping to pass from Lake Pontchartrain to the booming Uptown neighborhood. By the mid-nineteenth century, as the New Orleans population expanded, pressures grew to open the areas along the lake to yachting, boating, and fishing. Lakeview became one of the first such tracts to be so developed, well situated as it was a canal ride away from Uptown and adjacent to the new, bucolic, 1,500-acre City Park. Between 1835 and 1876, real estate firms and developers transformed the area into an upscale resort known as New Lake End. Between the 1880s and 1900, thanks to the city's construction of an embankment atop the New Basin and 17th Street Canals and subsequent routing of trains to the embankment, the area expanded to become the West End resort. With ornate and fanciful design typical of the era, the resort included a hotel, restaurant, casino, garden, concert hall, and amusement park, all built on a large wooden platform constructed over Lake Pontchartrain.[102]

Lakeview's early reputation as a destination for well-to-do pleasure-seekers, developers, and city boosters prompted planners and developers to consider the possibility of transforming the area into an affluent residential neighborhood along the lake. Like most areas of the city, however, the omnipresent threat of seasonal flooding and hurricanes dampened real estate dreams of converting low-lying land for profitable uses. During the first decade of the twentieth century, the city financed swamp drainage, and sewerage and street construction opened up new areas for residential and commercial investment.[103] The new West End and Spanish Fort streetcar lines further encouraged residential development. By 1909, the New Orleans Land Company began selling lots, advertising the area as the Southern equivalent of Chicago's "Gold Coast" on Lake Michigan. However, due to a series of storms, including a destructive hurricane in 1915, significant development was stalled until the 1920s.

Like much of New Orleans, Lakeview's development was inextricably connected with racial inequality and segregation. In 1927, the Louisiana Supreme Court overturned state laws prohibiting blacks from renting or buying residential property in a white community. Shortly thereafter, private real estate firms began using racially restrictive covenants to limit the housing options of African Americans and reinforce and perpetuate racialized residential segregation.[104] In spite of the state supreme court ruling, the New Orleans Swamp Land Reclamation Company, for example, assembled and sold newly drained areas in Lakeview to private developers with restrictive covenants that prohibited sales of lots and homes to "negroes or colored people."[105] Because of these restrictions, Lakeview developed as a racially segregated neighborhood reserved for upper- and middle-class whites. Residential and commercial development accelerated after World War II, with the paving of more streets and the introduction of bus service in 1950. During these decades, Lakeview exhibited the features of a relatively prosperous and conflict-free suburban community with newly built, low-density single-family homes.[106]

Though the Lower Ninth Ward sat just a few miles to the south on the shores of the Mississippi, the neighborhood's history and development provided a dramatic contrast to Lakeview. Much older than Lakeview, the Ninth Ward started as a marshland community that existed on the outskirts of the city in the early nineteenth century. During the early to mid-twentieth century, African American families and white families with Irish, Italian, and German heritage created a culturally diverse community in the area.[107] As immigrants and free blacks settled the area, the neighborhood soon developed a reputation as the "ignored stepchild" of New Orleans and as an "isolated backwater" that was neglected by the city.[108] Well into the twentieth century, the neighborhood contained no sewerage or electrical services.[109]

Thereafter, three major events contributed to the area's social and historic marginalization within the city while exacerbating the Ninth Ward's vulnerability to flood and storm damage. First, the construction of the Industrial Canal during the 1920s split the neighborhood, disrupting community life and creating a predominantly white Upper Ninth Ward and a predominantly black Lower Ninth Ward.[110] Second, a protracted battle over school desegregation in the early 1960s triggered a demographic transformation in the neighborhood, as the token integration of white schools in the Lower Ninth Ward led to a mass exodus of whites to neighboring St. Bernard Parish.[111] Third, levee breaks caused by Hurricane Betsy in 1965 further traumatized the neighborhood with 6 to 8 feet of water. Over 80 percent of the neighborhood flooded, leading to further out-migration by whites and wealthier African Americans. One historian summed up the devastating impact of Hurricane Betsy on the Ninth Ward:

> In the Lower Ninth Ward's collective memory, Hurricane Betsy was the catalyst that drove remaining whites, already inflamed by school integration, to St. Bernard Parish. The storm also came to symbolize long-standing municipal indifference to the Ninth Ward. The hurricane's devastation of the Lower Ninth Ward contrasted sharply with minimal damage to the rest of the city, and residents, accustomed to decades of neglect, were certain that officials purposefully blew up the Industrial Canal to spare the "richer upriver areas."[112]

Insufficient recovery funds and lackluster relief efforts contributed to widespread disinvestment in the neighborhood. These actions, combined with the larger deindustrialization of New Orleans in the 1970s and 1980s, decimated the neighborhood's commercial base, projecting an image of concentrated poverty and social malaise. By 2000, the Lower Ninth Ward was nearly 95 percent African American, with a poverty rate of 36.4 percent, compared to 27.9 percent for Orleans Parish as a whole.[113]

In sum, a long history of racial discrimination and residential segregation guided the development of each neighborhood contributing to unequal patterns of real estate investment and socio-spatial isolation. By 2000, Lakeview was 96 percent white with a poverty rate of only 4.9 percent, one of the lowest in the city. Average household income in Lakeview stood at $63,984, compared to $27,499 for the Lower Ninth Ward and $43,124 for Orleans Parish.[114] These neighborhood, class, and racial differences reflected the larger racial polarization of New Orleans linked to a historically entrenched system of segregation and discrimination. Thus, on the eve of Hurricane Katrina, these two neighborhoods were starkly different in terms of their socio-economic status and demographic characteristics. By this time, institutionalized forms of racial discrimination had evolved into a web of practices for creating and reinforcing the color line in housing as well as racializing the dimensions of risk versus resilience in the built environment. What the levee breaks of Hurricane Katrina revealed was the integrated and interlocking nature of race and class with vulnerability, and the spatiality of risk and resilience.

Race and class differences between the neighborhoods also influenced the scale and duration of the post-Katrina diaspora, as many poor African

Americans were forced to flee, and far fewer were able to freely return to the area. After fleeing the storm, New Orleans's African American residents were much more likely than displaced white residents to end up living far from the region. Many African American displacees ended up in cities such as Houston and Atlanta. For these people, the forced movement to another state destabilized generations-old networks of kinfolk and close-knit communities. Even years after the deluge, long distances and the cost of travel back to New Orleans restricted the ability of poor and middle-class African Americans to return to their neighborhoods to repair their homes and rebuild their lives and communities. In contrast, middle-class whites typically had access to automobiles and did not have to travel far. Many of them rented apartments, bought houses, or moved in with friends or relatives in the New Orleans suburbs. Over the years, these New Orleans residents were able to remain close enough to get building permits, deal with insurance agents, and hire contractors to rebuild their houses.[115]

Since the levee breaks, disparities in wealth, distance of displaced residents, and level of public and private investment have been major drivers of repopulation and commercial revitalization in Lakeview and the Ninth Ward. The number of housing units in both neighborhoods has plummeted and are well below the average for Orleans Parish. Yet while Lakeview experienced a 29 percent loss in housing units, the Ninth Ward experienced a 64 percent decline (see table 5.6). Then, as residents were struggling to clean up the neighborhood after Hurricane Katrina, the Lower Ninth Ward was re-flooded by Hurricane Rita in September 2005. During 2006 and 2007, many of the flooded homes in the Ninth Ward were bulldozed rather than repopulated by homeowners, a development that caused a large drop in the percentage of total housing units in the neighborhood. Because many residents in the Lower Ninth Ward were poor, they had limited savings and low levels of insurance to cover their flood-induced losses. Reflecting larger racial disparities, residents of the Lower Ninth Ward were less likely to have to have their homes insured due to the insurance redlining of black neighborhoods throughout the United States. Overall, huge yet unequal declines in total and occupied housing units reflect uneven landscapes of risk and reslience in the two neighborhoods and across the city and region.

"Green Dot By Neglect": Uneven Redevelopment and the Lower Ninth Ward

We can view the unevenness of the pace and trajectory of the post-Katrina redevelopment as a result of the interaction between preexisting racial,

Table 5.6 TOTAL HOUSING UNITS AND VACANCY STATUS: LOWER NINTH WARD, LAKEVIEW, AND NEW ORLEANS, 2000–2010

	2000			2010			Change 2000–2010		
	Total Housing Units	Occupied Housing Units	Vacant Housing Units	Total Housing Units	Occupied Housing Units	Vacant Housing Units	Total Housing Units (% change)	Occupied Housing Units (% change)	Vacant Housing Units (% change)
New Orleans MSA*	548,629	498,587	50,042	538,239	455,146	83,093	-10,390 (-2.0%)	-43,441 (-9.0%)	33,051 (66%)
Orleans Parish	215,091	188,251	26,840 (12%)	189,896	142,158	47,738 (25%)	-25,195 (-12.1%)	-46,093 (-24%)	20,898 (78%)
Lakeview	4,805	4,524	281 (6%)	3,399	2,672	727 (21%)	-1,406 (-29%)	-1,852 (-41%)	446 (159%)
Neighborhood Lower Ninth Ward	5,601	4,820	781 (14%)	2,039	1,061	978 (48%)	-3,562 (-64%)	-3,759 (-78%)	197 (2.5%)

Source: U.S. Census Bureau, 2010 Census Public Law 94-171 File and 2000 Census SF1 Population Division. Greater New Orleans Community Data Center analysis of data from Census 2000 and 2010 and USGS National Landcover Database 2001. *MSA stands for Metropolitan Statistical Area.

class, and neighborhood disparities and inequalities in access to post-disaster recovery resources. Since the levee breaks, dispersed residents all shared a profound attachment to place and desire to rebuild homes and community. Yet their neighborhoods soon became competitive and embattled zones, as residents struggled with widely varying success to access the resources required to rebuild. Even in those spaces that governments and capital marked as ripe for reinvestment and rebuilding, conflict over the form of redevelopment unfolded, as residents jockeyed for a seat at the decision making table. Like post-9/11 redevelopment efforts in New York, neighborhood redevelopment in post-Katrina New Orleans reflects the creative-destructive nature of crisis-driven urbanization. The destructive character is evident in policies, socio-legal regulations, and framing strategies that undermine extant institutional arrangements, neighborhood identifications, and collective attachments to place. The creative aspect manifests in public-private efforts to attract investments and jobs and mobilize neighborhood space as an arena for market-oriented growth.

In the months after the levee breaches, city leaders raised serious doubts about the viability of some flooded neighborhoods and questioned whether governments should devote resources to rebuild them. The first indication that things were to be particularly hard for the Lower Ninth Ward was when city leaders refused to allow residents to return to their homes for three months after the flood. Through 2006, under the "Look and Leave Program," the city and the Red Cross bused residents into the neighborhood but only allowed them to visit their former homes to salvage whatever they could. In the first year after the disaster, the few returning residents faced a situation of widespread disinvestment with no nearby churches, banks, grocery stores, or restaurants. Throughout 2006, bodies were still being found in neighborhood houses.

Early decisions not to invest in the Lower Ninth Ward and to maintain a de facto policy of exclusionary displacement via the Bring New Orleans Back (BNOB) and Urban Land Institute (ULI) plans—i.e., the "green-dot" map—discouraged residents and businesses from returning to the area. The ideology that New Orleans was a blank slate ready for new forms of investment, combined with calls to "green" neighborhoods and adopt a policy of urban triage, served as powerful mechanisms for reinforcing inequalities and uneven development. While the green-dot idea was never implemented, the BNOB and ULI plan and map played an important role in raising doubts among residents and businesses about the long-term viability and sustainability of the city—and in particular areas slated for elimination.

The piecemeal, uncoordinated, and contradictory policies implemented in the years after Hurricane Katrina gave shape to a culture of uncertainty that had a decisive effect in creating widespread confusion and misunderstanding of the causes of the deluge and the future of urban neighborhoods. Robert Bullard and Beverly Wright contend that what residents in the Lower Ninth Ward and other low-income neighborhoods experienced was a "second disaster" of environmental and racial injustice defined by class and race inequalities. In many low-income neighborhoods, residents became convinced that government officials would not prioritize their communities for recovery and rebuilding.[116] According to our interviews and long-term ethnographic field observations, some residents maintain that the green-dot map dissuaded insurance companies from writing new policies and discouraged some residents from returning to the city. "Neighbors had been complaining about problems with the city before Katrina, so the green dot and lethargy of rebuilding gave them an excuse not to return," according to one Lower Ninth Ward resident.[117] The Nagin commission's map also had an effect on older residents, some contend. "Some elderly people were just not up for the battle. I think seeing that map made some people think, 'I'm not fighting that fight,'" one person remembered.[118]

With much of the Lower Ninth Ward still struggling to recover, some residents suspect the Nagin administration adopted a policy of "green dot by neglect," whereby no reinvestments were made unless residents returned first. "No residents, no city services," as one resident put it.[119] For residents observing this, the green-dot map served as a self-fulfilling prophecy: negative perceptions and low expectations about the recovery of the Lower Ninth Ward affected public and private actions toward the neighborhood that then caused those expectations and perceptions to be fulfilled. Planners' decisions to treat the Lower Ninth Ward and other neighborhoods with green dots communicated a powerful message that capital should be disinvested from these areas, an expectation that elicited that very response by insurance companies, small businesses, government officials and policymakers, and some residents.

In addition, Road Home procedures delayed or prevented many homeowners in the Lower Ninth Ward from accessing funds to rebuild their flooded homes. To qualify for Road Home funds, homeowners had to provide the title indicating that they were the rightful owner. For many homeowners in New Orleans, family members had passed down their property to younger relatives who agreed to occupy the home but never completed a formal succession in court. In many situations, residents of flooded homes whose families had "owned" the home for several generations did not have a clear title of ownership and therefore could not qualify for Road Home funds to rebuild their homes. Given that many residents were elderly and low-income, many homeowners gave up, abandoned their homes, and relocated elsewhere.

For many Lower Ninth Ward residents, this problem of heirship—property owned by multiple relatives—complicated resettlement and redevelopment efforts. This precarious but longstanding practice, based on informal kinship networks rather than formal markets, might be considered a "distinctive characteristic" of this low-income community akin to the precarity of employment for workers in Chinatown. One lawyer who represented several Road Home applicants explained the hardships that residents faced in dealing with the heirship problem.

> All these people after the storm went to get their Road Home money and couldn't prove they had cleared titles. In many low-income areas of the city, people lived in grandma's house, but they never had the property cleared in the legal system. It was always okay that cousin so-and-so lived in the house. But if you don't have a title the Road Home would not give you money because they did not think you owned the house. Even if you paid taxes, you may not "own" the house. So we had to go through the proper paperwork, we had lawyers look at how to streamline the process. The Road Home Program helped opened our eyes to this heirship problem, which not only plagues Louisiana, but really the Deep South.[120]

On top of heirship, one long-time activist and Lower Ninth Ward homeowner listed the obstacles that residents faced:

> There were many things that hurt families. Some family members died or took sick. There were endless waits for Road Home money. There was no money to rebuild because banks demanded repaid mortgages, taking entire Road Home grants. There were also crooked contractors who didn't finish the job or thieves who stripped houses of new cabinets, plumbing and aluminum windows. These are the major issues that have slowed people from moving back. It is not that they did not want to come back but they just could not move back given all the roadblocks that were in their way.[121]

Another neighborhood leader reflected on the struggles facing Lower Ninth Ward residents and noted the special problems elderly residents suffered.

> A lot of the elderly Lower Ninth Ward population suffered greatly. Most of them did not receive enough Road Home money. And their children lived outside of New Orleans. It has been said that they got a free bus ride out. But there was no free ride back. Many of them were not up to fighting with the government to get back to the Lower Ninth Ward. They were forced to evacuate and then forced to stay out because of funding shortfalls for the Road Home program.[122]

The above points draw our attention to the travails of Road Home victims and illustrate how the "private trouble" of rebuilding home and

Figure 5.6
Images of Post-Katrina Lower 9th Ward
In the Ninth Ward, thousands of flooded homes were demolished rather than rebuilt, and many others stand vacant and blighted. Many years after the destruction, it is more common to see empty lots.

neighborhood intersects with the "public issue" of post-Katrina urban redevelopment. Prior to Hurricane Katrina, the Lower Ninth Ward had an owner occupancy rate of almost 60 percent, well above the rate of home-ownership for the city as a whole (46 percent).[123] Important, this high rate of homeownership established a critical mass of stable residents and social networks interconnecting diverse people with local institutions. Interviews with residents suggest that the physical wrenching of homeowners and residents from their long-time homes generated a host of personal conse-quences, including damaging psychological distress, fear, humiliation, bit-terness, and anger. Not the least among the consequences was the collective toll on individual lives through the fragmentation of the community caused by government actions and inactions.

Today, irony, paradox, and contradiction define the Lower Ninth Ward. On one hand, returning and new residents have formed close ties and net-works to rebuild home and community in the midst of widespread dis-investment and blight. On the other hand, years of abandonment weigh heavily on residents, pushing them to the brink of despair as they frus-tratingly attempt to navigate the labyrinth of government bureaucracy to secure scarce rebuilding resources. Ultimately, the Lower Ninth Ward has become a landmark of catastrophe, the subject of films and books, a talk-ing point for aspiring politicians, and a must-see place on any disaster tour. The neighborhood also gained a reputation as a fledging urban forest due to the mass thicket of foliage reaching 7 feet high or more in places (see figure 5.6a and b). Years after floodwaters overwhelmed the neighborhood, the Lower Ninth Ward now includes three urban farms and more "green" houses than any other neighborhood in the United States, as reported by the Sierra Club (see figure 5.6c).[124] In addition to typical neighborhood calls for repaired streets and code enforcement, Lower Ninth Ward resi-dents must now regularly lobby for sustainable development, including structurally sound levees, bayou restoration, and environmentally sensitive construction, in hopes of one day bringing their neighborhood and com-munity back.

---

with weeds than rebuilt houses. In the photograph at the bottom (5.6c), a new home manufactured by actor Brad Pitt's Make It Right Foundation exists alongside a vacant lot. Since the levee breaks, neighborhood organizations in the Lower Ninth Ward have created new networked connections with sustainability advocates around the world to build green homes with radiant barriers, solar panels, and other technologies that conserve energy. For some residents and neighborhood leaders, these new sustainability efforts have become sources of resident pride and indicators of resilience. In the words of one resident, solar energy is now a "marquee issue for the neighborhood." While others celebrate these new sustainability efforts, they also note that such efforts are typically piecemeal and fail to explicitly address the systemic problems of long-term displacement of residents, poverty, and widespread blight (Photographs by Kevin Gotham).

Resources Drive Resilience: Rebuilding Community in Lakeview

Lakeview offers a very different picture of the rebuilding effort, one that is marked by revitalization and resilience. Unlike the Lower Ninth Ward, Lakeview was not targeted with a green dot, and residents therefore did not have to contend with insecurities and doubts concerning whether the city would support the area's recovery. Lakeview did not face the heirship problem, because many of its residents were younger and did not have a long history of family and kinship ties to the neighborhood. While redevelopment efforts were slow during the first few years after the deluge, in recent years, resettlement and repopulation have accelerated, and rebuilding is happening on many streets. Lakeview exudes enthusiasm and triumph over hardship and adversity. Many residential streets reveal new but strikingly mismatched housing, such as a brand new Acadian cottage next to an original 1940s bungalow, next to a modular home raised 8 feet on concrete piers. Optimism rather than despair characterizes the neighborhood as new residents join others in a momentum of return that seems unstoppable. "The people from Lakeview are not poor," according to Rev. Donald Dvorak, pastor of St. Dominic Catholic Church, the largest church in Lakeview. "They all had the means to leave on their own terms and a place to go—and the means to come back. That is the difference between us and the Lower Ninth Ward."[125]

Like the Tribeca and the Battery Park City-Lower Manhattan areas, Lakeview stands out for the economic rebirth it has experienced even as the national economic downturn from 2007 through 2011 stymied growth around the nation. A much younger demographic has moved into the area, and census figures show that the median age of residents has fallen from 41.4 in 2000 to 36.9 in 2010. Lakeview has seen a major decline in the percentage of residents over age 65 living in the neighborhood, from 19.1 percent in 2000 to 8.4 percent in 2010. The decline in the percentage of elderly residents stands in contrast to the increase in percentage of young adults living in the neighborhood, from 21 percent in 2000 to almost 30 percent in 2010. As of 2010, there was a higher percentage of children living in the neighborhood than there was before the storm. In 2000, 20 percent of the residents living in Lakeview were children. Ten years later in 2010, the percentage of children had increased to 22 percent, slightly higher than the city average of 21 percent. In fact, Lakeview is the only flood-ravaged neighborhood in New Orleans that had a higher percentage of children in 2010 than before the storm. These neighborhood figures provide a striking contrast to the Lower Ninth Ward, which has roughly the same percentage of elderly residents and young adults in 2010 as it had before the storm.[126]

Figure 5.7
Entrance to Lakeview on Harrison Avenue with Hynes Charter School in the background.
Floodwaters from the breached 17th Street Canal destroyed schools, businesses, libraries, and more than 9000 homes in the Lakeview neighborhood. But today, the neighborhood stands out for its community and economic rebirth. By 2011, commercial space in Lakeview had reached a saturation point with business leaders calling the neighborhood "a clean slate begging for development." The newly rebuilt Hynes school opened in January 2012 in a state-of-the-art building with computer labs, an art room, black-box theatre, and band room. According to some residents, the opening of Hynes symbolized the neighborhood's hard-fought recovery from the disaster (Photograph by Kevin Gotham).

One major driver of these changing demographic and resettlement patterns in Lakeview has been the disproportionate amount of federal aid that the neighborhood has received compared to the Lower Ninth Ward. In June 2010, the neighborhood received $21 million from FEMA for construction of the 106,000 square foot, 2-story Hynes Charter School, along with another $7 million to cover architectural, engineering, and project-management fees. In December 2011, the lavish, state-of-the-art school opened with computer labs, an art room, black-box theatre, and a band room for children prekindergarten through eighth grade. In addition to the construction of a new school, the abundance of affordable Road Home properties has attracted young homeowners into the neighborhood. According to one leader of the Lakeview Civic Improvement Association:

We've sold probably 400 out of 600 Road Home properties.... Lakeview has been built back because people who buy these properties have to build within a year. We created a waiting list database for [Road Home] properties, and [as of September 2011] there were over a thousand people on it.... Since Katrina, a lot of dollars being invested have been creating beautiful structures that weren't there before, like the public library at

Canal and Harrison and the Hynes School. When businesses see those federal and state dollars put to use like that, it makes their investments seem wise.[127]

"This young 27-to-35 group saw an opportunity to get into Lakeview, an area they thought was safe and sure to come back," according to one major real estate developer and long-term Lakeview resident. "They saw it was less expensive after the storm, and they were able to buy a piece of property for $70,000 a lot. You've seen this tremendous influx of retailers saying this demographic is where I want to be."[128] "Before the hurricane, the neighborhood was a lot older. It was my grandparents and their friends who unfortunately didn't have the means to come back," remarked one Lakeview resident and owner of local ice cream shop. "Now, there's a different business opportunity than there was before."[129]

Although Lakeview's population declined 34 percent between 2000 and 2010, home construction is booming, and businesses are returning to former commercial corridors such as Harrison Avenue, Robert E. Lee Boulevard, and Canal Boulevard. As one person told us in November 2011, "it is great having a grocery store again on Harrison Avenue because it is not only a place to get food to feed your family but it is a meeting place for neighbors that signals we are back, emotionally invested in making the community prosper."[130] Along Harrison Avenue, a string of commercial enterprises and community institutions have all reopened, including Hynes Charter School (see figure 5.7), St. Dominic Catholic Church, and St. Paul's Episcopal Church, as well as restaurants such as Reginell's, Lakeview Deli, the Steak Knife, Lakeview Harbor, and Mondo. From 2005 through 2009, FEMA trailers and construction dumpsters dominated the area. Since then, the pace of community redevelopment and repopulation has increased, and returning and new residents celebrate the phoenix-like rebirth of the community. "We never doubted, from that grim period in the fall of 2005, that we would have what we have today, thanks to all who have believed and invested," remarked a Lakeview Civic Improvement Association leader in November of 2010.[131] As another resident told us:

> The community atmosphere is very attractive to homeowners, businesses, and families with children. We have a sense of community that is resilient, and I think that is something that appeals to lots of different kinds of people. Everyone looks out for one another and there is a strong feeling of community pride.[132]

Overall, like investments made by the LMDC in schools, parks, and community centers in New York City, the investments in Lakeview in schools, parks, and businesses are propelling the growth and influx of young homeowners who are the pioneers in the rebuilding of the neighborhood.

The divergent repopulation and resettlement trends in Lakeview and the Lower Ninth Ward are not an outcome of group preferences or a reflection of market laws of supply and demand. Rather, neighborhood differences in the pace and magnitude of neighborhood repopulation and resettlement reflect the vestiges of past racial discrimination and housing segregation combined with the recent actions of government officials and real estate developers interested in maximizing the exchange-value of space. The grassroots actions of residents are vital in shaping the culture and economic fortune of a neighborhood. How residents channel their motivation and vision to build resilient neighborhoods and gain access to resources can be transformative. Yet individual desires and actions take place within a larger historic and spatial context of race and class that constrains their options. Just as uneven redevelopment is a consequence of the unequal distribution of power and resources, the fate of a disaster-ravaged neighborhood is tied to public policies and flows of funding and economic resources that predate the disaster and follow in its wake.

HISTORY, CRISIS, AND UNEVEN REDEVELOPMENT

Scholars have long recognized the centrality of political power, public policy, and resource control in understanding the historical development of U.S. cities and metropolitan areas. In *Place Matters: Metropolitics for the Twenty-First Century*, Peter Dreier, John Mollenkopf, and Todd Swanstrom maintain that the "spatial organization of American metropolitan areas is not the simple result of individuals making choices in free markets. Instead, federal and state policies have biased metropolitan development in favor of economic segregation, concentrated urban poverty, and suburban sprawl."[133] These outcomes are not just shaped by policy actions but by policy inactions, including the failure to enforce antidiscrimination statutes, build moderately priced rental housing, and create socially integrated schools and communities. People make decisions based on the choices available to them. But previous political decisions shape these choices to a great extent, influencing what options people have pertaining to where to live, what jobs are available, and what resources (housing, schools, health care, and so on) will be made available.

These basic points about the political economy of place are extremely relevant to post-disaster urban redevelopment efforts in New York City and New Orleans. Attempts to anchor capital in the built environment in the midst of crisis express conflicts and struggles inherent to what Lefebvre calls the "production of space." That is, socio-spatial patterns of uneven redevelopment are not simply the result of the aggregate decisions of actors in urban housing and real estate markets. Rather, as our comparison of neighborhood redevelopment in New York and New Orleans highlights, the role of history, race, social class, and public policy is decisive in shaping localized forms of uneven redevelopment. Obviously, some neighborhood differences in the speed of repopulation and redevelopment reflect differences in the scale and intensity of destruction caused by the disaster trigger. But variations in redevelopment outcomes are also due to each neighborhood's past socio-economic status and racial and class disparities, as well as residents' subsequent access to material resources for resettlement and community rebuilding. Moreover, while the valiant actions of enthusiastic residents have been crucial to recovery efforts, institutional decisions outside their control have played an outsized role in shaping the pace and pattern of neighborhood revival.

Ultimately, post-disaster redevelopment actions have produced a stark new landscape of risk and resilience. What we might call "leading" neighborhoods like Lower Manhattan and Lakeview that were advantaged before 9/11 and Hurricane Katrina have become more resilient in the face of future crises. "Lagging" neighborhoods that were disadvantaged prior to the disasters have been further weakened by displacement and rendered more vulnerable to future crises and hazards. By identifying and analyzing these differences and commonalities in the redevelopment trajectories of urban neighborhoods, our account draws attention to how local institutions, federal disaster aid policies, socio-legal regulations, and political struggle create and distribute not only risks in the built environment but socio-spatial variations in neighborhood resilience as well. As we have demonstrated, such uneven post-disaster redevelopment has the capacity to accelerate and intensify pre-existing processes of uneven development and thereby reinforce socio-spatial polarization. Indeed, relatively brief periods of crisis and redevelopment, even at the local neighborhood scale, play a catalytic role in the longer-term history, and wider scale dynamics, of uneven urban development writ large.

Rebranding the "Big Apple" and the "Big Easy": Representations of Crisis and Crises of Representation

On August 9, 2007, New Orleans Mayor Ray Nagin was asked by a TV reporter whether the city's high murder rate and escalating violence hurt the local tourism economy and slowed recovery efforts. In a city where the tourism industry is the lifeblood of a fragile economy, the wave of violence had threatened to derail efforts to bring visitors—and former residents—back. Crime is a "two-edged sword," Nagin answered. "Do I worry about it? Somewhat. It's not good for us, but it also keeps the New Orleans brand out there and keeps people thinking about our needs." Antiviolence activist Baty Landis shot back, calling Nagin's remarks "stunningly insensitive." "New Orleans is not a brand, it's a city," exclaimed Landis, "We're not products. We're people with lives, some of which are being taken by other people." Kelly Schulz, spokeswoman for the New Orleans Metropolitan Convention and Visitors Bureau (NOMCVB) did not disagree with Nagin's specific comments but suggested that the city must strike a "delicate balance" between drawing attention to its recovery needs and supporting the tourism industry—a "multibillion dollar, perception-driven industry," as she put it. "One good thing you can look at," according to Schultz, "is a lot of visitors have come to the city and their expectations were so lowered that they were pleasantly surprised."[1]

After the disasters, New Orleans and New York City both found themselves saturated with spectacular images of death and destruction—a seemingly infinite loop of New York's exploding towers and ash-shrouded citizens and of New Orleans's flooded neighborhoods and desperate residents waiting for aid in horrific conditions. As reflected in the above debate and similar ones that took place in New York City, these representations presented a dilemma for the cities' official marketing bodies—those like the NOMCVB that were tasked with creating and managing the cities' commercial image, or "brand," for tourism and economic development. On the one hand, disaster coverage posed a major obstacle for place branding, grounded as this practice is in the cities' sunny reputation for business and pleasure. Indeed, from experiences in previous eras of upheaval, marketers realized that such frames could provoke an "image crisis"—whereby negative representations, in and of themselves, undermined their economic development strategy, eroded their competitive edge, and exacerbated economic decline.[2] The simple solution to this crisis for these officials was the elaboration of new representational strategies and the strategic and commercial reimagining of urban space, or what is generally referred to as *urban rebranding.* As reported in the *Wall Street Journal* following 9/11, "for the city's official marketers New York isn't just a wounded city, but a challenged brand... [and] like all challenged brands, it needs...an overarching scheme to reposition itself in the American popular consciousness."[3] People in post-Katrina New Orleans harbored similar concerns. "We need to restore the brand that is New Orleans," according to Alfred Groos, general manager of the Royal Sonesta Hotel. "That is the biggest challenge that we all have."[4] As the NOMCVB reported, "[w]hen Hurricane Katrina struck...the [CVB] was forced to cancel $2 billion in business, relocate all meetings through May 2006 and then begin to overcome unprecedented brand impairment."[5]

In both cities, the circulation of disaster-related imagery reflected a crisis of representation that demanded new representations of crisis. Yet, in creating these representations, disaster-related imagery could not so simply and easily be erased. Beyond providing visual evidence for aid appeals, post-disaster media and popular culture also documented historic degrees of civic engagement and solidarity. In addition to the "visioning sessions" and town halls addressed in Chapter 4, both New York City and New Orleans experienced an upsurge in collective creative expression—to locate loved ones, raise relief funds, and give a complex voice to the diverse impacts of the disasters. Thus, the cities' visual and symbolic landscape—their "urban imaginary"—was to be forever altered. Some expressions, like missing-people walls after 9/11 and refrigerator graffiti after Katrina, were desperate, ad hoc responses that became iconic. Others, like hip-hop poetry slams, RIP murals, jazz funerals, and second line parades—drew on and transformed locally rooted forms of artistic expression and mourning. Still others, including award-winning documentaries, novels, and dramatic portrayals in television and film, reframed and reimagined local experiences and circulated across social, alternative, and mainstream media channels nationally and globally.[6] Through multiple voices, these cultural interventions attempted to answer a question on the minds of so many in the two cities and beyond: how to represent the enormity of the disasters, and how these two complex, beloved cities would survive in their aftermath.

City marketers faced a dilemma. They recognized the power and resonance of these frames and the benefits they could provide in attracting disaster-related conventions, corporate donations, and "voluntourism." Yet they also recognized the painful memories, volatile emotions, and contentious politics they stirred up and hence their limitations in meeting the long-term commercial demands of urban branding. Such demands include the development of simple, noncontroversial, and consistent messaging, vetted by marketing consultants and a range of corporate stakeholders, and easily circulated through an array of global media networks. Moreover, urban branding must counter "negatives"—of the cities in general and disasters in particular—so as to promote redevelopment driven by investments in real estate and tourism. To resolve this dilemma, we discovered that marketers did strategically invoke certain aspects of collective creative expression related to the disasters—often without ever mentioning the disasters explicitly. Rather, rebranding campaigns drew on some of the powerful affective and aesthetic qualities underlying this expression—including affects of hope and love and aesthetics of authenticity, resilience, and solidarity. As we shall explore, these were then used to craft utopian, post-crisis city campaigns, emphasizing frames of *cultural diversity* and *urban sustainability*. Yet despite the appearance of inclusivity, any and all aspects of the original forms of cultural expression that did not meet the commercial demands of the new brand—for example, those too emotionally raw, demographically undesirable, or politically radical—were to be excluded from this new vision of urban utopia.

In fact, these campaigns were used to further preexisting, market-oriented objectives held by members of branding coalitions. This included arguing—as marketing agencies long had—that current approaches to urban branding were woefully out-of-date, uncoordinated, small-scale, and poorly funded. If this did not change, they held, they would be unable to address the challenge of rebranding in response to crisis. This contention became the new common sense. City marketing became a major fiscal priority, despite competing demands for urgently needed public resources. As we shall see, a massive infusion of capital enabled both cities to mount a new, ambitious agenda. On the one hand, this agenda involved the retooling of marketing infrastructure, the creation of new institutional "synergies" between the public and private sectors, and the incorporation of cutting-edge creative, technological, and corporate expertise. On the other hand, the new agenda entailed redesigning the representational universe of both cities such that a market-oriented versions of "recovery" and "redevelopment" could be viewed as "utopian" and, therefore, necessary, legitimate, and universally beneficial.

RETOOLING THE POST-CRISIS BRANDING INFRASTRUCTURE

In analyzing urban rebranding in response to crisis, the first thing we learn is the enormous, and mostly hidden, work that it requires. As compared to city marketing during "normal" times, developing the capacity to extend and manage complex new brands in times of crisis and to tailor these to broader redevelopment initiatives requires the retooling of the entire branding "mode of production." Retooling involves significant institutional realignments and the creation of new "synergies," or forms of integration within government agencies and between these agencies and the private sector; increased funding to mount larger-scale, multimarket campaigns; the recruitment of new talent, from C-suite marketing managers to designers and other creative workers; and the leveraging of new technologies and media platforms to reimagine urban space and thereby shape and influence how people think about and understand a particular locale. While we cannot deduce their outcomes ahead of time, we can say that such corporate-style retooling acts on particular agendas long pursued by powerful members of branding coalitions, yet which could not be fully implemented previously due to lack of funding or political support. In times of crisis, it is easier to push through these reforms without public debate.

While we identify retooling for urban rebranding as a common development in both of our cases, we also recognize significant variation between them. We see this perhaps most dramatically in levels of funding available for rebranding, as measured by the annual revenues and expenses of major economic development organizations and convention and visitors bureaus. In the decade after 9/11, average annual revenue was $600 million for the New York City Economic Development Corporation (NYCEDC) and $30 million for NYC & Co., the city's official tourism marketing arm., whereas, since Hurricane Katrina, average annual revenue for comparable organizations in New Orleans—Greater New Orleans, Inc. and the NOMCVB—was $3.3 million and $13 million respectively.[7] Another obvious difference is found in the degree of restructuring of city agencies. A hallmark of post-9/11 retooling and increased funding for urban branding was the merging of major marketing operations and the high degree of bureaucratic centralization under "CEO-Mayor" Michael Bloomberg. Meanwhile, efforts at centralization by New Orleans's marketing agencies did not bear much fruit due to inherited conflicts within these agencies and a different mayoral vision under successive Democratic administrations. Yet, as we shall see, these divergent funding and organizational factors have not been all-determining. Expenditures for New York City and New Orleans both increased exponentially in response to crisis, albeit from a different base. Meanwhile, agencies in the two cities all moved toward integrated, citywide campaigns, although at different scales and degrees of integration. Thus, the retooling of city branding capacity in a crisis context reveals, on the one hand, the heterogeneous influence of local contexts and place-based branding coalitions and, on the other hand, the homogenizing pressure of larger scale forces like interurban competition and the increasing standardization of corporate models of urban governance.

New York: Public-Private Governance and the Pursuit of "Synergy"

That Mayor Bloomberg was the ideal political leader to take on the task of post-crisis urban rebranding in New York City was continually emphasized in our interviews with agency officials. As a senior official at NYC & Co. put it: "Bloomberg is a master at creating brands and an extraordinary businessperson. He really knew [after 9/11] that if you're going to do the best that you can do for the city…you have to create the city in the likes of how you would create a successful business."[8] Essentially, from the perspective of city marketers, Bloomberg's vaunted business and branding experience, developed at his eponymous firm, Bloomberg L.P., positioned him particularly well to seize the opportunity presented by 9/11.[9]

This argument also reflected the extent to which Bloomberg was able to identify with the post-crisis concerns and aspirations of elites in this global media, financial, and real estate capital. Indeed, the extreme nature of this identification—Bloomberg was among the top ten wealthiest people in New York upon taking office, and he became the second wealthiest by his third term—makes it hard to avoid an analysis of "the Bloomberg way," at least in part, as a significant element in a broader, urban-based "class project," as Julian Brash has cogently argued.[10] New York elites gained invaluable experience in mobilizing as a class "in and for itself" during the crisis of the 1970s, when they formed highly effective partnerships to facilitate the branding and urban redevelopment campaigns that countered image crisis and fueled the growth of wealth across a range of sectors in the 1980s. Post-9/11 New York elites—now primarily drawn from the ranks of finance, real estate, and the corporatw sector—again saw the necessity to reestablish their global reputation in association with the reputation of New York City. But, unlike in the 1970s, they had the opportunity to work with a newly elected mayor who was "one of their own" to make this happen. Even in an era of "urban entrepreneurialism," Bloomberg's profile put him in a class by himself; with the possible exception of former Italian Prime Minister Silvio Berlusconi, no media magnate had risen to so high a political office. Thus, not surprisingly, more than any mayor in New York City's history, Bloomberg sought to apply his governance skills toward taking "direct coordinated custody of the city's image," transforming this image into a global brand.[11]

To do so, Mayor Bloomberg first did what he did best at Bloomberg L.P.: "vertically integrating" city marketing operations by creating a complex hierarchy that controlled all aspects of the production and distribution of the brand and, in the process, creating new "synergies" between the creative and financial aspects of branding. In the 1970s, the main groups in the branding coalition were public-private partnerships and state agencies that were relatively independent of City Hall. After 2001, campaigns were created by public-private partnerships appointed and overseen by the mayor's office, representing a new stage in the entrepreneurialism of city government and the professionalism of its branding operation. These partnerships included, primarily, the New York City Economic Development Corporation (NYCEDC), charged with stimulating business development for the city through corporate retention and attraction, and NYC & Co., the city's official tourism marketing arm.[12]

In the aftermath of 9/11 and during his first two terms in office, Bloomberg greatly enlarged these agencies in size, budget, and purview, while creating cabinet-level positions that enabled them to interface directly with the mayor's office. Both groups were integral to the creation of the Lower Manhattan Development Corporation (LMDC)—the private-sector-led group that drove the redevelopment of Lower Manhattan from 2002–2006, discussed in Chapters 3 and 4—and helped guide the use of federal funds for the LMDCs own extensive marketing operations and their integration within broader economic development initiatives to sell the "new Lower Manhattan." Bloomberg personally oversaw the staffing of these agencies with professionals from the private sector, ensured that their efforts were guided by strategic planning and market research, and integrated all of this via Bloomberg L.P.'s hallmark computer terminals—a device commonly known as "The Bloomberg."

New Orleans: Decentralization and Institutional Segmentation

In comparing New Orleans with New York, we find several similarities and differences in the former's response to crisis and the subsequent retooling of the post-crisis image infrastructure. Unlike Mike Bloomberg, neither Ray Nagin nor Mitch Landrieu, New Orleans' two post-Katrina mayors, had the distinction of being a multibillionaire or former CEO of a Fortune 500 corporation with the capacity to bring diverse public and private elements of the branding apparatus into coalition. Rather, both mayors were relatively traditional, if entrepreneurial, Democratic party politicians, with the latter the son of a prominent political dynasty. Unlike New York City, New Orleans did not experience increased centralization and vertical integration of city marketing operations or the formation of tightly unified branding campaigns after Hurricane Katrina—despite considerable effort.[13] Like Bloomberg's office, the City of New Orleans Mayor's Office created new public-private partnerships for business development and tourism marketing. These organizations included the Mayor's Office of Cultural Economy and the New Orleans Business Alliance, which, like the NYCEDC and the NYC & Co., emerged in a context of crisis in which the global circulation of negative imagery motivated people to form new organizations, networks, and synergies to reshape public perceptions of the city.

The decentralized organization of New Orleans's tourism infrastructure did not just happen after Hurricane Katrina, but was a product of decisions made over a long span of time. In 1960, political and economic elites formed the Greater New Orleans Tourist and Convention Commission (GNOTCC), the precursor to the contemporary NOMCVB. Unlike NYC & Co., which was a public institution within the city government, the GNOTOCC emerged from the New Orleans Chamber of Commerce and embraced a militantly privatist ideology founded on deep skepticism of the public sector and distrust of public officials. In 1990, African Americans, civil rights leaders, and entrepreneurs formed the Greater New Orleans Black Tourism Network (GNOBTN) to represent the interests of minority businesses and campaign for the inclusion of African American history and culture in the city's tourist narrative.[14] In 1999, the GNOBTN was renamed the New Orleans Multicultural Tourism Network (NOMTM) in an effort to "encourage multicultural visitation" and "identify and promote the cultural diversity of New Orleans."[15] Also during the 1990s, political and economic elites established the New Orleans Tourism Marketing Corporation (NOTMC), a development that further divided tourism marketing operations along public-private and marketing lines, with the privately funded NOMCVB primarily handling conventions and business travel and the NOTMC, a city agency, primarily handing leisure travel. By the time Katrina roared ashore, tourism marketing operations and promotions were segmented among several different organizations including the NOMCVB, NOTMC, and the NOMTN.

In the first year after the deluge, each of the three major tourism organizations in the region—the New Orleans Metropolitan Convention and Visitor's Bureau, the New Orleans Tourism Marketing Corporation, and the New Orleans Multicultural Tourism Network—adopted separate and autonomous rebranding campaigns. In April 2006, the Louisiana Recovery Authority earmarked $30 million for tourism and convention marketing, with the NOMCVB using a portion of this money to "reimage and rebrand" the Ernest N. Morial Convention Center, the site of an internationally televised humanitarian crisis in the days after Hurricane Katrina. In addition, the NOTMC joined forces with the Louisiana Office of Tourism to launch a new branding campaign with "Fall in Love with Louisiana All Over Again" as the main slogan. The New Orleans Multicultural Tourism Network adopted the slogan "Do You Know What It Means to Miss New Orleans? We Know You Do" to rebrand New Orleans as a multicultural destination. Thus, unlike New York City, where the post-9/11 rebranding effort was centrally organized and characterized by vertical integration, New Orleans's campaigns were relatively diffuse, uncoordinated, and lacking in direct public-sector leadership. Yet despite these differences, and in a sign that local contexts shape variegated approaches to market-oriented redevelopment strategies, both cities were to embrace a post-disaster "tourism solution" with equal gusto.

THE TOURISM SOLUTION

The emphasis on tourism and consumption as the driver of recovery and a long-term solution to crisis has become common-sensical in the contemporary global urban marketplace. The popularity of the "tourism solution" began in the late 1970s when the "I♥NY" tourism marketing campaign found unexpected success and became an instant model for other crisis-torn cities. The rhetoric is backed up by three often-repeated arguments. The first is that tourism is one of the last place-based job creators in an era of hypermobile global capital. The second is that tourism comes cost-free and produces powerful economic "multiplier effects," namely, that investment in tourism and related branding can benefit nontourism aspects of the economy, including business development, retail, and real estate investment. Third, tourism is an attractive tax-exporting opportunity, as cities can impose the tax burden on visitors to government operations and activity. The notion of exporting taxes to nonresidents often draws considerable support from elected officials and the public interested in financing public services. For these reasons, urban boosters argue that tourism services should have a special status among local industries. New Orleans officials state that "hospitality, tourism, sports, and special events are the business of New Orleans and have more national and international impact on the brand of New Orleans than any other industry or business sector," while New York's tourism boosters make much the same claim, in particular highlighting the symbiotic relationship between the tourism, media, and real estate complex.[16]

The competitive frenzy to increase tourism reached fever pitch following 9/11, when so many cities saw the impact of sharp declines in air travel.[17] The first major public appeal by Mayor Rudolph Giuliani and Governor Pataki was aimed at tourists and consumers, imploring "visitors to come back to New York City" from around the world and "go shopping," as a means of displaying patriotism and civic pride. Of course, much of this turn in public discourse was driven by the tourism industry itself, as leading officials attempted to link patriotic sentiment with consumption-based activities.

In response to Hurricane Katrina, New Orleans tourism officials and their staff explicitly positioned themselves as the saviors and master planners of a "new" New Orleans. Among an August 2010 list of "story ideas" for media and publicity, NOMCVB officials noted that one idea, "Overcoming Crisis," implored city officials to alert all stakeholders to "how the CVB convinced visitors that it was safe to visit post-Katrina New Orleans and managed the destination's reputation... in a perception and image-driven tourism business."[18] Carefully plotted and disseminated, this salvation theme was intended to mollify critics and reposition an industry often seen as ancillary to citywide economic recovery. "The future of New Orleans has never been brighter thanks to the renaissance of the tourism industry," according to the NOMCVB.[19]

Absent is any public recognition, let alone analysis, of potential downsides of a tourism-driven approach. For instance, rising rents drive out low-income residents while the redirection of social service priorities toward amenities that benefit visitors, like shopping and recreation areas, can mean less funds available for services for local residents, like libraries, affordable housing, and healthcare. However, in what appears to be a tacit response to critique, growing attention is paid to the public perceptions of the industry, with an increased focus on *internal* political branding as well as *external* urban branding. Indeed, as we see in the case of NYC & Co. most strikingly, tourism marketing agencies can now double as PR firms for the mayor's office. Within this environment, a "tourism solution" to crisis, requiring costly restructuring and retooling of the infrastructure and technology, advanced rapidly in the aftermath of 9/11 and Katrina, despite a fiscal environment stretched thin by many competing and arguably greater post-disaster needs.

NYC & Co.

The high-profile epicenter of tourism-driven rebranding in New York was New York City and Company, renamed "NYC & Co.," the city's official city marketing arm. In 2003, with his pursuit of the 2012 Olympic Games and other mega-events a cornerstone of his post 9/11 tourism solution, Mayor Bloomberg created two new marketing groups: NYC Big Events and NYC Marketing (themselves modeled on larger tourist cities like Las Vegas). In 2006, in a highly publicized move, he merged these two groups with NYC & Co. and moved the entire operation, under the new NYC & Co. name, to large new Midtown offices.[20] Guiding the expensive move was a new goal: attracting 50 million tourists by 2015—or five tourists for every resident (the city reached the goal in 2011).[21] Bloomberg doubled NYC & Co.'s city funding to $22.5 million—more than five times what the agency received under the previous administration of Mayor Giuliani. This largesse diluted the amount of funds coming from member dues such that, for the first time in the agency's history, control of the city's promotional efforts shifted from travel and tourism industry leaders to the mayor's office.[22] Total revenue and expenses for NYC & Co. skyrocketed, with revenue growing from $19 million in 2006 to $40 million a year later, and expenses increasing from $17 million to $42 million in the same time period.[23] Next, the mayor placed two veteran advertising executives, George Fertitta and Jane Reiss, both with backgrounds managing some of the world's biggest luxury brands—including Godiva chocolates, Remy Martin cognac, and Cunard cruises—as well as major corporate accounts like American Express, in the newly created positions of chief executive officer and chief marketing officer, respectively.

Now, as agency leaders had long sought, NYC & Co. finally had the organizational structure, funds, and expertise to operate as a full-fledged marketing department for the city. Within the new organization were ten interacting departments modeled on a professional marketing firm. The media department expanded beyond the production of brochures and guides to launch a full-service website, complete with original content, updated hourly, written and photographed by an in-house staff of thirty, translated into nine different languages by another staff of five, and able to compete with established online guides like *Time Out NY* and *New York* magazine among tourists and locals alike. This enabled the advertising department to sell advertising space on the website, which could host interactive ads that helped to generate revenue.

Behind the scenes, a new partnerships department was put in charge of creating "synergistic" deals, exchanges, and co-branding opportunities with external companies linked to the tourist and convention trade—from global billboard display companies to credit card companies—and who also agreed to barter, partner, or co-brand with NYC & Co., and so extend the reach of its advertising. The entertainment department was charged with pursuing product placement opportunities, that is, seeing that New York City and its logo were shown prominently and in a good light on television and films. This entailed getting product placement deals akin to other corporate brands. To this end, the agency was to create its first ever official logo, the hip and versatile "NYC," to be analyzed below. As the NYC & Co. official we interviewed explained: "We just treat the [NYC] brand how other brands are treated. If [a TV show is] going to put an Apple computer on someone's desk—why shouldn't someone say something about NYC?"[24]

Meanwhile, the new structure of the agency facilitated the use of "NYC" as an internal political brand. A new "government communications" department handled rebranding 124 city agencies and offices—from "adult education" to "youth services"—now all sharing the official "NYC" logo. Further, this political branding was integrally intertwined with Bloomberg's own efforts to market his image as mayor, as one can see in his controversial but successful 2009 bid to overturn term limits in order to run for a third term in office, at a record-breaking cost of $108 million. The campaign logo, "MikeNYC" incorporated the iconography and narrative of the newly developed NYC brand, highlighting the increasing degree to which urban and political branding campaigns were, and are now, intertwined.[25]

Forever New Orleans: Building Networks to Revitalize the Damaged Brand

A major feature of New Orleans's post-Katrina rebranding efforts was the formation of new synergies among the leading tourism organizations in the region. In 2007, the NOTMC and the NOMCVB unveiled the "Forever New Orleans" rebranding campaign, the result of a joint public-private partnership to attract visitors to the city, "preserve the city's leading industry (hospitality) and overcome misperceptions about New Orleans among consumers."[26] Joining with Harrah's New Orleans Hotel and Casino, the two agencies adopted each other's advertisements, merged their visitor guidebooks, and settled on this shared slogan for their campaigns. The agencies' two locally based advertising agencies—Trumpet for the NOMCVB and Peter A. Mayer for the NOTMC—collaborated to develop the slogan, logo, and design, as well as to select the shared focus on local culture and cuisine. One tourism official elaborated on the synergistic relationships established between the NOMCVB and the NOTMC for cross-promotional purposes:

> The city's rich culture and signature events gave ample opportunity/concepts for the industry to rally around and provide a loose but powerful form of cohesion. Our food, our music, our culture—Jazz Fest, French Quarter Fest, Mardi Gras—all these were easily used by all for marketing and branding purposes. Because we have different tourism organizations each could draw on their own strengths and expertise as well as connect with one another. We have one agency focused on leisure tourism (NOTMC) and one on meetings and international leisure (CVB). But they both needed to be on the same page with their campaigns![27]

Increases in federal funding for tourism promotion catalyzed the formation of the new branding coalition. After Hurricane Katrina, HUD directed $28.5 million in federal funds for tourism to the state-level Louisiana Tourism Marketing Program, which in turn distributed the funds to seventeen tourism entities in thirteen parishes.[28] New Orleans area tourism organizations and marketing agencies received 71 percent of the total— $20.2 million—with funding going to numerous organizations. For the NOMCVB, funds increased markedly as total revenue increased from $9.3 million in 2006 to $17.3 million a year later in 2007. Total expenses also shot up, going from $10.3 million in 2006 to $15.4 million the next year.[29]

The "Forever New Orleans" rebranding campaign was part of a broader post-Katrina redevelopment strategy to retool the image infrastructure using both intensive place marketing and pro-business economic reforms. By 2009, the Landrieu administration and leaders of the major tourism organizations were calling for long-term and comprehensive planning and coordination to reinvigorate the tourism sector. In April of 2009, Lt. Governor Mitch Landrieu along with tourism leaders formed the New Orleans Hospitality Strategic Task Force to create a master plan to guide the resurgence and long-term growth of tourism. The seventeen-member group included representatives from the NOMCVB, NOTMC, NOMTN, Harrah's New Orleans Hotel and Casino, the Audubon Nature Institute, and the Ernest N. Morial Convention Center. Major restaurateurs, hotel operators, and associations representing them were also on the panel, which was created by Lt. Gov. Landrieu to provide "one team that has one vision and one fight."[30] The Task Force selected The Boston Consulting Group (BCG), a global management consulting firm and adviser on business strategy, to lead a $2 million study and planning effort. In January 2010, after eighteen weeks of meetings between BCG and the Task Force, they released the report, "Celebrate Our History, Invest in Our Future: Reinvigorating Tourism in New Orleans." Similar to New York, BCG set a goal for New Orleans to exponentially increase the number of annual visitors within a decade, in this case from 7.6 million in 2008 to 13.7 million by 2018, the city's tricentennial celebration.

UPGRADING ECONOMIC DEVELOPMENT

One might consider tourism and economic development marketing to be the twin arms of urban branding campaigns. Tourism waves dramatically to audiences "front stage" using billboards, websites, cable dramas, T-shirts, and so forth. The economic development arm beckons more covertly from the "backstage," using tax breaks and other pro-business incentives targeted at particular industries. The two efforts are not separate. Raising tourism numbers is also a major goal of economic development agencies. Tourism marketing, meanwhile, with its catchy slogans, iconic images, and emphasis on the "quality of life" of particular locales, is highly relevant for place consumers interested in developing businesses in and/or moving operations to a city. Tourism officials we spoke to described the "reciprocity" between these two types of marketing, as in this interview with an official from the NOMCVB:

> What's interesting is the reciprocal relationship between tourism and economic development. Tourism acts as a gateway for investors just as new residents to the city or those investing then become ambassadors- bringing associates, family and friends to the city. The city's fresh stock was also a big theme—restaurants were always mentioned but also the fresh hotel stock and newly renovated convention center and newly renovated Superdome, those were often touted as part of the "new" New Orleans.[31]

This synergistic dynamic has been understood since the fiscal crises of the 1970s, and increasingly since the latest round of disaster- and recession-driven crises, as cities ramp up their efforts to woo a young, culturally savvy "creative class," and so to spark economic growth and investment.[32] In this sense, tourism investment is seen as leading the way toward catalyzing both a "cultural renaissance" and "new entrepreneurialism" that will be mutually sustaining. As the above official continued, in reference to their promotion of New Orleans's "Idea Village" new economic zone: "The entrepreneurial movement was a common theme we promoted to journalists in efforts to shape ideas about the city as a vibrant, creative place attractive to young adults, investors and entrepreneurs."[33]

Meanwhile, and mostly behind the scenes, agencies devoted specifically to economic development marketing—extending beyond the tourism industry—greatly expanded the scope and scale of their operations in the post-crisis period. The work of such agencies typically entails the promotion of a "good business climate" and investment opportunities of a locale to targeted audiences—including the promotion of local entrepreneurial talent and technological infrastructure; a lax regulatory environment enabling low labor costs and taxes; and the ease of "cutting red tape" in dealings with the public sector.

Since the disasters, the nature of economic development marketing has undergone dramatic restructuring akin to that experienced by tourism. This restructuring has entailed new synergies and expanded geographical scale of externally targeted campaigns. Also like tourism, it has been met with the expansion—or wholesale innovation—of "internal marketing," which in this case involves the direct and indirect lobbying of local officials to push through tax cuts, rezoning, and other pro-business and development deals.

NYCEDC

The post-9/11 period witnessed a major repurposing of the New York City Economic Development Corporation (EDC) and a dramatic expansion of its role. Based in Lower Manhattan, the agency was itself displaced by 9/11 and immediately became involved in the new LMDC, aiding in the design and implementation of the Liberty Zone tax incentive programs and developing some of the first provisional post-disaster branding campaigns. Mayor Bloomberg, meanwhile, saw the opportunity after the disaster to reorient the EDC beyond this immediate task. His vision was to strategically expand the financial scale and geographic scope of EDC deals by targeting top-tier global firms, particularly in real estate investment, through what has become known as the "luxury city" model.[34] To accomplish this, the agency hired a new "C-Suite" of upper management—CEOs, CFOs, and CMOs—with experience in global finance to guide the city's development priorities in a way that would be attractive to such elite business. Almost all of the new recruits were drawn from investment banking, primarily from powerful firms like Goldman Sachs and JP Morgan, unlike the more eclectic mix of sectors represented previously.[35] Their first move was to spin off the EDC's "small business unit," turning it into a fully public city agency, so as to focus EDC energies on deals with big business. They then devised a "5-Borough Economic Opportunity Plan," through which some eighty different pieces of city-owned property would be redeveloped and turned into potential investment assets through the use of rezoning and tax incentives. These new strategic steps were continuous with the market-oriented Liberty Zone strategy that EDC helped to craft, now on a larger scale.

Furthering this "luxury city" direction, the reorientation of the EDC had another goal: to create a new public face of the agency and its projects for both *external* markets and *internal* political lobbying efforts. To this end, a new position of senior vice president of marketing and communications was created (SVP), for which a seasoned marketing executive with an extensive background in corporate brand management was hired. The SVP's first move was to create a new brand logo, "NYCEDC"; a new tagline, "New York. Make It Here"; and more than one hundred unique yet compatible "sub-brands" to market existing city-owned commercial properties as well as the many multibillion dollar, public-private development projects that were proposed by the city post-9/11—from Willets Point to Coney Island to Long Island City. The EDC created separate brochures for each project, and Local Development Corporations (LDCs) handed them out to businesses being approached to invest and move in (replete with tax break information); to businesses being forced out through eminent domain (replete with move-out instructions and new possible destinations); and to those politicians—from local representatives to city planning officials—whose backing and vote the EDC sought to gain.[36] To support this, a raft of designers were hired to create brochures and staff a new Interactive Media Department.

In addition, as was uncovered through an audit by the New York State Attorney General's office, the EDC paid political insiders, including former Queens borough president Claire Shulman, to directly lobby-elected officials using these materials through the offices of EDC-created, supposedly "independent," "grassroots" LDCs. Ultimately, the Attorney General's office found these claims to be fraudulent and the EDC to be engaged in illegal lobbying and use of propaganda on behalf of private developers in an effort to overcome often strong community and political opposition. The finding led to the forced restructuring of the EDC, the primary effect of which was to prevent lobbying and sever the agency's ties with LDCs.[37] However, this "mild tap on the wrist," as opponents of the projects called it, included no financial penalties and could not stop the EDC from continuing to conduct branding campaigns in-house, on behalf of the same developers.[38]

Greater New Orleans, Inc. (GNO, Inc.), and the New Orleans Business Alliance

The New Orleans economic development scene post-Katrina was similarly mired in behind-the-scenes political dealing on behalf of major business and developer interests. The difference, however, was that there was no large-scale official entity like the EDC to carry these out. New Orleans was distinct from New York City, and many others, in its lack of an economic development entity—at least one that reached beyond the visitor industry and the domain of the NOMCVB and the NOTMC. For decades, local economic elites had opposed a strong public sector, and up through the 1980s, New Orleans "was known as one of the last cities in the United States where an old, long-established social aristocracy still controlled politics and business."[39] Throughout the twentieth century, business leaders served on many nonelected boards and commissions that governed areas like the port, the lakefront, sewerage and water, and the city debt. These boards and commissions were independent of the city administration and aggressively protected their insularity and autonomy as a source of power and influence. Moreover, corruption and mismanagement had long afflicted New Orleans's public bureaucracy, especially its school system, aggravating community tensions and contributing to adversarial relations among private-sector elites and publicly elected officials. In the 1980s and 1990s, longstanding antagonisms between the public and private sectors had begun to soften as existing business leaders and corporate newcomers to the city were successful in creating the Business Council, a coalition of corporate elites, the Audubon Institute, a private nonprofit organization, and later, Metrovision, a planning arm of the New Orleans Chamber of Commerce.[40]

The damage and destruction caused by the Corps' levee breaks accelerated efforts to transform relationships between public and private sectors and created a new opportunity for political and economic elites to push for a more "entrepreneurial" vision for New Orleans. In 2007, the city, in conjunction with Greater New Orleans, Inc. (GNO, Inc.), a regional economic development alliance, hired the International Economic Development Council (IEDC) to "help in developing and implementing a public-private model for the city that included expanded focus on economic development."[41] Fueling this effort to create a new public-private model was also the new demographics of the region, for instance, the loss of nearly 50,000 poor residents between 1999 and 2008–2010 and a decline in the percentage of African Americans living in the city from 67 percent before the storm to 59 percent in 2010.[42] Political and economic elites viewed these demographic trends as presenting "big opportunities" for investment and advancement of pro-business reforms and a new urban business agenda. Comments by members of the new regional growth coalition about the "clean slate" presented by the flood as a result of the destruction of low-cost housing and underfunded schools, and the displacement of poor, black New Orleanians, were common, if usually made in private.[43]

More publicly, political and economic elites formulated an ambitious strategy to rebrand New Orleans as a center of biosciences, software and digital technology, and sustainable industries, all part of a campaign to steer public resources into new economic development areas in addition to the traditional sectors of oil, tourism, and shipping. Within a year, IEDC officials reported that "a common agenda is emerging to address the city's long-term economic positioning."[44] Aided by this new "Regional Economic Development Strategy," as GNO, Inc. framed it, business leaders and elected officials rallied around far-reaching pro-business reforms that included and extended beyond tourism and linked New Orleans more to the business interests of those in the suburbs. Initiatives, all proposed by the IEDC and modeled on regional approaches elsewhere, included an "Urban Biomedical District," the Silicon Valley-inspired "Idea Village," and the ecotech-oriented "Green New Orleans" plan.

The largest area of targeted economic development was in the "cultural economy." Here, synergies were created between the city of New Orleans and the state of Louisiana, with the goal of rebranding both the city and state as a "cultural hub." As originally defined in a 2005 report titled "Louisiana: Where Culture Means Business," the cultural economy consisted of six segments: culinary arts, design, entertainment, literary arts and humanities, preservation, and visual arts and crafts. In 2007, the Louisiana legislature passed several regulations and tax incentive packages to further the development of culinary, entertainment, and artistic enterprises. Specifically, the legislature created "cultural products districts," which could sell works of art without sales tax, grant tax credits to redevelopers to renovate historic buildings, and grant refundable income tax credits to musical or theatrical productions and musical or theatrical facility infrastructure projects.[45] As of 2011, fifty-nine state-designated cultural districts had been created in thirty-four towns and twenty-four parishes across the state, over a third of which were in the New Orleans metropolitan area.[46]

Related to the development of cultural products districts was the use of city and state tax incentives and subsidies to build new economic infrastructure dedicated to film, television, music, and theatrical productions—a move that also required a new message and promotion. "Louisiana has cemented its reputation as Hollywood South, thanks to the most generous incentive package in the nation," proclaimed The Times-Picayune newspaper in 2007, echoing language used by the new state office of Entertainment Industry Development and the city's new Film New Orleans office. While New Orleans has long been a setting of movies and had seen local production increase rapidly in the early 2000s, this spiked in 2007 when the state began offering a tax credit program that paid 30 percent of a production's expenses so long as the project spends $300,000 in Louisiana—a controversial program that also met with a fair share of corruption.[47] Nonetheless, in the years since Katrina, the number of film program applications surged, according to state figures, nearly doubling from 79 in 2007 to almost 150 in 2011 and catapulting Louisiana to the third-ranked film-producing state in the nation, behind only New York and California.[48]

A central force in the production of this new aestheticized environment was the Mayor's Office of Cultural Economy, created to market and rebrand New Orleans as a place of artistic and creative industries. Through a program of advertising and public relations, the new office worked with other city agencies, including the NOTMC, to identify funding streams for cultural programming and incentives to expand the cultural economy and secure access to capital for cultural producers and others to expand an arts- and entertainment-based economy.[49] This new cultural economy served a dual purpose: providing jobs for cultural workers and promoting the city's quality of life for tourists, business, and new residents. As Scott Hutcheson, the mayor's new adviser on the Cultural Economy explained, culture offers "incredible value" to "our City's fabric—indeed the very heartbeat of what makes New Orleans the unique, rich place that it is, and why this is a great place to live, work and visit."[50] This sentiment was commonly voiced by then Mayor Mitch Landrieu as well. As he put it in 2010:

> Culture is inseparable from our way of life in New Orleans. We enjoy a diversity of cultural riches that most cities can only dream about.... New Orleans is one of the leading centers in the world for the intersection of creativity and commerce. The cultural economy in New Orleans...drives our tourism industry...contributing to the life of the city both culturally and economically. My administration will partner with cultural workers, businesses, non-profits, and institutions in order to best tap the valuable resource that is the cultural economy and to benefit both those who work within it and the communities that benefit from it. As Mayor, I have created the Mayor's Office of Cultural Economy to both quantify the cultural economy and to steer my administration's policy in this area.[51]

Then, in August 2010, Mayor Mitch Landrieu announced the creation of the city's first formal public-private partnership, the New Orleans Business Alliance—thus realizing the primary recommendation of the IEDC post-Katrina. The new agency, modeled on the NYCEDC, now helps to "incentivize" and "cut red tape" for business retention, expansion, and relocation; entrepreneurship initiatives; international business development; and strategic planning. Reflecting the outsized role of private trade groups, "[t]he charge of the New Orleans Business Alliance is to take most of the economic development function away from the city," according to Leslie Jacobs, vice chairperson of the Business Alliance. In addition, the "Alliance will have a primary responsibility to attract retail," a focus that reflects efforts to promote the growth of a consumption-oriented economy.[52] The new group was outfitted with a professional marketing and media arm that has helped market the city regionally and globally. We would argue that this reflects one of the key purposes of urban rebranding: the blurring of boundaries between the public and private sectors and between the marketing of culture and economic development.

Technology and New Media

A crucial aspect of the retooling of branding in both New Orleans and New York City for tourism and economic development was technological upgrades, and with this, new possibilities for mounting multiscalar, multimarket campaigns. In New York City, again, this was linked to the leadership of a former CEO of a global financial media corporation. Officials at NYC & Co. made two points repeatedly: "Bloomberg is a technology man," and "Bloomberg is all about customer service." To demonstrate, they revealed how, with the aid of "Bloomberg" terminals and software, branding efforts were coordinated via sophisticated back-end technology and new, state-of-the-art user-friendly websites: nycgo.com and nycedc.com. Innovations include the creation of a content management system (CMS) that funnels all fresh content to the multiple platforms, both online and offline; software to track references to the city's campaigns on social networking sites to gauge the impact of advertising for the research department; and, for nycgo.com, a partnership with Google Maps to enhance the navigability and manageability of the site.

The latter feature was key to NYC & Co.'s expansion into a "5-Borough Tourism Plan"—a major departure from the city's historic focus on the "tourist bubble" of Manhattan south of 116th Street.[53] This strategy mirrored and helped to market the 5-Borough Economic Opportunity Plan of NYCEDC, helping promote a "global city" image to tourists and corporations from around the world by featuring the city's far-flung multiethnic neighborhoods as well as new city-sponsored development projects. To promote this new tourist- and real estate-centered geography, the city realized the need for new forms of cartography. This began with a state-of-the-art visitor center replete with "smart tables" and wall screens with giant interactive maps of New York City—all designed by NYC & Co. staffers employing original proprietary software and powered by Bloomberg databases.[54] Ultimately, this led to a partnership between NYC & Co. and tech startup CityMap, and to their launch of a free smart phone application that enables residents, visitors, realtors, and apartment buyers to digitally and visually navigate the five boroughs via the brand logos of their storefronts[55]—at least insofar as they have brand-name stores that can be mapped.[56]

A major impact of the upgrade at both agencies has been the ability to globalize the city's marketing efforts internally and externally. This was linked to the international business networks of the new upper echelon of employees as well as that of Mayor Bloomberg himself. In its first two years of operations, NYC & Co. established new global linkages by opening eleven full-service offices in cities around the world, bringing its total to eighteen offices serving twenty-five countries.[57] Modeled on strategies of global media firms like Bloomberg L.P., reporters and sales representatives in these offices are bilingual, culturally savvy locals—rather than transplanted New Yorkers—who sell and extend the New York City brand in their own markets. This international staff is coordinated by the "International Tourism Office" in New York, an impressive command center with walls lined with clocks set to local times and televisions tuned to local stations. Far-flung "journalists" communicate weekly via teleconference and, through consultation with New York staffers, develop story ideas that publicize the city for audiences back home. These foreign offices also serve as an "extension of the sales force" for NYC & Co.'s 2,000 corporate members.[58] They market New York City-based attractions and businesses to tourists and business travelers abroad, and cross-promote the services of those members—like Loews Hotels and Time Warner—that are global corporations with operations in these same eighteen cities.

Like New York City, New Orleans's rebranding also entailed venturing into new media and technology terrain. Reminiscent of the new style of commercials used for the original "I♥NY," the NOMCVB launched a professional thirty-minute travel television show, hosted by local celebrities, that represented a new direction for city marketing. Originally called "A Whole New Orleans" and renamed "Forever New Orleans" to tie in with the larger campaign, the show was distributed nationally and globally via the Travel Channel, greatly expanding the campaign's reach.[59] The NOMCVB also took its first step toward "corporate reputation" monitoring, a branding heuristic that larger cities, states, and nations had begun adopting after the economic crash of the early 2000s. The NOMCVB hired the Cision Corporation to provide media monitoring software to "analyze key message delivery, frequency and tone of media coverage about the New Orleans brand."[60] Tourism officials also developed the new 24NOLA.com website for bookings, integrated with new websites created by the Louisiana Office of the Lieutenant Governor and the Louisiana Department of Culture,

Recreation and Tourism (CRT). These websites were linked to a series of advertisements for outdoor and print media, developed by London-based GlobalCastmedia, Inc.

In 2007, the NOMCVB went further, joining with the state of Louisiana to hire Weber Shandwick, then one of the largest global PR firms (now the largest) and a specialist in crisis communications, "to strategically re-brand and reposition the city and State." In particular, they sought to expand beyond regional marketing by disseminating their campaign nationally and internationally. Promoting the "New Orleans destination" for "leisure travelers, conventions and meetings" as well as for "meeting professionals, associations and corporate decision makers," Weber Shandwick mounted a ten-city media tour. Leveraging a portion of the $28.5 million distributed by HUD in September 2006 to fund the Louisiana Tourism Marketing Program, the NOMCVB staff in New York, Chicago, Washington, DC, Tokyo, London, Paris, and Frankfurt strengthened and expanded long-term relationships with "influencers" such as meeting professionals, corporate and association decision-makers, and travel professionals worldwide.[61]

REPRESENTING POST-CRISIS CITIES: FROM DISASTER TOURISM TO UTOPIAN NARRATIVES

Fueled by entrepreneurial, retooled marketing agencies flush with public monies, the post-crisis branding coalitions of New York and New Orleans entered a new creative phase, developing elaborate and all-encompassing representational frames to reposition their two cities. These frames can be grouped into two historical phases: those of the immediate post-disaster period and those of the longer-term period of urban redevelopment. In the former, marketing efforts were necessarily *sui generis*, responding to the different disasters and image crises with which the cities had to contend, and drawing on local cultural referents to do so. These campaigns emphasized appeals for "disaster tourism," recasting terrible recent events via tropes of patriotism, humanitarian concern, and/or love of cities as a reason for, rather than an obstacle to, tourism and consumption. Over the longer term, large-scale campaigns were developed that no longer referenced the disasters at all. Instead, in this second phase, campaigns featured urban redevelopment as a triumphant monument signaling post-crisis transcendence and the attainment of an ideal, utopian urbanism of cultural diversity and environmental sustainability. We address each of these phases in turn.

Phase I: Disaster Tourism

Immediately following the attacks of September 11, 2001, the dominant mode of rebranding New York City was as a patriotic destination, depending largely on images of the Statue of Liberty to replace the once central image of the Lower Manhattan skyline. Advertisements, events, and conventions—most notably the Republican National Convention of 2004, but also including annual campaigns—directly referenced the terrorist strike, highlighted the city's triumphant strength and ability to rise again, and, in the name of patriotism, invited tourists and conventioneers to come to New York City, visit Ground Zero, and shop.[62] Rebranding after Hurricane Katrina, meanwhile, addressed images of storm and flood damage via their own version of phoenix-like recovery. The initial "Forever New Orleans" campaign, launched as a series of billboards, cleverly acknowledged Katrina while celebrating the city's unwavering spirit by using headlines like "Soul is waterproof," over a picture of a jazz musician; "We've never been dry," next to an image of a woman with a glass of wine; and "Open for just about anything," with a shot of Mardi Gras revelers on stilts.[63]

Yet despite their particularities, both New York's and New Orleans's new urban brands shared the peculiar affective qualities of post-disaster campaigns. Having to address the recent trauma created a strange openness, with marketers drawing on a rare degree of pathos in their commercial appeals. They knew they couldn't deny or ignore people's fears of witnessing the devastation of the disasters or cater simply to voyeuristic curiosity—though they did this as well. In general, they discovered ways of responding to fears by focusing on what, arguably, was underlying them: emotional attachment to and desire for the survival of two beloved and wounded cities. Much like "I♥NY" in the 1970s, new campaigns responded to palpable desires— now raised in listening and visioning sessions and rampant in popular culture—for the survival of the irreplaceable urban qualities and culture that the two cities represented as well as for the solidarity and mutual aid across lines of race and class that was so needed and frequently displayed in the aftermath of disaster. "I don't know why I've been coming here, except that I'm confused," one young man in Union Square told a reporter from the *New York Times*. "Also a sense of unity. We all feel differently about what to do in response, but everybody seems to agree that we've got to be together no matter what happens. So you get a little bit of hope in togetherness."[64] Immediate post-crisis campaigns responded to this, appealing to visitors' desire for human connection and unity and for those urban qualities and public spaces that make this possible.

Thus, initial crisis campaigns used powerful emotional appeals that foregrounded disaster and the capacity to overcome. As Kelly Schulz, vice president of Communications and Public Relations at the NOMCVB, put it, "the one thing that Katrina did not wash away is our culture and the experience and emotional connection people have with this city and each other."[65] To this end, "Forever New Orleans" stressed "Beauty Out of Chaos." According to Scott Couvillon, Trumpet's director of brand strategy, a mix of "optimism" and "honesty" was crucial: "Yeah, it's worth coming and seeing and no don't cancel your convention, but the expectation has to be real.... You are going to see the water lines... you are going to see a modern city that was hit by something we've never seen before." This prompted the agency's creative department to research New Orleans's history of struggle going back to the 1600s.[66] Robbie Vitrano, cofounder and director of brand design at Trumpet, described the epiphany that sparked their creative process: "[Adversity] is the secret... to this place. It's a city that built creativity around overcoming challenges and difficulties, be it jazz, from poverty, or the fact that the city was built out of a swamp."[67]

Similarly, Milton Glaser, the pathbreaking graphic designer who created the original "I♥NY" in 1977, was inspired to create a new logo and slogan for the city after 9/11, one that could capture some of the feelings of those New Yorkers who had lived through this tragedy, as well as prospective visitors. This was "I♥NY More Than Ever," which took the original iconic logo and added a small black mark on the bottom left side of the heart, approximating the site on the island of Manhattan where the attacks took place. As he explained: "A powerful giant is one thing. A vulnerable giant is much more loveable. Once we realized how vulnerable we were, all these people's hearts just opened."[68] This campaign never became official—indeed it provoked the threat of a lawsuit from the Empire State Development Corporation (ESDC) for copyright infringement and was shut down. Nonetheless, its creation was in keeping with initial efforts endorsed by the ESDC, LMDC, and NYC & Co., for example, through the promotion of "quasi-spiritual tours," to bring people back to New York based on their desire to participate in a process of healing and to reaffirm their love for the city.

The epitome of this was the turn to "disaster tourism," a new tourism genre that had the effect of transforming the tourism map and narrative in both cities. In New York, tourists rarely traveled to Lower Manhattan for anything but a view atop the World Trade Center and trip to the Statue of Liberty; by 2002 the "ruins" and the surrounding financial district had become the city's major tourist destination. As one *New York Times* article proclaimed, "the fallen trade center site has done what it could not do when standing: turn the financial district into one of the city's top attractions."[69] The ESDC and LMDC helped to fund a multimillion dollar "Ground Zero Viewing Platform" on Church Street to accommodate the thousands of visitors and locals who traveled there to see the site; NYC & Co. included the many daily tours of the ruins in its listings and revamped its tourist brochures and website accordingly. Lower Manhattan marketing became second only to Midtown in resources, while images of the cleanup, rebuilding, and neighborhood solidarity struck a new, poignant note.

The impact on the tourist experience of post-Katrina New Orleans was equally profound. By 2007, every major tour company across a broad spectrum of genres offered some type of Hurricane Katrina-related tour.[70] The proliferation of disaster tours had profound effects on the standard New Orleans tourism narrative, which emphasized New Orleans customs, traditions, food, and architecture in a heavily nostalgic fashion, harkening back to a romanticized history of the antebellum period. In particular, New Orleans's purported "exceptionalism" as a culturally hybridized, polyglot, and racially mixed city was celebrated, thus eliding complex histories of exclusion and inequalities based in race and class.[71] This was reinforced by a cartography that focused on relatively affluent areas—the French Quarter, Warehouse District, and Garden District—while avoiding poor and disproportionately African American neighborhoods such as the Lower Ninth Ward. The latter neighborhood was heavily impacted by the storm and became a primary destination for disaster tourists, thus challenging the racial imaginary of New Orleans. As cultural historian Lynnell Thomas has put it: "At the very least, this spatial rerouting of the tourist map" forced visitors to "physically and psychically confront both the presence and absence of African Americans in the city."[72]

Eventually, however, urban rebranding efforts and campaigns completely jettisoned the disaster frame, and appeals to compassion and solidarity were replaced by declarations of full recovery, emphasizing resilience and redevelopment. These recalibrations were made largely in response to studies by market research firms and crisis communications consultants who convinced both cities that emphasizing the disasters could deter the city's most valued demographics. Focus group research by D. K. Shifflet and Associates showed the Bloomberg administration that its patriotic rhetoric was wearing thin among wealthy business travelers and corporations considering relocation.[73] Even slight reference to national symbols, let alone emphasis on the actual events of 9/11, made New York City appear "desperate" and repelled these affluent and highly coveted target markets.[74]

A similar concern was raised by New Orleans in response to early studies by Weber Shandwick in 2007 and Boston Consulting in 2008, which showed that reference to Katrina would contribute to a sense of "unending crisis." This was compounded by the downturn in the national economy in 2008 and the BP oil spill in April 2010. "I think what we're seeing now is the national economy has impacted our industry and it has created a sense of nervousness," remarked Doug Thornton, senior vice president of SMG, the company that operates the Superdome and the New Orleans Arena for the state of Louisiana, in April 2009.[75] "[A]ll the brand damage that we are suffering in Louisiana this summer with the [BP] spill is devastating," remarked NOMCVB president, Stephen Perry in June 2010. "It [is] urgent for us to move forward."[76] By 2010, marketers sought to move away from "brand mitigation campaigns" altogether, whether involving reference to Hurricane Katrina or the BP oil spill.

The shift to banish the stigma of disaster showed in the way the cities dealt with their disaster sites, and the conflicts over this. In New York, marketers of the World Trade Center's ruins factionalized into the "pile fetishizers" seeking to package pilgrimages to Ground Zero and the "pile minimizers" seeking to downplay the tragedy and focus on New York's victorious spirit. Already by 2002, the latter group had won out, convincing the city to avoid emotional references to the events of 9/11 in its marketing of the city.[77]

Similar factionalization occurred in the New Orleans Lower Ninth Ward neighborhood. During the first several years after the flooding, tour guides carefully designed their bus tours to present visitors with images of damage and destruction along with images of renewal and rebuilding, such as the revitalization of several blocks of the neighborhood with homes built by actor Brad Pitt's Make It Right (MIR) Foundation. The juxtaposition of ruin and recovery was strategic and methodical. The troubling experience of visiting the Lower Ninth Ward and viewing the destruction was neatly resolved through presentation of the MIR homes as beacons of hope and optimism. By 2012, the number of bus tours was dwindling due to growing resident opposition and increased enforcement of a city ordinance passed in 2006 banning tour buses in the Lower Ninth Ward.

Also by this time, many tour guides were attempting to shift visitors' focus away from Hurricane Katrina altogether. Tom Nagelin, president of the Tour Guides Association of Greater New Orleans, noted that his tours avoided the Lower Ninth Ward. Voicing a position becoming mainstream within the city's tourism and city marketing agencies, he put it plainly: "We're tired of hearing about Katrina. We want to move on as a city. My tours focus on cuisine, art and architecture—not hurricanes."[78]

One sees this drive to exorcise representations of destruction most dramatically during the major commemorations for 9/11 and Katrina—that is, the five- and ten-year anniversaries that once again attracted national and international media attention to New York and New Orleans. While the cities' immediate post-disaster framing couldn't have been more different—one becoming a site of national pride, the other of national shame—the effort on the part of elected officials, philanthropists, and marketers to move on from mournful memorials and toward celebratory monuments couldn't have been more similar. Art historian Arthur Danto, writing about the Vietnam Veterans Memorial, analyzed the important distinction between these two forms of commemoration: "Monuments commemorate the memorable and embody the myths of beginnings. Memorials ritualize remembrance and mark the reality of ends....The memorial is a special precinct, extruded from life, a segregated enclave where we honor the dead. With monuments we honor ourselves."[79] The monuments to 9/11 and Katrina were not the war monuments Danto imagined and did not take the classic form of obelisk or statue. Rather, they were to be found in the buildings that rose from the rubble of disaster, like the proverbial phoenix from the ashes—whether iconic skyscrapers in Lower Manhattan or imaginatively designed, brightly colored homes in the Lower Ninth Ward.

In essence, the branded monument to 9/11 and Katrina—in functional if not literal terms—was *urban redevelopment* itself. The commemoration of the fifth anniversary of the Hurricane Katrina disaster in New Orleans, held August 29, 2010, was a case in point. Whereas the national news media emphasized the still-devastated Lower Ninth Ward and the failure of government policy at multiple scales, local commemorative events sought to recast the city as a site of extraordinary "recovery" and "resilience," using a code that was firmly forward facing, uplifting, and fixated on physical signs of growth. Mayor Mitch Landrieu, standing in a refurbished Marriott Hotel ballroom, celebrated the New Orleanians who "stood up and took the future into their hands, house by house, neighborhood by neighborhood, community by community." Five years after Katrina, Landrieu proclaimed that the spirit of determination was as strong as ever: "The singular message to the nation and to the rest of the world is: We're here. We're unbowed. We're unbroken.... And we will continue to move forward in our recovery step by step, not looking backward, but looking toward the city that we can create."[80] The evidence of revival was found in rebuilt neighborhoods, schools, and, especially, tourist destinations, all of which symbolized the "can-do" spirit of New Orlenians.

City boosters went so far as to speak of a "New Orleans Miracle" that offered lessons for the rest of the country. As Michael Hecht, president and CEO of Greater New Orleans, Inc. (GNO, Inc.), put it: "We are sitting in the middle of one of the greatest urban revivals of our lifetime.... There is a real lesson in rebirth and recovery here for the entire nation. All you have to do is believe in miracles."[81] If New Orleans could emerge from such a catastrophe with new opportunities for profitable economic development, Hecht seemed to say, so too could the United States at the height of recession.

The tenth anniversary of 9/11 in New York City elicited similar declarations of resilience by leaders from around the city and the nation. On the one hand, while the events themselves were far from conflict free,[82] a patriotic code of remembrance was revived and prevailed in the news media. There was the flag-lined, multibillion dollar World Trade Center Memorial and Museum, completed just days before the ceremonies and the shots of former President Bush standing alongside President Obama, emphasizing a patriotism that transcended politics: "Debates about war and peace, about security and civil liberties, have often been fierce these last 10 years. But it is precisely the rigor of these debates, and our ability to resolve them in a way that honors our values and our democracy, that is a measure of our strength."[83]

Yet meanwhile, work was also being done to replace the backward gaze—mournful, condemnatory, or patriotic—with one looking triumphantly forward toward complete recovery. Like the "New Orleans Miracle" inaugurated five years after Katrina, New York City's effort was epitomized by "One World Trade Center," which, ten years later, while still only 50 percent complete, played a central role in the events. The gleaming, flag-draped, 11,000 square foot tower was presented as a monument to the victory of ambition and was intended to complete, even overshadow, the memorial at its base. Indeed, beyond the giant flag, overtly patriotic associations were avoided. Based on research conducted by Wordsearch, the U.K. based global real estate branding agency hired by the Port Authority to craft a new identity for the building, such associations, including the original "Freedom Tower" name chosen by architect Daniel Libeskind, sounded too "jingoistic" to prospective tenants and investors, many of whom were not from the United States and felt that the building should not be turned into a target.[84] This led to the renaming and reframing of the building to "One World Trade Center" to emphasize its "essential purpose": a proud display of ambition, power, and global city status.[85]

Phase II: Utopian Narratives

Within a scant year to two years after each disaster, a new proactive generation of post-disaster campaigns had set in, emphasizing urban resilience and signaling that New York and New Orleans had both permanently moved on. In this phase, the two cities came to employ a remarkably similar narrative and representational strategy, which we will refer to as that of *urban utopia*. With the partial exception of disaster tours and commemorative events, the disasters themselves—and all the complexities they stirred up—were largely erased. New campaigns presented cities that had not only recovered but had also been propelled into a transcendent and ideal urban future, leaving class, racial, and environmental troubles behind. Beneath the surface sparkle, these campaigns were more narratively complex and emotionally charged than standard city branding or immediate post-disaster rebranding—and were arguably more powerful as well. With recent history as backdrop, they responded implicitly and subtextually to the disaster-linked themes mentioned above: concern for the survival of irreplaceable urban qualities and desire for solidarity and mutual aid across lines of race and class. At the explicit level of the text itself, meanwhile, new campaigns focused on the opportunity, now apparently realized, to experience and consume a *better*, even *ideal*, city created out of the ashes of the old.

Another key aspect of this new representational universe was its geographic and scalar dimension. In both cases, branding campaigns were created to reimagine cities reshaped and remapped as a result of crisis and redevelopment. This reimaging involved the creation of a citywide brand umbrella that could be applied to the new urban landscape. Related to this, "sub-brands" were created to apply to particular neighborhoods targeted for redevelopment—such as "Downtown New Orleans," "New Lower Manhattan," and Chinatown. Thus, multiscalar urban rebranding and commodification of space was occurring in a highly rationalized fashion, with efforts made to ensure that framing at all scales represented unity and diversity simultaneously.

The production of these relatively complex utopian and multiscalar imaginaries required significant creative labor. This was harnessed via a "creative revolution" in city marketing in both cities—one reminiscent of similar upheavals in post-crisis corporate marketing, as well as in previous rounds of post-crisis urban rebranding.[86] There was a "shakeup" of the workforce at NYC & Co., NOMCVB, and NOTMC, all of which replaced older advertising firms in favor of young, avant-garde talent. The hope was that the private-sector experience and "youth cultural capital" of the new talent would enable them to tap into the zeitgeist of a new generation and demonstrate the city's vigorous tourism and business climate—and so confound the predictions of demise that haunted the new vision. NYC & Co. created the new position of creative director (CD) and hired a recent star graduate of the Yale master of fine arts program to fill it. They also hired cutting-edge branding firms with experience in branding for mega-events and lifestyle media, like London-based Wolff Olins and New York City-based Two Twelve. In New Orleans, old guard ad firms were replaced with new local firms—Trumpet and Calliope Consulting—staffed with recent design school graduates.

Looking at the new crop of creative urban rebranding projects, we found two dominant utopian narratives shared across our cities, albeit in locally distinct ways. The first is that of *cultural diversity*—a revamped and heightened version of a longstanding narrative. The second is what we identify as an entirely new narrative for both cities, that of *greening* and *sustainability*.

As with most influential and resonant concepts, the discursive and semi-otic power of these terms lies in their denotative simplicity and connotative elasticity, allowing room for vastly different interpretations and articu-lations.[87] Over the past two decades, both sets of polysemous terms have emerged as discursive devices that test extremely well across broad cross-sections of potential place consumers, from visitors to home buy-ers to corporate relocators, as well as among affluent demographics across lines of race and nationality. In the context of the post-crisis moment, they are used to respond to particular anxieties and aspirations—yet, we would argue, in contradictory ways. Here, utopian themes are deployed to frame and advance a process of uneven redevelopment—a process that, arguably, threatens the very diversity and sustainability they invoke.

Culture, Diversity, Urbanity

The merger of culture and diversity was the overriding theme of both New York City's first official post-9/11 tourist marketing campaign, "This is New York City," and of "Forever New Orleans." Here, "culture" was under-stood not as exclusive "High Culture," but rather as an inclusive popular culture rooted in local artistic forms, creative practices, and lifestyles. Campaigns celebrated local culinary, musical, and performative traditions as practiced by a broad mix of race, class, and ethnic identities, and includ-ing groups and practices not previously featured in city marketing, for instance, African Americans and hip-hop in New York and Hispanics and LGBT festivals in New Orleans. The use of culture was not new—indeed "culture-led development" had been a prevailing urban strategy since the 1980s.[88] It is also not an entirely "top-down" strategy; arguably, city agen-cies were catching up with a multicultural tourism trend started by grass-roots entrepreneurs and nonprofit organizations that sought to exploit the growing tourist trade by creating locally owned businesses in marginalized neighborhoods like Harlem and the Treme.[89] Yet here, in what we would argue is a post-crisis shift, ethnic and racial diversity and the neighbor-hoods that represent this were explicitly emphasized by official, centralized campaigns.

With a redeveloped city as the backdrop, these campaigns helped pro-duce a "post-race" and "post-class" understanding of diversity that rendered the term utopic, that is, transcending the inequalities, discriminatory prac-tices, uneven development, and social frictions with which race and class were once associated.[90] Indeed, the latter two terms were not used at all in the campaigns. Rather, diversity is represented primarily in neoliberal terms, that is, as a depoliticized form of cosmopolitanism and multiculturalism.[91]

Its historically rooted meaning in the United States as a pluralistic response to racial exclusion and racism was displaced and rendered obsolete—particularly in the "age of Obama." We found that the preferred mode of representation of the post-race and post-class city was that of montage—the seemingly infinite juxtaposition, listing, and mosaic of racialized aesthetic forms, sites, products, and experiences.

In this way, the two cities were also tapping into broader trends. Depoliticized, "cultural diversity" has proven quite useful in attracting a wide range of pleasure-seeking place consumers to redeveloped cities, particular in an era of expanding global mobilities. Marketers are savvy to the fact that international tourists explicitly seek authentic local cuisines and gritty urban experiences and are less prone to U.S.-based racial and ethnic prejudices.[92] Realtors have discovered that affluent overseas populations may be more inclined to buy expensive real estate in redeveloped neighborhoods when their language is spoken and familiar cultural products are nearby—that is, wealthy Chinese in New York's "new Chinatown" and the French in New Orleans's Faubourg Marigny.[93] And whether on a national or international level, branding coalitions understand that cultural diversity attracts new middle classes and elites—particular those in the coveted younger demographic seeking to put down roots. The latter increasingly seek to distinguish themselves through the eclecticism and multiculturalism of their taste.[94]

A first case in point is "NYC," a campaign designed in 2005–2006 by Wolff Olins, which, as mentioned above, became New York's first official logo for both external and internal marketing purposes. See figure 6.1. In stating the "ambition" for the campaign, Wolff Olins took a seemingly counterintuitive step (albeit one the firm had taken in a number of other city branding campaigns elsewhere).[95] They asserted that a fixed, monolithic identity for all New Yorkers was an impossible idea:

> There's only one New York City. But within that one city are five boroughs, approximately 191 neighborhoods, nearly a million buildings and over 8.2 million people. Each individual has their own New York. Within the mind of every single New Yorker resides a different version of New York City. It's a city loved in 138 different languages and viewed through an almost infinite mix of cultures, ideologies, and ways of life. Everyone living side by side. This kaleidoscopic quality is one of the greatest things about this city. It's the very thing we love. But it also makes it difficult to represent. There is no one symbol, no one logo or brand that means New York City to everyone.[96]

Rather, the very impossibility of isolating a single image of New York became the conceit of the campaign. It was a savvy and sensitive move that seemed to give voice to the consensus reached at myriad post-9/11 vision-ing sessions. The solution they found was the following:

> Wolff Olins made sturdy letterforms that are thick, rugged—a little on the tough side—just like a New Yorker. The mark is durable and will represent New York for a long time. And the mark functions as a window into infinite complexity. Imagine what you'd see peering in a typical masonry façade—perhaps a fashion designer, a recording engineer or someone crusading for social justice. Like a window this symbol can reveal images of every culture, profession and activity of this city. The NYC brand is a transparent pane of glass that offers a view of real New Yorkers and real NYC neighborhoods. It's a venue for the very ideas that make NYC strong—8 million brands.[97]

Making the subtlest possible reference to 9/11, the shape and weight of the letters emphasized the city's "toughness," "ruggedness," and "dura-bility"—thus responding affectively to the trauma of that event while also asserting the city's resilience. Meanwhile, in selling the mark to NYC & Co., Wolff Olins filled the bulky letterforms with a montage of "authentic," race- and class-diverse, New York-specific snapshots—including a chubby cop, white fashion models, and African American hip-hop performers, as seen in Figure 6.1.[98] If the sturdy proportions of "NYC" implicitly responded to 9/11 by assuring target markets of New York's toughness, their con-tents also transcended this history, invoking utopian visions of a post-crisis city. Here, the branding campaign explicitly celebrated New York's famed "diversity"—in the post-class, post-race, post-conflict sense that is typical of utopian fantasy.[99] Wolff Olins even referenced the city's "crusading for social justice" in their passionate rationale for the campaign.[100]

NYC & Co. ran with the Wolff Olins idea through their "This is New York City" campaign (see figure 6.2). With NYC's block logo in the bottom right corner, the campaign used whimsical, hand-drawn characters and iconic sites. Significantly, this approach also reframed the city historically and geo-graphically: scrambling the skyline such that the Empire State and Chrysler buildings stand next to the Brooklyn Bridge and Statue of Liberty and jux-taposing cultural references of multiple eras and genres—from Chinese New Year to the Mermaid Parade. Thus, the campaign transcended the still-scarred ground of Lower Manhattan and the recent past of 9/11.

Another innovative, utopian component of the campaign was the incor-poration of hip-hop and graffiti to sell the city. This was seen, for instance, in a new line of T-shirts evoking subway graffiti, with Day-Glo colors dripping from the black NYC logo like subway lines.[101] This might not seem a sur-prising move for a city aiming to attract the young—especially New York. Hip-hop—from rap, to mc'ing, to b-boying, to graffiti—was created by African American and Latino teenagers from the Bronx and Brooklyn at the

Figure 6.1
Composite of new "NYC" logo for post-9/11 New York rebranding
"NYC" was the first official logo developed for New York City in its history. Designed for NYC & Co. by Wolff Olins in 2005, these images show the original concept behind the logo. Bulky letterforms signaled the city's resilience in the face of past disaster, while cultural diversity provided edgy, future-facing, and utopian content. (*Source*: NYC & Co.)

Figure 6.2
"This is New York City" Campaign
Launched in 2006, this was NYC & Co.'s first post-9/11 tourism campaign, and the first to use the new "NYC" logo.
Whimsical illustrations celebrated cultural diversity and a utopian, inclusive post-crisis future. (*Source*: NYC & Co.)

height of the 1970s fiscal crisis and, over the course of the 1980s and 1990s, became the paradigm of global youth culture, essential to youth marketing as well as a magnet for "birthplace of hip-hop" tours to New York City. Yet New York's own city marketing agencies never before incorporated the art form nor invoked this moniker. To the contrary, they saw graffiti as a crime and the other three hip-hop elements tarred by association. The hostility dated to the 1970s when subway graffiti gained publicity in the press and, branding coalitions believed, reified an image of New York as an "asphalt jungle" run by lawless teenagers that precipitated an image crisis for the city.[102] Yet the newly hired creative team at NYC & Co. appreciated that the hip hop aesthetic could reach demographics "anywhere from teenagers to 30-somethings," and could also easily be delinked from this conflictual local history. In an article on the t-shirts Wong "dismissed the notion that [NYC t-shirts] might have been inspired by graffiti, which as of this writing, remains illegal," instead reducing the campaign to aesthetics: "colors overlap or forms overlap as a representation of that mixing of different cultures or different times."[103] Such campaigns—like broader branding efforts—harnessed a racialized urban imaginary, with all its friction but none of its fangs, to make New York appear resilient, youthful, and reborn in a new era.

In New Orleans, the urban imaginary of tourism marketing had long been multiracial and polyglot, yet focused primarily on "traditional"—that is, antebellum—Cajun, Creole, and white southern arts and culture, as well as classic New Orleans jazz. "Forever New Orleans" broke new ground by emphasizing the city's more diverse demographics—with particular inclusion of Asians—as well as its contemporary, "experimental" arts and culinary scene. Here is how one tourism official expressed the city's new montage of culture and diversity in an interview:

> [A] main theme in our work of branding the city had to do with the cultural renaissance the city was experiencing. The palpable energy of rebuilding that visitors' embrace. Explosion of new restaurants and culinary experimentation was taking place in neighborhoods across the city, ranging from high-end eateries such as Sylvain to neighborhood eateries like Dat Dog. John Besh is one of the celebrity chefs that the city rallied around to illustrate the culinary boom. *And a big part of this story-line was how the scene was diversifying.* New Orleans food is not just Cajun and Creole. It is Vietnamese Fanco, sushi, gastro pubs, and mixologist driven cocktails. We also emphasized the diversity of the art scene, for example, St. Claude Arts District, Prospects 1, 1.5, and 2, the Music Box by Swoon. We also stress the diversification going on in the dance movement and jazz. Young jazz artists such as Meshiyea Lake and the Little Big Horns, Trombone Shorty, Shamarr Allen. They represent the next generation of New Orleans Jazz. A new spin on an old idea.[104]

Montage techniques juxtaposed not only an array of diverse cultures, but historical periods and geographic sites as well. Again, despite the appearance of inclusivity, they did so selectively and strategically. They linked an avant-garde cultural future with an idealized historic past, and old tourist districts with new, "up-and-coming" (i.e., gentrified) neighborhoods. Meanwhile, as in New York, New Orleans leapfrogged over the disaster period as well as over still-devastated areas and poorer, less desirable destinations (see figure 6.3a, 6.3b, 6.3c). In so doing, these post-crisis campaigns provided a mechanism for both reframing and remapping the two cities.

A short commercial created for "This is New York City" exemplifies this aesthetic work. With the soundtrack of Billy Strayhorn's "Take the A-Train" lilting in the background, the commercial features recently landed tourists—a white American mother and daughter looking out their cab window at a Manhattan skyline that has been transformed through animation into bobbing lipsticks, ice cream cones, and Coney Island Ferris wheels. Jazz-era jubilance is invoked through clips of the Rockettes dancing and saxophone players swinging atop Midtown spires, while biplanes fly in circles overhead.[105] Similar alchemy was achieved through the New Orleans campaigns "Fall in Love All Over Again" and "Forever New Orleans." Both encouraged visitors and investors to associate the city's "most celebrated and historic core" with a thriving and cutting-edge future, in part by expanding this core to include new destinations like the "revitalized Warehouse and Arts District," a.k.a "the Soho of the South"[106]

The campaigns thus visually and affectively linked contemporary cultural consumption with a timeless, pre-crisis past—and so eclipsed poorer urban areas and communities ostensibly less historical and celebrated. Through playful montage, city marketers borrowed the emotional charge of the Jazz Age in both cities, and in the case of New York City, hip hop as well, while maintaining a safe distance from these genres' critical edge. They sought to exorcise the ghosts of one city under attack and another under water through these utopian, post-racial narratives. Thus, branding campaigns responded to the anxieties and desires of crisis while turning New York City and New Orleans into a consumer paradise once again.

Clean and Green: Discourses of Sustainability in Crisis Cities

Crises inspire the search for "perception-changing" marketing devices that can attract big business and affluent residents without undermining key aspects of the city's brand. Both New York and New Orleans achieved this, in part, through expanded marketing of local culture and authenticity and with this, increased emphasis on cultural diversity. Yet cultural diversity was, to a large extent, familiar territory for the two cities. Although reassuring to apprehensive travelers and investors—particularly given its new post-racial and post-political framing—this revamped version of culture was not sufficiently perception changing to overcome the negative associations of disaster and so to rebrand the two cities as post-crisis.

Figure 6.3
Composite of "Forever New Orleans" for post-Katrina NOLA rebranding
Tourism officials in New Orleans designed the "Forever New Orleans" campaign to overcome negative perceptions of the city using ironic and sarcastic themes meant to celebrate the city's "sprit of swagger." Like the rebranding of New York City, the goal was to counter negative images of urban crisis, disaster, and destruction by promoting a vision of cultural resilience. As shown above, the rebranding campaign featured several print ads and photographs of various New Orleansesque scenes emblazoned with satirical slogans to neutralize people's doubts about the recovery of the city.
Source: New Orleans Metropolitan Convention and Visitors Bureau.

To alter perceptions and reinvigorate their brands, we argue, the two cities developed what for them was a new tactic: combining the marketing of culture with the marketing of "nature," with the latter understood in terms of the "sustainability" and "greening" of urban development. These concepts were increasingly viewed as competitive indicators of modern urban lifestyle and governance in other parts of the United States and globally—for example, in western states like California and Oregon as well as in northern Europe and China. Yet such concepts had not historically been embraced by nor associated with either city. To the contrary, both cities had earned reputations, deserved or not, as decidedly unsustainable.

In the post-disaster environment, however, marketing officials discovered that focusing on a clean, green urban discourse dramatically "flipped the script" on the public's perception of the cities and their ability to respond to crisis. With this, ironically, came the realization that post-crisis redevelopment can offer a competitive advantage in terms of urban brand value. This is because cities can and do exploit their post-disaster condition to argue that, compared to competitor cities, their process of sustainability planning and innovation 'from the ground up' will be more transformative as well as more high profile and in the news, thus offering investors, corporations, and the city itself a brand-enhancing opportunity. Whether using a human-centric narrative of a post-disaster "clean slate" followed by rational rebuilding or a nature-centric narrative of ecological collapse followed by organic and cyclical new growth, disasters provide an unusual opportunity for sustainable urban marketing campaigns. The branding coalition in New York had all of this in mind when, in 2008–2012, they rapidly embraced the discourse of urban sustainability and, within their broader post-crisis utopian imaginary, elevated it to a new level.

"Sustainability" is a utopian concept in the sense that it points to an ideal future state in which a balance between environmental, economic, and social needs has been achieved, and in which the planet has been liberated from environmental, economic, and social conflicts and constraints. In association with urban development, discourses of sustainability advanced through a series of international commissions and conferences as well as grassroots activism beginning in the late 1980s in response to an understanding that mounting environmental, economic, and social crises were linked, at the local and global scale.[107] By the late 1990s, sustainability had become a new, if contested, common sense in global policy circles. At the same time, the corporate sector and marketing consultants began to embrace the term, in conjunction with a new and potentially profitable movement in green industry, design, and consumption, as well as the development of socially responsible investment indicators and the correlation of the latter to brand valuation and equity. This sudden embrace may be viewed as an effort to de-link critique of the environmental crisis—and related economic and social crises—from that of capitalism more broadly. Indeed the sustainability of capitalism in the face of these crises, and specifically of real estate markets, became a central aim. Thus, similar to "diversity," "sustainability" became a market-oriented discourse: culturally resonant, retaining a flavor of its radical past, yet fundamentally depoliticized.[108]

In this context, cutting-edge entrepreneurial cities and regions, habituated as they were to adapting to the private-sector vogue, began to use urban sustainability frameworks as part of broader efforts at attracting new industries and the creative class. The "conceptual travels" of urban sustainability was pushed by a range of powerful actors: the local real estate industry, wishing to reap the 35 percent mar-up possible with LEED Gold Star certification; marketing consultants like McKinsey and Co. and Boston Consulting Group, which began issuing urban sustainability reports, rankings, metrics, and guides; and international bodies like the International Olympics Committee, which obliged cities submitting bids to include sustainability as an aspirational principle in development and marketing plans. Cities wishing to market themselves as modern, global cities felt increasingly compelled to make use of the concept.[109]

Like the many cities adopting such policies in the face of mounting risks, New York and New Orleans were also motivated by rational, parochial concerns: the fact that sound urban environmental policies had long been advocated by citizens groups and social movements, the vulnerabilities revealed by recent disasters, and hence the urgency of sustainability for local industries, residential communities, ecosystems, and long-term development plans. Yet, as our cases also reveal, interurban competition, and the opportunity the disasters presented to reposition both cities and gain a "sustainable edge," was also a deciding factor.

The relevance of this approach to crisis cities became apparent in New York City after 9/11. Powerful private-sector players had already been advocating a market-oriented approach to sustainability prior to the crisis. Specifically, Daniel Doctoroff, who was to become deputy mayor under Bloomberg, first became aware of the concept through his role as leader of the private sector "NYC 2012" committee bidding for the Olympics, launched in 2000, when the committee faced the International Olympic Committee requirement of framing the "sustainable legacy" of the games on a citywide scale.[110] To the committee, this was an easy case to make. The Olympics would provide the opportunity for changes to urban infrastructure, amenities like parks and bike paths, and iconic new architecture that powerful businesses in Midtown had long sought for themselves and their employees. In this sense, the Olympics would be sustainable environmentally as well as in terms of the future needs of local industries in real estate and finance.

After 9/11, once Doctoroff and Bloomberg took office and after New York City lost its Olympic bid, the citywide ambitions of this plan were channeled in new directions.[111] First, this manifest as the "5-boro development plan," geared toward rezoning one hundred neighborhoods and developing central business districts in all five boroughs. After winning his third term, Bloomberg rebranded this plan in greener terms as the "long-range sustainability vision," called "PlaNYC 2030." To effectuate the new plan, the deputy mayor hired Two Twelve, the branding firm that designed the Olympic bid, working in conjunction with the EDC and gathering data collected by the consulting firm McKinsey and Co. through focus groups with environmental organizations and businesses.

PlaNYC was, like its predecessor, essentially a growth plan, but now was geared toward managing this growth. It was premised on the fact that New York was going to grow by 1 million people within the decade, a fact with no basis in existing demographic prognostics, yet envisioning the scale of urbanization that would be necessary to sustain such imagined growth. It was not a real plan produced by the Department of City Planning; rather, it produced "the aura of a plan," using fonts and layouts and a blue color scheme to make it look like an "official blueprint."[112] In this sense, it was a powerful perception-changing document: showing a future, ecotopian New York City liberated from traffic congestion and grime, with greenways linking the New Lower Manhattan to the five boroughs, and with a skyline of luxury and LEED-certified office and residential buildings on par with any other global city.

Thus, the post-crisis benefits of sustainability marketing were fully realized. As the EDC senior vice president explained: "If you think of a city as being sustainable and green, you think of it as cleaner, safer, friendlier—it does a lot to undermine negative perceptions of the city, whether from the media world or from the events of the day." The senior vice president continued: "If you are going to be moving big businesses with all of their upper level employees, you have to show them that their kids will be provided for, that they're going to be able to breathe clean air, ride their bikes somewhere.... It works really well for us, in everything we do, to have this kind of reputation."[113] This helps explain PlaNYC's rather contradictory graphics, showcasing park space at the base of newly built skyscrapers. In highly resonant if indirect ways, sustainability rebranding communicates that the city is open for business and has risen above the past trauma and future risk of crisis.

Similar framing processes are apparent in New Orleans where political and economic elites have attempted to link the discourse of sustainability with the promotion of market-centered notions of free enterprise, entre-preneurial city governance, deregulation of industry, and renewed calls for generous capital subsidies and tax incentives for "green" business growth. Since 2007, the mayor's office, the chamber of commerce, Greater New Orleans (GNO), Inc., and other organizations have attempted to rede-fine New Orleans as place of "clean" industry, including art-based com-merce, biotechnology, and film and media production. The formation of the "Green Committee" of the New Orleans Chamber of Commerce in 2011 reflects an interest in developing sustainability strategies; increasing business-to-business relationships; raising the profile of green commerce in New Orleans; and assisting "New Orleans businesses to build local politi-cal support for the green industries while elevating our reputation on the regional and national stage."[114] In recent years, the NOMCVB created a meeting planner resources guide and assembled information on greening efforts and other ecofriendly attractions from the City of New Orleans and the local hospitality community.[115]

In 2011, GNO Inc. unveiled its "Sustainable Industries Initiative" (SII), aimed at rebranding Southeast Louisiana the "Silicon Valley" of environ-mental solutions. GNO, Inc.'s sustainability initiative seeks to diversify the economy by "developing sustainable services" that "will help companies not only manage environmental issues but even profit from them (e.g., waste-to-energy technology)."[116] In addition, the SII attempts to "catalyze business activity within sustainable industries by leveraging the regional assets." These assets include, for example, "federal, state and local incen-tives available to sustainable businesses in the Greater New Orleans region." Sustainability's potential as a catalyst for economic growth lies in cultivat-ing what GNO, Inc. calls a "sustainable entrepreneurial culture" premised on the use of "green incentives" to spur development and target businesses that specialize in water management/hydrology, sustainable building, renewable energy, coastal restoration, and disaster mitigation. Green incen-tives include tax credits, tax exemptions, and enterprise zones to "make the region an ideal place to build sustainable technologies, products and services."[117] "There's no question the New Orleans area has an experience and a brand that is inextricably linked to the environment," according to Michael Hecht, president and CEO of GNO, Inc. "We have an opportunity to leverage that brand and that experience."[118]

Symbolically and affectively, "sustainability" helps to connect anxiety-ridden post-crisis landscapes and real estate markets to stable, secure ecomodernist futures. The term provides a facelift for cities that might otherwise be considered risky investments due to ongoing threats like climate change and terrorism. This rearticulation of sustainability was also an instance of discursive depoliticization. As in the case of "diversity," which emerged out of earlier waves of political and cultural activism, the sustainability cosncept was previously linked to environmental social movements as well as to slow growth, ecological, and/or social justice-oriented critiques. Here, it was rearticulated with tech-futurist and market-oriented urbanization for leading global cities and regions. And so it became a key discursive tool in countering post-disaster image crisis and rebranding crisis cities so as to enable them to compete globally for tourists, investment, and new talent.

CONCLUSION

Post-crisis redevelopment in New York and New Orleans has been as much about accumulating brand value as about rebuilding storm and flood defense systems, restoring business districts, and repopulating neighborhoods. Indeed, we argue, these processes of redevelopment and rebranding are integrally intertwined and mutually reinforcing. Such conjoined efforts reflect strategic decisions in the midst of potential image and economic crisis to mobilize culture, finance capital, and public policy in a synergistic way. The goal and outcome is to protect and enhance property and commercial values for business and real estate owners and to provide political capital for governing agencies. Such large-scale efforts merge tourism and economic development marketing and use tax breaks, rezoning, and deregulation to speed the transformation of the built environment to more faithfully reflect the urban imaginary of brand campaigns. To do so, these campaigns create new cross-promotional networks and political coalitions among entrepreneurial city and state agencies, public-private partnerships, and the creative industries. In addition, transnational consultancies are increasingly employed by local branding campaigns to teach best practices for market-oriented growth, while elevating the status of cities for the purpose of interurban competition—thus contributing to the production and dissemination of the urban brands themselves.

The proliferation of urban branding strategies and campaigns expresses a profound preoccupation, growing since the 1970s, with the use of imagery, rhetoric, and symbols to manage perceptions of cities. Indeed, the increasing financial support of city marketing campaigns in New York and New Orleans, together with neoliberal reforms like austerity, privatization, deregulation, and pro-business incentives, suggests that city leaders are more concerned with reimagining and redesigning urban space for visitors, investors, and real estate developers than for the city's own inhabitants. Certainly this branding strategy produces benefits for inhabitants, such as jobs in tourism, construction, and security, and the creation of urban amenities that both tourists and residents can enjoy. Yet it also produces significant costs, such as gentrification and displacement, cuts to vital social services, and, when linked to a broader free-market ideology, a weakened hand for organized labor.

The shift to urban branding has come in fits and starts over this forty-year period, catalyzed by periodic crises, as new campaigns and alliances have mobilized amid the chaos and consensus of those extraordinary moments. Today, city agencies that were once dedicated separately to the promotion of local attractions for visitors or to the creation of incentives for business retention, attraction, and the development of city-owned land, have moved toward coordinated efforts driven by the interests of global investors in finance, real estate, tourism, and entertainment. These conjoined branding efforts aim to distinguish entire cities as unique and valuable commodities in a national and global marketplace. In so doing, they seek not only to change popular perceptions but also to transform the urban-built environment.[119]

Our analysis of the cases of New York City and New Orleans allow us to draw further conclusions about the dynamics—both material and cultural—that drove this shift on the ground in the immediate years following crisis. Processes of urban rebranding—in particular, the production and circulation of post-crisis brand values—have been invigorated by new infrastructure, technology, and funding as well as aesthetic innovation and the incorporation of new narratives and imagery. The latter includes a move from memorials to monuments, featuring redeveloped neighborhoods and iconic architecture as metonyms for urban resilience and global competitiveness. Over the longer term, these narratives have encompassed broader utopian and post-crisis themes of cultural diversity and environmental sustainability. These inspirational and uplifting notions respond to the solidarities, imaginations, and affective experiences sparked in the aftermath of crisis. Yet, as we've observed, the discourse of diversity and sustainability that post-crisis urban rebranding constructs is a nominal one, which decontextualizes and erases normative references to social justice, equity, environmentalism, and democratic inclusion. Once appropriated by public private growth coalitions, diversity and sustainability are rearticulated and redeployed, ironically, to legitimize the exclusivity and class-specific pleasures of the rebranded city.

CHAPTER 7

Conclusion: Lessons in the Wake of Crisis

"God gave Noah the rainbow sign/no more water but fire next time"
—American spiritual[1]

One of the central premises of our book has been that urban crises lay bare the underlying power structures, long-neglected injustices, and unacknowledged inequalities of contemporary cities. Moreover, such crises reveal certain forms of decision-making and organized action that tend to go unnoticed when everyday routines are stable and secure. These painful yet revelatory periods have the potential to create *radical ruptures*—opportunities to experience events collectively, build new solidarities, rethink the status quo, and, through a democratic process of urban redevelopment, imagine ways to build a future, post-crisis city on a more just, equitable, and sustainable foundation. And yet just as crises uncover submerged disparities and catalyze demands for change, so too can they reproduce and greatly exacerbate these disparities, serving as legitimating "states of exception" for elites to expand their power. Here, too, the process of redevelopment can be instrumental, enabling emboldened growth coalitions to extend their influence and realize long-held ambitions to rebuild the city in their own image—architecturally, infrastructurally, culturally, and in class terms.

All of these potential outcomes, the radical and the revanchist, were realized in the multiyear process of urban rebuilding and redevelopment following the 9/11 and Katrina disasters. The two cities that were built on the ashes of the old represent in myriad ways these hopes, solidarities, conflicts, and ongoing struggles. The fruits of these struggles, for the time being, have gone overwhelmingly to the powerful and have served to exacerbate inequality and crisis tendencies. It is our hope that a critical and comparative reassessment of dynamics in these cities, and others like them elsewhere, can be helpful in creating a different set of outcomes for the urban crises that are to come. We think of these future crises in terms or what James Baldwin once called, in reference to the classic spiritual, and wisely anticipating the urban uprisings of the late 1960s, "the fire next time."[2] If we do not learn from the flood, the fire will follow. In this concluding chapter, we highlight the main findings of the text and discuss how and why we think redevelopment trends in New York and New Orleans matter for other cities, and future crises, in the United States and around the world.

CRISIS-DRIVEN URBANIZATION

We have developed the theoretical framework of *crisis-driven urbanization* to help conceptualize the historic, spatial, and environmental dynamics that precede and are set in train by contemporary modes of uneven post-disaster redevelopment. This framework is premised on the basic assumption that disasters need not lead to large-scale crises, and that whether or not they do depends on the broader contexts in which they occur. In the case of New York and New Orleans, and a great many cities like them today, this context is one of market-oriented or "neoliberal" urbanization, uneven development, and what we have come to call uneven landscapes of risk and resiliency. All of these dynamics emerged out of previous rounds of crisis and redevelopment and, by not resolving the contradictions within this preexisting context, have similar effects in new rounds of crisis and redevelopment. In short, a market-oriented and uneven approach to redevelopment, however justified it may seem in the face of crisis, helps generate new landscapes of inequality and risk, and with them, yet greater potential for and vulnerability to future crisis. We have studied the 9/11 and Hurricane Katrina disasters through this analytic framework, revealing the contentious dynamics of uneven redevelopment as well as their powerful, catalytic role in processes of capitalist urbanization more broadly.

Within this framework, we have conceptualized "crises" in two distinct yet interrelated ways: as historic *events* and as discursive *frames*. As events, we understand crisis as a form of social breakdown, destabilization, and rupture triggered by sudden disasters, while always interwoven with preexisting contradictions and new forms of political intervention. These historic moments of rupture cannot be acted upon, however, without discursive frames, which enable political and economic elites and other organized interests to assess causality, attribute blame, and define "recovery." Through use of these frames, different kinds of post-crisis interventions are either legitimized or contested. As we have documented throughout the book, the questions of *who* does the framing, and within what broader historical and local context, is enormously consequential. The frames created by powerful actors play a major role in constructing "deserving" versus "undeserving" recipients of aid and targeting particular areas for rebuilding over others. As we saw in the case of urban re-branding campaigns, disaster frames also help legitimize this uneven redevelopment process, and so lay the ground for long-term trajectories of urbanization.

As explored in Chapters 1 and 3, the framing of the terrorist attacks of 9/11 as an "act of war" led to the public celebration of the victims of the 9/11 disaster as national heroes, which in turn led to many contradictory impacts. Most famously, it aided the Bush White House in launching a "global war on terror," despite broad-based opposition, and the fact that Iraq had nothing to do with the attacks. At the same time, New York's patriotic framing helped overcome conservative antipathy towards the city and opposition to the securing of an unprecedented amount of disaster aid—$32 billion, or 50 percent more than any previous disaster—in the form of Community Development Block Grants (CDBGs) and spatially targeted Private Activity Bonds (PABs), dubbed "Liberty Bonds."

In some ways, the framing and response to Hurricane Katrina represents a contrast to the 9/11 case. Conservative politicians, think tanks, and the mainstream media framed this storm as a natural rather than man-made disaster. They also framed Katrina's victims as refugees, akin to persons outside their own country, rather than national heroes. The mostly poor and nonwhite residents who could not afford to flee ahead of the storm were depicted as antisocial, deviant, and unworthy of national concern, invoking deep-rooted American narratives of race-based citizenship. This finding resonates with those of a great number of disasters, such as Eric Klinenberg's poignant analysis of the deadly 1995 Chicago heat wave, where explanations for the crisis offered by political officials and media outlets also laid blame on the victims for their irresponsible behavior.[3] Such portrayals helped legitimize the limited delivery of public aid and resources to New Orleans, placing the disproportionate burden of rebuilding on state and local governments and providing opportunities to private business to fill the breach. With some justification, many came to see 9/11 and Katrina as diametrically opposing cases—contrasting the generosity of the federal government when those in need include the white and wealthy, versus its stinginess when they were disproportionately black and poor.

Yet with the benefit of a broader time frame and more rigorous comparative analysis, we found this contrast led to a false dichotomy. Despite multiple differences—in the scale of rupture and initial frames of these two crises, in local demographics, and in the lobbying power of local growth coalitions—we found that both cities ultimately experienced quite similar forms of discrimination. This began with FEMA's initial disaster declaration following 9/11, which covered affected areas that were primarily wealthy and white—the Financial District and Tribeca—while excluding those that were majority working class and nonwhite—Chinatown and the Lower East Side. And it continued over the longer term, as poor neighborhoods in both cities were framed as a "tabula rasa," wiping away the particular histories of the two disasters and preparing the ground for more market-oriented rede-velopment. We argue that these unexpectedly similar outcomes following extreme difference in the immediate experience of disaster had to do with the longer-term dynamics of crisis-driven urbanization.

Particularly significant in our findings was the fact that New York City managed to not only secure an enormous package of recovery and redevel-opment funds but also the sweeping deregulation in how these funds were to be distributed and for what purpose. As explored in Chapter 4, "flexibil-ity" changes won for Lower Manhattan fundamentally transformed the fed-eral Community Development Block Grant (CDBG) and Private Activity Bond (PAB) programs from which the funds were derived, the original intent of which was to prioritize rebuilding in sites of greatest public benefit and to target aid to those who were lowest-income and hence most in need. Following 9/11, all provisions regarding "public benefits," "means-testing," and "public oversight" were waived—since, lobbyists argued, funds had to flow freely to disproportionately wealthy, financial sector victims, and be designed to incentivize private, market-rate real estate development. This ignored the impacts of the disaster on low-income residents and small businesses as well as the inequities this use of funds would generate. These sweeping waivers were then used as a precedent in the deregulation of aid for the entire Gulf Coast region following Katrina. The Gulf Opportunity (GO) Zone was modeled on the Liberty Zone for spatially targeted PAB tax relief, and the Louisiana Recovery Agency (LRA) became a conduit for CDBGs just as the Wall Street-backed Lower Manhattan Development Corporation (LMDC) did before it. Despite all of the differences men-tioned above—in the scale of the destruction, demographics of victims, and so on—few questioned whether a business-friendly tax, bond, and grant package designed for Lower Manhattan could be retrofitted for this vast, low-income region.

The similarity in these "flexibilities" and inequities helps explain the unfortunately similar outcomes experienced by the two cities. As explored in Chapter 5, redevelopment served to steer billions of dollars in public resources to industries, real estate developers, individual corporations, and already wealthy neighborhoods at the expense of low-income residents, small businesses, and poor neighborhoods, greatly exacerbating preexisting disparities. Thus "temporary" emergency responses like the Liberty Zone and the GO Zone, the LRA and LMDC, using the tax code and direct subsidies, produced long-lasting and deeply inequitable socio-spatial change, or what we refer to as *uneven redevelopment.*

The policies and regulatory strategies designed to rebuild New York City and New Orleans had a limited relationship to the damage and destruction unleashed by terrorist strike and levee breaches. As we argued in Chapter 2, both the vulnerability of particular communities to 9/11 and Katrina and the market-oriented logic of official responses to them were outgrowths of the political, economic, environmental, and socio-spatial contradictions associated with past forms of uneven development inherited from the fiscal crises of the 1970s. The ostensible "spatial fixes" to the latter for New York and New Orleans—the financialization of Manhattan and the urbanization of the wetlands in New Orleans—were vehicles of uneven development that spawned new crisis tendencies. These included urban disinvestment and poverty related crises, ecosystem collapse, and increased risk and vulnerability to hazards. By the time of the terrorist strike of 2001 and the levee breaches of 2005, both cities had been suffering from decades of such inequitable policy and planning. In New York, the concentration of FIRE activities, heightened fiscal austerity, and public-sector retrenchment that emerged during the 1970s and 1980s actually intensified vulnerability to future economic downturns. In New Orleans, the urbanization of the wetlands, flood insurance policies, and federal levee building actually intensified storm and flood risks throughout the metropolitan region.

A final contribution of our theory of crisis-driven urbanization has been to reveal the striking role of the state in these dynamics. The state is instrumental in the creative destruction of institutional, regulatory, and policy arrangements, out of which arise new coalitions, agencies, laws, and programs that have an enduring effect on the political field of the post-crisis city. Also significant is the role of the state in the reproduction of crisis itself. By engaging in patchwork reform rather than deep structural change, state interventions create a vicious cycle. "Old" policies and forms of development produce the conditions for crises that bring forth calls for "new" policies that, once implemented, create further contradictions and crises, a situation that then generates a new round of calls for "reform," and so on.

In both cities, urban disinvestment, deindustrialization, and the concentration of poverty meant that those most negatively affected by crises would be the poor and working class, thus institutionalizing the unequal distribution of risk within socio-physical space. These historic conditions have combined with the uneven redevelopment policies described above. Thus, we must understand both the prelude and aftermath of disaster, and the interactions between them, if we are to grasp how such different events in such different cities could create such similar and problematic outcomes.

NUANCING NEOLIBERALIZATION

Our project has embraced comparison not just as a method of analysis but as a mode of thought that can help us fashion new critical theories of urban transformation and take seriously the potential of a range of cities, social actors, and events to play a role in history. To this end, we have employed Charles Tilly's "encompassing" and "variation-finding" comparisons, which help scholars of history and social change to "make sense of social structures and process that never recur in the same form yet express common principles of causality."[4] In addition, we hope that our work might contribute to the ongoing "comparative turn" in geography, which has been so helpful, as Colin McFarlane says, "for revealing the assumptions, limits and distinctiveness of particular theoretical or empirical claims," and "for formulating new lines of inquiry and more situated accounts."[5] The possibility for challenging the status quo and building new theory has been particularly generative within urban geography, sociology, and related fields. Robert Beauregard' and Neil Brenner's concern that urban scholars move beyond boosterish and under-theorized notions of "superlative" or "prototypical" cities[6] is powerfully echoed by Jennifer Robinson's call for a "comparative gesture" in the study of cities. Hers is an invitation to consider a more nuanced, outward-looking, and inclusive research strategy than is typical within the single-city focus of self-identified schools (e.g., Chicago School, Los Angeles School, and so on) and the comparative but overly macro, hierarchical, and "northern" frameworks of leading "global cities" or "world systems" approaches.[7]

Such critical, comparative approaches freed us to better theorize the dynamics shaping our particular cities by identifying the significant processes, networks, and flows within which these cities are enmeshed. We now could analyze two cities—one "global" and the other "regional"—and two disasters—one "man-made" and the other "natural"—that, within earlier paradigms, would have been rendered incomparable. Probing more deeply into early evidence of a relationship between the two cities in their use of disaster aid, the comparative approach turned our attention to similarities and differences in their recent history and longer-term response, and led us to the discovery of common dynamics of pre- and post-crisis redevelopment.

These findings in turn helped us contribute to what we hope will be a more nuanced understanding of broader socio-spatial dynamics of neoliberal urbanization through which redevelopment is typically understood. First, rigorous comparative analysis confirmed our sense that neither New York City nor New Orleans—nor any other city—is a fixed arena or generic site on which the exogenous, singular, and inexorable forward march of neoliberalization produces "effects." Supporting theorists who argue for a "variegated" or even "exceptional" understanding of neoliberalism when situated in particular cultural, historical, and geographic contexts, we found that such factors all matter greatly.[8] In particular, we became attuned to how the particularities of place and time can create opportunities and constraints that shape and influence different urban outcomes, with special focus on the spatial dynamics of urban redevelopment.[9] As Lefebvre argued, cities and the urban and natural landscapes within and beyond them, at multiple scales, are continually produced and reproduced in and through the conscious and concerted actions of designers, movements, and the state, all of whom seek to represent their vision of the future through space.[10] Crucial to these spatial dynamics, we would argue, are the vagaries and contingencies of disasters and social upheavals and the crisis dynamics that they entrain. As a result, we see that the very nature of urban space, including how it is imagined, restructured, and put into relationship to other, equally dynamic spaces, has been in constant flux in conjunction with post-1970s forms of crisis-driven urbanization.

Thus, the study of urban crisis complicates generalizations about neoliberalization. We affirm the point made by Jamie Peck and Alan Tickell that neoliberalization "is neither monolithic in form nor universal in effect," but rather "exists in historically and geographically contingent forms" that are contradictory and prone to incessant regulatory crises and market breakdowns.[11] We would add to this the suggestion that the nature and dynamics of these crises and breakdowns should themselves become a focus of study. In short, place, history, and culture, as well as crisis, matter in the study of neoliberalism. Put another way, an analysis of the *why, where, and how* of neoliberalization will need to analyze particular dynamics and events at the urban scale to reveal how the process of neoliberal urbanization is fought out.

At the same time, and in dialectical fashion, we found that urban-scale transformations and battles had an impact on broader processes and scales of neoliberal urbanization. Our conceptualization of these dialectics was aided by Philip McMichael's method of "incorporating comparison," which points to ways in which local and extra-local processes of social change are mutually constituted.[12] Specifically, the formulation and ultimate implementation of "neoliberalized" disaster and urban policies, including those entailing privatization in disaster response, market-oriented re-regulation, and entrepreneurial economic development strategies, were the result of both top-down and bottom-up processes. Moreover, they occurred in response to a contingent event, set precedents, and had long-lasting impact on policy. Simply put, were it not for the local impact of 9/11 on Lower Manhattan as well as the power and newfound legitimacy of New York's elite coalitions, federal policymakers would not have had the opportunity to so dramatically "roll back" low-income targeting and benefits of the CDBG. And were it not for Katrina's massive devastation of New Orleans and the Gulf Coast, and the lack of power and legitimacy of the residents and workers impacted there, lawmakers would not have had the opportunity to then "roll out" new redevelopment policies on a far wider and more transformative scale—with the significant addition of privatized, anti-union disaster response as well as attacks on public housing.[13] This leads us to pose the possibility that, under the right circumstances, crisis cities have the potential to become particularly significant sites, or laboratories, for generating broader forms of neoliberalization globally. Thus, rather than making static claims that particular events or cities are paradigmatic, future comparative research should be focused on paradigmatic *processes* and *dynamics* that are emerging out of a range of cities, often "off the map" of mainstream urban research, yet that are transforming our increasingly interconnected urban world.[14]

Finally, our emphasis on contingency, agency, and social conflict suggests that trends and patterns of post-disaster recovery and rebuilding do not emerge out of an inevitable structural necessity or neoliberal logic, or preclude alternative futures. Nor do they predict a mechanical process of urban uprising and transformation. Rather, they develop in an indeterminate manner through the conscious and contested actions of individuals, organizations, and movements, within particular historical and spatial contexts. While neoliberalization may be understood as a broad, macrostructural trend, its local manifestations, and their limits, have to do with the interaction of preexisting social, cultural, and environmental conditions in particular places together with new political interventions—or what we have called the spatial politics of redevelopment. Even within the neoliberal heartland of the United States, the move toward market-oriented reform has not been an unchanging process producing homogeneous effects across diverse territories. Nor are local effects total. Rather, they generate uneven patterns of risk and resiliency, as well as evolving forms of crisis organizing, with diverse, volatile, and as yet unpredictable consequences. It is our hope that a better understanding of these dynamics can inform the creation of new politics. And if crisis cities are particularly significant sites of broader neoliberalization and social change, so too might be the politics that emerge in them.

QUESTIONING DISCOURSES OF URBAN RESILIENCE AND SUSTAINABILITY

A significant feature of post-disaster politics that emerged in the redevelopment process was a novel and near-exclusive focus on goals of resilience and sustainability, as pointed out in Chapters 5 and 6. Indeed, discourses of resilient and sustainable urbanization permeate public debates in New York and New Orleans to this day and have spread considerably farther afield. While these are important orienting concepts and political goals, it is vital to acknowledge the contradictions of redevelopment patterns and the continuing risks and vulnerabilities that both cities face—whether from ecological collapse, market downturns, or other unforeseen catastrophes. As we have pointed out in our chapters, this continuing risk is a result of the production of urban space itself, that is, uneven redevelopment that reproduces rather than redresses deep structural inequalities and socio-spatial vulnerabilities.

Our analysis highlights the fact that risk and recovery are neither static conditions nor objective states of an uncontested reality. Rather, both are power-laden concepts whose definition reflects bureaucratic decision-making processes and institutional actions related to the production and control of knowledge about cities and urban life. This point has been made in regard to risk by theorists like Ulrich Beck, who stated the matter succinctly: "Risk definition, essentially, is a power game."[15] That is, social, economic and political structures and movements construct risk, shape the territorial spread of risk, determine the impact and severity of risk, and can reduce risk through changes in public policies, socio-legal regulations, and other interventions.

The same could be said of resilience, a term that is fast becoming a dominant discourse in urban management circles, where it is embraced as a reassuring, quasi-biological, and depoliticized explanatory framework for guiding cities in the aftermath or face of disasters. Since the 1980s, ecologists and social scientists have applied a concept of "resilient adaptation," borrowed from the bionatural world and applied to social and built environments, to explain how all "systems" respond to traumatic events. Advanced by the Resilience Alliance through their journal *Ecology and*

Society, this "adaptive capacity" is seen as an essential characteristic of what are inherently resilient urban ecosystems. These systems are able to adapt to uncertainty and surprise; absorb recurrent disturbances; retain essential structures and processes; and build capacity for learning, improvement, and advancement over predisturbance conditions. In *Resilient City: How Modern Cities Recover From Disaster*, for example, it is argued that "although cities have been destroyed throughout history they have, in almost every case, risen again like the mythic phoenix."[16] Some of this thinking has come to influence analysis of our cases, as in economist Howard Chernick's *Resilient City: The Economic Impact of 9/11*, which maintains that the hardships of the 9/11 disaster were short-lived and New York has made a "strong recovery" based on its ability to absorb economic shocks, or Campanella's early and influential "Urban Resilience and the Recovery of New Orleans."[17] These approaches, while nuanced in many ways, presume the possibility of "total recovery," and to achieve this, privilege social capital and market solutions over explicitly political interventions.

A related if more varied discourse of "urban sustainability" has also arisen over the last forty years and become heavily associated with recovery from disasters of all kinds. The call for sustainability originated within environmentalist circles in the 1970s and then was popularized through its usage by the United Nations as an integrative social-economic-environmental development goal in the late 1980s.[18] Facing environmental strain as well as federal government inaction on climate change, urban managers and elites in the last decade, including major players in the "global city" network, have also embraced an urban sustainability framework. Yet the "environment" emphasized in this market-oriented version of sustainability is the competitive environment for capital, thus narrowing the definition and depoliticizing its usage.[19] Lifestyle amenities for the creative class, like bike paths, are privileged. Emphasis is placed on the heavily marketed urbanisms of "smart growth," "new urbanism" and "eco-city development."[20] Advances in sustainable technology and design, for example, transit-oriented development and LEED certification, are increasingly framed as a fix for the environmental, economic, and social contradictions and crisis tendencies of capitalist urbanization and, as we saw in Chapter 6, are used to rebrand cities and promote growth.[21]

Ultimately, we found that emphasis on sustainability in post-crisis city branding campaigns, as well as vision plans and new planning initiatives, fit within broader utopian appeals and efforts to upgrade the city's image. These responded to the radical interventions fought for and often created by social movements in the aftermath of disaster. Yet within a neoliberal paradigm, the implementation of these solutions was handed to the private sector, whether paid directly through grants or incentivized through tax breaks. Some of these solutions—from bike lanes to wetland restoration—can be argued to have social and ecological benefits. Some—like the concomitant privatization of parks and the subsidization of corporate office complexes whose owners carry out the restoration—cannot so easily. Ultimately, however, the overriding concern of the market-oriented state is whether redevelopment projects boost competitiveness and growth— whether or not they produce greater potential for social and ecological benefits, or crises, in the process. This has generated intense struggles over democratic accountability, planning, and what has come to be called, after Lefebvre, the "right to the city"—and made the state a central battleground of the crisis city.

Our comparison cautions against the application of functionalist and naturalized notions of resilience, or vague and depoliticized uses of sustainability, to explain and frame post-disaster outcomes. The post-9/11 and post-Katrina changes that have occurred and are emerging in New York City and New Orleans do not lend themselves to explanations that emphasize the universality of recovery. Instead of viewing resilience and sustainability as a generic condition or end state, our comparison suggests a reality that is far more complex, especially at the neighborhood scale. Political interventions, newly created institutions, newly drafted policies and regulations, and so forth nurture some forms of resilience and sustainability (e.g., economic revitalization), undermine other kinds of resilience and sustainability (e.g., neighborhood social networks and community ties), and contribute to the long-term erosion of still other kinds of resilience and sustainability (e.g., socio-economic, environmental, etc.).[22] Consequently, some policies may produce resilience to particular types of disturbances (but not others) and promote the sustainability of certain urban qualities and communities (and not others), while also producing new vulnerabilities to hazards and institutional breakdown. In exploring the resilience and sustainability of different neighborhoods, cities, and regions, we confront a diversity of organizations, social networks, institutions, and actors with varying degrees of political and representational power and access to material and cultural resources. In this situation, scholars need always to ask the question: the resilience and sustainability of what, for whom, and for what purpose?

Rather than viewing resiliency and sustainability as universal and inevitably beneficial, we believe it is necessary to emphasize the ways in which policies often reinforce and perpetuate resilient inequalities, unjust sustainabilities, and systemic risks and vulnerabilities. Accounts of post-9/11 Tribeca and Battery Park City that rejoice over these neighborhoods' resilience—remarkable and uplifting though their resurgence has been—gloss over the uneven nature of resilience in the New Lower Manhattan and ignore the ongoing struggle and displacement of poorer neighborhoods. And while a small number of New Orleans neighborhoods and sectors did weather the storm to come back "stronger than ever," the all-encompassing "Miracle" touted by boosters confronts residents still forced to deal with the triple crises of Hurricane Katrina, the BP oil spill, and the Great Recession with a sense of bitter irony, if not betrayal.

We have found that the most salient post-disaster characteristic shared by New York and New Orleans is not growing resilience and sustainability, but highly uneven and divergent paths of neighborhood recovery and redevelopment. We would argue that the residents of the Ninth Ward and Chinatown have more in common with each other than they do with their neighbors in Lakeview and the Financial District, respectively. While resources flowed into the latter two neighborhoods and residents there rightfully heralded their victories in the face of disaster, the former neighborhoods continue to struggle with cycles of neglect and disinvestment as well as gentrification and displacement, even as residents there also valiantly organized themselves and fought for the same resources.

Looking closer still, extreme differences in outcome are to be found even within these neighborhoods. The Make It Right Foundation houses in the Lower Ninth Ward, built with $31 million in private money, certainly responded to a dire need for housing in this devastated neighborhood largely deprived of redevelopment assistance. Yet these state-of-the-art homes—currently 90 of the planned 150 have been built—represent a fraction of the tens of thousands still without financing, rebuilt amid vacant lots and struggling against widespread blight and disinvestment. And with its focus on creating a "sustainable model community" as opposed to comprehensive neighborhood rebuilding, many argue that MIR has only helped legitimize the piecemeal, private-sector-led approach to redevelopment that has facilitated the exodus of New Orleans's most vulnerable, poorest, and disproportionately African American residents.

Similarly, inequality has grown even within the most heavily reinvested Lower Manhattan neighborhoods. When the LMDC awarded Goldman Sachs $1.65 billion in Liberty Bonds—or 20 percent of the total—combined with $150 million in tax breaks and cash grants to build their lavish new $2.1 billion headquarters across from Ground Zero, this not only set them miles apart from the hundreds of small businesses who had difficulty getting Small Business Administration loans, let alone bonds, but it also gave Goldman a significant advantage over its wealthy neighbors—including luxury condo tenants experiencing gentrification for the first time as a result of the company's move.[23] These points suggest that the formal administrative boundaries of cities are not the relevant scale for comparison on questions of risk and resilience. Instead, we should look to the circulation of financial resources exceeding a city's boundaries as well as the dynamics of socio-spatial inequality that operate within them at the scale of neighborhoods, blocks, and even buildings.

Cities and regions do not recover or rebuild en masse in the aftermath of a major disaster, because they are not coherent or organic entities with unified subjectivities. Intense struggles over urban space and collective memory dominate the rebuilding process as different residents, groups, and city leaders claim to represent the "spirit" and "culture" of the city. In New York City, conflicts over rebuilding Ground Zero, and the map of Lower Manhattan beyond this 16 block area, reveal urban space as contested terrain. The displacement of groups that have lived and worked in the area for a century, as in the case of Chinatown, complicates simplistic and conjoined narratives of "diversity" and "sustainability." Likewise, it would be wrong to assume that New Orleans, with its exploited, low-wage hospitality sector and historically disinvested neighborhoods, will simply recover from the Katrina disaster through natural processes of urban "resilience." One of the signal accomplishments of such framing in both cities has been the further legitimation and dissemination of the market-centered policies of recovery and redevelopment—from disaster aid to tax-break-funded rebuilding—on a national and global scale. Yet there is no evidence to suggest that such policies reduce hazard risk and vulnerability or generate sustainable, resilient communities. To the contrary, our book demonstrates that policies and regulatory strategies primarily geared towards promoting and enhancing markets are the aorta of crisis formation and portend a future of increasing risk and vulnerability for New York, New Orleans, and cities writ large.

"THIS IS OUR KATRINA": HURRICANE SANDY HITS NEW YORK

With "Superstorm Sandy" in 2012, an extreme weather event reflected the above patterns everywhere it touched down, from Atlantic City to Port Au Prince, where health impacts were by far the most severe.[24] Yet it was in its impact on New York City that Sandy brought our two cases together in the most unsettling way. Following on the heels of Hurricane Irene in 2011, Sandy presented the very real possibility that New York is now as vulnerable to extreme weather as New Orleans has long been. Some claim that this is due, in part, to the effects of global warming and sea level rise for the coastal cities in which the bulk of the world's population now lives.

Yet the lessons of Sandy extend beyond the likelihood of similar storms. In its ongoing effects on vulnerable, low-income communities, Sandy is also a reminder of the legacies of crisis-driven urbanization.

In Sandy we saw an event that directly and indirectly embodied the contradictions of both of the disasters we have been studying. Most immediately, the devastation Sandy caused in Lower Manhattan was a result of shortsighted, market-driven, post-9/11 redevelopment in that waterfront neighborhood. Billions in federal rebuilding dollars fueled the meteoric construction of luxury residential and commercial towers on the southern tip of Lower Manhattan—with proximity to waterfronts actually boosting real estate values. In addition to ignoring the needs of neighboring low-income populations, this construction placed new, wealthy residents and their subsidized buildings at risk of storm surges. That this risk was known was revealed by the city's response to Hurricane Irene, of August 20–27, 2011. Irene was seen as a "wake-up call" for New York, revealing that extreme weather had posed a major risk to the city for the first time in its history. The Bloomberg administration was commended for creating emergency evacuation zones for low lying areas—including Lower Manhattan—and actually evacuating over 300,000 people in those areas. Yet this known risk in no way inspired a change in course for downtown real estate development. Indeed, at the official unveiling of the "New Lower Manhattan" for the ten-year anniversary of 9/11, coming just one week after Irene, the only official allusion to the storm was Mayor Bloomberg's assurance that it would have *no impact* on rebuilding. Speaking at a breakfast at Cipriani Wall Street sponsored by the Association for a Better New York, the mayor predicted the continual expansion of waterfront towers "come hell or high water."[25]

Deeper relationships between Hurricane Sandy and our case studies were to be revealed in the days, weeks, and months following this initial inundation. It was then that we saw how the preexisting, uneven landscape of risk versus resiliency—worsened by post-9/11 redevelopment— enabled the storm to have such starkly uneven economic, human, and environmental impacts. The New Lower Manhattan—wealthier, more heavily insured, with superior infrastructure, and more well-connected politically than ever—was able to withstand the storm's initial impact better than most and then repair and rebuild with remarkable speed. Some fared better than others—illustrated most dramatically when the only building on the Lower Manhattan skyline to stay lit on the night of the storm was the infamous new Goldman Sachs tower (see figure 7.1). Nonetheless, the entire Financial District and Battery Park City were to get essential services like electricity, heat, and hot water back within days, and 99 percent of that area's commercial, residential, hotel, and retail inventory "back to business"

Figure 7.1
The Lower Manhattan Skyline after Hurricane Sandy
Hurricane Sandy brought immediate comparisons to both 9/11—due to representing a return of disaster to Lower Manhattan—and Hurricane Katrina—due to it being a hurricane whose citywide devastation exposed deepening class-, race-, and space-based inequalities. These comparisons were crystallized by widely a circulating image of the new Goldman Sachs building—recipient of $1.65 billion in Liberty Bonds—as one of the only buildings illuminated on the Lower Manhattan skyline due to its private electrical grid. (*Source*: Reuters)

within weeks.[26] This stood in stark contrast to poorer storm-affected neighborhoods throughout the city, including those in the towering co-ops and public housing of the "old" Lower Manhattan in the Lower East Side and Chinatown, whose buildings lacked basic services for weeks, as well as for the hardest hit coastal areas of Red Hook, Coney Island, Far Rockaway, and Staten Island. With woefully inadequate responses by FEMA and city agencies, and with little by way of private resources, the streets of these neighborhoods remained flooded, their schools and clinics closed and their apartments and businesses without light, heat, or working plumbing, creating public health hazards due to mold and exposure during an extremely cold winter. The massive scale and degree of race and class inequality in the recovery effort created widely felt shock that defied local comparison, even to 9/11. Rather, as Red Hook public housing resident Toni Khadijah James put it in a widely circulated statement: "This is our Katrina."[27]

This comparison to Katrina in the post-Sandy recovery period raises the question of whether similarly uneven redevelopment is soon to follow. As of this writing, it is unclear what lessons will be learned from Katrina, or 9/11, in this regard—and as we know, a longer-term historic frame will be necessary for such analysis. Nonetheless, early evidence was provided on June 11 when Mayor Bloomberg announced "A Stronger, More Resilient New York," his administration's $20 billion plan to increase the resilience of infrastructure and buildings citywide in the face of climate change and sea level rise.[28] Sustainability experts suggested that New York City could now end up looking like New Orleans, mainly because of the heavy involvement of the Army Corps of Engineers in the design of this new plan.[29] This is of concern since, as we explored in Chapter 3, the Corps had a very poor track record in New Orleans. It is possible that that the enlightened self-interest of New York's finance-driven growth coalition will produce different results than that of the energy industry-driven coalition of the Mississippi Delta. It is also possible that a recent shift in Mayoral leadership plus public pressure will impose more checks and balances on the Corps. Yet, if its track record of levee building in New Orleans is a model, it is also possible that whatever flood control systems New York creates will be instrumentalized to serve powerful interests, and be compromised as a result. While they may make flood-prone areas like the New Lower Manhattan, and the city as a whole, appear safe for habitation, investment, and further growth, such systems may mask the vulnerabilities produced by such unevenness. Meanwhile, a technological fix—however state of the art—will not address the broader social and environmental inequalities that produce vulnerability and lay the ground for future crisis.

Such troubling developments are not the only history we see repeating after Sandy. There are renewed signs that the post-disaster landscape in New York City creates opportunities for hope, reinvention, and solidarity—by first responders, residents, public housing residents, aid organizations, local governments, and newly formed networks of all kinds. In August–September 2011, shortly after the tenth anniversary of 9/11, Occupy Wall Street formed in reaction to the fallout from the 2008 economic crises set off by the Downtown financial and real estate firms that benefited so disproportionately from 9/11 redevelopment aid. This movement, in turn, created fertile ground for the formation of the Occupy Sandy relief effort—the efforts of which proved more effective than FEMA in bringing aid to the most distressed communities in the outer reaches of Brooklyn, Queens, and Staten Island. In later months, it also led to the formation of a broad new coalition focused explicitly on redevelopment, the Alliance for a Just Rebuilding (AJR). Through conferences, seminars and community meetings, this new labor-community alliance carefully studied the uneven redevelopment following both 9/11 and Katrina. They now seek to not only redress the wrongs of Sandy but also explicitly to transcend and transform the post-crisis histories and geographies we have explored in

Figure 7.2
Alliance for a Just Rebuilding
Alliance for a Just Rebuilding formed in New York City after Hurricane Sandy in 2013 to demand transparency, equity, and just sustainability in the recovery and redevelopment process in this particular instance, and for other disasters moving forward. Learning from the experiences of coalitions formed in the aftermath of 9/11 and Katrina, the Alliance represents a new scale of and long-term commitment to crisis organizing. (*Source*: Alliance for a Just Rebuilding)

this book. On July 31, 2013, AJR led a massive march of Sandy survivors, laborers, and community organizations, from all five boroughs, through the canyons of a refurbished, publicly subsidized Financial District and to the steps of City Hall, demanding the city "turn back the tide" of market-oriented post-disaster redevelopment.[30] See figure 7.2. En route, the march stopped at Zuccotti Park, across the street from the World Trade Center complex, both to pay homage to the site of Occupy Wall Street and to speak pointedly to the Lower Manhattan Development Corporation, whose shiny black headquarters was being built on the park's northern edge. As Bobby Tolbert of Vocal New York called out, shaking a fist at the tower, the recovery efforts following both 9/11 and Katrina "were a disaster inside of a disaster," displacing the poor and enriching the powerful, and they must not be repeated.[31] This historical insight and broader political vision both build on and exceed that of the post-disaster coalitions that we studied in the book. It reminds us how these moments of radical rupture are also cumulative. If we can learn from and draw connections between past processes of crisis-driven urbanization, perhaps these can be the "ideas lying around" to inform a more just and sustainable vision of rebuilding.

URBAN FUTURES IN AN AGE OF
CONCATENATED CRISES

Moving beyond these resonant local examples in the United States, we can view redevelopment trends following 9/11, Katrina, and Sandy as symptomatic of a new era of globally connected urban crises. On the one hand, we daily witness confirmation of the famous prediction made by Henri Lefebvre in 1970: our planet is becoming progressively and irreversibly urbanized.[32] For the first time in human history, over 50 percent of the global population is urban, with 75 percent projected by 2050. In addition to demographic forces, this urbanization is driven by neoliberal global markets that depend upon the production of new spaces for growth and that contribute to deregulation and inequality at the metropolitan scale. The pace, scale, and market-oriented mode of this urbanization is also a leading contributor to the interconnected and unevenly distributed environmental and social risks facing the world today. In the global south, where the pace and scale of urbanization has been most extreme, this mode has been characterized by "informality," that is, the rapid, unregulated growth of both the high-rise urban core and of shantytowns at the urban periphery, creating what some consider a near permanent state of crisis.[33] It is thus not surprising that urban crises of all kinds as well as crisis-related political uprisings and social upheaval have become less the exception than the norm.

Recent research has termed the growing interrelation of various forms of breakdown "concatenated crises." Shocks or disturbances can emerge in different parts of the world, spread rapidly, interact with existing vulnerabilities, and have contagious effects in unpredictable ways.[34] We would agree that the growing extension, magnitude, velocity, complexity, and volatility of global flows are increasing, raising the potential for crises to spread and interact in novel ways. The global financial crisis of 2008, propagated by the consequences of the deregulation of the U.S. housing market, quickly infected the banking sector in the developed world, ultimately affecting availability of credit globally and impacting urban residents in both developed and less-developed regions. The oil price spike of 2007 and the food price crisis of 2008 are other examples of globally coupled crises that affected diverse cities and economic sectors. More recently, a massive earthquake and tsunami that battered Japan in 2011 killed over 19,000 people and unleashed the world's worst nuclear crisis in a quarter century. Enormous risks and challenges lie ahead at the Fukushima plant and surrounding region, which could take forty years to decontaminate.

The increasing accumulation of crises has exposed a new insecurity about the future of cities and revealed how urban disasters can wreak havoc at multiple scales across the globe. Our attention has been drawn to the wide range of hazardous, even deadly, conditions that now face urban citizens—the majority of the world's population—as well as the ecosystems of which they are a part. Yet cities are not merely localized arenas in which crises become concatenated through systems that span the globe. On the contrary, through the process of crisis-driven urbanization, cities have become central to the reproduction, mutation, and reconstitution of crises during the last several decades. On this broader planetary scale, we might speak of this dynamic as the *urbanization of crisis*—whereby crises of all kinds increasingly are impacted by urbanization or have a pivotal urban dimension. Understanding the drivers and consequences of the increasing interconnectedness, intensity, and proliferation of diverse crises through urban space is an essential task for researchers, policymakers, and global citizens.

Meanwhile, in the midst of these crises, new and dramatic forms of urban-based political intervention have spread and reverberated globally. We are witnessing a new age of urban uprisings in central squares, plazas, and capital buildings from New York to New Orleans, Cairo to Istanbul, Buenos Aires to Rio de Janeiro. These might be thought of as "concatenated" mobilizations, drawing inspiration from, interacting with, and building on one another. What the outcome of these emerging solidarities might be for urban planning, policy, and social movements is impossible to predict. What is increasingly apparent, however, is that growing numbers are using the contested spaces of crisis-torn cities to make broader social, political, and planetary demands.

Since the 9/11 and Hurricane Katrina disasters, the establishment of new institutional forms, resource streams, and socio-legal regulations have provided growth coalitions with powerful political and economic instruments through which to reproduce market-centered forms of urban redevelopment long beyond the period of immediate "disaster." In turn, they have further insulated urban governance from popular-democratic control and intensified long-term dynamics of uneven development. Yet consistently, these dynamics have been characterized by disruption and contestation, helping to create new forms and scales of political consciousness and connection—both *intra-urban* and *inter-urban*—among the growing numbers finding themselves excluded and marginalized by processes of urbanization that shape their everyday lives.

While retooled urban growth coalitions continue to exercise significant control over what enters the local redevelopment agenda, mobilized communities of all kinds are poised to marshal considerable local and extra-local opposition to particular proposals as well as to shape alternative political agendas. Progressive coalitions have attempted to harness redevelopment initiatives to enhance democratic accountability, to counteract racist and class-based forms of residential segregation, to foster just and sustainable forms of urban development, and to promote a more egalitarian distribution of public resources and investments at all spatial scales. Urban insurrections and occupations have arisen in city streets and public squares across the globe, creating prefigurative spaces through which to imagine radically different urban and planetary futures. For all of these reasons, we believe, nascent debates about crisis and redevelopment—post-9/11, post-Katrina, and beyond—have the potential to become lightning rods for broader struggles over the future of cities, urban ecosystems, and urban communities around the world.

NOTES

ACKNOWLEDGMENTS

1. For New Orleans, given the smaller size of the city and larger scale of Katrina's devastation, these special entities were frequently created at the state level.
2. We collected and analyzed interview data following the widely used steps and procedures outlined in the work of Howard Becker; Nancy Charmaz; Margaret LeCompte and Jean Schensul; Robert Emerson and colleagues; Mario Small, and John Lofland and colleagues. This scholarship suggests that researchers focus their research on asking "process" questions to illuminate how people construct meaning about events and activities, and how social structure and local context shape action and decision-making. Process questions lend themselves to the use of interpretive inquiry to seek out information about intentions, motivations, constraints, opportunities, and consequences of social action. See, e.g., Becker, *Tricks of the Trade*; Charmaz, "Grounded Theory in the 21st Century," 507–35; Emerson, Fretz, and Shaw, *Writing Ethnographic Fieldnotes*; LeCompte and Schensul, *Analyzing & Interpreting Ethnographic Data*; Lofland et al., *Analyzing Social Settings*; Small, *Unanticipated Gains*.

CHAPTER 1

1. Hartman and Squires, *There Is No Such Thing as a Natural Disaster*; see also Marcuse, "Ignoring Injustice in Disaster Planning."
2. Perrow, *The Next Catastrophe*; McQuaid and Schleifstein, *Path of Destruction*; Flynn, *The Edge of Disaster*.
3. Biggs et al., "Are We Entering an Era of Concatenated Global Crises?," 27.
4. The Long-Term Ecological Research (LTER) Network's Decadal Plan notes that "Human vulnerability to storms—due to growing numbers of people living in exposed and marginal areas—is increasing the risks associated with climate change, while human endeavors (such as local governments) try to mitigate possible effects." U.S. Long Term Ecological Research Network (LTER), *The Decadal Plan for LTER*, II-15; Nicholls, "Coastal Flooding and Wetland Loss in the 21st Century," 69; Törnqvist and Meffert, "Sustaining Coastal Urban Ecosystems," 805–07.
5. Cutter, *American Hazardscapes*; Bankoff et al. *Mapping Vulnerability*; Pelling, *The Vulnerability of Cities*; Graham, *Disrupted Cities*.
6. United Nations Habitat, *Risky Cities*.
7. For a review of literature in sociology, see Tierney, "From the Margins to the Mainstream." In anthropology, see Hoffman and Oliver-Smith, *Catastrophe & Culture*. In environmental sociology and environmental justice scholarship, see Szasz and Meuser, "Environmental Inequalities," 99–120; Sze and London, "Environmental Justice at the Crossroads," 1331–54.
8. See, e.g., Vale and Campanella, *The Resilient City*; Comfort et al., *Designing Resilience*.

9. See Tierney et al., *Facing the Unexpected*; Cutter, *American Hazardscapes*; Hewitt, "The Idea of Calamity in a Technocratic Age," 3–32; Hewitt, *Regions of Risk*; Bankoff, "Rendering the World Unsafe," 19–35; Bankoff, *Cultures of Disaster*; Pelling, *The Vulnerability of Cities*; Sen, *Poverty and Famines*.

10. This is a common phrase in the literature. See the "Disasters Waiting to Happen" series in the *Natural Hazards Observer*, published at the University of Colorado; see also Cable et al., "Risk Society and Contested Illness."

11. Exemplary studies in this regard include: Klinenberg, *Heatwave*; Auyero and Swistun, *Flammable*.

12. Beck, *Risk Society*; Beck, *Ecological Enlightenment*; Beck, *World Risk Society*; Luhmann, *Risk: A Sociological Theory*.

13. Beck, *Risk Society*; Giddens, *The Consequences of Modernity*.

14. The scholarship on the institutional, organizational, and political processes surrounding the production of risk and vulnerability to disaster is extensive. For overviews, see Tierney, "Toward a Critical Sociology of Risk"; Tierney, "From the Margins to the Mainstream?" For frequently cited works, see Erikson, *Everything in Its Path*; Clarke, *Acceptable Risk*; Clarke, *Mission Improbable*; Perrow, *Normal Accidents*; Perrow, *The Next Catastrophe*; Cutter, *American Hazardscapes*; Blaikie et al., *At Risk*; Hewitt, *Regions of Risk*; Pelling, *The Vulnerability of Cities*; Auyero and Swistun, *Flammable*.

15. Perrow, *Normal Accidents* and *The Next Catastrophe*.

16. On critical urban studies, see Brenner, "What Is Critical Urban Theory?"

17. We are inspired here by recent proposals that future research be directed toward the spatial distribution and mapping of socio-environmental risk. See Morello-Frosch et al., "Environmental Justice and Southern California's 'Riskscape'"; Fitzpatrick and LaGory, "'Placing' Health in an Urban Sociology," 33–46. Thanks to Raoul Lievanos for this reference.

18. Hay, "Narrating Crisis." We are indebted to Kris Olds for reference to Hay's work.

19. Sewell, "Three Temporalities."

20. Marx and Engels, "The Manifesto of the Communist Party."

21. Schumpeter, *Capitalism, Socialism and Democracy*, pt. 2, ch. 7, 83.

22. Sewell, "The Temporalities of Capitalism," 517–37.

23. Goffman, *Frame Analysis*, 21.

24. Hall, "Race, Articulation, and Societies Structured in Dominance," 305–45.

25. Hall et al., *Policing the Crisis*.

26. Agamben, *State of Exception*; In using this phrase, Agamben is responding to the work of German juridical theorist Carl Schmitt who, in his analysis of the Nazi State, famously defined the sovereign as he who has the power to declare the state of exception.

27. Benjamin, "On the Concept of History."

28. Beauregard, *Voices of Decline: The Postwar Fate of U.S. Cities*, 37. On anti-urbanism, racism, and discourses of urban crisis, see Sugrue, *The Origins of the Urban Crisis*. For a comparative analysis, see Steinberger, *Ideology and the Urban Crisis*.

29. Harvey, *A Brief History of Neoliberalism*.

30. Garrett and Stobel, "The Political Economy of FEMA Disaster Payments."

31. Tierney, "From the Margins to the Mainstream?," 507.

32. The term "disaster gerrymandering" comes from Dymon and Platt, "U. S. Federal Disaster Declarations," 47–67.

33. Robert D. Bullard and Beverly Wright, "The Real Looting: Katrina Exposes a Legacy of Discrimination and Opens the Door for 'Disaster Capitalism,'" *SeeingBlack.com*, Oct. 5, 2005, accessed July 10, 2013, http://www.seeingblack.com/2005/x101105/411_oct05.shtml; Klein, *The Shock Doctrine*.

34. Klein, *The Shock Doctrine*.

35. The literature on neoliberalism is vast. For important contributions, see Antonio and Bonanno, "Periodizing Globalization"; Brenner and Theodore, *Spaces of Neoliberalism*; Fourcade-Gourinchas and Babb, "The Rebirth of the Liberal Creed"; Hackworth, *The Neoliberal City*. For a perspective focused on the global south, as well as one emphasizing the Foucauldian dimension of neoliberalism as a mode of governance, see Ong, *Neoliberalism as Exception*.

36. See Hackworth, *The Neoliberal City*; Ong, *Neoliberalism as Exception*.

37. Brenner and Theodore, *Spaces of Neoliberalism*; Brenner, Peck, and Theodore, "After Neoliberalization?"

38. See, for example, Heynen, Kaika, and Swyngedouw, *In the Nature of Cities*.

39. Peck and Tickell, "Neoliberalizing Space."

40. Municipal privatization initiatives proliferated during the 1990s as Phoenix, San Diego, Charlotte, Cleveland, and Milwaukee, to name a few cities, adopted large urban privatization programs (see Cooke, *Rethinking Municipal Privatization*). For an overview of the implementation of market-centered policies, see Gotham, *Critical Perspectives on Urban Redevelopment*.

41. For overviews, see Gottdiener, *The Social Production of Urban Space*; Logan and Molotch, *Urban Fortunes*; Squires and Kubrin, *Privileged Places*; Squires, *Urban Sprawl*; Smith, *Uneven Development*; Harvey, *The Limits to Capital*; Harvey, *Spaces of Global Capitalism*; Massey, *Spatial Divisions of Labor*; Lefebvre, *The Production of Space*.

42. For critical insights and empirical examples of the public consequences of privatization, including the privatization of citizenship and risk, see Calhoun, "The Privatization of Risk"; Hacker, "Privatizing Risk Without Privatizing the Welfare State"; Hacker, *The Great Risk Shift*; Somers, *Genealogies of Citizenship*.

43. Harvey, "The Right to the City."

44. While neoliberal paradigms are influential within contemporary debates in urban studies, scholars disagree whether it is possible to conceive of "neoliberalism" as a coherent theoretical, political, or geographical project. Scholars also disagree on the ideal typical features of a putative singular neoliberalism, and debates rage over the indicators of contingent forms and variants of neoliberalism. For insights into these debates, see Wilson, "Toward a Contingent Urban Neoliberalism"; Gough, "Neoliberalism and Socialisation in the Contemporary City"; Mitchell, "Transnationalism, Neoliberalism, and the Rise of the Shadow State"; Mitchell, *Crossing the Neoliberal Line*; Newman and Ashton, "Neoliberal Urban Policy and New Paths of Neighborhood Change in the American inner city"; Hackworth, *The Neoliberal City*.

45. This understanding of contestation is indebted to the approach of a new generation of critical urban geographers. See Leitner, Peck, and Sheppard, *Contesting Neoliberalism*.

46. Abu-Lughod, *New York, Chicago, Los Angeles*; Abu-Lughod, *Race, Space, and Riots in Chicago, New York, and Los Angeles*. For other historically rigorous and theoretically informed urban comparisons, see also Halle and Beveridge, *New York and Los Angeles*; Nijman, "Introduction—Comparative Urbanism"; Zukin, *Landscapes of Power*.

47. See Robinson, "Cities in a World of Cities"; McFarlane, "The Comparative City."

48. For an overview and important comparative perspective on urban connections and flows, see Robinson, "Cities in a World of Cities"; McCann and Ward, *Mobile Urbanism*.

49. Robinson, "Cities in a World of Cities," 15.

50. Tilly, *Big Structures, Large Processes, Huge Comparisons*, 82, 147; McMichael, "Incorporating Comparison within a World-Historical Perspective," 326, 388.

51. McMichael, "Incorporating Comparison within a World-Historical Perspective," 386.

52. Schneider and Susser, *Wounded Cities*.

CHAPTER 2

1. "Mayors Urge Congress to Vote Assistance to Cash-Short Cities Such as New York," *Wall Street Journal*, September 25, 1975.
2. Edward Ranzal, "Beame and Other Mayors to Meet with Ford Tomorrow," *New York Times*, August 13, 1974; Douglas Kneeland, "Mayors Step Up Appeals for Federal Aid to Cities," *New York Times*, March 24, 1975, 24.
3. Martin Tolchin, "Simon Is Scored on Fiscal Policy: Congressional Leaders Call Him 'Callous' to City—Ford Rebuffs Mayors," *New York Times*, September 25, 1975, 52.
4. Editorial, "No Help," *New York Times*, September 25, 1975, 42; Hobart Rowen, "Cities' Fiscal Crisis Grows, Mayors Say," *Washington Post*, September 25, 1975, A1.
5. Martin Tolchin, "Simon is Scored on Fiscal Policy: Congressional Leaders Call Him 'Callous' to City—Ford Rebuffs Mayors," *New York Times*, September 25, 1975, 52.
6. Ibid.
7. Ronald G. Shafer, "Mayors Group Warns That U.S. Tax Cuts May be Offset by Local Government Rises," *Wall Street Journal*, January 31, 1975, 23.
8. Ernest Holsendolph, "Beame Bids U.S. Operate All Projects to Aid Income," *New York Times*, May 1, 1975, 26. Included in the mayors' recovery plan was the call for an immediate $5 billion package of emergency aid for "rapidly deteriorating local economies" and to pay for "damages caused by inflation and higher energy costs." Their plan included another $5 billion the following year if the economy failed to recover, an additional $5 billion for 500,000 public service jobs that would offer longer-term employment, financial aid to rehabilitate rapidly deteriorating urban facilities and to build "urban multi-family housing," $650 million for summer youth job programs, an end to anti-urban tax incentives that encouraged corporate flight to the suburbs, and national responsibility for all welfare programs to avoid migration of people to areas that offered higher benefits.
9. "Cities Ask $16 billion 'Crisis Aid,'" *Chicago Tribune*, February 1, 1975, 6.
10. For critical discussions and overviews of postwar deindustrialization and urban crisis, see Darden et al., *Detroit: Race and Uneven Development*; Squires et al., *Chicago: Race, Class, and the Response to Urban Decline*; Gotham, *Race, Real Estate and Uneven Development*; Smith and Feagin, *Bubbling Cauldron*; Gottdiener and Komninos, *Capitalist Development and Crisis Theory*; Gottdiener, *Cities in Stress*; Sugrue, *Origins of the Urban Crisis*.
11. Morris, *Origins of the Civil Rights Movement*.
12. Piven and Cloward, *Regulating the Poor*; Mollenkof, *Contentious City*.
13. Quadagno, *The Color of Welfare*.
14. Kerner Commission, *The Kerner Report*, 38, 40, 56–69, 84–108, 112–113.
15. Bainfield, *The Unheavenly City*; Wilson, *Metropolitan Enigma*.
16. President Richard Nixon, "Address to the Nation on Domestic Programs," Public Papers of the Presidents, Richard Nixon, Augusts 8, 1969, 637–38. Nixon's quotes appear in Prichett, "Which Urban Crisis?," 278.
17. Conte and Karr, *An Outline of the U.S. Economy*.
18. Prichett, "Which Urban Crisis?"
19. On the mix of negative representations of urban crisis across multiple forms of media, especially the press, see Beauregard, *Voices of Decline*.
20. For an overview and critical analysis of the "image crisis" in New York City, see Greenberg, *Branding New York*, 43–70.
21. Martin Tolchin, "Simon is Scored on Fiscal Policy," *New York Times*, September 25, 1975.
22. This was the title of a documentary film, shot in 1977 and directed by Martin Lucas, James Gaffeney, and Jonathan Miller (*Tighten Your Belts, Bite the Bullet*, Icarus Films, 1980). The film depicts the fiscal crises occurring simultaneously in New York City and Cleveland and seeks to demonstrate that such crisis was now common throughout urban America.

23. Freeman, *Working-Class New York*, 7–8.

24. Figures cited in Smith and Keller, "'Managed Growth' and the Politics of Uneven Development in New Orleans," 130.

25. Bobo, *The New Orleans Economy: Pro Bono Publico?*, 1–3.

26. Quante, *The Exodus of Corporate Headquarters*, 42, describes a decline from a high in 1956 of 140 firms to a low in 1974 of 64, or a loss of 76. The Department of Commerce's office of Metropolitan Area Operations, on the other hand, estimated in 1972 that 200 of the nation's 750 largest corporations had their headquarters in New York City. In 1973, the number had dropped to 112 out of 500, or a loss of 88 (New York State Comptroller's Office, "Audit Report on Financial and Operating Practices: New York State Department of Commerce." Albany, NY: Office of the State Comptroller, Division of Audits and Accounts, December 31, 1974).

27. Quante, *The Exodus of Corporate Headquarters*, 62–63.

28. Matteson, *Dimensions and Solutions of New Orleans' Financial Dilemma*, i–ii.

29. Ibid.

30. Board of Directors Meeting, September 24, 1968, 8. Volume 114. MS 66. Chamber of Commerce of the New Orleans Area. University of New Orleans.

31. For an overview of population and demographic trends in New Orleans, see Lewis, *New Orleans: Making of an Urban Landscape*.

32. Mollenkopf and Castells, *Dual City*.

33. The phrase "sunbelt in the swamp" refers to the title of Arnold Hirsch's article, "New Orleans: Sunbelt in the Swamp," which discusses the deindustrialization of the New Orleans economy in the postwar period.

34. Piore et al., "Public Expenditures and Private Control?"

35. Soffer, *Ed Koch and the Rebuilding of New York City*, 151.

36. For more on the welfare rights movement, see Piven and Cloward, *Regulating the Poor*. As Bellush and Netzer write in *Urban Politics*, by 1965, an unprecedented 500,000 New Yorkers were receiving welfare.

37. Maier, *City Unions*, 137, 154–55; Freeman, *Working-Class New York*.

38. Newton E. Renfro, "Federation Given Right to Represent Custodians," *The Times-Picayune*, December 4, 1974.

39. Schumpeter, *Capitalism, Socialism, and Democracy*; Harvey, *The Limits to Capital*; Harvey, *Spaces of Capital*. In Harvey's work, "spatial fix" refers to capitalism's insatiable drive to resolve its inner crisis tendencies through geographical expansion and the reorganization of space and land uses. See Harvey, *Limits to Capital*, 427–28.

40. Regional Plan Association, *Regional Plan of New York and its Environs*. Much of the research on the role of finance, insurance, and real estate elites in reshaping New York's planning priorities in order to build the World Trade Center (WTC) was done by Fitch, *The Assassination of New York*. Other background can be found in Darton, *Divided We Stand*.

41. Moody, *From Welfare State to Real Estate*.

42. See "Manhattan New Office Building Construction (1960–1992)," in Fitch, *The Assassination of New York*, 280. Fitch draws on data from the Real Estate Board of New York, Research Department. Totals do not include additions, reconstructions, or mixed-use buildings.

43. Ruchelman, *The World Trade Center*, 25.

44. Greenberg, *Branding New York*.

45. Ruchelman, *The World Trade Center*, vii.

46. "2 in Legislature Scare Restaurant at Trade Center," *New York Times*, January 30, 1976, 58.

47. As Peter Marcuse states in reference to the historic role of Midtown: "the notion that New York City's office sector is dependent on its location in Lower Manhattan is a myth." See Marcuse, "What Kind of Planning after September 11?," 155.

48. Caro, *The Power Broker*; Fitch, *The Assassination of New York.*

49. The greatest example of the use of rent to subsidize private real estate is the World Trade Center. When it was unable to rent its 10 million square feet of office space, the city and state governments, along with the New York and New Jersey Port Authority, stepped in to rent over half of the space. Greenberg, *Branding New York*, 289.

50. Fitch, *The Assassination of New York*, ix.

51. Moody, *From Welfare State to Real Estate.*

52. According to the *New York Times*, if the Port Authority had chosen to occupy the $30 million building it had built for new offices at 1166 Avenue of the Americas, vacant since 1974, it could have saved $4.2 million a year in rent. It was also found that the state of New York was being charged above-market rates for its offices. See C. Kaiser, "State Told It Can Save by Leaving Trade Center," *New York Times*, June 7, 1976, 33.

53. K. Rothmyer, "Troubled Towers: New York Port Unity Battles Big Problems at Its Trade Center," *Wall Street Journal*, July, 1, 1975, 3.

54. For a critical account of the impact of Hurricane Betsy on the passage of legislation to develop the post-1960s levee system in New Orleans, see Colten, *Perilous Place, Powerful Storms.*

55. For information on Hurricane Betsy as the nation's first billion dollar hurricane, see Eric S. Blake et al., "The Deadliest, Costliest, and Most Intense United States Tropical Cyclones from 1851 to 2010," NOAA Technical Memorandum NWS NHC-6, National Weather Service/National Hurricane Center, Miami, Florida, August 2011, accessed June 26, 2013, http://www.nhc.noaa.gov/pastcost.shtml.

56. Prior to the 1930s, the building of levees and floodwalls to regulate land uses related to water flow was a local responsibility. After extensive flooding of the Mississippi River in 1927, Congress authorized the Army Corps of Engineers to assume responsibility for constructing flood control structures including dams, dikes, levees, and floodwalls. Several years later, the Flood Control Act of 1936 declared flood control a "proper" federal activity in the "national interest" and ushered in a modern era of federal flood control investment. For an overview, see Barry, *Rising Tide.*

57. In 1966, the governor of Louisiana designated the Orleans Levee District (OLD) to lead the local cooperation effort for the Orleans, Jefferson, St. Charles, and St. Tammany Parishes. Other local sponsors became involved in the 1970s, including the Pontchartrain Levee District (PLD) and the Lake Borgne Basin Levee District. See Woolley and Shabman, *Decision-Making Chronology*, 27–28.

58. Ibid., Executive Summary, 10.

59. Ibid., Executive Summary, 26.

60. Ibid., A5, referring to United States Army Corps of Engineers, "Interim Survey Report."

61. Memo for the Chief of Engineers from William R. Gianelli, Assistant Secretary of the Army (Civil Works) regarding Level of Protection for Urban Areas, February 27, 1984, accessed June 26, 2013, http://library.water-resources.us/docs/hpdc/docs/19840227_ASAtoCG_re_LOP_urban_areas.pdf.

62. Comptroller General of the United States, Cost, Schedule, and Performance Problems of the Lake Pontchartrain and Vicinity, Louisiana, Hurricane Protection Project, Report to Congress, PSAD-76-161, August 31, 1976, 8, 21, accessed June 29, 2013, http://archive.gao.gov/f0402/098185.pdf.

63. Houck, "Rising Water."

64. Burby, "Flood Insurance and Floodplain Management," 111–22.

65. U.S. Army Engineer District, Final Environmental Statement, iii.

66. Schumpeter, *Capitalism, Socialism, and Democracy*, 82–83.

67. R. H. Caffey and B. Leblanc, "'Closing' the Mississippi River Gulf Outlet: Environmental and Economic Considerations," Interpretive Topic Series on Coastal Wetland Restoration

in Louisiana, Coastal Wetland Planning, Protection, and Restoration Act, accessed June 26, 2013, http://lacoast.gov/new/Data/Reports/ITS/MRGO.pdf.

68. Woolley and Shabman, *Decision-Making Chronology*, 17.
69. Rounsefell, "Preconstruction Study of the Fisheries."
70. Colten, *An Unnatural Metropolis*.
71. Burby, "Hurricane Katrina and the Paradoxes of Government Disaster Policy," 175.
72. Hacker, *The Great Risk Shift*.
73. The most prominent of Carey's consultants was Felix Rohatyn of the financial advisory and asset management firm, Lazard Freres. In addition, Carey consulted with Simon H. Rifkind, former federal judge, Richard Shinn, president of Metropolitan Life Insurance Corporation, and Donald B. Smiley, CEO of R. H. Macy & Co. As Freeman, *Working-Class New York*, 260, observes: "In [consulting with these men], he was asking leaders of large capital, who had a national and international orientation that left them normally oblivious to day-to-day city affairs, to shape a solution to the fiscal crunch."
74. Newfield and DuBrul, *The Abuse of Power*, 178–82; Bailey, *The Crisis Regime*, 27–29. Lichten, *Class, Power and Austerity*, 129–34.
75. As Freeman, *Working-Class New York*, 265, points out, while MAC had succeeded in selling two $1 billion bond issues, there was little interest in subsequent offerings. This is why Carey and his advisers, Rohatyn, Simon Rifkind, and William Ellinghouse (NY Telephone president), drafted an omnibus bill for the Emergency Financial Control Board (EFCB) in "another effort to reopen private capital markets."
76. See, for example, Lichten, *Class, Power and Austerity*; Rohatyn, "New York and the Nation," *New York Review of Books*, January 21, 1982, 28; Tabb, *The Long Default*.
77. Ferretti, *The Year the Big Apple Went Bust*.
78. On the split between union leaders and their rank-and-file membership on concessions during the fiscal crisis, see Maier, *City Unions*.
79. Freeman, *Working-Class New York*.
80. Orlebecke, "Saving New York," 321. According to William Simon's memoir, *A Time for Truth*, President Ford's only two concerns in allowing the city to go into bankruptcy were "avoiding civil unrest, and preserving confidence in the financial structure, particularly the banking system."
81. Newfield and DuBrul, *The Abuse of Power*.
82. "Rohatyn Urges a City Plan for Industry," *New York Times*, March 16, 1976.
83. Ibid.
84. Freeman, *Working-Class New York*, 275, cites one example from 1975 in which the Dollar Savings Bank, then the largest mortgage lender in the city and the fifth largest in the country, issued only thirty-two mortgages in the entire borough of the Bronx.
85. Greenberg, *Branding New York*, ch. 5.
86. Wallace and Wallace, *A Plague on Both Your Houses*.
87. Ibid. Health and safety experts Deborah and Roderick Wallace conducted the most extensive study of the history, scope, and distribution of the city's cuts in fire service and the relationship this had to the increase in fires in particular neighborhoods. In their study, they found that social engineers, some of them from the Rand Corporation Fire Project, supervised the deliberate degradation of fire control resources in areas the engineers of shrinkage had slated for clearance. Ultimately, over the course of two years, about 10 percent of New York's fire companies were eliminated, 20 percent of manpower was cut back, and emergency response systems were whittled down. This occurred primarily in ten of the city's poorest neighborhoods, located mainly in the Bronx and Brooklyn. As response times fell in these still heavily populated neighborhoods by between five and ten minutes (a deadly amount in fire terms), an "inevitable fire epidemic" resulted. This then exacerbated the problem of housing abandonment by landlords. The Wallaces calculated that

when the dust settled, about 2 million poor people had been uprooted by the end of the decade.

88. According to the City and County Data Book for 1983 (Bureau of the Census, 1983), between 1970 and 1980, New York City lost 825,000 residents while the New York metropolitan area lost 915,000, or 20 percent of its population.

89. For an overview of Reagan administration cutbacks, see Gaffikin and Warf, "Urban Policy and the Post-Keynesian State"; Boger, "Race and the American City," 33; Rubin, Wright, and Devine, "Unhousing the Urban Poor"; Dreier, "Reagan's Legacy."

90. Smith and Keller, "'Managed Growth' and the Politics of Uneven Development in New Orleans," 150–54.

91. For an overview of the New Orleans fiscal crisis during the 1970s and 1980, see Julian, "The New Orleans Fiscal Crisis"; Smith and Keller, "'Managed Growth' and the Politics of Uneven Development in New Orleans," 126–66.

92. City of New Orleans Operating Budget, 1964 and 1984. Calculations by the Commission on the Future of the City. April 1985. "Recommendations for the Future of New Orleans," 44. City of New Orleans. Box 3, Folder 86 (MS 804-A, Blanche F. Mysing Papers, Louisiana Collection, Howard-Tilton Memorial Library, Tulane University).

93. Memo to All Members of the City Council from Richard Kernion, Chief Administrative Officer, June 3, 1975. Subject: Projected Operating Budget Deficit in 1976 and Subsequent Years, Landrieu Collection, Box 105, folder 4, Loyola University.

94. For an overview and summary of the impact of federal cutbacks on New Orleans, see Smith and Keller, "'Managed Growth' and the Politics of Uneven Development in New Orleans," 156, 157.

95. Joe Massa, "City Trying to Figure Out Where to Cut Work Force," *The Times-Picayune*, April 2, 1980.

96. Wright, "Black New Orleans," 61.

97. For a historical overview of the finances of the City of New Orleans from the 1960s through the 1990s, see Bureau of Governmental Research, *BGR Outlook on Orleans: Status Report on the 1998 City Operating Budget.*

98. Canak and Miller, "Gumbo Politics," 267.

99. Ibid., 266.

100. Ibid.

101. Ashton Phelps, "As The Publisher Sees It," *The Times-Picayune*. March 22, 1976, sec. 1, 3

102. Canak and Miller, "Gumbo Politics," 267.

103. "Letter from the Beachfront Retreat: Organized Labor Fights the Battle of the Brunches," *Washington Post*, February 22, 1986, A03.

104. New Orleans Chamber of Commerce, Economic Development Council, Program of Work, 1974. Vol. 124 (MS 66. Chamber of Commerce of the New Orleans Area. University of New Orleans).

105. Image Development Luncheon, June 15, 1982, International Ballroom, Fairmont Hotel. Program Agenda. Frank H. Walk, "New Images—Past, Present, and Future"; Dolnald E. Moore, "Image Campaign Program Benefits." New Orleans Image Development, 1982–1984 (Vertical File. Howard-Tilton Memorial Library. Tulane University); Commission on the Future of the City, April 1985, "Recommendations for the Future of New Orleans," City of New Orleans. Box 3, Folder 86 (MS 804-A. Blanche F. Mysing Papers. Louisiana Collection. Howard-Tilton Memorial Library. Tulane University).

106. Greenberg, *Branding New York.*

107. For critical overview and analysis of the historical development of tourism in New Orleans, see Gotham, *Authentic New Orleans.*

108. Figures are cited in Whelan, "New Orleans: Public-Private Partnerships and Uneven Development," 225.

109. *Baton Rouge Morning Advocate,* "NO Center Boosts Tourism Hopes," January 14, 1985.

110. "City Quietly Becoming World Tourist Haven," *City News,* August 29, 1978, 33.

111. Brookings Institution, *New Orleans after the Storm.*

112. Tobier, *Changing Face of Poverty.*

113. Mollenkopf and Castells, *Dual City.*

114. Ibid., 11.

115. Smith and Keller, 1983, and Gotham, 2007, 14–16.

116. Mark Levitan, "Poverty in New York, 2002: One-Fifth of the City Lives Below the Federal Poverty Line," *Community Service Society,* September 30, 2003, accessed March 5, 2012, http://www.cssny.org/userimages/downloads/2003_09poverty.pdf.

117. "Most of the City's Workers Fall into Service Jobs; Orleans' Poverty Rate Among the Worst in the U.S." *The Times-Picayune,* November 20, 2001, 1.

CHAPTER 3

1. National Commission on Terrorist Attacks in the United States, *The 9/11 Commission Report.*

2. Fiscal Policy Institute, *The State of Working New York.*

3. Fiscal Policy Institute, *The Employment Impact of the September 11 World Trade Center Attacks;* Damiani and Greenwood, *The LMDC: They're In the Money.*

4. For a critical overview of the impact of the terrorist strike on New York, see Foner, *Wounded City* and Chernick, *Resilient City.*

5. Figures from Brookings Institution, *New Orleans after the Storm,* 13–16.

6. Ibid.

7. Paul Rioux, "World's Largest Drainage Pumping Station Roars to Life on West Bank," *The Times-Picayune,* June 3, 2011.

8. Mark Schleifstein, "As Hurricane Season begins June 1, New Orleans Has Unprecedented Protection," *The Times-Picayune,* May 29, 2011.

9. U.S. Army Corps of Engineers, *Performance Evaluation of the New Orleans and Southeast Louisiana Hurricane Protection System.*

10. Harvey, *The New Imperialism.*

11. Hall, *Cultural Representations and Signifying Practices.*

12. White House, Office of the Press Secretary to President George W. Bush, "Remarks by the President in Photo Opportunity with the National Security Team."

13. The full text of President Bush's State of the Union address is published in the *Washington Post,* http://www.washingtonpost.com/wp-srv/onpolitics/transcripts/sou012902.htm, accessed March 12, 2012.

14. For a overview of the hero narrative and framing, see Brian A. Monahan, *The Shock of the News.*

15. George W. Bush, ""Remarks at the 9/11 Heroes Medal of Valor Award Ceremony."

16. George W. Bush, "Remarks at the Dedication Ceremony for the 9/11 Pentagon Memorial in Arlington, Virginia."

17. Erika Kinetz, "Small, Shocked," *New York Times,* December 2, 2001, 1.

18. Dreier, "Katrina and Power in America," 532n2.

19. Perrow, "The Disaster after 9/11," 17–18.

20. Center for International Policy, "Privatizing Homeland Security."

21. Since 1979, FEMA has been the main executive branch agency responsible for organizing and coordinating disaster relief and aid among government agencies and between government and the private and nonprofit sectors (for historical overviews and critical analyses of FEMA, see Stehr, "The Political Economy of Urban Disaster Assistance"; Morris, "Whither FEMA?"; Moss, Schellhamer, and David, "The Stafford Act and Priorities for Reform").

22. Peter Gosselin and Alan Miller, "Why FEMA Was Missing in Action," *Los Angeles Times*, September 5, 2005; Farhad Manjoo, "Why FEMA Failed," *Salon*, September 7, 2005, accessed June 30, 2013, http://dir.salon.com/story/news/feature/2005/09/07/fema/index.html.

23. Gary Fields and David Rogers, "Already Under Scrutiny, FEMA Is in the Spotlight," *Pittsburgh Post-Gazette*, August 31, 2005.

24. Brian Thevenot and Gordon Russell, "Rape. Murder. Gunfights; For Three Anguished Days the World's Headlines Blared that the Superdome and Convention Center had Descended into Anarchy," *The Times-Picayune*, September 26, 2005.

25. Brian Thevenot, "Myth-making in New Orleans," 36.

26. Tierney, Bevc, and Kuligowski, "Metaphors Matter," 36.

27. Robert E. Pierre and Ann Gerhart, "News of Pandemonium May Have Slowed Aid; Unsubstantiated Reports of Violence Were Confirmed by Some Officials, Spread by News Media," *Washington Post*, October 5, 2005, A8; Jim Dwyer and Christopher Drew, "Fear Exceeded Crime's Reality in New Orleans," *New York Times*, September 29, 2005, 1A; Dynes and Rodriguez, "Finding and Framing Katrina."

28. John M. Broder, "Amid Criticism of Federal Efforts, Charges of Racism are Lodged," *New York Times*, September 5, 2005. For an overview of the application of the stigma of "refugee" to New Orleans residents, see Kromm and Sturgis, *Hurricane Katrina and the Guiding Principles on Internal Displacement*.

29. For critical analyses of the rumor mongering and false stories that were disseminated through media outlets, see Brezina and Kaufman, "What Really Happened in New Orleans?"; Brezina, "What Went Wrong in New Orleans?"

30. Quote appears in Quigley, "What Katrina Revealed," 366. A pointed break from such reporting, including local reaction to Bill O'Reilly's comments, can be found on This American Life, episode 296 "After the Flood" September 9, 2005. http://www.thisamericanlife.org/radio-archives/episode/296/after-the-flood

31. For one view of the role of conservative think tanks in framing Katrina, including supplying policy ideas and rationales to the Bush administration, see Peck, "Neoliberal Hurricane."

32. Peck, "Neoliberal Hurricane," 693 (quoting Gelinas, "Will New Orleans Recover? Weak and Struggling before Katrina, the Good-Time City Now Teeters on the Brink, *City Journal*, August, 31, 2005, http://www.city-journal.org/html/eon_08_31_05ng.html).

33. Peck, "Neoliberal Hurricane," 703–04.

34. Sean D. Hamill, "Santorum Suggests Penalties for Some Who Don't Evacuate," Associated Press News Wire, September 7, 2005.

35. U.S. Senate, Far From Home, 82

36. FEMA, FEMA Winds Down Year of Compassionate Sheltering, 2.

37. Bob Kemper and Tom Baxter, "Deficit-conscious GOP Cringes at Katrina Plan," Atlanta Journal-Constitution, September 17, 2005.

38. Associated Press, "Hastert Questions Proposed Efforts to Rebuild; House speaker Says Rebuilding New Orleans Under Sea Level Makes No Sense," Press Release, September 1, 2005. Accessed June 29, 2013. http://www.nbcnews.com/id/9164727/

39. Andante Higgins, "McCain to Tour Katrina-Damaged New Orleans Neighborhood," CBS News, April 24, 2008, Aaccessed April 16, 2013, http://www.cbsnews.com/8301-502443_162-4040391-502443.html

40. In December 2005, Rep. Richard H. Baker (R-La.) proposed legislation (H.R. 4100) (the "Baker Bill") to create a government-run corporation to buy out damaged or flooded properties in the hardest-hit areas of Louisiana, thus enabling the owners to pay off their mortgages and avoid foreclosure. The corporation would have been empowered to sell the properties to developers for rebuilding, with right of first refusal going to the

former homeowners. The Baker Bill proposed that the U.S. Treasury issue up to $30 billion in bonds to finance the program, with some costs recouped from the eventual resale of property. The White House opposed the bill as a "needless layer of bureaucracy" (Martin H. Bosworth, "Controversy Swirls Around Louisiana Reconstruction Plan," *ConsumerAffairs.com*, January 29, 2006, accessed August 11, 2006, http://www.consumeraffairs.com/news04/2006/01/nola_reconstruction.html).

41. Lewis, *The Politics of Presidential Appointments*, 161; Hollis, "A Tale of Two Federal Emergency Management Agencies"; Roberts, "FEMA and the Prospects for Reputation-Based Autonomy."

42. White and Eisinger, *Cities at Risk*, 8, 9.

43. Government Accountability Office, *Disaster Assistance*, 7.

44. Government Accounting Office. Written Statement, presented by Jay Etta Z. Hecker.

45. Diana Henriques and David Barstow, "Change in Rules Barred Many from Sept. 11 Disaster Relief," *New York Times*, April 26, 2002.

46. Government Accountability Office. *September 11: Overview of Federal Disaster Assistance to the New York City Area*, 33.

47. Ibid.

48. Diana Henriques and David Barstow, "Change in Rules Barred Many from Sept. 11 Disaster Relief," *New York Times*, April 26, 2002.

49. Ibid.

50. David W. Chen, "More Get 9/11 Aid, but Distrust of U.S. Effort Lingers," *New York Times*. August 27, 2002.

51. Letters to the Editor, "Terror's Other Victims," *New York Times*, May 2, 2002.

52. "The Incomplete and Uneven Federal Response to New York after 9/11," prepared by the Office of Congresswoman Carolyn Maloney, accessed November 7, 2013, http://maloney.house.gov/sites/maloney.house.gov/files/documents/olddocs/Sept11/FedResponse.pdf

53. David W. Chen, "More Get 9/11 Aid, but Distrust of U.S. Effort Lingers," *New York Times*, August 27, 2002.

54. Letter from Carolyn Maloney, Member of Congress, et al. to the Honorable Dennis Hastert, Speaker of the House et al., May 21, 2003, accessed July 11, 2012, http://maloney.house.gov/sites/maloney.house.gov/files/documents/olddocs/Sept11/052103Hearings.pdf.

55. U.S. House of Representatives, *Federal 9/11 Assistance to New York: Part I, II and III*, 67.

56. David Barstow and Diana B. Henriques, "Sorting Out Why U.S. Agency Spent So Little," *New York Times*, April 26, 2002.

57. Michael Chertoff, interview by Soledad O'Brien, *CNN.com, American Morning*, September 1, 2005, http://transcripts.cnn.com/TRANSCRIPTS/0509/01/ltm.03.html: NBC Photojournalist Describes Horrific Situation in New Orleans," MSNBC, updated September 1, 2005, accessed October 30, 2005, http://www.msnbc.msn.com/id/9160710.

58. "'Can I Quit Now?' FEMA Chief Wrote as Katrina Raged," *CNN.com*, November 4, 2005, http://www.cnn.com/2005/US/11/03/brown.fema.emails/.

59. White House, "President Arrives in Alabama, Briefed on Hurricane Katrina."

60. Three major class action claims against FEMA resulted in Court ordered extensions of housing assistance under FEMA's programs: (1) McWaters, et al. v. FEMA, et al. 408 F.SUPP.2d 221, 225-6 (E.D.La In Acorn, e 2005), opinion modified (January12, 2006); (2) ACORN, et al. v. FEMA, 463 F.Supp.2d 26 (D.D.C. 2006), stay granted in part, 2006 WL 3847841 (D.D.C. December 22, 2006); and (3) Ridgely, et al. v. FEMA, Civil Action No. 07-2146 (E.D.La. 2007), reversed in part, 512 F.3d 727 (5th Cir., 2008). These cases all involved legal challenges to FEMA termination and/or denial of benefits under Sections 403 and 408 of the Stafford Act for immediate and temporary housing needs after Katrina. See also U.S. Senate, *Far From Home*, 211–19.

61. McWaters v. FEMA, 408 F. Supp. 2d 221, 233 n.15 (E.D. La. 2005), *op. modified*, 436 F. Supp. 2d 802 (E.D. La. 2006); see also U.S. Senate, *Far from Home*, 214.

62. *McWaters*, 408 F. Supp. 2d at 234; see also U.S. Senate, *Far from Home*, 214.

63. For an overview of the role of multinational contractors in responding to Hurricane Katrina, see Eric Klinenberg and Thomas Frank, "Looting Homeland Security."

64. Jeffrey Kaye, "Controversy Continues over Post-Katrina Spending on Trailers."

65. Federal Emergency Management Agency, *IA-TAC Program Status and Performance Assessment*, 10–11.

66. U.S. Senate, *Far From Home*, 111.

67. Ibid., 111–12.

68. Ibid., 8.

69. Ibid.

70. Federal Emergency Management Agency, "Formaldehyde and Travel Trailers"; U.S. House of Representatives, "Toxic Trailers: Have the Centers for Disease Control Failed to Protect Public Health?"

71. Robert T. Stafford Disaster Relief and Emergency Assistance Act, Pub. L. No. 93-288 (1988), as amended by the Disaster Mitigation Act of 2000, 42 U.S.C. §§ 5121 et seq.

72. Government Accountability Office, *Disaster Assistance*.

73. Disaster Mitigation Act of 2000, Pub. L. No. 106-390.

74. Department of Homeland Security, *A Performance Review of FEMA's Disaster. Management Activities in Response to Hurricane Katrina*; Bruce Alpert and Jonathan Tilove, "On The Hill; News from the Louisiana Delegation in the Nation's Capital. D.C. Delegate Takes No Prisoners with FEMA," *The Times-Picayune*, September 26, 2010.

75. Christine Hauser, "Mayor Announces Layoffs of City Workers," *New York Times*, October 5, 2005, A24.

76. Written testimony of Walter Leger, Member of the Board of the Louisiana Recovery Authority, Before The U.S. Senate Subcommittee on Response and Recovery. January 29, 2007, accessed May 15, 2011, http://lra.louisiana.gov/assets/docs/searchable/Newsroom/2007/WalterLegerTestimony012997.pdf.

77. The federal Community Disaster Loan (CDL) program is intended to "provide funds to any eligible jurisdiction in a designated area. " The program is authorized by Section 417 of the Stafford Act and administered by the Federal Emergency Management Agency (FEMA). See FEMA, Community Disaster Loan Program, http://www.fema.gov/media-library/assets/documents/33726, accessed November 7, 2013.

78. Nonna Noto, FEMA's Community Disaster Loan Program: Action in the 110th Congress.

79. Bruce Alpert, "Federal Cash Would Help Cities Pay Workers; But Money Would Have to Be Repaid," *The Times-Picayune*, October 8, 2005.

80. Michelle Krupa, "$1.7 Billion in Relief of State Debt Urged; Blanco Raising 'Issue of Fairness' with Feds," *The Times-Picayune*, February 6, 2007.

81. Bruce Nolan, "Biden Announces Decision to Forgive Disaster Loans; $705 Million Was to Be Due at Year's End," *The Times-Picayune*, January 16, 2010.

82. Department Of Homeland Security. Federal Emergency Management Agency. Special Community Disaster Loans Program.

83. Jonathan Tilove, "Louisiana Officials Ask the Federal Government to Forgive Loans," *The Times-Picayune*, May 23, 2011; Richard Rainey, "FEMA's Decision Is Costly to Jeff; Parish Still Has to Pay Almost $55 Million," *The Times-Picayune*, March 31, 2011; Christine Harvey, "St. Tammany Still Hoping for Katrina Loan Forgiveness," *The Times-Picayune*, September 1, 2010.

84. Bruce Alpert, "Road Blocked for Jeff Loan; FEMA Rejection Can't be Arbitrated," *The Times-Picayune*, February 21, 2010.

85. Bruce Alpert, "House Approves Budget Bill that Can Lead to Forgiveness of Katrina Disaster Loans," *The Times-Picayune*, March 21, 2013.

86. For discussions, see U.S. Senate, *Far From Home*, 5, 12; Waugh, *Shelter from the Storm*; Cooper and Block, *Disaster*; Heerden and Bryan, *The Storm*; Birch and Wachter, *Rebuilding Urban Places after Disaster*; Daniels, Kettl, and Kunreuther, *On Risk and Disaster*; Brasch, *"Unacceptable": The Federal Government's Response to Hurricane Katrina*.

87. Comfort, "Crisis Management in Hindsight"; Comfort et al., "Retrospectives and Prospectives on Hurricane Katrina."

88. SRA International Inc., *FEMA Recovery Division 2005 Hurricane Season After-Action Report*.

89. U.S. House of Representatives, *Implementation of the Road Home Program Four Years after Hurricane Katrina* 4.

90. See FEMA, Private Sector Division, accessed April 16, 2013, http://www.fema.gov/private-sector.

91. Zack Phillips, "FEMA Looks to Private Sector for Disaster Provisions."

92. Government Accountability Office, *Actions Taken to Implement the Post-Katrina Emergency Management Reform Act of 2006*.

CHAPTER 4

1. John Esterbrook, "New Orleans Mayor Takes Swipe At NYC," CBSNews.com, August 24, 2006, accessed June 1, 2010, http://www.cbsnews.com/stories/2006/08/24/60minutes/main1933092.shtml.

2. "NYC Unveils 9/11 Memorial Hole," *The Onion* 43, no. 26, September 11, 2006, accessed September 12, 2006, http://www.theonion.com/articles/nyc-unveils-911-memorial-hole,2038/.

3. Mike Pesca, "Ground Zero Rebuilding Delays Irk New Yorkers," NPR News, September 11, 2006, accessed June 1, 2010. http://www.npr.org/templates/story/story.php?storyId=6053448&ps=rs.

4. Henri Lefebvre, "Space: Social Product and Use Value," in *Critical Sociology: European Perspectives*, ed. J. Freiberg (New York: Irvington Publishers, 1979), 292.

5. Swyngedouw, "Neither Global nor Local," 141.

6. Gottdiener, "A Marx for Our Time," 130.

7. Lefebvre, "Space: Social Product and Use Value," 289–90.

8. Angotti, *New York for Sale*, 183.

9. Robin Pogrebin, "Culture Raises Its Head and Heart," *New York Times*, January 16, 2006, E1.

10. For an evocative description of how such spaces were created and used in Battery Park City, see Smithsimon, *September 12*, 118–61.

11. Luft, "Beyond Disaster Exceptionalism," 501–02. Following Chetkovich and Kunreuther, Luft defines grassroots groups as "grounded in a local community" where the community is composed of people without access to many resources, the leadership comes from this community, and the group operates with minimal infrastructure (see Chetkovich and Kunreuther, *From the Ground Up*).

12. Luft, "Beyond Disaster Exceptionalism," 509.

13. On December 13, 2007, over a hundred protestors gathered at City Hall for a rally against the demolition of housing complexes in New Orleans. Protesters blocked one entrance to the federal courthouse building on Poydras Street at noon for about thirty minutes, chanting criticism of the U.S. Department of Housing and Urban Development's plans to demolish four thousand public housing units (Eliot Kamenitz, "Protesters Block HUD

Offices Downtown," *The Times-Picayune*, December 13, 2007). For a critical analysis of the history of public housing in New Orleans, see Arena, *Driven From New Orleans*.

14. These coalitions represented dozens of groups, including longstanding organizations and service providers in Chinatown like Chinese Staff and Workers Association, CAAAV, and Asian Americans for Equality, and in the Lower East Side, groups like Good Old Lower East Side, Educational Alliance, and University Settlement. They were joined by groups like the Fiscal Policy Instiute and Pratt Institute Center for Community and Environmental Development (PICCED). For overviews, see PICCED, A "Map" of the Civic Planning Initiatives to Rebuild New York, Reconstruct Lower Manhattan and the World Trade Center Site, January 23, 2002; and Regional Plan Association, *A Civic Assessment of the Lower Manhattan Planning Process*.

15. On the role of coalitions led by middle-class professionals, see Woods, *Democracy Deferred*. For a comparative analysis of how these coalitions were situated vis-à-vis elite-oriented and low-income-oriented coalitions, see Angotti, *City for Sale*, ch. 7.

16. B. Nolan, "Katrina's Devastation Rewrote the Playbook; Local Groups Say Relief about Half Finished," *The Times Picayune*, July 26, 2009.

17. By "elite groups," we refer to groups with powerful political connections, ready access to economic resources, and operating with ample infrastructure. These groups may be rooted in particular geographic communities—as in the case of wealthy neighborhoods surrounding Ground Zero or in New Orleans; or they may not be—as in the case of elites living outside the city but who have a financial and political interest in it. Our comparative analysis of elite mobilization is informed by the work of G. William Domhoff, C. Wright Mills, Francis Fox Piven, Richard Cloward (see Domhoff, *Who Rules America?*; Mills, *The Power Elite*; Piven and Cloward, *Regulating the Poor*).

18. Joseph Giovanni, "Architecture Review: Fixing the Whole," *New York Magazine*, November 12, 2001.

19. The Baker quote appears in Bill Quigley, "New Orleans: Leaving the Poor Behind Again!"

20. Douglas A. Blackmon and Thaddeus Herrick, "New Urbanist Tries to Rebuild New Orleans." *Wall Street Journal*, May 3, 2006.

21. Gretchen Morgenson, "Attorney General of N.Y. Is Said to Face Pressure on Bank Foreclosure Deal." *New York Times*, August 21, 2011, A1. In addition to her role as NYCP president and CEO, Wilde was also on the board of the New York Federal Reserve at the time of this quote.

22. For overviews of the four planning commissions, see Burns and Thomas, "A 'New' New Orleans?"; Olshansky et al., "Planning for the Rebuilding of New Orleans"; Kates et al., "Reconstruction of New Orleans after Hurricane Katrina."

23. For an overview of the planning debates and controversies, see Olshansky and Johnson, *Clear as Mud*; Laska, "'Mother of Rorschachs'"; Nelson, Ehrenfeucht, and Laska, "Planning, Plans, and People."

24. Edward Soja, "Economic Restructuring and the Internationalization of Los Angeles," 187.

25. Real Estate Board of New York, *Key Principles in Rebuilding Lower Manhattan* (NY: REBNY, n.d.) (cited in Angotti, *New York For Sale*, 270).

26. Tom Angotti, "The Make-Up of the Lower Manhattan Development Corporation," *Gotham Gazette*, December, 2001; Reconstruction Watch Publication #1—February 2002 "Profiles of the Members of the Lower Manhattan Development Corporation: Who Are These People and Where Did They Come From?," accessed November 11, 2013, http://www.gothamgazette.com/images/pdf/rebuildingnyc/ReconstructionWatch1. PDF

27. Edward Wyatt, "Everyone Weighs in with Rebuilding Ideas," *The New York Times*, January 11, 2002.

28. Port Authority of New York and New Jersey, "Port Authority and Lower Manhattan Development Corporation Unveil Six Concept Plans."

29. Ada Huxtable, " 'Downtown' Is More than Ground Zero," *Wall Street Journal*, August 7, 2002.

30. For a critical analysis of Bloomberg's ambitions and views of government as well as designs on Midtown, see Brash, *Bloomberg's New York.*

31. Civic Alliance to Rebuild Downtown New York, "Listening to the City."

32. Ibid., 1.

33. America *Speaks*, "About Us," accessed February 17, 2012, http://americaspeaks.org/about/.

34. Civic Alliance to Rebuild Downtown New York 5.

35. Ibid., 3. See chart on pg.21 showing that 66% of participants were less than confident that their voices would be heard.

36. Ibid.

37. Edward Wyatt, "A Forum on Rebuilding Lower Manhattan," *New York Times*, July 20, 2002.

38. Civic Alliance to Rebuild Downtown New York 17.

39. Civic Alliance to Rebuild Downtown New York 16.

40. Author interview with LCAN member KD.

41. "Listening to the City." Opinion. *New York Times*. July 23, 2002, accessed February 5, 2012.

42. Civic Alliance to Rebuild Downtown New York 21. It was well known that Doctoroff himself was never a fan of the Beyer Blinder Belle plan and that by "something great," he meant architecture and urban design. See Angotti, *New York for Sale*, 189.

43. Author interview with DB.

44. Martha Carr, "Citizens Pack Rebirth Forum; Experts Urged to Use N.O. History as Guide," *The Times-Picayune*, November 15, 2005; Martha Carr, "Rebuilding Should Begin on High Ground, Group Says; Planners Warn Against Haphazard Development," *The Times-Picayune*, November 19, 2005. For a description of the NAACP and Louisiana ACORN opposition to BNOB's proposal, see Gordon Russell and Frank Donze, "Rebuilding Proposal Gets Mixed Reception; Critics Vocal, But Many Prefer to Watch and Wait," *The Times-Picayune*, January 12, 2006.

45. For overviews of the controversy surrounding BNOB's green-dot plan, see Burns and Thomas, "A 'New' New Orleans?"; Campanella, *Bienville's Dilemma*, 344–54.

46. Bruce Eggler, "Lower 9th Ward, East N.O. Endorsed; Rebuilding Panel Says They Must Be Included." *The Times-Picayune*, October 25, 2005.

47. Michelle Krupa, "Many Areas Marked for Green Space after Hurricane Katrina Have Rebounded," *The Times-Picayune*, August 23, 2010.

48. Michelle Krupa, "The Dreaded Dot: After the Flood, a Map of the City with Large Green Dots Representing Proposed Green Spaces Sent Homeowners into a Panic," *The Times-Picayune*, August 24, 2010.

49. Gordon Russell, "On Their Own; In the Absence of Clear Direction, New Orleanians Are Rebuilding a Patchwork City," *The Times-Picayune*, August 27, 2006.

50. Ibid.

51. Ibid.

52. Author interview with GFK, October 17, 2010.

53. Author interview with BFG, October 7, 2010.

54. Author interview with ALF, October 29, 2010.

55. Stephanie Grace, "Will Plan Lift the Curse of the Green Dot?" *The Times-Picayune*, April 1, 2007.

56. HUD's recommendation that Louisiana adopt the LMDC as a model for the LRA is discussed in Allocations and Common Application and Reporting Waivers Granted to and

Alternative Requirements for CDBG Disaster Recovery Grantees Under the Department of Defense Appropriations Act, 2006 71 Fed. Reg. 7666, 7667 (February 13, 2006).

57. Governor Kathleen Blanco appointed a board that included prominent Louisiana businesspeople, such as shipbuilder Boysie Bollinger, trucking executive James Davison, and lawyer Walter Leger Jr., along with former *Time* magazine and CNN chief Walter Isaacson and political consultants Mary Matalin and Donna Brazile. The LRA was initially chaired by Xavier University President Norman Francis, followed by New Orleans area investor David Voelker. In September 2008, eleven out of twelve members of the board of directors of the LRA were business owners and executives (see Louisiana Recovery Authority, bios of board members, http://lra.louisiana.gov/index.cfm?md=pagebuilder& tmp=home&pid=87) and fourteen out of twenty-seven former members of the LRA were business owners and executives (see Louisiana Recovery Authority, bios of past board members, http://lra.louisiana.gov/index.cfm?md=pagebuilder&tmp=home&pid=83), accessed June 10, 2013.

58. Louisiana Recovery Authority, Executive Order KBB 05-63, accessed April 17, 2012, http://doa.louisiana.gov/osr/other/kbb05-63.htm.

59. Public Affairs Research Council of Louisiana, "PAR Says Embed Recovery Authority in Law," January 17, 2006, accessed June 26, 2013, http://www.parlouisiana.com/explore. cfm/parpublications/commentariesandletters/100059.

60. Department of Housing and Urban Development, CDBG Disaster Recovery Assistance, accessed June 10, 2013, http://portal.hud.gov/hudportal/HUD?src=/program_offices/ comm_planning/communitydevelopment/programs/drsi.

61. See Good Jobs New York, "Memo: Community Development Block Grant Waivers." For notices and descriptions of HUD waivers, see Statutory and Regulatory Waivers Granted to New York State for Recovery from the September 11, 2001 Terrorist Attacks, Docket No. 02-1936, 67 Fed. Reg. 4163–4166 (January 28, 2002); Statutory and Regulatory Waivers Granted to New York State for Recovery from the September 11, 2001 Terrorist Attacks: Technical Correction, Docket No. FR-4732-C-02, 67 Fed. Reg. 5845–5846 (February 7, 2002).

62. Ibid.

63. Edward Wyatt and Joseph P. Fried, "Two Years Later; The Money; Downtown Grants Found to Favor Investment Field," *New York Times*, September 8, 2003.

64. Ibid.

65. Katia Hetter, "Big Money to Stay Near World Trade Center," *Newsday*, June 3, 2002.

66. Reconstruction Watch, The LMDC: They're in the Money; We're in the Dark: A Review of the Lower Manhattan Development Corporation's Use of 9/11 Funds 21. New York: Good Jobs New York, August 2004, accessed June 10, 2013, http://www.goodjobsfirst.org/ sites/default/files/docs/pdf/lmdc_report.pdf.

67. Daniel H. Bush, "Talking Point: Equity and Faith Needed in Community Spending Plan."

68. Lower Manhattan Development Corporation, "Governor Pataki Announces Major Progress on Lower Manhattan Transportation Initiatives."

69. Errol Louis, "The 9/11 Black Hole: LMDC's Secret Ways Keep Little Guys from Getting Rebuilding Bucks," *Daily News*, July 6, 2004.

70. Lower Manhattan Development Corporation, "Neighborhood Outreach Workshop Report Comments."

71. Author interview with DB.

72. New York City Independent Budget Office, "Mayor's Housing Plan: Progress to Date; Prospects for Completion."

73. Eric Jaffe, "New York's 'Affordable Housing' Isn't Always Affordable."

74. Lower Manhattan Development Corporation, "LMDC Announces More than $37 Million in Grants: Funds Will Go to Non-Profits for Community Enhancements."

75. Aid recipients included the Educational Alliance, Grand Street Settlement, University Settlement, the Museum of Chinese in the Americas, Charles B. Wang Community Health Center, New York Downtown Hospital, New York City Parks Foundation, Downtown Manhattan Little League, and competitive grants for Lower Manhattan's forty-four public schools. In awarding the grants, LMDC Chairman Avi Schick echoed the language of grassroots coalitions, saying he was "committed to improving all of Lower Manhattan, not just the 16 acres of Ground Zero." Ibid.

76. Ibid.

77. Lower Manhattan Development Corporation, "Governor Pataki, Mayor Bloomberg Hail President Bush's Support of Tax Conversion Proposal to Re-Direct Federal September 11th Aid."

78. These are designated in Section 141(a) of the Internal Revenue Code (defining private activity bonds). See also Reconstruction Watch Publication #3, "An Analysis of the 'Job Creation and Worker Assistance Act of 2002' Private Activity Bonds: An Opportunity for Public Input?" New York: Good Jobs New York. April 2002, accessed June 10, 2013, http://goodjobsny.org/sites/default/files/docs/rwatch_3.pdf.

79. "Public benefit" restrictions were an essential feature of PABs when this category of bond was first designated in 1984. See U.S. Congress, Joint Committee on Taxation, General Explanation of the Revenue Provisions of the Deficit Reduction Act of 1984, H.R 4170, 98th Congress; Pub. L. No. 98-369 (December 31 1984), at 931, accessed June 10, 2013, http://www.jct.gov/jcs-41-84.pdf.

80. Ibid., 930. As the report explains: "Congress was extremely concerned with the volume of tax exempt bonds used to finance private activities. The volume of these bonds has increased sharply over the past few years, from $6.2 billion in 1976 to $62.4 billion in 1983. During this same period, private activity bonds increased from 21 percent of total borrowing by State and local borrowings in 1975 to 68 percent in 1983." Governments issued so many, and prices were bid down so low, that the interest rates local governments had to pay began to increase, threatening their fiscal solvency. In addition, all kinds of private enterprises began to be given tax exemption regardless of public benefit. This led Congress to draft legislation limiting PABs, which was ultimately codified in the Tax Reform Act of 1986. We are indebted for these insights to Timothy L. Jones, Senior Counsel in the Internal Revenue Service Office of Assistant Chief Counsel.

81. When qualified PABs are used for private rental housing, for instance, 20 percent or more of rental units must be affordable to low-income tenants for a minimum of fifteen years. See U.S. Tax Code, 26 U.S.C. § 142d.

82. Allowable uses for Liberty Bonds were restricted to the "cost of acquisition, construction, reconstruction, and renovation of commercial real estate, residential rental property and public utility property located in the Liberty Zone." See Internal Revenue Service (IRS).
    "New York Liberty Zone Bonds." Accessed November 11, 2013. http://www.irs.gov/Government-Entities/New-York-Liberty-Zone-Bonds

83. Section 1301 of the Federal Tax Reform Act of 1986 and Section 146 of the Internal Revenue Code impose a limit on the amount of tax-exempt private activity bonds a state may issue in a calendar year ("the annual state ceiling"). In calendar year 2001, when the federal statute in question was enacted, Section 146(d), as amended by the Community Renewal Tax Relief Act of 2000, permitted a state to set its annual ceiling at $187.5 million or an amount equal to $62.50 per capita of its population, whichever was higher. In New York's case, with a population of 18,976,457, the former was higher. For national figures on total amount of PABs see Cynthia Belmont, "Tax-Exempt Bonds, 1996–2002."

84. Kallick, "Rebuilding a High Road Economy," 34.

85. Charles Bagli, "Chase Bank Set to Build Tower by Ground Zero," *New York Times*, June 14, 2007.

86. Michael Powell and Michelle Garcia, "After Attacks Changed the World, the Recovery Changed a City; Near Ground Zero, a New Version of Life Goes On," *Washington Post*, September 9, 2006, A01.

87. Martin Z. Braun, "New York's Post-9/11 Liberty Bond Program Gets Mixed Grades," *Bloomberg.com*, September 11, 2006, accessed June 29, 2013, http://www.bloomberg.com/apps/news?pid=email_en&refer=munibonds&sid=a.3Ce4rZER9M.

88. *9/11 Federal Assistance to New York: Lessons Learned in Fraud Detection, Prevention, and Control: Hearing Before the U.S. House of Representatives, Comm. on Homeland Security Subcomm. on Management, Integration, and Oversight*, 109th Cong. 172 (July 13, 2006) (testimony of Bettina Damiani, Project Director, Good Jobs New York), accessed June 10, 2013, http://www.goodjobsny.org/sites/default/files/docs/testimony_congress_2006.pdf.

89. Federal waivers are printed in the Federal Register, published by the National Archives and Records Administration (NARA). For CBDG waivers related to Hurricane Katrina, see National Archives and Records Administration, Department of Housing and Urban Development [Docket No. FR-5051-N-01], Allocations and Common Application and Reporting Waivers Granted to and Alternative Requirements for CDBG Disaster Recovery Grantees Under the Department of Defense Appropriations Act, 2006, 71 Fed. Reg. 7668 (February 13, 2006); National Archives and Records Administration, Department of Housing and Urban Development [Docket No. FR–5089–N–03], Additional Waivers Granted to and Alternative Requirements for the State of Louisiana, Under Public Laws 109-148 and 109-234," 72 Fed. Reg. 10014 (March 6, 2007).

90. In summer 2007, the state of Louisiana projected a $3 billion to $5 billion shortfall due to inaccurate estimates by FEMA of the number of damaged and flooded homes. In response, the state committed an additional $1 billion, and Congress eventually added $3 billion to a defense spending bill in November. See Finger, "Stranded and Squandered."

91. Bruce Eggler, "Blanco Launches Road Home Office on Poydras Street," *The Times-Picayune*, August 23, 2006.

92. David Hammer, "Closings Stopped, but Not for Long; Road Home's Leading Contractor Changing," *The Times-Picayune*, April 15, 2009.

93. Jeffrey Meitrodt, "State blasts Road Home firm, But Top Exec Defends ICF's Performance." *The New Orleans Times-Picayune*, December 24, 2006.

94. David Hammer, "ICF Raise Was No Secret," *The Times-Picayune*, December 11, 2008.

95. David Hammer, "Blanco Spurred Plea from Legal Aid," *The Times-Picayune*, March 26, 2008.

96. David Hammer, "Road Home Can Lead to Big Payday; 3 Contractors Paid Over $200 million," *The Times-Picayune*, April 6, 2008, 1.

97. Greater New Orleans Fair Housing Action Center v. U.S. Department of Housing & Urban Development, No. 08-01938 (District Court for D.C. 2008). See Complaint for Declaratory and Injunctive Relief, accessed February 17, 2012, http://www.gnofairhousing.org/wp-content/uploads/2012/02/11-12-08_RoadHomeComplaint.pdf.

98. Hartman and Squires, "Lessons from Katrina."

99. Rose, Clark, and Duval-Diop, *A Long Way Home* 47.

100. *The Road Home? An Examination of the Goals, Costs, Management, and Impediments Facing Louisiana's Road Home Program: Hearing Before the Ad Hoc Subcomm. on Disaster Recovery of the Comm. on Homeland Security and Governmental Affairs*, 110th Cong. 8, 37 (May 24, 2007) (testimony of Andrew D. Kopplin, Executive Director of the Louisiana Recovery Authority; testimony of Isabel Reiff, Senior Vice President of ICF International, Inc., and

Chief Program Executive, Louisiana Road Home Program), accessed July 1, 2010, http://www.gpo.gov/fdsys/pkg/CHRG-110shrg36609/html/CHRG-110shrg36609.htm.

101. Government Accountability Office, *Gulf Opportunity Zone*.
102. Ibid., 13.
103. "'This Great City Will Rise Again,' Bush Promises," *New York Times*, September 16, 2005 (publishing excerpts from President Bush's September 15, 2005, speech about Hurricane Katrina) (emphasis added).
104. Ariella Cohen, "New Orleans Gets Table Scrap in GO Zone Lending Feast," *The Lens*, December 17, 2010.
105. Louisiana Department of Treasury, Louisiana Bond Commission. Data on Louisiana Go Zone Projects by Issued Amount was released through public records request initiated by the authors.
106. Graham, "Permanently Failing Organizations?"
107. Letter from Good Jobs First et al. to Members of Congress, Concerned Individuals, and Groups on the Gulf Coast, September 15, 2005, "An Open Letter from Civic Groups in New York on 9/11 and Katrina," accessed June 26, 2013, http://www.fiscalpolicy.org/openletterontherebuildingprocess.pdf.

CHAPTER 5

1. See, for example, Smith, *Uneven Development*; Massey, *Spatial Divisions of Labor*.
2. On urban obsolescence in relation to redevelopment see Weber, "Extracting Value from the City."
3. Klein, *The Shock Doctrine*, 7.
4. On the early native American, African American, Dutch, and British history of Lower Manhattan, see parts I and II of Wallace and Burrows, *Gotham*.
5. For descriptions of these neighborhoods, see the Federal Writers' Project, *The WPA Guide to New York City*. Historical portraits can also be found in Diner, *Lower East Side Memories*; Bayoumi, "Letter to a G-Man"; and Kwong, *The New Chinatown*.
6. NTAs are combinations of adjoining census tracts arranged according to commonly designated neighborhoods or neighborhood clusters. These were originally designed by the New York City Department of City Planning for the 2010 U.S. Census. We reconstructed these NTAs for the 2000 U.S. Census. The Chinatown NTA (MN27) includes census tracts 8, 16, 18, 25, 27, 29, 30.01, and 36.01. The Lower East Side NTA (MN28) includes census tracts 2.01, 2.02, 6, 10.01, 10.02, 12, 14.01, 14.02, 20, 22.01, 22.02, 24, 25.01, 26.02, and 28. The SOHO-Tribeca-Civic Center-Little Italy NTA (MN24) includes census tracts: 21, 31, 37, 39, 41, 43, 45, 47, and 49. The Battery Park City-Lower Manhattan NTA (MN25) includes census tracts 7, 9, 13, 15.01, 15.02, 317.03, and 317.04.
7. New York City, Office of the Mayor. "Mayor Bloomberg Delivers Major Address."
8. Ibid.
9. On this dual approach, see ch. 3 of Greenberg, *Branding New York*. Marketing efforts included the "Big Apple" Bicentennial celebrations of 1976 and the early "I Love New York" campaign in 1979.
10. Author interview of WC, September 15, 2011. This doomsday fear was based in an understanding of the "agglomeration effect" for firms working within well-connected business districts, and an understanding that without this critical mass, the raison d'être of the district might be lost. As Saskia Sassen argued at the time, the geographic and social concentration for finance, insurance, and real estate (FIRE) and business services was a powerful incentive for agglomeration, one that made physical "downtowns" not only still relevant in the midst of transportation and communication upgrades but also advantageous as hubs of prosperous economic development. Sassen, *The Global City*.

11. Author interview of WC, September 15, 2011

12. Construction of Battery Park City began in 1982, with the first phase completed in 1989 on the cusp of the recession. The original complex had 5,574 residents. By 2000, this had grown relatively slowly, to 7,951 residents.

13. Author interview of WC, September 15, 2011.

14. Ibid.

15. Aaron Donovan, "If You're Thinking of Living In/The Financial District; In Wall Street's Canyons, Cliff Dwellers," *New York Times*, September 9, 2001.

16. Jacobs, *The Death and Life of Great American Cities*, 155.

17. This was according to Andrew S. Heiberger, chief executive of the large rental broker Citi Habitats. See Aaron Donovan, "If You're Thinking of Living In/The Financial District; In Wall Street's Canyons, Cliff Dwellers," *New York Times*, September 9, 2001.

18. Ibid.

19. Author interview of WC, September 15, 2011. This former DA president noted that one exception to this was the goal of creating rail service to Westchester and Connecticut, which did not occur after September 11. However, the explosion of residential development was to bring so many senior executives in from the suburbs to live within walking distance of their jobs downtown that "in a peculiar way," this goal was "no longer as pressing."

20. Kwong, *The New Chinatown*.

21. Ibid., 39–40.

22. Mele, *Selling the Lower East Side*; Abu-Lughod, "The Battle for Tompkins Square Park," 233–66; Smith, "New City, New Frontier," 61–93.

23. On policies involved, see Sites, *Remaking New York*.

24. Peter Kwong, "Answers about the Gentrification of Chinatown, Part 3," *City Room* (blog), *New York Times*, September 18, 2009, accessed April 18, 2012, http://cityroom.blogs.nytimes.com/2009/09/18/answers-about-the-gentrification-of-chinatown-part-3/.

25. Kwong, *The New Chinatown*, 172–73.

26. John Freeman Gill, "The Land of the $800 Stroller," *New York Times*, May 6, 2011.

27. "Ground One: Voices from Post-9/11 Chinatown," accessed April 18, 2012, http://911chinatown.mocanyc.org/oralhistory.html.

28. John Freeman Gill, "The Land of the $800 Stroller," *New York Times*, May 6, 2011.

29. For documentation of the health impacts on office workers north of Chambers, the GAO notes: "[Community and labor] representatives have noted that the geographic boundaries used by the [WTC Health] Registry exclude office workers...between Chambers and Canal...who may have been exposed to the cloud of dust and smoke." See Government Accountability Office, *September 11: Health Effects in the Aftermath of the World Trade Center Attack*. For an account and discussion of the broader health impacts, see Beyond Ground Zero, *We Count!*

30. On immediate impacts to Chinatown and the Lower East Side, see Asian American Federation of New York, "Chinatown One Year after September 11th"; Barbara Ross, "Chinatown's Garment Biz Shrivels, Tourist Traffic Dwindles in Lasting Blow of 9/11," *New York Daily News*, September 5, 2011. The article notes: "Law enforcement commandeered 1,000 parking spots—on the street and at a nearby municipal garage."

31. For a report on the economic impact of 9/11 in Chinatown and the Lower East Side, see Fiscal Policy Institute, *The Employment Impact of the September 11 World Trade Center Attacks*.

32. Asian American Federation of New York, "Chinatown One Year After September 11," April 4, 2002.

33. Ibid., 30.

34. Ibid., 2–4.

35. Fewer surveys were done of residents and businesses in the Lower East Side, but organizations cited similar effects. See Victor J. Papa's "Foreword" in *"A Divided Community": A Study of Gentrification of the Lower East Side Community.*

36. Edward Wyatt, "At Ground Zero, a New Divide; Some of 9/11's Neediest Get the Least Government Aid," *New York Times,* June 5, 2002.

37. Ibid.

38. Ibid.

39. Asian American Federation of New York, "Chinatown One Year After September 11," November 2002, p. 2. Other distinctive characteristics included a cultural aversion to seek government aid among some immigrant groups, as well as a fear that doing so might threaten immigration status.

40. Ibid., 20; Barbara Ross, "Chinatown's Garment Biz Shrivels, Tourist Traffic Dwindles In Lasting Blow of 9/11," *New York Daily News,* September 5, 2011.

41. Liu, "Blank Slates and Disaster Zones."

42. The original designation covered all five boroughs of New York City but policymakers soon changed the designation to areas "south of Canal." See Government Accountability Office, *September 11: Overview of Federal Disaster Assistance to the New York City Area.*

43. On the environmental health implications of this restriction, see Beyond Ground Zero, *We Count! Documenting the 9/11 Health Crisis 8 Years Later.*

44. The residential program apportioned $14,500 for residents in Zone I, south of Chambers and west of Broadway; $7,750 for those in Zone 2, south of Canal; and just $1,750 for those in Zone 3, north of Canal, east of Broadway, and south of Delancey. Average income west of Broadway was $125,000; east of Broadway it was $40,000, meaning the wealthiest residents got the most aid. For a reproduction of the LMDC map of these zones, and reporting on the controversy surrounding this inequity, see: Edward Wyatt, David W. Chen, Charles V. Bagli "After/9/11, Billions From Washington, and Dismay in New York" *New York Times,* December 30, 2002, A1.

45. Other important service providers included the historic settlement houses of the Lower East Side: University Settlement and Henry Street Settlement. On CWE and Safe Horizons, see Alyssa Katz, "Help Wanted." *City Limits,* August 15, 2003. A program called the "Center for Workforce and Economic Development" (the Center) was funded by $32.5 million from Congress, secured through joint lobbying by New York City business and labor groups. Center grants kept more than 2,800 workers employed following 9/11; helped nonprofits like the tenant advocacy group Good Old Lower East Side to retain staff; and recruited companies in targeted sectors, making sure that the dollars got spent quickly and effectively on jobs that carried decent wages and benefits. After two years, in 2003, Congress ceased funding to the Center.

46. Waheed et al., *Ripple Effect.*

47. Kallick, "Rebuilding a High Road Economy."

48. Alyssa Katz, "Help Wanted," *City Limits,* August 15, 2003.

49. Andrew Beveridge, "Census Wounded City's Pride but Probably Got the Numbers Right," *Gotham Gazette,* April 2011, accessed April 8, 2012, http://www.gothamgazette.com/article/demographics/20110426/5/3515.

50. The $136,000 median household income figure is reported in John Freeman Gill, "The Land of the $800 Stroller," *New York Times,* May 6, 2011.

51. U.S. Census Bureau. Figures on racial change in New York City neighborhoods (2000–2010), generated by Social Explorer, March 24, 2012.

52. Barbara Ross, "Chinatown's Garment Biz Shrivels, Tourist Traffic Dwindles In Lasting Blow of 9/11," *New York Daily News,* September 5, 2011.

53. Barbara Ross, ibid., notes other impacts on tourism. Unable to park temporarily near the old historic section, tourist buses wrote Chinatown off their itineraries for years to come.

The number of tourists visiting Chinatown numbered 2,000 a day in 2000; in 2010, a daily average was half that number, according to tourism officials. Three subway stops serving Chinatown—Grand St., Canal St., and East Broadway—have lost 3.5 million riders a year since 2000, MTA records show. Barbara Ross, "Chinatown's Garment Biz Shrivels, Tourist Traffic Dwindles in Lasting Blow of 9/11," *New York Daily News*, September 5, 2011.

54. Alliance for Downtown New York, *The Lower Manhattan Retail Sector: One Year Later*; Alliance for Downtown New York, *The Lower Manhattan Retail Sector: Beginning to Recover*.

55. Graham, "Permanently Failing Organizations? Small Business Recovery after September 11, 2001."

56. Edward Wyatt and Joseph P. Fried, "Two Years Later; The Money; Downtown Grants Found to Favor Investment Field," *New York Times*, September 8, 2003.

57. Diane Cardwell, "Mayor Says New York Is Worth the Cost," *New York Times*, January 8, 2003.

58. David W. Dunlap, "Liberty Bonds' Yield: A New Downtown," *New York Times*, May 30, 2004, A1.

59. Patrick McGeehan, "Near Ground Zero, a Mixed-Use Revival," *New York Times*, September 9, 2007.

60. Alliance for Downtown New York 2011. *State of Lower Manhattan 2011*, 13–18.

61. For discussions of which companies benefited from post-9/11 aid, see Nicole Gelinas, "Liberty Misspent," *New York Post*, September 6, 2011; New York City Independent Budget Office, *The Aftermath*.

62. Charles Bagli, "Chase Bank Set to Build Tower by Ground Zero," *New York Times*, June 14, 2007.

63. "At Duane Reade's Newest Outpost, Sushi and Hairstyling," *New York Times*, July 5, 2011.

64. Alliance for Downtown New York, *State of Lower Manhattan 2011*, 13.

65. Alyssa Katz, "Gentrification Hangover," *American Prospect*, January 6, 2010.

66. Right to the City Alliance, *People Without Homes and Homes Without People*.

67. Following the crash of 2008, the Bloomberg administration did attempt a limited, market-based version of such a policy, which soon failed. See: Cara Buckley, "City's Affordable Housing Program Faces Trouble Finding Buyers." Feb 18, 2010. http://www.nytimes.com/2010/02/19/nyregion/19affordable.html?pagewanted=all

68. Already by 2003, retailers surveyed in the financial district remarked that fewer customers came from business and more were residential. For a description of the early stage of this Liberty Bond-financed residential boom and the debates around it, see David Dunlap, "Liberty Bonds Yield a New Downtown," *New York Times*, May 30, 2004.

69. Michael Powell and Michelle Garcia, "After Attacks Changed the World, The Recovery Changed a City; Near Ground Zero, a New Version of Life Goes On," *Washington Post*, September 9, 2006, A01.

70. Alliance for Downtown New York, *State of Lower Manhattan 2011*.

71. David Dunlap, "Liberty Bonds Yield a New Downtown," *New York Times*, May 30, 2004.

72. Lower Manhattan Development Corporation. *Revised Partial Action Plan Number 6 for Affordable Housing*.

73. Michael Powell and Michelle Garcia, "After Attacks Changed the World, the Recovery Changed a City; Near Ground Zero, a New Version of Life Goes On," *Washington Post*, September 9, 2006, A01.

74. John Freeman Gill, "Land of the $800 Stroller," *New York Times*, May 6, 2011.

75. U.S. Census Bureau. Figures on Change in Lower Manhattan Neighborhood Population by Residents under 18 Years (2000–2010), generated by Social Explorer, March 24, 2012.

76. For a description of the role of organized tenants of Battery Park City in LMDC projects, see Smithsimon, *September 12*.

77. John Freeman Gill, "Land of the $800 Stroller," *New York Times*, May 6, 2011.

78. CAAAV and Urban Justice Center, "Converting Chinatown: A Snapshot of a Neighborhood Becoming Gentrified and Unlivable," December 2008. A related project "documenting and fighting the gentrification and displacement of tenants, street vendors, and youth in New York City's Chinatown" is *Chinatown Gentrification Watch* (blog), http://nogentrification.blogspot.com/. On the rezoning of the East Village and Lower East Side, see New York City Department of City Planning, http://www.nyc.gov/html/dcp/html/evles/index.shtml. A similar rezoning was planned for Chinatown but is currently being debated, with local groups demanding a greater voice in its design. See Chinatown Working Group, "Community Planning Its Future," http://www.chinatown-workinggroup.org/.

79. U.S. Census Bureau. Figures on Change in Lower Manhattan Neighborhood Population by Residents under 18 Years (2000–2010), generated by Social Explorer, March 24, 2012.

80. Community Board No. 1, Manhattan, New York City, District Needs Statement, Statement of Community District Needs—Fiscal Year, 2011, accessed April 19, 2012, http://www.nyc.gov/html/mancb1/html/archives/needs.shtml.

81. Lower Manhattan Development Corporation. "Mayor Bloomberg Unveils Plans for East River Waterfront"; New York City Department of City Planning, "East River Waterfront Study, Concept Plan," accessed March 25, 2012, http://www.nyc.gov/html/dcp/html/erw/erw.shtml. The East River Waterfront redevelopment was part of a plan to develop a thirty-two-mile greenway around the island of Manhattan.

82. O.U.R. Waterfront Coalition, "A People's Plan for the East River Waterfront," n.d., accessed March 25, 2012, http://www.urbanjustice.org/pdf/publications/peoples_plan.pdf.

83. Ibid, 22, 37.

84. Ibid, 14, 48.

85. Ibid., 2, 3.

86. Ibid., 32–33.

87. See The East River Waterfront Esplanade page at http://www.nycedc.com/project/east-river-waterfront-esplanade, accessed November 1, 2011. As the site mentions: "The project has received critical acclaim and recognition in national and international award ceremonies." This includes the Excellence on the Waterfront Award from the Waterfront Center (2006), which recognizes high-quality waterfront plans and projects from all over the world; the 55th Annual P/A Award granted to SHoP Architects (2008); and the Design Award from the NYC Public Design Commission to the project team for the Reconstruction of Pier 35 (2009).

88. Liu and Plyer, "An Overview of Greater New Orleans: From Recovery to Transformation."

89. Ibid., 2.

90. Greater New Orleans Community Data Center, "Facts for Features: Hurricane Katrina Recovery."

91. Liu and Plyer, "An Overview of Greater New Orleans: From Recovery to Transformation."

92. Greater New Orleans Community Data Center, "Facts for Features: Hurricane Katrina Recovery."

93. For an overview, see William Freudenberg et al., *Catastrophe in the Making*.

94. van Heerden et al., *The Failure of the New Orleans Levee System during Hurricane Katrina* 2.

95. Louisiana Department of Transportation and Development, "Executive Summary," xii (quoting Bob Bea, co-director of University of California, Berkeley, Center for Catastrophic Risk Management, and an ILIT member).

96. R. G. Bea, "Reflections on the Draft Final U.S. Army Corps of Engineers Interagency Performance Evaluation Task Force (IPET) Report Titled Performance Evaluation of the New Orleans and Southeast Louisiana Hurricane Protection System," June 2, 2006, accessed June 29, 2013, http://cbr.tulane.edu/PDFs/IPETBEAreview.pdf.

97. Plyer, Ortiz, and Pettit, "Post-Katrina Housing Affordability Challenges Continue in 2008."

98. Figures reported in Allison Plyer, *What Census 2010 Reveals about Population and Housing in New Orleans and the Metro Area.*

99. For insights into the scale limitations of the resilience concept, see Laska, "'Mother of Rorschachs.'"

100. Lakeview contains four census tracts: 56.01, 56.02, 56.03, and 56.04. The Lower Ninth Ward contains five census tracts: 7.01; 9.01, 9.02, 9.03, and 9.04.

101. Figures on Change in Total and Ethnic/Racial Population for New Orleans, Lakeview, and the Lower Ninth Ward (2000–2010), generated by Social Explorer, March 24, 2012.

102. For overviews of the historical development of Lakeview, see Campanella, *Time and Place in New Orleans*; Campanella, *Bienville's Dilemma*; Lewis, *New Orleans: The Making of an Urban Landscape.*

103. See Colten, "Basin Street Blues," 237–57; Colten, *An Unnatural Metropolis.*

104. See Colten, *Unnatural Metropolis*, 81, 99, 189.

105. Ibid., 251.

106. For an overview of the developmental history of Lakeview, see Lakeview Civic Improvement Association, accessed July 15, 2011, http://www.lakeviewcivic.org/

107. For overviews of the history of the Lower Ninth Ward, see Landphair, "The Forgotten People of New Orleans"; Landphair, "Sewerage, Sidewalks, and Schools: The New Orleans Ninth Ward and Public School Desegregation.".

108. Landphair, "Sewerage, Sidewalks, and Schools," 37.

109. E. J. Morris Senior Center, "Oral Recollections of the Ninth Ward Elderly, 1900–1950."

110. Landphair, "The Forgotten People of New Orleans," 839; Thomas Ewing Dabney, "The Industrial Canal and Inner Harbor of New Orleans," esp. 6 and 16.

111. Wieder, "The New Orleans School Crisis of 1960"; Spain, "Race Relations and Residential Segregation In New Orleans."

112. Landphair, "The Forgotten People of New Orleans," 841.

113. Census 2000 figures available from Greater New Orleans Community Data Center, "Holy Cross Neighborhood: People and Household Characteristics," accessed July 19, 2011, http://www.gnocdc.org/orleans/8/20/people.html.

114. Poverty and income figures for Lakeview and the Lower Ninth Ward were compiled by and obtained from the Greater New Orleans Community Data Center, Pre-Katrina data center website, "Lakeview Neighborhood: Income & Poverty," accessed July 11, 2011, http://www.gnocdc.org/orleans/5/37/income.html.

115. For critical analyses and overviews of the racial impacts of the forced out-migration from New Orleans, see Institute for Southern Studies, "One Year After Katrina: The State of New Orleans and the Gulf Coast"; Liu, Fellowes, and Mabanta, *Special Edition of the Katrina Index*; Gabe et al., "Hurricane Katrina: Social-Demographic Characteristics of Impacted Areas."

116. Bullard and Wright, *Race, Place, and Environmental Justice after Hurricane Katrina.*

117. Author interview of JNN, December 29, 2010.

118. Author interview of GFK, November 7, 2010.

119. Author interview of WHD, July 22, 2011.

120. Author interview of CK, December 16, 2010.

121. Author interview of PHG, October 3, 2010.

122. Author interview of DMW, October 27, 2010.

123. Greater New Orleans Community Data Center, "Lower Ninth Ward Neighborhood: Housing & Housing Costs."

124. Katy Reckdahl, "Sierra Club Trumpets 'Green Wave' in Lower 9th Ward," *The Times-Picayune*, February 25, 2012.

125. Blaine Harden, "A City's Changing Face; Wealth, Race Guiding Which New Orleanians Stay, and Which Never Return," *Washington Post*, May 17, 2006, A01.

126. U.S. Census Bureau, Change in Age, by Number and Percent, for Lakeview and the Lower Ninth Ward, 2000–2010, generated by Social Explorer, April 25, 2012.

127. Allison Good, "Lakeview Sees Flood of Young Homeowners, New Businesses Since Hurricane Katrina Nearly Wiped the Slate Clear," *The Times-Picayune*, September 27, 2011.

128. Ibid.

129. Ibid.

130. Author interview of CCC, November 1, 2011.

131. Stephanie Bruno, "Harrison Ave. Feasts on Recovery; New Grocery Boosts Lakeview Corridor," *The Times-Picayune*, November 22, 2010.

132. Author interview of MVG, November 30, 2011.

133. Dreier, Mollenkopf, and Swanstrom, *Place Matters*, 1.

CHAPTER 6

1. Becky Bohrer, "Mayor: Crime Part of New Orleans 'Brand,'" *Washington Post*, August 10, 2007.

2. Greenberg, *Branding New York*, "Prologue."

3. Ruth Shalit, "Brand New: How Do You Sell New York Now? Great Minds Are Working on It," *Wall Street Journal*, November 9, 2001, W17.

4. "A Year after the Storm, Business Remains Unusual," *New York Times*, August 25, 2006, 14.

5. New Orleans Metropolitan Convention and Visitors Bureau, press release, "New Orleans Tourism Industry Fact Sheet: Six-Year Anniversary of Hurricane Katrina," August 2011, accessed July 5, 2013, http://www.neworleansonline.com/pr/releases/releases/Sixth%20Anniversary%20Katrina%20tourism%20fact%20sheet.pdf.

6. There is a wealth of literature on the impacts of 9/11 and Katrina on popular culture. For some excellent examples, see Melnick, *9/11 Culture*; Gray, "Recovered, Reinvented, Reimagined;" Porter and Watts, *New Orleans Suite*.

7. Revenue figures for the organizations come from IRS Form 990, supplied by Guidestar (http://www.guidestar.org/). Guidestar reports generated June 28, 2012.

8. Author interview of NYC & Co. marketing official, 2009. In making this comment, the official referenced a similarly themed Bloomberg quote from a *New Yorker* cover story that had come out the week prior to the interview. Ben McGrath, "The Power of Michael Bloomberg: Can a Good Mayor Amass too Much Power?" *New Yorker*, August 24., 2009.

9. For discussion of the success of brand management techniques at Bloomberg L.P., see, for example, B&Q, "Case Study: Bloomberg." This report profiled models of "global thought leadership in the management of intangibles." See also the *New York Times* business profile, documenting how Bloomberg L.P. weathered the financial crisis and sought to extend its brand. Stephanie Clifford and Julie Creswell, "At Bloomberg, Modest Strategy to Rule the World," *New York Times*, November 15, 2009.

10. Brash, *Bloomberg's New York*.

11. Michael R. Bloomberg, "State of the City Address," press release, PR- 024-03, January 8, 2003.

12. The NYCEDC is a renamed version of the Office of Economic Development, created in 1976 during the fiscal crisis. NYC & Co. is a renamed version of the Convention and Visitors' Bureau, created in 1934 at the height of the Depression.

13. For coverage of these efforts, see the reporting of Jaquetta White for *The Times-Picayune* (available at nola.com business news archives), for example, Jaquetta White, "Proposal to Merge Two New Orleans Tourism Groups Is Voted Down," *The Times-Picayune*, December 8, 2010, http://www.nola.com/business/index.ssf/2010/12/proposal_to_ merge_two_new_orle.html.

14. For more on the role of race in the history of New Orleans tourism, see Souther, *New Orleans on Parade*; Gotham, *Authentic New Orleans*.

15. New Orleans Multicultural Tourism Network, "The Network," accessed June 14, 2013, http://www.soulofneworleans.com/thenetwork/.

16. New Orleans Metropolitan Convention and Visitors Bureau, "Tourism: The Silent Majority of American Industry Is Taking to the Streets in Cities Nationwide Including New Orleans," press release, 2009, accessed June 24, 2013, http://www.neworleanscvb. com/articles/index.cfm?action=view&articleID=3572&menuID=1604.

17. M. W. Walsh, "Urban Pain, from Sea to Sea: Many Once-Thriving Cities Are Suddenly Hurt," *New York Times*, September 30, 2001.

18. New Orleans Metropolitan Convention and Visitors Bureau, "Tourism, Hospitality and Cultural Economy Fact Sheet: Five-Year Anniversary of Hurricane Katrina," 2, press release, August 2010, accessed June 28, 2013, http://www.neworleansonline.com/pr/ releases/releases/Tourism,%20Hospitality,%20and%20Cultural%20Economy%20 Fact%20Sheet_1.pdf.

19. Ibid., 4.

20. New York City & Co., "Mayor Bloomberg and NYC & Company Chairman Tisch Announce City's Plan to Create Single Marketing and Tourism Organization," press release PR 190-06, June 8, 2006, accessed June 20, 2013, http://www.nyc.gov/portal/site/nyc-gov/menuitem.c0935b9a57bb4ef3daf2f1c701c789a0/index.jsp?pageID=mayor_press_ release&catID=1194&doc_name=http%3A%2F%2Fwww.nyc.gov%2Fhtml%2Fom%2F html%2F2006a%2Fpr190-06.html&cc=unused1978&rc=1194&ndi=1.

21. Ibid. The previous high was 43 million tourists in 2005.

22. Patrick McGeehan, "Near Ground Zero, a Mixed-Use Revival," *New York Times*, September 9, 2007.

23. Expenses and Revenue from the NYC & Co. are from IRS Form 990, supplied by Guidestar (http://www.guidestar.org/). Guidestar reports generated June 28, 2012.

24. Author interview of RJ, August 17, 2009.

25. Greenberg, "Branding, Crisis, and Utopia."

26. New Orleans Metropolitan Convention and Visitors Bureau, "New Orleans CVB Announces Aggressive Rebranding Campaign to Focus on Authentic and Dynamic Culture of New Orleans," press release, January 25, 2007, accessed June 20, 2013, http:// www.hotel-online.com/News/PR2007_1st/Jan07_NewOrleansCVB.html.

27. Author interview of DS, May 16, 2012.

28. State of Louisiana, Office of Lieutenant Governor, "Gov. Blanco, Lt. Gov. Landrieu, Sen. Landrieu, Sen. Vitter, and LRA Announce $28.5 M for Tourism Recovery," Press Release, September 19, 2006, accessed October 16, 2010, http://www.crt.state.la.us/ltgovernor/ media_view.aspx?id=131.

29. Expenses and Revenue from NOMCVB come from IRS Form 990, supplied by Guidestar (http://www.guidestar.org/). Guidestar reports generated June 28, 2012.

30. Jaquetta White, "Hospitality Task Force Created to Boost Tourism," *The Times-Picayune*, April 1, 2009.

31. Author interview of DS, May 16, 2012.

32. Greenberg, *Branding New York*, ch. 7.

33. Author interview of DS, May 16, 2012.

34. Cardwell, Diane, "Mayor Says New York Is Worth the Cost." *New York Times*, January 8, 2003.

35. Author interview of PR at EDC, July 27, 2009.This point is underscored by Brash, *Bloomberg's New York*. According to our interview, the new "C-suite" contrasted dramatically with the previously varied corporate backgrounds of EDC leadership.

36. Author interview of SP at EDC, July 27, 2009.

37. New York State Attorney General's Office, "A.G. Schneiderman Ends Illegal Lobbying of NYC Officials by Three Local Development Corporations," press release, July 3, 2012, accessed June 28, 2013, http://www.ag.ny.gov/press-release/ag-schneiderman-ends-illegal-lobbying-nyc-officials-three-local-development; Michael Howard Saul, "City Agency Admits Illegal Lobby Effort." *Wall Street Journal*, July 2, 2012, A17. The state statute governing LDCs stipulates that "no such corporation shall attempt to influence legislation by propaganda or otherwise." The audit uncovered illegal dealings by the EDC itself, as an LDC, as well as by two other LDCs created by the EDC and representing two of the largest-scale private development projects backed by the EDC: Coney Island and Flushing-Willets Point-Corona. The investigation was carried out at the instigation of a dissenting community group, Willets Point United.

38. For criticism of the limitations of the ruling, see Willets Point United, "It's Official: Entire Willets Point Development Rests on Illegal Lobbying," July 3, 2012, Accessed June 20, 2013, http://www.willetspoint.org/2012/07/its-official-entire-willets-point.html.

39. Whelan, Young, and Lauria, "Urban Regimes and Racial Politics," 15.

40. For scholarly accounts of the history and development of public-private relationships and business-government conflicts, see Gotham, *Authentic New Orleans*; Gotham, "Selling New Orleans to New Orleans"; Gotham, "Destination New Orleans"; Miron, "Corporate Ideology and the Politics of Entrepreneurialism in New Orleans"; Whelan and Young, "New Orleans: The Ambivalent City"; Whelan, "New Orleans: Mayoral Politics and Economic Development Policies in the Postwar Years, 1945–1986"; Whelan, Young, and Lauria, "Urban Regimes and Racial Politics in New Orleans."

41. New Orleans City Council, "Council Continues Effort to Move Towards New Public-Private Partnership Model of Economic Development for the City of New Orleans," press release, February 27, 2008, accessed June 25, 2012, http://archive.nolacitycouncil.com/newsfiles/2008/2008Feb27CouncilContinuesEffortEconomicDevelopment.pdf.

42. Plyer and Ortiz, "Poverty in Southeast Louisiana Post-Katrina."

43. This *New York Times* profile on Joseph Canizaro, real estate magnate and head of Mayor Ray Nagin's "Bring New Orleans Back Commission," originally brought such views into the national spotlight: Gary Rivlin, "A Mogul Who Would Rebuild New Orleans," *New York Times*, September 29, 2005.

44. Berlin, Burns, and Anderson, "Economic Development in Post-Katrina New Orleans."

45. Louisiana Department of Culture, Recreation, and Tourism. *Report of the Louisiana Rebirth Accountability Panel*.

46. Louisiana Department of Culture, Recreation, and Tourism, "Cultural Districts Program."

47. "2007: Louisiana Cements Its Reputation as Hollywood South," *The Times-Picayune*, January 19, 2012. As Anya Kamenetz reported in "The Short, Shady History of Hollywood South," *Fast Company*, December 19, 2007, http://www.fastcompany.com/60350/short-shady-history-hollywood-south, many film deals were legally questionable, including companies fudging accounts to get larger state handouts, ultimately leading to investigations by the FBI.

48. Figures reported in the *Louisiana Economic Quarterly*, Q3 and Q4 2011, 18.

49. City of New Orleans, "Mayor Landrieu Releases Report on Cultural Economy," press release, May 2, 2013, accessed November 11, 2013, http://www.nola.gov/mayor/press-releases/2013/20130502-mayor-landrieu-releases-report-on-city-s/

50. ibid.

51. City of New Orleans, Mayor's Office of Cultural Economy. *2010 New Orleans: Cultural Economy Snapshot,* 8.

52. Jaquetta White, "Orleans Alliance Will Focus on Retail; Public-Private Push Discusses Its Strategy," *The Times-Picayune,* February 9, 2011.

53. Judd, "Constructing the Tourist Bubble."

54. Author interview of NYC & Co. marketing official, 2009. Tim Armstrong, then CMO of Google and now at AOL, said at the launch: "What you have done with the site [technologically] is just unprecedented in terms of what's being done for a city." See also: NYC & Co., "NYC & COMPANY Announces Major Renovation of Visitor Information Center in Midtown Manhattan," press release, July 1, 2008, accessed July 17, 2013, http://www.nycandcompany.org/press/press-releasevisitor-information-center-07-01-08.

55. NYC & Co., "NYC & COMPANY Partners with CityMaps to Launch NYC Map," press release, April 2, 2012, http://www.nycandcompany.org/press/nyc-company-partners-with-citymaps-to-launch-nyc-map. A few months before joining NYC & Co., CityMap was embraced by the local real estate industry and received $2.5 million in investment. On the real estate potential of this application, see Alison Gregor, "A New York Map Service Saves Brokers' Shoe Leather," *New York Times,* December 6, 2011.

56. As the editor of the *New York Observer's* technology blog noted after reviewing the application: "While more popular areas like Manhattan were easily populated with logos, the further out in the boroughs you got, the less helpful the map became. NYC Map claims to serve as a digital toolkit for all five boroughs, but considering that the app is primarily aimed at tourists, we won't hold our breath on places like Bushwick getting a fleshed-out map tool any time soon." See Jessica Roy, "Betabeat: There's a Map for That: NYC & Company and CityMaps Team Up to Launch Free Mobile Map App," *New York Observer,* April 2, 2012, http://betabeat.com/2012/04/nyc-company-and-citymaps-team-up-to-launch-free-mobile-map-app/.

57. NYC & Co., "Mayor Bloomberg and NYC & Company Open New Office in India as Strength of—and Reliance on—New York City's $30 Billion Tourism Industry Grows," press release PR- 406-08, October 13, 2008, accessed June 22, 2013, http://home.nyc.gov/portal/site/nycgov/menuitem.c0935b9a57bb4ef3daf2f1c701c789a0/index.jsp?pageID=mayor_press_release&catID=1194&doc_name=http%3A%2F%2Fhome.nyc.gov%2Fhtml%2Fom%2Fhtml%2F2008b%2Fpr406-08.html&cc=unused1978&rc=1194&ndi=1. Since March 2007, NYC & Co.'s new offices include Spain (Madrid), the Benelux countries (Amsterdam), Scandinavia/Finland (Stockholm), Russia (Moscow), China (Shanghai), Korea (Seoul), Japan (Tokyo), Brazil (São Paulo), Canada (Toronto), Australia (Sydney), and India (Mumbai).

58. This point was made by Jennifer Ackerson of Alon Consulting for the promotional video, "This is NYC & Company Membership," uploaded to YouTube by nycgo.com, Oct 1, 2009, http://www.youtube.com/watch?v=mHcpWQUqwuM.

59. New Orleans Metropolitan Convention and Visitors Bureau, "New Orleans CVB Announces Aggressive Rebranding Campaign to Focus on Authentic and Dynamic Culture of New Orleans," press release, January 25, 2007, accessed June 20, 2013, http://www.hotel-online.com/News/PR2007_1st/Jan07_NewOrleansCVB.html.

60. Ibid.

61. State of Louisiana, Office of Lieutenant Governor, "Gov. Blanco, Lt. Gov. Landrieu, Sen. Landrieu, Sen. Vitter and LRA Announce $28.5 M for Tourism Recovery," press release,

September 19, 2006, accessed June 22, 2013,.http://www.crt.state.la.us/ltgovernor/media_view.aspx?id=131.

62. Greenberg, "The Limits of Branding."

63. Gotham, "(Re)Branding the Big Easy."

64. Michael Kimmelman, "In a Square, a Sense of Unity; A Homegrown Memorial Brings Strangers Together," *New York Times*, September 19, 2001, E1.

65. Eleftheria Parpis, "New Orleans, Revisited," *Adweek*, August 8, 2007, accessed November 12, 2013, http://www.adweek.com/news/advertising/new-orleans-revisited-89870.

66. Ibid.

67. ibid.

68. Author interview, 2003.

69. Jayson Blair, "Here Dignity Rubs Elbows with Demand: Ground Zero Crowds Don't Please Everyone," *New York Times*, June 26, 2002, B1, B4.

70. For an ethnography of these tours, see Thomas, "Roots Run Deep Here."

71. See Gotham, *Authentic New Orleans*.

72. Thomas, "Roots Run Deep Here," 754

73. Wirthlin Worldwide, "Post 9/11 Assessment of E.D.C. Communications"; Shifflet and Associates, *USA Travel Recovery/Monitor*.

74. Wirthlin, ibid.

75. Jaquetta White, "Task Force Tackles Tourism Study; 17-member Group Has 10 Year Vision," *The Times-Picayune*, April 2, 2009.

76. Jaquetta White, "La. Takes 3-Pronged Attack; Angelle Reveals How BP Aid Will Be Split," *The Times-Picayune*, June 10, 2010.

77. Ruth Shalit, "Brand New: How Do You Sell New York Now? Great Minds Are Working on It," *Wall Street Journal*, November 9, 2001.

78. Robbie Brown, "New Orleans Limits Hurricane-Themed Excursions," *New York Times*, October 11, 2012.

79. Arthur Danto, "The Vietnam Veterans Memorial," *The Nation*, August 31, 1985, 152–55. Cited in Marita Sturken, *Tangled Memories*.

80. Frank Donze, " 'We're Unbowed,' N.O. Mayor Declares; Landrieu Addresses Global News Media," *The Times-Picayune*, August 27, 2010.

81. Ron Starner, "The New Orleans Miracle: Led by an Innovative Mayor, a Resilient City Offers Lessons for the Rest of the United States," *Site Selection*, n.d., accessed July 19, 2011, http://www.siteselection.com/ssinsider/snapshot/new-orleans.cfm.

82. Conflict arose, in particular, around the exclusion of first responders and other survivors from the events, due to "space constraints." First responders and their representative organizations took this as "an affront" and linked it to the embarrassing fact that many still hadn't received adequate medical treatment for 9/11-related health problems. They saw the decision "as evidence of the city's attempt to push to the background their untreated ailments in the official narrative of recovery and renewal." See Jeff Stein, "First Responders Decry Exclusion from 9/11 Ceremony," *CNN*, August 30, 2011, accessed September 16, 2011, http://www.cnn.com/2011/US/08/16/new.york.911.memorial/index.html?hpt=hp_t2.

83. White House, "Remarks by the President at 'A Concert for Hope,'" press release, September 11, 2011, accessed November 8, 2012, http://www.whitehouse.gov/the-press-office/2011/09/11/remarks-president-concert-hope.

84. Author interview of Wordsearch executive, April 5, 2010.

85. Ibid.

86. The original "creative revolution" in advertising and commercial media arose along with the 1960s counter culture—particularly its embrace of an anticorporate ethos and burgeoning consumer movement. It was then that younger, more "creative" firms were able

to tap into the zeitgeist and challenge Madison Avenue stalwarts through use of more intelligent, experimental, and ironic messaging. This new talent began working on campaigns for the nation's struggling corporations and struggling cities, as it had in 1977 when New York State hired the upstart Wells, Rich, Greene and leading pop-art graphic designer Milton Glaser to create the "I♥NY" campaign. See Greenberg, *Branding New York*, chs. 2 and 7; Frank, *The Conquest of Cool*.

87. Roland Barthes, *The Semiotic Challenge*.
88. For overview and analysis, see e.g. Ann Markusen and Anne Gadwa, "Arts and Culture in Urban or Regional Planning;" and Sharon Zukin, *The Cultures of Cities*.
89. For an overview and description of the New Orleans Urban Conservancy's "Stay Local!" program to support grassroots business growth, see http://www.staylocal.org/about (accessed August 6, 2012).
90. For discussion of the evolution of the concept of diversity in a post-race context, see Perry, *More Beautiful and More Terrible*; Gray, *Cultural Moves*; Bell and Hartmann, "Diversity in Everyday Discourse"; Goldberg, "When Race Disappears."
91. There is a growing literature on the neoliberal "post-racial." See David Theo Goldberg, *The Threat of Race: Reflections on Racial Neoliberalism*; and Aihwa Ong, *Neoliberalism as Exception*.
92. Author interview of NYC & Co. marketing official, 2007. See also Liz Robbins, "Follow That Tourist" *New York Times*, July 21, 2012, MB1.
93. CAAV, "Converting Chinatown: A Snapshot of a Neighborhood Becoming Unaffordable," report of CAAV Organizing Asian Communities and Community Development Project of the Urban Justice Center, December 2008, accessed June 28, 2013, http://www.urban-justice.org/pdf/publications/ConvertingChinatown_dec08.pdf; see also Adrian Leeds, "The Cost of Real Estate: The Big Easy, the Rich Coast or the City of Light."
94. There is growing interest in the elite embrace of multiculturalism and diversity as a form of cultural capital and self-cultivation in the current global era. See, for example, Shamus Khan, "The New Elitists," *New York Times*, July 7, 2012.
95. For a similar campaign, see, for example, "London 2012" at http://www.wolffolins.com/search?q=london+2012, accessed June 28, 2013.
96. Wolff Olins, "New York City Case Study," accessed June 22, 2010, http://www.wolffolins.com/work/new-york-city.
97. The "NYC Case Study" was originally hosted at wolffolins.com. It may be found, cached, at "NYC: One for Many," 2008, fall2008.g-ap.org/uploads/NYC_case_study.pdf.
98. On the desire for cross-class New York authenticity, see Sharon Zukin, *Naked City*, ch. 7.
99. On this point, see, for instance, Jameson, "Reification and Utopia in Mass Culture."
100. Wolff Olins, "New York; One for Many."
101. Other aspects of the campaign included banners and wall art. On T-shirts, see Adrian Quinlan, "With New Official T-Shirts, City Shoots for the Hip." *New York Times*, August 19, 2011, accessed June 22, 2013, http://cityroom.blogs.nytimes.com/2011/08/19/with-new-official-t-shirts-city-shoots-for-the-hip/.
102. Through successive mayoral administrations from the 1980s through the 2000s, New York maintained a $500 million "war on graffiti," and launched various efforts, some shot down in court, to censor any expression of the art form, legal or not, in public space. See Greenberg, *Branding New York*; Austin, *Taking the Train*.
103. Adrian Quinlan, "With New Official T-Shirts, City Shoots for the Hip."
104. Author interview of SD, May 2, 2012.
105. See video at: https://www.youtube.com/watch?v=kmvTcFWWhmc
106. For representations of the Arts District, see http://www.neworleansonline.com/tools/neighborhoodguide/artsdistrict.html (accessed June 28, 2013).
107. Gro Harlem Bruntland, *Our Common Future*.

108. For discussion of the depoliticization of sustainability as a discourse, see Melissa Checker, "Wiped Out by the 'Greenwave' "; for an overview of the appropriation of sustainability rhetoric by powerful interests, see Parr, *Hijacking Sustainability*.

109. Greenberg, "The Sustainability Edge."

110. Author interview of Two Twelve, July 2012. Two Twelve is the branding firm hired to design the NYC 2012 campaign, as well as PlaNYC 2030.

111. For the extent to which the original vision for redevelopment from the Olympic bid was realized through subsequent development efforts, see Mitchell Moss, *How New York City Won the Olympics*, Rudin Center for Transportation Policy and Management, New York University, November 2011, accessed June 22, 2013, http://wagner.nyu.edu/rudincenter/publications/Olympics_in_NYC%202012_REPORT_110711.pdf.

112. Description of fonts and layout from author interview of Two Twelve, July 2012. "Aura of a plan" from Peter Marcuse presentation on the panel, "Bloomberg's 2030 Plan for New York City," hosted by the Progressive Planners Network, American Academy of Geographers conference, February26, 2012. See also C. J. Hughes, "A Critical Look at PlaNYC, Four Years After Its Launch," *Architectural Record*, September 29, 2011.

113. Author interview with SP, ibid.

114. New Orleans Chamber of Commerce, "Green Committee," accessed November 11, 2013, http://neworleanschamber.org/article/greencommitee.

115. New Orleans Metropolitan Convention and Visitors Bureau, "Sustainability and Green Meetings," accessed July 1, 2012, http://www.neworleanscvb.com/meeting-planners/plan-your-meeting/sustainability-green/.

116. Greater New Orleans, Inc., "SII the Future," *News and Publications*, 26: June 17, 2011, accessed July 1, 2012, http://gnoinc.org/news/publications/region-report/sii-the-future/.

117. Greater New Orleans, Inc., "Sustainable Industries," Industry Sectors, accessed November 11, 2013. http://m.gnoinc.org/sustainable-industries.php

118. Stephanie Riegel, Greater New Orleans, Inc., "Looking On the Green Side," *News and Publications*, August 1, 2010, accessed July 2, 2012, http://gnoinc.org/news/region-news/looking-on-the-green-side/.

119. A growing literature explores the implications of city efforts to imagine "the standpoint of the out-of-towner" alongside of, and often instead of, the standpoint of the daily urban inhabitant in various urban redevelopment and urban branding campaigns. See, for example, Gotham, *Authentic New Orleans*; Greenberg, *Branding New York*; Eisinger, "The Politics of Bread and Circuses"; Judd, *The Infrastructure of Play*.

CHAPTER 7

1. Lyrics found on the Carter Family, *My Clinch Mountain Home: Their Complete Victor Recordings 1928–1929*.

2. Baldwin, *The Fire Next Time*.

3. Klinenberg, *Heat Wave*.

4. Tilly, *Big Structures*, 146.

5. McFarlane, "The Comparative City," 726; McFarlane, *Learning the City*. Also, see especially *Urban Geography*, 33(6), 2012, a particularly helpful special issue on comparative urbanism.

6. Beauregard, "City of Superlatives"; Brenner, "Stereotypes, Archetypes and Prototypes."

7. Robinson, *Ordinary Cities*; Robinson, "Cities in a World of Cities." For a critical overview of recent theorizing on urban paradigms, see Judd and Simpson, *The City, Revisited*.

8. Brenner, Peck, and Theodore, "Variegated Neoliberalization"; Ong, *Neoliberalism as Exception*.

9. Abu-Lughod, *New York, Chicago, Los Angeles*; Abu-Lughod, *Race, Space, and Riots in Chicago, New York, and Los Angeles*; Brenner, "World City Theory, Globalization, and the Comparative-historical Method."

10. Lefebvre, *The Production of Space*.

11. Peck and Tickell. "Neoliberalizing Space," 36; Brenner and Theodore, eds. *Spaces of Neoliberalism*.

12. McMichael, "Incorporating Comparison Within a World-historical Perspective."

13. As explored in Chapter 3, here one sees the importance of the relative strength of public-sector unions in New York versus in New Orleans. The latter are located within a "right-to-work" state and became a softer target for the rollout of legislation that empowered FEMA to disregard prevailing wage, benefit, and health and safety regulations in the hiring of temporary emergency workers.

14. Robinson, "Global and World Cities"

15. Beck, "Living in the World Risk Society," 331.

16. Vale and Campanella, *Resilient City*; Campanella, "Urban Resilience and the Recovery of New Orleans."

17. Chernick, *Resilient City*; Campanella, "Urban Resilience and the Recovery of New Orleans." See also, Aldrich, *Social Capital in Post-Disaster Recovery*.

18. On anti-urban origins of modern environmental discourse, see Gandy, *Concrete and Clay*. On the U.N. definition, see World Commission on Environment and Development, *Our Common Future*, 43.

19. On sustainability as competitive urban strategy, see Greenberg, "The Sustainability Edge."

20. Calthorpe, *The Next American Metropolis*. Note: Contemporary "eco-city" discourse references but departs from countercultural and conservation-oriented models of eco-architecture and urban design that arose in the 1960s and later, particularly in Northern California. On the latter, see Register, *Ecocity Berkeley*.

21. In response, there has been a move to reclaim and reframe concepts of sustainability and growth within the environmental justice movement, and so to keep alive the social and cultural sustainability of vulnerable communities at risk of contamination and displacement. See, for example, Agyeman, Bullard, and Evans, *Just Sustainabilities*.

22. For a critical account of the loss of resilience and increased vulnerability of New Orleans to hurricanes and flooding, see Colten, *Perilous Place, Powerful Storms*.

23. James Quinn, "Goldman Sachs Faces Public Anger over Plan to Replace Shops with Designer Restaurants Near HQ," *The Telegraph*, August 1, 2010. As landlord of the 200 West block, Goldman promised to rent to tenants who could provide needed retail services like a grocery and hardware store in this newly developed residential neighborhood. Not only did it renege on this promise, but it also replaced the existing pizzeria, shoe store, gym, and budget hotel with "a trio of restaurants run by Danny Meyer—the New York City restaurant wunderkind—as well as a new ballroom and conference centre, attached to the hotel which will be upgraded." Even within the building, "a new class of haves and have-nots" emerged, as outside offices were reserved for the firm's three hundred partners; managing directors got windowless inside offices, and lowly vice presidents lost offices altogether and were relegated to benches in a common area. See Suzanne Craig, "Goldman Sachs's New Palace Creates Princes, Serfs," *Wall Street Journal*, April 16, 2010, http://online.wsj.com/article/SB10001424052702303828304575180581255747658.html.

24. Jonathan Watts, "Aftermath of Hurricane Sandy Leaves Haiti Facing New Disaster: While the World's Attention Has Focused on the US, the Suffering and Consequences for the Caribbean Nation are Far Greater," *The Guardian*, November 2, 2012.

25. Kate Taylor, "Bloomberg Hails Lower Manhattan's Revival Since 9/11," *New York Times*, September 6, 2011, Accessed August 6, 2013, http://cityroom.blogs.nytimes.com/2011/09/06/bloomberg-hails-lower-manhattans-revival-since-911/.

26. Downtown Alliance, "Back to Business: The State of Lower Manhattan Four Months After Hurricane Sandy," March 6, 2013, accessed August 6, 2013, http://www.downtownny.com/sandy#sthash.UXVsfdNT.dpuf.

27. Nick Pinto, "Hurricane Sandy Is New York's Katrina: Floods, Fear, and FEMA Failures," *Village Voice*, November 21, 2012, accessed August 6, 2013, http://www.villagevoice.com/2012-11-21/news/hurricane-sandy-is-new-york-s-katrina/.

28. The report is available at http://www.nyc.gov/html/sirr/html/report/report.shtml. While dubbed a "plan," there is nothing binding about this report, nor has it passed through City Planning. Rather, like PlaNYC, it may be viewed more as a "vision plan" and as a form of marketing and PR intended to build internal political consensus and attract investment. Moreover, given its issuance in the final months of the Bloomberg administration, there is no assurance it will become policy. Nonetheless, it represents a significant effort to advocate for a Bloomberg model of urban resilience that will protect and ensure the continuance of his administration's redevelopment agenda.

29. Mark Fishetti, "New York Could Look Like New Orleans, Due to Storm Protection," *Scientific American*, June 12, 2013.

30. For images and description of the rally, see Somala Diby, "Groups March to City Hall for Fairness in Rebuilding," *City Atlas*, August 8, 2013, http://newyork.thecityatlas.org/lifestyle/turning-tide/, accessed August 15, 2013.

31. From notes taken by Miriam Greenberg at the rally, July 31, 2013.

32. Lefebvre, Henri, *The Urban Revolution*.

33. Roy and AlSayyad, *Urban Informality*.

34. Biggs et al., "Are We Entering an Era of Concatenated Global Crises?"

SELECTED BIBLIOGRAPHY

Abu-Lughod, Janet L. "The Battle for Tompkins Square Park." In *From Urban Village to East Village: The Battle for New York's Lower East Side*, edited by Janet L. Abu-Lughod, 233–66. Cambridge, MA: Blackwell, 1994.

Abu-Lughod, Janet L. *New York, Chicago, Los Angeles: America's Global Cities*. Minneapolis and London: University of Minnesota Press, 1999.

Abu-Lughod, Janet L. *Race, Space, and Riots in Chicago, New York, and Los Angeles*. New York: Oxford University Press, 2007.

Agamben, Giorgio, *State of Exception*. Translated by Kevin Attell. Chicago: University of Chicago Press, 2004.

Agyeman, Julian, Robert D. Bullard, and Bob Evans, eds. *Just Sustainabilities: Development in an Unequal World*. Cambridge: MIT Press, 2003.

Aldrich, Daniel P., *Social Capital in Post-Disaster Recovery*. Chicago: University of Chicago, 2012.

Alliance for Downtown New York. *The Lower Manhattan Retail Sector: One Year Later*. New York: Audience Research and Analysis, 2002.

Alliance for Downtown New York. *The Lower Manhattan Retail Sector: Beginning to Recover*. New York: Audience Research and Analysis, 2003.

Alliance for Downtown New York. *State of Lower Manhattan 2011*. New York: Alliance for Downtown New York, 2011, accessed June 29, 2013, http://www.downtownny.com/sites/default/files/pdfs/SOLM_2011_9.20.11.pdf.

Angotti, Tom. *New York for Sale: Community Planning Confronts Global Real Estate*. Cambridge: MIT Press, 2008.

Antonio, Robert, and Alessandro Bonanno. "Periodizing Globalization: From Cold War Modernization to the Bush Doctrine." In *Current Perspectives in Social Theory; Between the Cold War and Neo-Imperialism*, edited by Jennifer Lehmann and Harry Dahms, 1–57. Binkley, UK: Emerald Group Publishing, 2006.

Arena, John. *Driven from New Orleans: How Nonprofits Betray Public Housing and Promote Privatization*. Minneapolis: University of Minnesota Press, 2012.

Asian American Federation of New York. "Chinatown One Year after September 11th: An Economic Impact Study." April 4, 2002 (an interim report in collaboration with the Federal Reserve Bank of New York, the Fiscal Policy Institute, Ralph and Goldy Lewis Center), accessed March 24, 2012, http://www.aafny.org/doc/ChinatownAfter911.pdf.

Asian American Federation of New York. "Chinatown One Year After September 11: An Economic Impact Study." November 2002 (in collaboration with the Federal Reserve Bank of New York, the Fiscal Policy Institute, Ralph and Goldy Lewis Center), p. 20, accessed November 12, 2013, http://www.aafny.org/doc/ChinatownOneYearAfter911.pdf

Auyero, Javier and Debora Swistun. *Flammable: Environmental Suffering in an Argentine Shantytown*. New York: Oxford University Press, 2009.

B&Q. "Case Study: Bloomberg." In *Unlocking the Hidden Wealth of Organisations: The Development and Communication of Intangible Assets* (2003), 33–40, accessed June 28, 2013, https://www.cass.city.ac.uk/__data/assets/pdf_file/0003/76980/Cass_UnlockingHiddenWealthofOrgnanisations.pdf.

Bailey, Robert. *The Crisis Regime: The M.A.C., the E.F.C.B., and the Political Impact of the New York City Financial Crisis*, Albany: State University of New York Press, 1985.

Bainfield, Edward. *The Unheavenly City.* New York: Little, Brown, and Company, 1970.

Baldwin, James. *The Fire Next Time.* New York, Penguin, 1963.

Bankoff, Greg, "Rendering the World Unsafe: 'Vulnerability' as Western Discourse." *Disasters* 25, 1 (2001): 19–35.

Bankoff, Greg, *Cultures of Disaster Society and Natural Hazard in the Philippines.* London: Routledge, 2004.

Bankoff, Greg, G. Frerks, and D. Hilhorst, eds. *Mapping Vulnerability: Disasters, Development and People.* London: Earthscan, 2004.

Barry, John. *Rising Tide: The Great Mississippi Flood of 1927 and How It Changed America.* New York: Touchstone, 1997.

Barthes, Roland. *The Semiotic Challenge.* Berkeley: University of California Press, 1994.

Bayoumi, Moustafa. "Letter to a G-Man." In *After the World Trade Centre: Rethinking New York City,* edited by Michael Sorkin and Sharon Zukin, 131–42. New York: Routledge, 2002.

Beauregard, Robert A. *Voices of Decline: The Postwar Fate of U.S.Cities.* New York: Blackwell, 1993.

Beauregard, Robert A. "City of Superlatives." *City and Community,* 2 (2003): 183–99.

Beck, Ulrich. *Risk Society: Towards a New Modernity.* London, UK: Sage, 1992.

Beck Ulrich, *Ecological Enlightenment: Essays on the Politics of the Risk Society.* Atlantic Highlands, NJ: Prometheus Books, 1995.

Beck Ulrich, *World Risk Society.* Oxford, UK: Blackwell, 1999.

Beck, Ulrich. "Living in the World Risk Society: A Hobhouse Memorial Public Lecture Given on Wednesday 15 February 2006 at the London School of Economics." *Economy and Society* 35 (2006): 329–45.

Becker, Howard S. *Tricks of the Trade: How to Think about Your Research While You're Doing It.* Chicago: University of Chicago Press, 1998.

Bell, Joyce M., and Douglas Hartmann. "Diversity in Everyday Discourse: The Cultural Ambiguities and Consequences of 'Happy Talk.'" *American Sociological Review* 72, no. 6 (2007): 895–914.

Bellush, Jewell, and Dick Netzer, *Urban Politics, New York Style.* New York: New York University Press, 1990.

Belmont, Cynthia. "Tax-Exempt Bonds, 1996–2002." *SOI Bulletin* (Summer 2005), at 174, Table 7 (Volume of Private Activity Bonds by Type, Term, and Issue Year, 1996–2002), accessed June 13, 2013, http://www.irs.gov/uac/SOI-Tax-Stats-SOI-Bulletin:-Summer-2005.

Benjamin, Walter. *On the Concept of History.* New York: Classic Books America, 2009.

Berlin, Anne, Katie Burns, and Louise Anderson. "Economic Development in Post-Katrina New Orleans—With Disaster Comes Opportunity and New Ways of Thinking." *Economic Development Now* 8 (February 25, 2008).

Beyond Ground Zero, *We Count! Documenting the 9/11 Health Crisis 8 Years Later.* New York: Beyond Ground Zero, September 2009, accessed June 29, 2013, http://www.urbanjustice.org/pdf/publications/wecount_sept09.pdf.

Biggs, D., R. Biggs, V. Dakos, R. J. Scholes, and M. Schoon. "Are We Entering an Era of Concatenated Global Crises?" *Ecology and Society* 16, no. 2 (2011), accessed June 29, 2013, http://www.ecologyandsociety.org/vol16/iss2/art27/.

Birch, Eugenia Ladner, and Susan M. Wachter, eds. *Rebuilding Urban Places after Disaster: Lessons from Hurricane Katrina.* Philadelphia: University of Pennsylvania Press, 2006.

Blaikie, P., T. Cannon, I. Davis, and B. Wisner. *At Risk: Natural Hazards, People's Vulnerability and Disasters.* London: Routledge, 1994.

Bobo, James R. *The New Orleans Economy: Pro Bono Publico?* New Orleans: Division of Business and Economic Research, College of Business Administration, University of New Orleans, 1975.

Bolin, Robert and Lois Stanford, editors. *The Northridge Earthquake: Vulnerability and Disaster.* London, UK: Routledge, 1998.

Brasch, Walter. *"Unacceptable": The Federal Government's Response to Hurricane Katrina.* Charleston, SC: Booksurge, 2006.

Brash, Julian. *Bloomberg's New York: Class and Governance in the Luxury City.* Athens, GA: University of Georgia Press, 2011.

Brenner, Neil. "World City Theory, Globalization, and the Comparative-Historical Method: Reflections on Janet Abu-Lughod's Interpretation of Contemporary Urban Restructuring." *Urban Affairs Review* 36, no. 6 (2001): 124–47.

Brenner, Neil. "Stereotypes, Archetypes and Prototypes: Three Uses of Superlatives in Contemporary Urban Studies." *City & Community* 2, no. 3 (2003): 205–18.

Brenner, Neil, "What Is Critical Urban Theory?" *City* 13, nos. 2–3 (June–September 2009), 198–207.

Brenner, Neil, Jamie Peck, and Nik Theodore. "After Neoliberalization?" *Globalizations* 7 (2010): 327–45.

Brenner, Neil, Jamie Peck, and Nik Theodore. "Variegated Neoliberalization: Geographies, Modalities, Pathways." *Global Networks* 10, 2 (2010): 182–222.

Brenner, Neil, and Nik Theodore, eds. *Spaces of Neoliberalism: Urban Restructuring in North America and Western Europe.* Malden, NJ: Blackwell Publishing, 2002.

Brezina, Timothy. "What Went Wrong in New Orleans? An Examination of the Welfare Dependency Explanation." *Social Problems* 55 (2008): 23–42.

Brezina, Timothy, and Joanne M. Kaufman. "What Really Happened in New Orleans? Estimating the Threat of Violence During the Hurricane Katrina Disaster." *Justice Quarterly* 25, no. 4 (2008): 701–22.

Brookings Institution, *New Orleans after the Storm: Lessons from the Past, a Plan for the Future.* Washington, DC: Brookings Institution, October 2005, accessed June 29, 2013. http://www.brookings.edu/~/media/research/files/reports/2005/10/metropolitanpol-icy/20051012_neworleans.pdf.

Bruntland, Gro Harlem. *Our Common Future: The World Commission on Environment and Development.* Oxford: Oxford University Press, 1987.

Bullard, Robert D., ed. *Dumping in Dixie: Race, Class, and Environmental Quality.* Boulder, CO: Westview Press, 2000.

Bullard, Robert D., and Beverly Wright. "The Real Looting: Katrina Exposes a Legacy of Discrimination and Opens the Door for 'Disaster Capitalism,'" 2005, http://www.see-ingblack.com/2005/x101105/411_oct05.shtml, accessed July 10, 2013.

Bullard, Robert D., and Beverly Wright, eds. *Race, Place, and Environmental Justice after Hurricane Katrina: Struggles to Reclaim, Rebuild, and Revitalize New Orleans and the Gulf Coast.* Boulder, CO: Westview Press, 2009.

Burby, Raymond J. "Hurricane Katrina and the Paradoxes of Government Disaster Policy: Bringing about Wise Governmental Decisions about Hazardous Areas." *The Annals of the American Academy of Political and Social Science* 604, no. 1 (2006): 171–91.

Bureau of Governmental Research. *BGR Outlook on Orleans: Status Report on the 1998 City Operating Budget.* New Orleans: Bureau of Governmental Research, March 1998.

Burns, Peter F., and Matthew O. Thomas. "A 'New' New Orleans? Understanding the Role of History and the State–local Relationship in the Recovery Process." *Journal of Urban Affairs* 30, no 3 (2008): 259–71.

Bush, Daniel H. "Talking Point: Equity and Faith Needed in Community Spending Plan," *Downtown Express.* 17, no. 47 (April 15–21, 2005), accessed June 29, 2013, http://www.downtownexpress.com/de_102/equityandfaith.html.

Bush, George W., "Remarks at the 9/11 Heroes Medal of Valor Award Ceremony." Public Papers of the Presidents of the United States: George W. Bush (2005, Book II), 1410–12. Washington, DC: Government Printing Office, September 9, 2005, accessed August 11, 2011, http://www.gpo.gov/fdsys/pkg/PPP-2005-book2/html/PPP-2005-book2-doc-pg1410.htm.

——, "Remarks at the Dedication Ceremony for the 9/11 Pentagon Memorial in Arlington, Virginia." Public Papers of the Presidents of the United States: George W. Bush (2008, Book II). 1193-1195. Washington, DC: Government Printing Office, September 11, 2008. Accessed August 11, 2011. http://www.gpo.gov/ fdsys/pkg/ PPP-2008 -book2/html/PPP-2008-book2-doc-pg1193.htm

Cable, Sherry, Thomas E. Shriver, and Tamara L. Mix. "Risk Society and Contested Illness: The Case of Nuclear Weapons Workers." *American Sociological Review* 73, no. 3 (2008): 380–401.

Calhoun, Craig. "The Privatization of Risk." *Public Culture* 18, no. 2 (2006): 257–63, doi:10.1215/08992363-2006-001.

Calthorpe, Peter, *The Next American Metropolis: Ecology, Community, and the American Dream.* New York: Princeton Architectural Press, 1995.

Campanella, Richard. *Time and Place in New Orleans: Past Geographies in the Present Day.* Gretna, LA: Pelican Publishing, 2002.

Campanella, Richard. *Bienville's Dilemma: A Historical Geography of New Orleans.* Lafayette, LA: Center for Louisiana Studies, 2008.

Campanella, Thomas. "Urban Resilience and the Recovery of New Orleans." *Journal of the American Planning Association* 72, no. 2 (2006): 141–46.

Canak, William, and Berkeley Miller. "Gumbo Politics: Unions, Business, and Louisiana Right-to-Work Legislation." *Industrial and Labor Relations Review* 43, no. 2 (1990): 258–71.

Caro, R. *The Power Broker: Robert Moses and the Fall of New York.* Vintage, New York, 1975.

Center for International Policy. "Privatizing Homeland Security." *Border Lines* (blog), *TransBorder Project, Center for International Policy.* October 28, 2009, accessed June 29, 2013, http://borderlinesblog.blogspot.com/2009/10/privatizing-homeland-security.html.

Charmaz, Kathy. "Grounded Theory in the 21st Century: Applications for Advancing Social Justice Studies," in *The Sage Handbook of Qualitative Research,* edited by Norman K. Denzin and Yvonna S. Lincoln. 3rd ed. Thousand Oaks, CA: Sage, 2005, 507–35.

Checker, Melissa. "Wiped Out by the 'Greenwave': Environmental Gentrification and the Paradoxical Politics of Urban Sustainability." *City and Society* 23, no. 2 (2011): 210–29.

Chernick, Howard, ed. *Resilient City: The Economic Impact of 9/11.* New York: Russell Sage Foundation, 2005.

Chetkovich, Carol, and Frances Kunreuther. *From the Ground Up: Grassroots Organizations Making Social Change.* Ithaca, NY: Cornell University Press, 2006.

City of New Orleans, Mayor's Office of Cultural Economy. *2010 New Orleans: Cultural Economy Snapshot.* City of New Orleans, New Orleans, LA, 2010.

Civic Alliance to Rebuild Downtown New York, "Listening to the City: Report of Proceedings." Jacob Javits Center, New York City. July 20 and July 22, 2002, http://americaspeaks.org/wp-content/_data/n_0001/resources/live/final_report_ltc3.pdf.

Clarke, Lee. *Acceptable Risk? Making Decisions in a Toxic Environment.* Berkeley: University of California. Press, 1989.

Clarke, Lee. *Mission Improbable: Using Fantasy Documents to Tame Disaster*. Chicago: University of Chicago Press, 1999.

Cohen, Ariella. "New Orleans Gets Table Scrap in GO Zone Lending Feast." *The Lens*. December 17, 2010, http://thelensnola.org/2010/12/17/go-zone-lending-program/.

Colten, Craig E. "Basin Street Blues: Drainage and Environmental Equity in New Orleans, 1890–1930." *Journal of Historical Geography* 28, no 2 (2002): 237–57.

Colten, Craig E. *An Unnatural Metropolis: Wresting New Orleans from Nature*. Baton Rouge: Louisiana State University Press, 2005.

Colten, Craig E. *Perilous Place, Power Storms: Hurricane Protection in Coastal Louisiana*. Oxford, MI: University of Mississippi Press, 2009.

Comfort, Louise K. "Crisis Management in Hindsight: Cognition, Communication, Coordination, and Control." *Public Administration Review* 67, no. 1 (2007): 189–97.

Comfort, Louise K. ed. *Designing Resilience: Preparing for Extreme Events*. Pittsburgh: University of Pittsburgh Press, 2010.

Comfort, Louise K., T. A. Birkland, B. A. Cigler, and E. Nance. "Retrospectives and Prospectives on Hurricane Katrina: Five Years and Counting." *Public Administration Review* 70, no. 5 (2010): 669–78.

Comptroller General of the United States. *Cost, Schedule, and Performance Problems of the Lake Pontchartrain and Vicinity, Louisiana, Hurricane Protection Project*. Report to Congress. PSAD-76-161, August 31, 1976. Washington, DC: Comptroller General of the United States, 1976, accessed June 29, 2013, http://archive.gao.gov/f0402/098185.pdf.

Conte, Christopher, and Albert R. Karr. *An Outline of the U.S. Economy*. Washington, DC: U.S. Department of State, 2001.

Cooke, Oliver D. *Rethinking Municipal Privatization*. New York: Routledge, 2007.

Cooper, Christopher, and Robert Block. *Disaster: Hurricane Katrina and the Failure of Homeland Security*. New York: Times Books, 2006.

Cutter, Susan. *American Hazardscapes: The Regionalization of Hazards and Disasters*. Washington, DC: Joseph Henry Press, 2001

Dabney, Thomas Ewing. "The Industrial Canal and Inner Harbor of New Orleans: History, Description and Economic Aspects of Giant Facility Created to Encourage Industrial Expansion and Develop Commerce." Howard Tilton Library, Louisisana Collection, Tulane University, 1921.

Damiani, Bettina, and Stephanie Greenwood. *The LMDC: They're in the Money; We're in the Dark: A Review of the Lower Manhattan Development Corporation's use of 9/11 funds*. New York: Good Jobs New York, 2004, accessed August 12, 2011, www.goodjobsfirst. org/sites/default/files/docs/pdf/lmdc_report.pdf

Daniels, Ronald Joel, Donald F. Kettl, and Howard Kunreuther. *On Risk and Disaster: Lessons from Hurricane Katrina*. Philadelphia: University of Pennsylvania Press, 2006.

Darden, Joe T., Richard Child Hill, June Thomas, and Richard Thomas. *Detroit: Race and Uneven Development*. Philadelphia: Temple University Press, 1987.

Darton, Eric. *Divided We Stand: A Biography of New York's World Trade Center*. New York: Basic Books, 1999.

Diner, Hasia, *Lower East Side Memories: A Jewish Place in America*. Princeton: Princeton University Press, 2000.

Domhoff, G. W. *Who Rules America? Power, Politics, & Social Change* (6th ed.). New York: McGraw-Hill, 2010.

Dreier, Peter. "Reagan's Legacy: Homelessness in America." National Housing Institute ShelterForce 135, May/June 2004, http://www.nhi.org/online/issues/135/reagan. html.

Dreier, Peter. "Katrina and Power in America." *Urban Affairs Review* 41, no. 4 (2006): 528–49, doi:10.1177/1078087405284886.

Dreier, Peter, John Mollenkopf, and Todd Swanstrom. *Place Matters: Metropolitics for the Twenty-First Century*. Lawrence, KS: University of Kansas Press, 2004.

Dymon, U., and R. Platt, "U.S. Federal Disaster Declarations: A Geographical Analysis." In *Disasters and Democracy: The Politics of Extreme Natural Events*, edited by R. Platt, 47–67. Washington, DC: Island, 1999.

Dynes, Russell R., and Havidan Rodriguez. "Finding and Framing Katrina: The Social Construction of Disaster." In *The Sociology of Katrina: Perspectives on a Modern Catastrophe*, edited by David L. Brunsma, David Overfelt, and J. Steven Picou, 23–33. New York: Rowman & Littlefield, 2007.

E. J. Morris Senior Center. Louisiana Collection. "Oral Recollections of the Ninth Ward Elderly, 1900–1950." 1983, vertical file "Ninth Ward," 44–47. Howard-Tilton Memorial Library, Tulane University.

Eisinger, Peter. "The Politics of Bread and Circuses: Building the City for the Visitor Class." *Urban Affairs Review* 35, no. 3 (2000): 316–33.

Emerson, Robert M., Rachel I. Fretz, and Linda L. Shaw. *Writing Ethnographic Fieldnotes*. Chicago: University of Chicago Press, 1995.

Erikson K. T. *Everything in Its Path: Destruction of Community in the Buffalo Creek Flood*. New York: Simon & Schuster, 1976.

Erikson, K. *A New Species of Trouble: Explorations in Disasters, Trauma, and Community*. New York: W.W. Norton, 1994.

Federal Emergency Management Agency. *IA-TAC Program Status and Performance Assessment*. Washington, DC: Federal Emergency Management Agency, January 2006.

Federal Emergency Management Agency. "FEMA Winds Down Year of Compassionate Sheltering." Press Release No. 1606-237, August 8, 2006, accessed April 18, 2012, http://www.fema.gov/news-release/2006/08/08/fema-winds-down-year-compassionate-sheltering

Federal Emergency Management Agency. "Formaldehyde and Travel Trailers." Press Release No.: FNF-07-028, July 20, 2007, http://www.fema.gov/news-release/2007/07/20/formaldehyde-and-travel-trailers

Federal Writers' Project. *The WPA Guide to New York City*. New York: New Press, 1995.

Ferretti, Fred. *The Year the Big Apple Went Bust*. New York: Putnam Publishing Group, 1976.

Finger, Davida. "Stranded and Squandered: Lost on the Road Home." *Seattle Journal for Social Justice* 7, no. 1 (2008): 59–100.

Fiscal Policy Institute. *The Employment Impact of the September 11 World Trade Center Attacks: Updated Estimates based on the Benchmarked Employment Data*. New York: Fiscal Policy Institute, March 2002, accessed March 29, 2012, http://www.fiscalpolicy.org/Employment%20Impact%20of%20September%2011_Update.pdf.

Fiscal Policy Institute. *State of Working New York: Unbalanced Regional Economies through Expansion and Recession*. New York: Fiscal Policy Institute, 2003.

Fitch, Robert. *The Assassination of New York*. New York: Verso, 1996.

Fitzpatrick, Kevin M., and Mark LaGory. "'Placing' Health in an Urban Sociology: Cities as Mosaics of Risk and Protection," *City & Community* 2, no. 1 (2003) 33–46.

Flynn, Stephen. *The Edge of Disaster*. New York: Random House, 2007.

Foner, Nancy, ed. *Wounded City: The Social Impact of 9/11*. New York: Russell Sage Foundation, 2005.

Fourcade-Gourinchas, Marion, and Sarah L. Babb. "The Rebirth of the Liberal Creed: Paths to Neoliberalism in Four Countries." *American Journal of Sociology* 108, no. 3 (2002): 533–79.

Frank, Thomas. *The Conquest of Cool*. Chicago: University of Chicago Press, 1997.

Freeman, Joshua. *Working-Class New York: Life and Labor Since World War II*. New York: New Press, 2001.

Freudenberg, William, Robert Gramling, Shirley Laska, and Kai T. Erikson. *Catastrophe in the Making: The Engineering of Katrina and the Disaster of Tomorrow.* Washington, DC: Island Press, 2009.

Gabe, Thomas, Gene Falk, Maggie McCarty, and Virginia W. Mason. Cong. Research Serv., RL33141, Hurricane Katrina: Social-Demographic Characteristics of Impacted Areas (2005), accessed July 25, 2011, http://gnocdc.s3.amazonaws.com/reports/crsrept.pdf.

Gaffikin, Frank, and Barney Warf. "Urban Policy and the Post-Keynesian State in the United Kingdom and the United States." *International Journal of Urban and Regional Research* 17, no. 1 (1993): 67–84.

Gandy, Matthew, *Concrete and Clay: Reworking Nature in New York City.* Cambridge: MIT Press, 2002.

Garrett, T.A., and R.S. Stobel. "The Political Economy of FEMA Disasters Payments." *Economic Inquiry* 41, no. 3 (2003): 496–509.

Giddens, Anthony. *The Consequences of Modernity.* Stanford, CA: Stanford University Press, 1990.

Goffman, Erving. *Frame Analysis: An Essay on the Organization of Experience.* Boston: Northeastern University Press, 1974.

Goldberg, David Theo. "When Race Disappears." *Comparative American Studies* 10, no. 2–3 (August 2012): 116–27.

Goldberg, David Theo. *The Threat of Race: Reflections on Racial Neoliberalism.* New York: John Wiley & Sons, 2009

Good Jobs New York, "Memo: Community Development Block Grant Waivers, Reporting Waivers: What Does the LMDC Have to Tell the Government and the Public?" (March 3, 2002), accessed June 10, 2013, http://www.goodjobsny.org/economic-development/memo-community-development-block-grant-waivers.

Gotham, Kevin Fox, ed. *Critical Perspectives on Urban Redevelopment.* New York: Elsevier Press, 2001.

Gotham, Kevin Fox. *Race, Real Estate and Uneven Development: The Kansas City Experience, 1900–2010.* Albany, NY: State University of New York Press, second edition, 2014.

Gotham, Kevin Fox. *Authentic New Orleans: Race, Culture, and Tourism in the Big Easy.* New York: New York University Press, 2007.

Gotham, Kevin Fox. "(Re)Branding the Big Easy: Tourism Rebuilding in post-Katrina New Orleans." *Urban Affairs Review.* 42, no. 6 (2007): 823–50.

Gotham, Kevin Fox. "Selling New Orleans to New Orleans: Tourism Authenticity and the Construction of Community Identity." *Tourist Studies* 7, no. 3 (2007): 317–39.

Gotham, Kevin Fox. "Destination New Orleans: Commodification, Rationalization, and the Rise of Urban Tourism." *Journal of Consumer Culture* 7, no. 3 (2007): 305–34.

Gottdiener, Mark, ed. *Cities in Stress: A New Look at the Urban Crisis (Urban Affairs Annual Reviews),* 30. Beverly Hills: Sage Publications, 1986.

Gottdiener, Mark. "A Marx for Our Time: Henri Lefebvre and the Production of Space." *Sociological Theory* 11, no. 1 (1993): 129–34.

Gottdiener, Mark. *The Social Production of Urban Space.* 2nd ed. Austin: University of Texas Press, 1994.

Gottdiener, Mark, and Nicos Komninos, editors. *Capitalist Development and Crisis Theory: Accumulation, Regulation, and Spatial Restructuring.* New York: St. Martin's Press, 1989.

Gough, J. "Neoliberalism and Socialisation in the Contemporary City: Opposites, Complements And Instabilities." *Antipode* 34, no. 2 (2002): 405–26.

Government Accountability Office. *Disaster Assistance: Information on FEMA's Post 9/11 Public Assistance to the New York City Area.* Report to the Committee on Environment and Public Works, U.S. Senate. GAO-03-926. Washington, DC: Government Accountability Office, August 2003.

Government Accounting Office. *Written Statement, Presented by Jay Etta Z. Hecker, GAO Director, Physical Infrastructure Issues.* U.S. Senate Committee on Environment and Public Works, Subcommittee on Clean Air, Climate Change, and Nuclear Safety Hearing. Federal Aid to New York City Following the Attacks of September 11 and Challenges Confronting FEMA. GAO-03-1174T. Washington, DC: Government Accountability Office, September 24, 2003.

Government Accountability Office. *September 11: Overview of Federal Disaster Assistance to the New York City Area.* GAO-04-72. Washington, DC: Government Accountability Office, October 2003.

Government Accountability Office. *September 11: Health Effects in the Aftermath of the World Trade Center Attack.* GAO-04-1068T. Washington, DC: Government Accountability Office, September 8, 2004.

Government Accountability Office. *Budget Issues: FEMA Needs Adequate Data, Plans, and Systems to Effectively Manage Resources for Day-to-Day Operations.* GAO-07-139. Washington, DC: Government Printing Office, January 2007.

Government Accountability Office. *Gulf Opportunity Zone: States Are Allocating Federal Tax Incentives to Finance Low-Income Housing and a Wide Range of Private Facilities.* Report to the Committee on Finance, U.S. Senate, and the Committee on Ways and Means, United States House of Representatives. GAO-08-913. Washington, DC: Government Accountability Office, July 2008.

Government Accountability Office. *Actions Taken to Implement the Post-Katrina Emergency Management Reform Act of 2006.* GAO-09-59R. Washington, DC: Government Printing Office, November 21, 2008.

Graham, Leigh. "Permanently Failing Organizations? Small Business Recovery after September 11, 2001." *Economic Development Quarterly* 21, no. 4 (2007): 299–314.

Graham, Stephen, ed. *Disrupted Cities: When Infrastructure Fails.* New York and London: Routledge, 2009.

Gray, Herman. *Cultural Moves: African Americans and the Politics of Representation.* Berkeley: University of California Press, 2005.

Gray, Herman. "Recovered, Reinvented, Reimagined: Treme, Television Studies and Writing New Orleans." *Television & New Media.* 13, no. 3 (2012): 268–78.

Greater New Orleans Community Data Center. "Lower Ninth Ward Neighborhood: Housing & Housing Costs." July 31, 2006, accessed July 15, 2011, http://www.gnocdc.org/orleans/8/22/housing.html.

Greater New Orleans Community Data Center. "Facts for Features: Hurricane Katrina Recovery." News Release, August 27, 2012, accessed November 4, 2012, http://www.gnocdc.org/Factsforfeatures/HurricaneKatrinaRecovery/index.html.

Greenberg, Miriam. "The Limits of Branding: The World Trade Center, Fiscal Crisis and the Marketing of Recovery." *International Journal of Urban and Regional Research* 27, no. 2 (2003): 386–416.

Greenberg, Miriam, *Branding New York: How a City in Crisis Was Sold to the World.* New York: Routledge, 2008.

Greenberg, Miriam. "Branding, Crisis, and Utopia: Representing New York in the Age of Bloomberg." In *Blowing Up the Brand: Critical Perspectives on Promotional Culture,* edited by Melissa Aronczyk and Devon Powers, 115–43. New York: Peter Lang, 2010.

Greenberg, Miriam. "The Sustainability Edge: Competition, Crisis, and the Rise of Green Urban Branding in New York and New Orleans." In Melissa Checker, Cindy Isenhour, and Gary McDonough, eds. *Sustainability as Myth and Practice in the Global City.* Cambridge, UK: Cambridge University Press, 2014.

Greenberg, Miriam. "The Disaster Inside the Disaster: Hurricane Sandy and Post-crisis Redevelopment." *New Labor Forum,* January/February 2014, 23: 44-52.

Hacker, Jacob S. "Privatizing Risk Without Privatizing the Welfare State: The Hidden Politics of Social Policy Retrenchment In The United States." *American Political Science Review* 98, no. 2 (2004): 243–60.

Hacker, Jacob. *The Great Risk Shift: The New Economic Insecurity—And What Can Be Done About It.* New York: Oxford University Press, 2006.

Hackworth, Jason. *The Neoliberal City: Governance, Ideology and Development in American Urbanism.* London and Ithaca: Cornell University Press, 2007.

Hall, Stuart, "Race, Articulation, and Societies Structured in Dominance." *Sociological Theories: Race and Colonialism.* Paris: UNESCO (1980). 305–45.

Hall, Stuart. *Cultural Representations and Signifying Practices.* Thousand Oaks, CA: Sage Publications, 1997.

Hall, Stuart, Chas Critcher, Tony Jefferson, John Clark, and Brian Roberts Macmillan. *Policing the Crisis: Mugging, the State, and Law and Order.* London: Holmes & Meier, 1978.

Halle, David, and Andrew Beveridge. *New York & Los Angeles: Politics, Society and Culture.* Chicago: University of Chicago Press, 2003.

Hartman, Chester, and Gregory Squires, eds. *There Is No Such Thing as a Natural Disaster: Race, Class, and Hurricane Katrina.* New York: Routledge, 2006.

Hartman, Chester, and Gregory Squires. "Lessons from Katrina: Structural Racism as Recipe for Disaster." In *Building Healthy Communities: A Guide to Community Economic Development for Advocates, Lawyers, and Policymakers,* edited by Roger A. Clay, Jr. and Susan R. Jones. New York: American Bar Association, 2009.

Harvey, David. *The Limits to Capital.* New York: Verso, 1982.

Harvey, David *Spaces of Capital: Towards a Critical Geography.* New York, Routledge, 2001.

Harvey, David. *The New Imperialism.* Oxford: Oxford University Press, 2003.

Harvey, David. *A Brief History of Neoliberalism.* Oxford: Oxford University Press, 2005.

Harvey, David. *Spaces of Global Capitalism: Towards a Theory of Uneven Geographical Development.* London and New York: Verso, 2006.

Harvey, David. "The Right to the City." *New Left Review* 53 (2008): 23–40.

Hay, Colin S. "Narrating Crisis: The Discursive Construction of the 'Winter of Discontent.'" *Sociology* 30, no. 2 (1996): 253–77.

Hewitt, Kenneth. "The Idea of Calamity in a Technocratic Age." In *Interpretations of Calamity from the Viewpoint of Human Ecology,* edited by K. Hewitt, 3–32. Boston: Allen and Unwin, 1983.

Hewitt, Kenneth. *Regions of Risk: A Geographical Introduction to Disasters.* Harlow, Essex, UK: Longman, 1997.

Heynen, Nik, Maria Kaika, and Erik Swyngedouw. *In the Nature of Cities: Urban Political Ecology and the Politics of Urban Metabolism.* London: Routledge, 2006.

Hirsch, Arnold. "New Orleans: Sunbelt in the Swamp." In *Sunbelt Cities: Politics and Growth Since World War II,* edited by Richard M. Bernard and Bradley R. Rice. Austin, TX: University of Texas Press, 1983.

Hoffman, Susanna M., and Anthony Oliver-Smith, eds. *Culture and Catastrophe: The Anthropology of Disaster.* Santa Fe, NM: The School of American Research Press, 2002.

Hollis, Amanda Lee. "A Tale of Two Federal Emergency Management Agencies," *The Forum* 3, no. 3 (2005): 1–14.

Houck, Oliver A. 1985. "Rising Water: The National Flood Insurance Program and Louisiana." *Tulane Law Review* 60, no.1 (October 1985): 61–164.

Institute for Southern Studies. "One Year After Katrina: The State of New Orleans and the Gulf Coast." *Facing South,* 2006, accessed July 25, 2011, http://www.southernstudies.org/iss/2008/11/one-year-after-katrina.html.

Intergovernmental Panel on Climate Change (IPCC). *Climate change 2007: Synthesis Report.* Contribution of Working Groups I, II and III to the Fourth Assessment Report of the

Intergovernmental Panel on Climate Change, edited by R. K. Pachauri, and A. Reisinger. Geneva, Switzerland: IPCC, 2007.

Jacobs, Jane. *The Death and Life of Great American Cities.* New York: Vintage Books 1961 (1992).

Jaffe, Eric. "New York's 'Affordable Housing' Isn't Always Affordable." *The Atlantic Cities* (February 21, 2013), accessed June 10, 2013, http://www.theatlanticcities.com/housing/2013/02/new-york-affordable-housing-isnt-always-affordable/4757/.

Jameson, Fredric. "Reification and Utopia in Mass Culture." *Social Text* 1 (Winter 1979): 130–48.

Judd, Dennis, R. "Constructing the Tourist Bubble." In *The Tourist City*, edited by D. R. Judd and S. S. Fainstein. New Haven: Yale University Press, 1999.

Judd, Dennis R., ed. *The Infrastructure of Play: Building the Tourist City.* Armonk, NY: M.E. Sharp, 2003.

Judd, Dennis R., and Dick W. Simpson, eds. *The City, Revisited: Urban Theory from Chicago, Los Angeles, and New York.* Minneapolis: University of Minnesota Press, 2011.

Julian, Peter Scott. "The New Orleans Fiscal Crisis: When Debt Ceilings and Taxing Limitations Really Pinch." *Tulane Law Review* 55 (1981): 850.

Kallick, David Dyssegaard. "Rebuilding a High Road Economy: What Works for Workers." In *Cities At Risk: Catastrophe, Recovery, and Renewal in New York and New Orleans*, edited by Andrew White and Peter Eisinger. New York: Milano The New School for Management and Urban Policy, 2006.

Kates, R.W., C. E. Colten, S. Laska, and S. P. Leatherman. "Reconstruction of New Orleans after Hurricane Katrina: A Research Perspective." *Proceedings of the National Academy of Sciences* 103, no. 40 (2006): 14653–660.

Kaye, Jeffrey. "Controversy Continues over Post-Katrina Spending on Trailers." *PBS Newshour*, April 9, 2007, accessed February 2, 2012, http://www.pbs.org/newshour/bb/weather/jan-june07/katrina_04-09.html.

Kerner Commission. *The Kerner Report: The 1968 Report of the National Advisory Commission on Civil Disorders.* New York: Pantheon, 1968.

Klein, Naomi. *The Shock Doctrine: The Rise of Disaster Capitalism.* New York: Henry Holt and Company, 2007.

Klinenberg, Eric. *Heat Wave: A Social Autopsy of Disaster in Chicago.* Chicago: University of Chicago Press, 2002.

Klinenberg, Eric, and Thomas Frank. "Looting Homeland Security." *Rolling Stone* 990/991 (December 15, 2005): 44–54, http://www.rollingstone.com/politics/story/8952492/looting_homeland_security.

Kromm, Chris, and Sue Sturgis. *Hurricane Katrina and the Guiding Principles on Internal Displacement.* Durham, NC: Institute of Southern Studies, 2008.

Kwong, Peter. *The New Chinatown.* New York: Hill and Wang, 1996.

Landphair, Juliette. "Sewerage, Sidewalks, and Schools: The New Orleans Ninth Ward and Public School Desegregation." *Louisiana History* 40 (1999): 35–62.

Landphair, Juliette. "'The Forgotten People of New Orleans': Community, Vulnerability, and the Lower Ninth Ward." *Journal of American History* 94, no. 3 (2007): 837–45.

Laska, Shirley. "'Mother of Rorschachs': New Orleans Recovery from Hurricane Katrina." *Sociological Inquiry* 78, no. 4 (2008): 580–91.

LeCompte, Margaret Diane, and Jean J Schensul. *Analyzing & Interpreting Ethnographic Data.* Walnut Creek, CA: AltaMira, 1999.

Lefebvre, Henri. "Space: Social Product and Use Value." In *Critical Sociology: European Perspectives*, edited by J. Freiberg. New York: Irvington Publishers, 1979.

Lefebvre, Henri. 1974. *The Production of Space.* New York: Blackwell, 1991.

Lefebvre, Henri. 1996. *Writings on Cities.* Cambridge, MA., Blackwell, 1996

Lefebvre, Henri, *The Urban Revolution.* Translated by Robert Bononno. Minneapolis: University of Minnesota Press, [1970] 2003.

Leeds, Adrian. "The Cost of Real Estate: The Big Easy, the Rich Coast or the City of Light," *French Property Insider* 10, no. 28 (July 19, 2012).

Leitner, Helga, Jamie Peck, and Eric Sheppard, eds. *Contesting Neoliberalism: Urban Frontiers*. New York: Guilford Press, 2006.

Lewis, David. *The Politics of Presidential Appointments: Political Control and Bureaucratic Performance*. Princeton: Princeton University Press, 2008.

Lewis, Peirce. *New Orleans: The Making of an Urban Landscape*. 2nd ed. Charlottesville, VA: Center for American Places, 2003.

Lichten, Eric. *Class, Power and Austerity: The New York City Fiscal Crisis*. New York: Bergin & Garvey, 1986.

Liu, Laura, "Blank Slates and Disaster Zones: The State, September 11, and the Displacement of Chinatown." In *Indefensible Space: The Architecture of the National Insecurity State*, edited by Michael Sorkin. New York: Routledge, 2007.

Liu, Amy, Matthew Fellowes, and Mia Mabanta. *Special Edition of the Katrina Index: A One-Year Review of Key Indicators of Recovery in Post-Storm New Orleans*. Washington, DC: Brookings Institution, August 2006, accessed June 29, 2013, http://www.brookings.edu/metro/pubs/2006_katrinaindex.pdf.

Liu, Amy, and Allison Plyer. "An Overview of Greater New Orleans: From Recovery to Transformation." In *The New Orleans Index at Five*. Washington, DC: Brookings Institution and Greater New Orleans Community Data Center, 2010.

Lofland, John, David Snow, Leon Anderson, and Lyn H. Lofland. *Analyzing Social Settings: A Guide to Qualitative Observation and Analysis*. 4th ed. Belmont, CA: Wadsworth/Thomson, 2006.

Logan, John, and Harvey Molotch, *Urban Fortunes: The Political Economy of Place*. 20th anniversary ed. Berkeley: University of California Press, 2007

Louisiana Department of Transportation and Development, "Executive Summary," *The Failure of the New Orleans Levee System during Hurricane Katrina* xii, December 8, 2006, http://www.dotd.louisiana.gov/administration/teamlouisiana/Team%20Louisiana%20-%20cov,%20toc,%20exec%20summ,%20intro.pdf.

Louisiana Department of Culture, Recreation, and Tourism. *Report of the Louisiana Rebirth Accountability Panel*. Baton Rouge, LA: State of Louisiana Department of Culture, Recreation, and Tourism, January 8, 2008.

Louisiana Department of Culture, Recreation, and Tourism. "Cultural Districts Program," accessed July 1, 2012, http://www.crt.state.la.us/culturaldistricts/.

Lower Manhattan Development Corporation. "Neighborhood Outreach Workshop Report Comments." January 20, 2004, accessed June 26, 2013, http://www.renewnyc.com/content/pdfs/Neighborhood_Outreach_Workshop_Report_Comments.pdf.

Lower Manhattan Development Corporation, "Governor Pataki, Mayor Bloomberg Hail President Bush's Support of Tax Conversion Proposal to Re-Direct Federal September 11th Aid." Press Release, July 29, 2004, accessed June 10, 2013, http://www.renewnyc.com/displaynews.aspx?newsid=270756c8-9ccd-4cff-b78b-114dea334472.

Lower Manhattan Development Corporation. "Governor Pataki Announces Major Progress on Lower Manhattan Transportation Initiatives: Calls on Port Authority to Commit $1 Billion for Lower Manhattan Rail Link." Press Release, May 12, 2005, accessed April 10, 2012, http://www.renewnyc.com/displaynews.aspx?newsid=3341e5b2-009c-4e89-b2f2-2492c1f9a832.

Lower Manhattan Development Corporation. "Mayor Bloomberg Unveils Plans for East River Waterfront," Press Release, June 2, 2005, accessed March 25, 2012, http://www.renewnyc.com/displaynews.aspx?newsid=bc1346ca-ddb8-43ad-a97b-b367e292d461.

Lower Manhattan Development Corporation. *Revised Partial Action Plan Number 6 for Affordable Housing*. June 29, 2005, accessed June 30, 2013, http://www.renewnyc.com/

content/pdfs/HUD/ENG_PAP_006_REV_Draft_for_Public_Comment_062905. pdf.

Lower Manhattan Development Corporation, "LMDC Announces More than $37 Million in Grants: Funds Will Go to Non-Profits for Community Enhancements." Press Release, November 8, 2007, accessed June 10, 2013, http://www.renewnyc.com/displaynews. aspx.

Luft, Rachel. "Beyond Disaster Exceptionalism: Social Movement Developments in New Orleans after Hurricane Katrina." *American Quarterly* 61, no. 3 (2009): 499–527.

Luhmann, Nicholas. *Risk: A Sociological Theory*. New York: Walter de Gruyter, 1993.

Maier, Mark, *City Unions: Managing Discontent in New York City*. New Brunswick, NJ: Rutgers University Press, 1987.

Marcuse, Peter, "What Kind of Planning after September 11th?" In *After the World Trade Center: Rethinking New York City*, edited by M. Sorkin and S. Zukin. New York: Routledge, 2002.

Marcuse, Peter. "Ignoring Injustice in Disaster Planning: An Agenda for Research on 9/11 And Katrina," *The Urban Reinventors Online Journal* 3/09 (2009), accessed June 30, 2013, http://www.urbanreinventors.net/3/marcuse/marcuse-urbanreinventors.pdf.

Markusen, Ann and Anne Gadwa, "Arts and Culture in Urban or Regional Planning: A Review and Research Agenda." *Journal of Planning Education and Research* 29, no. 3 (2010); pgs 379–391.

Marx, Karl, and Friedrich Engels. 1848. "The Manifesto of the Communist Party." *Marx/Engels Selected Works*. Vol. 1. Translated by Samuel Moore. Moscow: Progress Publishers, 1969.

Massey, Doreen. *Spatial Divisions of Labor*. London: MacMillan, 1985.

Matteson, Robert John Montgomery. *Dimensions and Solutions of New Orleans' Financial Dilemma*. Study Report to the Bureau of Governmental Research. Bennington, VT and New York: Matteson Associates, Public Administration Council, distributed by the Bureau of Governmental Research, 1966.

McCann, Eugene, and Kevin Ward, eds. *Mobile Urbanism: Cities and Policymaking in the Global Age*. Minneapolis: University of Minnesota Press, 2011.

McFarlane, Colin. "The Comparative City: Knowledge Learning, Urbanism." *International Journal of Urban and Regional Research* 34, no. 4 (2010): 725–42.

McFarlane, Colin. *Learning the City: Knowledge and Translocal Assemblage*. Oxford: Wiley Blackwell, 2011.

McMichael, Philip. "Incorporating Comparison Within a World-Historical Perspective: An Alternative Comparative Method." *American Sociological Review* 55, no. 3 (1990): 385–97.

McQuaid, John, and Mark Schleifstein. *Path of Destruction: The Devastation of New Orleans and the Coming Age of Superstorms*. New York: Little, Brown and Company, 2007.

Mele, Christopher, *Selling the Lower East Side: Culture, Real Estate, and Resistance in New York City*. Minneapolis: University of Minnesota Press, 2000.

Melnick, Jeffrey P. *9/11 Culture: America under Construction*. New York: Blackwell, 2009.

Mills, C. W. *The Power Elite*. New York: Oxford University Press, 1956.

Miron, Louis. "Corporate Ideology and the Politics of Entrepreneurialism in New Orleans." *Antipode* 24, no. 4 (1992): 263–88.

Mitchell, K. "Transnationalism, Neoliberalism, and the Rise of the Shadow State." *Economy and Society* 30, no. 2 (2001): 165–89.

Mitchell, K. *Crossing the Neoliberal Line: Pacific Rim Migration and the Metropolis*. Philadelphia: Temple University Press, 2004.

Monahan, Brian A. *The Shock of the News: Media Coverage and the Making of 9/11*. New York University Press, 2010.

Mollenkopf, John, ed. *Contentious City: The Politics of Recovery in New York City.* New York: Russell Sage Foundation, 2005.

Mollenkopf, John, and Manuel Castells, eds. *Dual City: Restructuring New York.* New York, Russell Sage Foundation, 1989.

Moody, Kim. *From Welfare State to Real Estate: Regime Change in New York City, 1974 to the Present.* New York: New Press, 2007.

Morello-Frosch, Rachel, Manuel Pastor, and James Sadd. "Environmental Justice and Southern California's 'Riskscape': The Distribution of Air Toxics Exposures and Health Risks among Diverse Communities." *Urban Affairs Review* 36, no. 4 (2001): 551–78.

Morris, Aldon. *Origins of the Civil Rights Movement: Black Communities Organizing For Change.* New York: Free Press, 1984.

Morris, John C. "Whither FEMA? Hurricane Katrina and FEMA's Response to the Gulf Coast." *Public Works Management and Policy* 10, no. 4 (2006): 284–94.

Moss, Mitchell, Charles Schellhamer, and David A. Berman. "The Stafford Act and Priorities for Reform." *Journal of Homeland Security and Emergency Management* 6, no. 1 (2009): 1–21.

National Commission on Terrorist Attacks Upon the United States. *The 9/11 Commission Report. Final Report of the National Commission on Terrorist Attacks Upon the United States.* New York: W.W. Norton & Company, 2004.

Nelson, Marla, Renia Ehrenfeucht, and Shirley Laska. "Planning, Plans, and People: Professional Expertise, Local Knowledge, and Governmental Action in Post-Hurricane Katrina New Orleans." *Cityscape: A Journal of Policy Development & Research* 9, no. 3 (2007): 23–52.

New York City Independent Budget Office. "Mayor's Housing Plan: Progress to Date; Prospects for Completion." *Inside the Budget* No. 153 (November 9, 2007), accessed June 10, 2013, http://www.ibo.nyc.ny.us/newsfax/insidethebudget153.pdf.

New York City Independent Budget Office. *The Aftermath: Federal Aid 10 Years after the World Trade Center Attack.* New York: New York City Independent Budget Office, August 2011, accessed June 30, 2013, http://www.ibo.nyc.ny.us/iboreports/wtc2011.pdf.

New York City, Office of the Mayor. "Mayor Bloomberg Delivers Major Address on the Rebirth of Lower Manhattan Since 9/11." Press Release No. 319-11, September 6, 2011, accessed March 24, 2012, www.nyc.gov/html/om/html/2011b/pr319-11.html.

Newfield, Jack, and Paul DuBrul. *The Abuse of Power.* New York: Penguin 1978.

Newman, K., and P. Ashton. "Neoliberal Urban Policy and New Paths of Neighborhood Change in the American Inner City." *Environment and Planning A* 36, no. 7 (2004): 1151–72.

Nicholls, R. J. 2004. "Coastal Flooding and Wetland Loss in the 21st Century: Changes Under the SRES Climate and Socio-economic Scenarios." *Global Environmental Change* 14 (2004) 69–78.

Nijman, J. "Introduction—Comparative Urbanism." *Urban Geography* 28, no. 1 (2007): 1–6.

Noto, Nonna A. Cong. Research Serv., RL34065, FEMA's Community Disaster Loan Program: Action in the 110th Congress (2007), accessed May 2, 2011, http://assets.opencrs.com/rpts/RL34065_20070627.pdf.

Olshansky, Robert B., and Laurie A. Johnson. *Clear as Mud: Planning for the Rebuilding of New Orleans.* New York: American Planning Association Planners Press, 2010.

Olshansky, Robert B., Laurie A. Johnson, Jedidiah Horne, and Brendan Nee. "Planning for the Rebuilding of New Orleans," *Journal of the American Planning Association* 74, no. 3 (2008): 273–87.

Ong, Aihwa. *Neoliberalism as Exception: Mutations in Citizenship and Sovereignty.* Durham, NC: Duke University Press, 2006.

Orlebecke, Charles J. "Saving New York: The Ford Administration and the New York City Fiscal Crisis." In *Gerald Ford and the Politics of Post-Watergate America,* edited by Bernard J. Firestone and Alexej J. Ugrinsky. Westport, CT: Greenwood Publishing Group, 1993.

Papa, Victor J. "Foreword" in *"A Divided Community": A Study of Gentrification of the Lower East Side Community, New York*. New York: Two Bridges Neighborhood Council, Inc., June 2004, accessed June 30, 2012, http://www.twobridges.org/images/PDFs/ADividedCommunity_Report.pdf.

Parr, Adrian. *Hijacking sustainability*. Cambridge, MA: MIT Press, 2009.

Peacock, Walter Gillis, Betty Hearn Morrow, and Hugh Gladwin, eds. *Hurricane Andrew: Ethnicity, Gender and the Sociology of Disasters*. New York: Routledge, 1997.

Peck, Jamie. "Liberating the City: Between New York and New Orleans." *Urban Geography* 27, no. 8 (2006): 681–713.

Peck, Jamie. "Neoliberal Hurricane: Who Framed New Orleans?" *Socialist Register* 43, no. 43 (2007): 102–29.

Peck, Jaime, and Adam Tickell. "Neoliberalizing Space." In *Spaces of Neoliberalism: Urban Restructuring in North America and Western Europe*, edited by Neil Brenner and Nik Theodore, 33–57. New York: Blackwell Publishing, 2002.

Pelling, Mark. *The Vulnerability of Cities: Natural Disasters and Social Resilience*. London, UK: Earthscan Publications, 2003.

Perrow, Charles. *Normal Accidents: Living with High Risk Technologies*. New York: Basic Books, 1984.

Perrow, Charles. "The Disaster after 9/11: The Department of Homeland Security and the Intelligence Reorganization." *Homeland Security Affairs Journal* 2, no. 1 (2006): 1-29

Perrow, Charles. *The Next Catastrophe: Reducing Our Vulnerabilities to Natural, Industrial, and Terrorist Disasters*. Princeton, NJ: Princeton University Press, 2011.

Perry, Imani. *More Beautiful and More Terrible: The Embrace and Transcendence Of Racial Inequality in The United States*. New York: New York University Press, 2011.

Phillips, Zack, "FEMA Looks to Private Sector for Disaster Provisions," *GovernmentExecutive.com*, August 24, 2007, accessed April 5, 2012, http://www.govexec.com/story_page.cfm?articleid=37855&dcn=e_gvet.

Piore, Nora, Purlaine Lieberman, and James Linnane. "Public Expenditures and Private Control? Health Care Dilemmas in New York City." *The Milbank Memorial Fund Quarterly. Health and Society*. 55, no. 1 (1977): 79–116.

Piven, Frances Fox, and Richard A. Cloward. *Regulating the Poor: The Functions of Public Welfare*. New York: Pantheon Books, 1971.

Plyer, Allison. *What Census 2010 Reveals About Population And Housing In New Orleans And The Metro Area*. Greater New Orleans Community Data Center. May 17, 2011, accessed June 30, 2013, http://www.gnocdc.org/Census2010/index.html.

Plyer, Allison, and Elaine Ortiz. "Poverty in Southeast Louisiana Post-Katrina." Greater New Orleans Community Data Center. June 2102, accessed July 7, 2013, https://gnocdc.s3.amazonaws.com/reports/GNOCDC_PovertyInSoutheastLouisianaPostKatrina.pdf.

Plyer, Allison, Elaine Ortiz, and Kathy Pettit. "Post-Katrina Housing Affordability Challenges Continue in 2008, Worsening among Orleans Parish Very Low Income Renters." Greater New Orleans Community Data Center. October 13, 2009, accessed June 20, 2013, https://gnocdc.s3.amazonaws.com/reports/GNOCDC_NewOrleansMetroAreaHousingAffordability2004-2008.pdf.

Port Authority of New York and New Jersey. "Port Authority and Lower Manhattan Development Corporation Unveil Six Concept Plans for World Trade Center Site, Adjacent Areas and Related Transportation." Press Release. July 16, 2002, accessed April 10, 2012, http://www.panynj.gov/press-room/press-item.cfm?headLine_id=197.

Porter, Eric, and Lewis Watts. *New Orleans Suite: Music and Culture in Transition*. Berkeley: University of California Press, 2013.

Prichett, Wendell E. "Which Urban Crisis? Regionalism, Race, and Urban Policy, 1960-1974." *Journal of Urban History* 34, no. 2 (2008): 266–86.

Quadagno, Jill. *The Color of Welfare: How Racism Undermined the War on Poverty.* New York: Oxford University Press, 1994.

Quante, Wolfgang. *The Exodus of Corporate Headquarters from New York City.* New York: Praeger, 1976.

Quigley, Bill. "New Orleans: Leaving the Poor Behind Again!" CommonDreams.org. October 11, 2005, accessed June 20, 2013, http://www.commondreams.org/views05/1011-20.htm.

Quigley, William P. "What Katrina Revealed." *Harvard Law & Policy Review* 2, no. 2 (2008): 361–84.

Regional Plan Association, *Regional Plan of New York and its Environs.* "Major Economic Factors in Metropolitan Growth and Development," Vol. 1. Regional Plan Association, New York, 1929–1931.

Regional Plan Association, *A Civic Assessment of the Lower Manhattan Planning Process: A Regional Plan Association Report to the Civic Alliance,* October 2004, accessed April 17, 2012, http://www.rpa.org/pdf/civicassessmentrpa.pdf.

Register, Richard, *Ecocity Berkeley: Building Cities for a Healthy Future.* Berkeley: North Atlantic Books, 1987.

Right to the City Alliance, *People Without Homes and Homes Without People: A Count of Vacant Condos in Select NYC Neighborhoods.* New York: Right to the City Alliance, New York City Chapter, 2010, accessed June 30, 2013, http://www.urbanjustice.org/pdf/publications/People_Without_Homes_and_Homes_Without_People.pdf.

Roberts, Patrick S. "FEMA and the Prospects for Reputation-Based Autonomy." *Studies in American Political Development* 20, no. 1 (2006): 57–87.

Robinson, Jennifer. "Global and World Cities: A View from Off the Map." *International Journal of Urban and Regional Research* 26 (2002): 531–54.

Robinson, Jennifer. *Ordinary Cities: Between Modernity and Development.* London: Routledge, 2006.

Robinson, Jennifer. "Cities in a World of Cities: the Comparative Gesture." *International Journal of Urban and Regional Research* 35, no. 1 (2011): 1–23.

Rose, K., A. Clark, and D. Duval-Diop. *A Long Way Home: The State Of Housing Recovery in Louisiana, 2008.* PolicyLink (2008), accessed July 1, 2013, http://www.policylink.org/threeyearslater/.

Rounsefell, G. A. "Preconstruction Study of the Fisheries of the Estuarine Areas Traversed by the Mississippi River-Gulf Outlet Project." *Fishery Bulletin* 63, no. 2 (1964).

Roy, Ananya, and Nezar Alsayyad, eds. *Urban Informality: Transnational Perspectives from the Middle East, Latin America, and South Asia.* Oxford: Lexington Books, 2004.

Rubin, Beth A., James D. Wright, and Joel A. Devine. "Unhousing the Urban Poor: The Reagan Legacy." *Journal of Sociology and Social Welfare* 19, no. 1 (1992): 111–48.

Ruchelman, Leonard I. *The World Trade Center: Politics and Policies of Skyscraper Development.* Syracuse: Syracuse University Press, 1977.

Sassen, Saskia. *The Global City: New York, London, Tokyo.* 2nd ed. Princeton: Princeton University Press, 2001.

Schneider, Jane, and Ida Susser. *Wounded Cities: Destruction and Reconstruction in a Globalized World.* Oxford: Berg Publishers, 2003.

Schumpeter, Joseph A. 1942. *Capitalism, Socialism, and Democracy.* 3rd ed. London: Routledge, 2006.

Sen, A. *Poverty and Famine: An Essay on Entitlement and Deprivation.* Oxford: Oxford University Press, 1982.

Sewell, William H. "Three Temporalities: Toward an Eventful Sociology." In *The Historic Turn in the Human Sciences,* edited by Terrence J. McDonald, 245–80. Ann Arbor: University of Michigan Press, 1996.

Sewell, William H. "The Temporalities of Capitalism." *Socio-Economic Review* 6 no. 3 (2008): 517–37.

Shifflet and Associates. *USA Travel Recovery/Monitor: A Blueprint for Rebuilding Travel.* New York: D. K. Shifflet & Associates Ltd., December 3, 2001–February 15, 2002.

Simon, William. *A Time for Truth.* New York: Reader's Digest Press, 1978.

Sites, William, *Remaking New York: Primitive Globalization and The Politics Of Urban Community.* Minneapolis: University of Minnesota Press, 2003.

Small, Mario. *Unanticipated Gains: Origins of Network Inequality in Everyday Life.* New York, NY: Oxford University Press, 2009.

Smith. Neil. *Uneven Development: Nature, Capital and the Production of Space.* 2nd ed. New York: Basil Blackwell, 1990.

Smith, Neil. "New City, New Frontier: The Lower East Side as Wild West." In *Variations on a Theme Park. The New American City and the End of Public Space,* edited by Michael Sorkin, 61–93. New York: Hill and Wang, 1992.

Smith, Michael Peter, and Joe R. Feagin, eds. *Bubbling Cauldron: Race, Ethnicity, and the Urban Crisis.* Minneapolis: University of Minnesota Press, 1995.

Smith, Michael Peter, and Marlene Keller. "'Managed Growth' and the Politics of Uneven Development in New Orleans." In *Restructuring the City: The Political Economy of Urban Redevelopment,* edited by Susan Fainstein, Norman I. Fainstein, Richard Child Hill, Dennis Judd, and Michael Peter Smith, 126–66. New York: Longman, 1986.

Smithsimon, Gregory. *September 12: Community and Neighborhood Recovery at Ground Zero.* New York: New York University Press, 2011.

Soffer, Jonathan. *Ed Koch and the Rebuilding of New York City.* New York: Columbia University Press, 2010.

Soja, Edward. "Economic Restructuring and the Internationalization of Los Angeles." In *The Capitalist City,* edited by Michael Peter Smith and Joe R. Feagin, 178–98. Cambridge, MA: Blackwell, 1987.

Somers, Margaret. *Genealogies of Citizenship: Markets, Statelessness, and the Right to Have Rights.* Cambridge: Cambridge University Press, 2008.

Sorkin, Michael, and Sharon Zukin, eds. *After the World Trade Center.* New York: Routledge, 2002.

Souther, J. Mark. *New Orleans on Parade: Tourism and the Transformation of the Crescent City.* Baton Rouge: Louisiana State University Press, 2006.

Spain, Daphne, "Race Relations and Residential Segregation in New Orleans: Two Centuries of Paradox." *Annals of the American Academy of Political and Social Science* 441, no. 1 (1979): 82–96.

Squires, Gregory D., ed. *Urban Sprawl: Causes, Consequences, and Policy Responses.* Washington, DC: The Urban Institute Press, 2002.

Squires, Gregory D., Larry Bennett, Kathleen McCort, and Philip Nyden. *Chicago: Race, Class, and the Response to Urban Decline.* Philadelphia: Temple University Press, 1987.

Squires, Gregory D., and Charis E. Kubrin. *Privileged Places: Race, Residence, and the Structure of Opportunity.* Boulder, CO: Lynne Rienner Publishers, 2006.

SRA International Inc. *FEMA Recovery Division: 2005 Hurricane Season After-Action Report,* prepared for the Federal Emergency Management Agency, Recovery Division, Department of Homeland Security. Arlington, VA: SRA International, Inc., June, 26, 2006, accessed July 1, 2013, http://studio.unitedway.org/211/FEMA_report.pdf.

Stehr, Steven D. "The Political Economy of Urban Disaster Assistance." *Urban Affairs Review* 41, no. 4 (2006): 492–500.

Steinberger, Peter. *Ideology and the Urban Crisis*. Albany: State University of New York Press, 1985.

Sugrue, Thomas. *The Origins of the Urban Crisis: Race and Inequality in Postwar Detroit*. Princeton: Princeton University Press, 1996.

Sturken, Marita, *Tangled Memories: The Vietnam War, the AIDS Epidemic, and the Politics of Remembering*. Berkeley: University of California Press, 1997.

Swyngedouw, Erik. "Neither Global Nor Local: 'Glocalization' and the Politics of Scale." In *Spaces of Globalization*, edited by K. R. Cox, 137–66. New York: Guilford Press 1997.

Szasz, Thomas, and Michael Meuser. "Environmental Inequalities: Literature Review and Proposals for New Directions in Research and Theory." *Current Sociology* 45, no. 3 (1997): 99–120.

Sze, Julie, and Jonathan K. London. "Environmental Justice at the Crossroads." *Sociology Compass* 2, no. 4 (2008): 1331-13541.

Tabb, William K. *The Long Default: New York City and the Urban Fiscal Crisis*. New York: Monthly Review Press, 1982.

Thevenot, Brian. "Myth-making in New Orleans." *American Journalism Review* 27, no. 6 (2005): 30–37.

Thomas, Lynnell L. "'Roots Run Deep Here': The Construction of Black New Orleans in Post-Katrina Tourism Narratives." *American Quarterly* 61, no. 3 (2009): 749–68.

Tierney, Kathleen. "Toward a Critical Sociology of Risk." *Sociological Forum* 14, no. 2 (1999): 215–42.

Tierney, Kathleen. "From the Margins to the Mainstream? Disaster Research at the Crossroads." *Annual Review of Sociology* 33 (2007): 503–25.

Tierney, Kathleen, Christine Bevc, and Erica Kuligowski. "Metaphors Matter: Disaster Myths, Media Frames, and Their Consequences in Hurricane Katrina." *Annals of the American Academy of Political and Social Science* 604 (2006): 57–81.

Tierney, Kathleen, M. K. Lindell, and R. W. Perry. *Facing the Unexpected: Disaster Preparedness and Response in the United States*. Boulder, CO: Natural Hazards Center, Institute of Behavioral Science, University of Colorado, 2001.

Tilly, Charles. *Big Structures, Large Processes, Huge Comparisons*. New York: Russell Sage, 1984.

Tobier, Emannuel. *Changing Face of Poverty: Trends in New York City's Population in Poverty, 1960–1990*. New York: Community Service Society, 1984.

Törnqvist, T. E., and D. J. Meffert. "Sustaining Coastal Urban Ecosystems." *Nature Geoscience* 1 (2008): 805–07.

United Nations Habitat, *Risky Cities: The Deadly Collision between Urbanization and Climate Change*. United Nations Global Report on Human Settlement, Geneva, Switzerland, 2011.

United Nations International Strategy for Disaster Reduction. *Global Assessment Report on Disaster Risk Reduction*. Chatelaine, Geneva: United Nations, 2009.

United States Department of Homeland Security. Office of Inspector General. *A Performance Review of FEMA's Disaster Management Activities in Response to Hurricane Katrina*. OIG -06-32. Washington, DC: DHS (Office of Inspections and Special Reviews), March 2006, accessed June 29, 2013, http://www.oig.dhs.gov/assets/Mgmt/OIG_06-32_Mar06.pdf.

United States Department of Homeland Security. Federal Emergency Management Agency. Special Community Disaster Loans Program. Action: Final Rule. Docket ID FEMA-2005-0051, RIN 1660–AA44, 44 C.F.R. pt. 206, 75 Fed. Reg. No. 11, 2800–2820, No. 11 (January 19, 2010).

United States Department of Homeland Security, Office of Inspector General, *Hurricane Katrina Temporary Housing Technical Assistance Contracts*, OIG 88-08, August 2008.

U.S. Army Corps of Engineers. *Performance Evaluation of the New Orleans and Southeast Louisiana Hurricane Protection System: Draft Final Report of the Interagency Performance Evaluation Task Force*. Vol. I—Executive Summary and Overview, June 1, 2006, accessed July 1,

2013, http://www.nytimes.com/packages/pdf/national/20060601_ARMYCORPS_SUMM.pdf.

U.S. Army Corps of Engineers. New Orleans District. August 1974. Final Environmental Statement: Lake Pontchartrain, Louisiana, and Vicinity Hurricane Protection Project. Prepared by U.S. Army Engineer District, New Orleans, Louisiana. August 1974, accessed July 1, 2013, http://biotech.law.lsu.edu/katrina/hpdc/docs/19740800_Final_EIS.pdf.

U.S. Congress. Joint Committee on Taxation. *General Explanation of the Revenue Provisions of the Deficit Reduction Act of 1984.* H.R 4170, 98th Congress, Pub. L. No. 98-369. December 31, 1984, accessed July 1, 2013, http://www.jct.gov/jcs-41-84.pdf.

U.S. Government Information Office. "Address Before a Joint Session of the Congress on the State of the Union." The United States Capitol. Washington, DC. Government Printing Office, January 29, 2002, accessed September 21, 2010, http://frwebgate.access.gpo.gov/cgi-bin/getdoc.cgi?dbname=2002_presidential_documents&docid=pd04fe02_txt-11.pdf.

U.S. House of Representatives. Committee on Homeland Security Subcommittee on Management, Integration, and Oversight. *9/11 Federal Assistance to New York: Lessons Learned in Fraud Detection, Prevention, and Control.* Washington, DC. Government Printing Office, 2006.

U.S. House of Representatives. *Federal 9/11 Assistance To New York: Part I, II and III;* Hearing before the Subcommittee on Management, Integration, and Oversight of the Committee on Homeland Security. House of Representatives. 109th Congress, 2nd Session. July 12 and 13, 2006. Serial No. 109-91. Washington, DC: Government Printing Office, 2007, accessed July 1, 2013, http://www.gpo.gov/fdsys/pkg/CHRG-109hhrg35501/html/CHRG-109hhrg35501.htm.

U.S. House of Representatives. Committee on Space, Science, and Technology. Subcommittee on Investigations & Oversight. *Toxic Trailers: Have the Centers for Disease Control Failed to Protect Public Health?* April 2008, accessed July 1, 2013, http://science.house.gov/sites/republicans.science.house.gov/files/documents/hearings/040108_charter.pdf.

U.S. House of Representatives, *Implementation of the Road Home Program Four Years after Hurricane Katrina,* Field Hearing before the Subcommittee on Housing and Community Opportunity of the Committee on Financial Services. Washington, DC: August 20, 2009.

U.S. Long Term Ecological Research Network (LTER). *The Decadal Plan for LTER: Integrative Science for Society and the Environment.* LTER Network Office Publication Series No. 24, Albuquerque, New Mexico, 2007.

U.S. Senate. Committee on Environment and Public Works, Subcommittee on Clean Air, Climate Change, and Nuclear Safety Hearing. *Federal Aid to New York City Following the Attacks of September 11 and Challenges Confronting FEMA.* GAO-03-1174T. Washington, DC: Government Printing Office, September 24, 2003.

U.S. Senate. Committee on Homeland Security and Governmental Affairs. Ad Hoc Subcommittee on Disaster Recovery. *Far From Home: Deficiencies in Federal Disaster Housing Assistance after Hurricanes Katrina and Rita and Recommendations for Improvement: Special Report.* Washington, DC: Government Printing Office, 2009.

White House. "President Arrives in Alabama, Briefed on Hurricane Katrina." Press Release. September 5, 2005, accessed September 19, 2010, http://georgewbush-whitehouse.archives.gov/news/releases/2005/09/20050902-2.html.

White House. *The Federal Response to Hurricane Katrina: Lessons Learned.* The White House, 2006, accessed. July 1, 2013, http://georgewbush-whitehouse.archives.gov/reports/katrina-lessons-learned/.

Vale, Lawrence J. and Thomas Campanella. *Resilient City: How Modern Cities Recover From Disaster.* New York: Oxford University Press, 2005.

van Heerden, I., and M. Bryan. *The Storm: What Went Wrong and Why During Hurricane Katrina.* New York: Viking, 2006.

van Heerden, Ivor, G. Paul Kemp, Hassan Mashriqui, Radhey Sharma, Billy Prochaska, Lou Capozzoli, Art Theis, Ahmet Binselam, Kate Streva, and Ezra Boyd (Team Louisiana). *The Failure of the New Orleans Levee System during Hurricane Katrina.* A report prepared for Secretary Johnny Bradberry, Louisiana Department of Transportation and Development, Baton Rouge, Louisiana. State Project No. 704-92-0022, 2006, accessed July 1, 2013, available at http://www.dotd.louisiana.gov/administration/teamlouisiana/.

Waheed, Saba, Laine Romero-Alston, Ray Brescia, Andrew Kashyap, and Wendy Bach. *Ripple Effect: The Crisis in NYC's Low-Income Communities after September 11.* New York: Urban Justice Center, 2002, accessed July 1, 2013, http://www.urbanjustice.org/pdf/publications/RippleEffect.pdf.

Wallace, Deborah, and Roderick Wallace. *A Plague on Both Your Houses.* New York: Verso, 1998.

Wallace, Mike, and Edwin G. Burrows. *Gotham: A History of New York City to 1898.* New York: Oxford University Press, 2000.

Waugh, W.L. (editor). 2006. *Shelter from the Storm: Repairing the National Emergency Management System after Hurricane Katrina.* Annals of the American Academy of Political and Social Science. 604 (MarcH). Thousand Oaks, CA: Sage Publications, 2006.

Weber, Sarah. "Extracting Value from the City: Neoliberalism and Urban Redevelopment." *Antipode* 34, no. 3 (2002): 519–40.

Whelan, Robert K. "New Orleans: Mayoral Politics and Economic Development Policies in the Postwar Years, 1945–1986." In *The Politics of Urban Development,* edited by C. N. Stone and H. T. Sanders, 219–29. Lawrence, KS: University of Kansas Press, 1987.

Whelan, Robert K. "New Orleans: Public-Private Partnerships and Uneven Development." In *Unequal Partnerships: The Political Economy of Urban Redevelopment in Postwar America,* edited by Greg Squires, 222–39. New Brunswick, NJ: Rutgers University Press, 1989.

Whelan, Robert K., and Alma Young. "New Orleans: The Ambivalent City." In *Big City Politics in Transition,* edited by H. V. Savitch and John Clayton Thomas, 132–48. Newbury Park: Sage Publications, 1991.

Whelan, Robert K, Alma H. Young, and Mickey Lauria. "Urban Regimes and Racial Politics: New Orleans During the Barthelemy Years." Working Paper No 7, Division of Urban Research and Policy Studies, College of Urban and Public Affairs, University of New Orleans, 1991.

Whelan, Robert K., Alma Young, and Mickey Lauria. "Urban Regimes and Racial Politics in New Orleans." *Journal of Urban Affairs* 16, no. 1 (1994): 1–21.

White, Andrew, and Peter Eisinger, eds. *Cities at Risk: Catastrophe, Recovery and Renewal in New York and New Orleans.* New York: Milano The New School for Management and Urban Policy, 2006.

Wieder, Alan. "The New Orleans School Crisis of 1960: Causes and Consequences." *Phylon* 48, no. 2 (1987): 122–31.

Wilson, David. "Toward a Contingent Urban Neoliberalism." *Urban Geography* 25, no. 8 (2004): 771–83.

Wilson, James Q. *Metropolitan Enigma.* Cambridge, MA: Harvard University Press, 1968.

Wirthlin Worldwide. "Post 9/11 Assessment of E.D.C. Communications: San Francisco." New York: Economic Development Corporation, 2002.

Woods, David W. *Democracy Deferred: Civic Leadership after 9/11.* New York: Palgrave Macmillan, 2012.

Woolley, D., and L. Shabman. *Decision-Making Chronology for the Lake Pontchartrain & Vicinity Hurricane Protection Project. Final Report for the Headquarters.* U.S. Army Corps of Engineers, Institute for Water Resources of the U.S. Army Corps of Engineers (2008).

World Commission on Environment and Development. *Our Common Future*. Oxford: Oxford University Press, 1987.

Wright, Beverly. "Black New Orleans: The City that Care Forgot." In *In Search of the New South: The Black Urban Experience in the 1970s and 1980s*, edited by Robert Bullard. Tuscaloosa, AL: The University of Alabama Press, 1989.

Zukin, Sharon, *The Cultures of Cities*. London: Blackwell, 1996.

Zukin, Sharon. *Naked City: The Death and Life of Authentic Urban Places*. Oxford: Oxford University Press, 2009.

INDEX

Note: Page numbers followed by *f* and *t* indicate figures and tables, respectively.